THE
COMPLETE
BOOK OF
Bicycle
Commuting

THE COMPLETE BOOK OF

Bicycle Commuting

BY JOHN S. ALLEN

With special contributions from
The Boston Area Bicycle Coalition and Sheldon Brown

Rodale Press  Emmaus, Pa.

Book design by Linda Jacopetti
Photographs by Sheldon Brown and John S. Allen
Illustrations by George Retseck

Printed in the United States of America on recycled paper, containing a high percentage of de-inked fiber.

Library of Congress Cataloging in Publication Data

Allen, John Stewart, 1946-
     The complete book of bicycle commuting.

     Includes index.
     1. Cycling.   2. Bicycle commuting.   I. Title.
GV1043.7.A43   629.28′772   80-28574

ISBN 0-87857-342-9 hardcover
ISBN 0-87857-344-5 paperback

2   4   6   8   10   9   7   5   3   1   hardcover
2   4   6   8   10   9   7   5   3   1   paperback

This book is thankfully dedicated to you, the new bicycle commuter. Only because you have chosen to read it does this book have any meaning, power, or importance.

CONTENTS

Acknowledgments xi

Introduction xiii

**Chapter One: Choosing and
      Adapting a Bike for
      Commuting** 1

Buy at a Full-Service Bike Shop
Use Manufacturers' Catalogs
Use Magazine Test Reports
Buy a Used Bike
Recycle a Bicycle
What to Look for in a
      Commuting Bike
Types of Bikes
Adapt Bicycles for Commuting

**Chapter Two: Accessories for
      Commuting** 11

Clothing
Gloves
Helmet
Eyewear
Mirrors
Shoes
Safety Flags

**Chapter Three: Fitting the Bike
      to You** 19

Fit of the Frame
Adjust Your Bike to Fit You

**Chapter Four: Understanding
      Gearing and Cadence** 29

Your Gears and How to Use
      Them
Using Derailleur
      Gearing

Chapter Five: Basic Riding Skills .. 39

Your Learning Bike
Riding in a Straight Line
Riding without Hands
Turns
How to Use the Brakes
A Straight, Quick Start
Uphill Riding
Downhill Riding
Know the Size of Your Bike
Bumps and Potholes
The Role Your Tires Play
Develop Sensitivity to the Road
      Surface
Things That Try to Steer Your
      Bike
Nonriding Skills
Tricks for Leaning Your Bike

Now That You've Learned the
Basics

Chapter Six: Driver Training **75**

Dispense with Your Fears
Safer Than Walking
How to Make Cycling Safer
Commuting: The Best Record
Riding on the Road
How to Enter Traffic (All Levels)
Ride with Traffic (All Levels)
In a Wide Lane, Keep to the
Right of Cars (All Levels)
Keep a Straight Line in Traffic
(All Levels)
Riding through Intersections
On-the-Road
Environments
Other Riding Environments
(All Levels)
Preventive Riding
Avoiding Accidents

**Chapter Seven: On-Road
Communication** **141**

Use Your Ears
Audible Signalling
Develop Widescreen Vision
How to Be Seen
Have You Been Seen? Rules
of Thumb
Should You Use a Rearview
Mirror?
Know Your Safety Zones
Predict What the Drivers
Will Do
Effective Signalling

Examine Your Feelings
Being in Control
Dealing with the Police
Bicycle Law
Dealing with Mistaken Drivers
You and the Law

Chapter Eight: Trip Planning **169**

Trip Planning Checklist
Distances and Times
Eat Right
Fatigue
Your First Commuting Trip

Chapter Nine: Finding Your Way ... **173**

Maps You Need if You Ride in
a City
Maps for the Country
Map Use
Two Measuring Devices
Route Selection and Exploration

**Chapter Ten: Parking, Storage,
and Security** **183**

Theft Is a Serious Problem
Get a Good Lock
Where to Park Your Bicycle
Theft Prevention
Insurance Against Theft and
Damage

Chapter Eleven: Carrying Loads ... **195**

Organizing the Load
Equipment to Get Started
Riding with a Load
Carrying Your Accessories
Using a Bicycle Trailer

Special Load-Carrying Bikes
Carrying Passengers
When Your Child Begins
   to Ride

**Chapter Twelve: Complete
   Transportation** 207
Bike and Walk
Car and Bike
Successful Combinations
Bike-Car Tradeoffs
The Right Car for a Cyclist
Carrying a Bike on or in a Car
Cost of Commuting
Public Transportation
Bike and City Bus, Trolley,
   Subway, or Commuter Rail
Other Transportation Options
Bike Disassembly
Tools and Supplies

Chapter Thirteen: Riding at Night .. 223
Equip Yourself for Night Riding
Riding on Dark Roads
Trials of Night Riding
Night Riding Rules of Thumb

**Chapter Fourteen: Riding in Rain,
   Snow, and Heat** 237
Riding in the Rain
Riding in Winter
Riding in Snow and Ice
Winter Falls and Accidents
Hot Weather Riding

The Bike for Bad Conditions
Special Conditions
Air Pollution
Carbon Monoxide
Wind

**Chapter Fifteen: Inspect, Maintain,
   and Repair Your Bicycle** 257
Who Should Repair Your Bike?
Learn to Fix Your Bike
Inspection
Tightness Test
Weekly Maintenance
Monthly Inspection
Yearly Overhaul
Brake Adjustment
Repairing Flat Tires

**Chapter Sixteen: Specialized
   Bicycle Adaptations** 281
A Custom-Made Bike
Heavy-Duty Bikes
Bikes for Handicapped Persons

Conclusion 289

**Appendix I: Some Straight Talk
   about Bicycle Planning** 291

**Appendix II: Bicycle Activist
   Organizations** 293

Index 299

ACKNOWLEDGMENTS

Boston Area Bicycle Coalition members who gave their time to read and add their suggestions to the manuscript include:

John Allis, Anita Brewer, Sheldon Brown, Cathy Buckley, Peter Campagna, Marie Cartier, John Debrowski, Nancy Early, Janice Gepner, Ed Gross, Doran Howitt, Jack Lee, John Leek, Katherine Long, Dave McClamrock, Doug Mink, Eric Newman, Nancy Peacock, Nick Peck, Jacek Rudowski, John Vanderpoel, Pm Weissenberg, Bob Williamson, and Rich Withers.

Other cyclists, members of other organizations or unaffiliated, who likewise contributed include:

John Dowlin, Nancy Drye, John English, Ralph Hirsch, Gihon Jordan, Ed Kearney, Mary Day Kent, Bonita Dostal Neff, Beth Perry, Bob Silverman, Judith Stellar, and Bob Thomas.

Those who posed for photographs or donated the use of their equipment include:

Bradford Connor, Calvin Crawford of the Marblehead Cycle Shop, Jeremiah Donahue, Harriet Fell, Susannah Fiering, Joyce Leja, Joe Levangie and Paul Simon both of the Open Air Cyclery, and Lori Meltzer.

Authors of books that showed the way include:

Ken Cross, Fred DeLong, John Forester, Archibald Sharp, Rowland Whitt, and David Gordon Wilson.

A special thanks to the Rodale Press staff, who worked long and hard beyond the call of duty, including:

Kathy Fones, Tom Gettings, Tina Klidonas, Ed Landrock, James C. McCullagh, Editor, Dolores Nash, and John Schubert.
    . . . and other people too numerous to mention.

INTRODUCTION

In 1975 approximately 500,000 Americans commuted to work by bicycle. The U.S. Department of Transportation estimates that by 1985 up to 2.5 million cyclists will be commuting.

With the price of gasoline headed toward $2 a gallon by 1981 and $3 by 1985, there is every reason to believe that the above estimates will be surpassed by a wide margin.

Beyond the other obvious benefits, bicycle commuting offers real savings. By cycling to work instead of driving you can pay for a $200 bicycle in two to four months. Put on another level, if you used a bike instead of a second car, you could save $2,500 per year.

And the savings that could be achieved on a national level are staggering. The Department of Transportation estimates that an increase in bicycle commuting could mean a $1 billion savings for our nation per year. By not buying foreign oil we would save a billion dollars. And that figure is based on very conservative estimates. What if ten million people commuted regularly?

The savings associated with bicycle commuting are real. So are the other benefits. A regular five-mile ride will provide good cardiovascular exercise. You are, in fact, getting your exercise while saving money and time.

Most people don't realize that cycling in typical city-traffic conditions is safe, quick, and efficient. And easy, once you learn the ropes, which is what this book is all about.

The Complete Book of Bicycle Commuting is intended to be the commuters' "bible," as it contains 16 chapters and two appendices on every aspect of commuting. This is indeed a practical guide for cycling in all traffic and under all road conditions.

The book contains detailed information on choosing and adapting a bike for commuting, no matter what your size, riding habits, or needs. It also contains comprehensive material on accessories for commuting, fitting the bike to you, and basic riding skills. But the heart of the book is the comprehensive sections on "Driver Training" and "On-Road Communications," which are no less than a rich course in all the skills you will need to operate effectively, confidently, and safely in traffic. Specifically, the rules of the road, traffic techniques, and traffic tips are organized in such a way that everyone from the beginner to the veteran cyclist can make immediate use of them.

But the book contains much more, including chapters on carrying loads, multimodal commuting, parking, storage and security, trip planning, riding at night, riding in the rain, riding in snow and sun, inspecting and maintaining your bike, and specialized bike adaptations.

Primarily, this book is very much a practical handbook for the bicycle commuter with particular emphasis on the skills needed to cycle in traffic. And there's nothing theoretical about this material, as all of it has been "road-tested" by the author and many members of the Boston Area Bicycle Coalition. And that explains the use of "we" throughout the book; this work is based on the knowledge, suggestions, and insights of many cyclists who have put the ideas in this book to the acid test of experience.

So read and enjoy this book with the knowledge that every suggestion is based on the experiences of practicing cyclists. To them, bicycle commuting is second nature.

We hope the same will be true of you after you have read this.

CHAPTER ONE

CHOOSING AND ADAPTING A BIKE FOR COMMUTING

You may be about to buy a bicycle, new or used, or you may already own one, in which case you will have to consider whether it can be adapted to serve your needs or whether you should buy another.

For any of these situations, there are some general rules to follow. These have to do not so much with the particular type of bike to ride—we'll get to that later—as with how to go about buying one.

BUY AT A FULL-SERVICE BIKE SHOP

Buy your bike at a full-service bike shop. Don't buy it at a discount, department, or auto parts store. Though these places can charge you less, you'll end up paying more. The bikes are usually of low quality to begin with, made

to be sold but not to be used as serious transportation. You assemble the bicycle yourself—the dealer doesn't check it out for you. And where bikes are sold only as a sideline, a guarantee is almost meaningless and spare parts must be ordered (which may take weeks).

Contrast this with the situation found at a good bike shop. Manufacturers of quality bikes will sell only through these shops, because they insist that the places which sell them assemble and check them. The people who work in the shop are bicyclists themselves and are proud of their work. A bike shop has a large stock of spare parts, so any modifications or repairs can be made quickly. The shop doesn't have to sell you the bike just as it came, but can change parts around to set it up just right for you. Your bike gets a free 30-day checkup, and a guarantee, backed up by an on-the-spot mechanic.

There are differences among bike shops. Talk with other bicyclists and hear what they

1

have to say about shops. Then take some time to look around at two or three shops. See which brands of bikes they sell, though often the service and the attitude are more important than the brands. Different brands often have models which are very much the same.

USE MANUFACTURERS' CATALOGS

Every manufacturer puts out a catalog of its bikes which is usually a small pamphlet or fold-out sheet printed in inviting colors. Bike shops are happy to give away these catalogs for free.

As you shop around, collect these catalogs. Mark down the prices the bike shop is asking for the bikes that interest you. When you get home, spend some time studying the catalogs to compare different brands. Compare prices and see which bikes have the features you need. If some equipment you will need is not standard on a bike that interests you, note this down, too. With the catalog, you can phone the bike shop and ask how much it would cost to add this equipment. Also ask whether the bike is in stock and how long it will take the shop to get it ready for you. The amount of time your bike takes may be an important factor in deciding which one to buy.

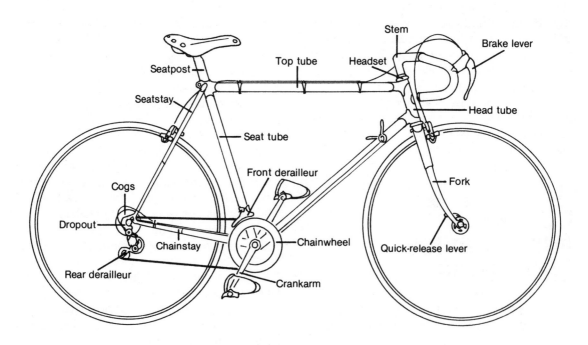

Side view of the bicycle, with major parts labeled.

USE MAGAZINE TEST REPORTS

Bicycling® magazine publishes a bicycle buyer's guide which is on sale at many bike shops. This lists comparable models of all common brands of bicycles, and gives much useful advice. Whether you are about to buy a new bike, a used one, or just fix up the one you already have, the *Bicycling Buyer's Guide* will be valuable in helping you make choices. For more information, write to *Bicycling* magazine, 33 E. Minor St., Emmaus, PA 18049.

Almost every month *Bicycling* magazine prints a road test report on one or two new bikes. It's worth your while to subscribe to this magazine. You'll get valuable information not only about new bikes, but about many other sides of bicycling.

Consumer's Reports magazine also tests bikes once every year or so; many different bikes are compared in the same article.

Many bicyclists keep back issues of *Bicycling* in case you need to look through past test reports. Your local public library has—or should have—both *Bicycling* and *Consumer's Reports*.

BUY A USED BIKE

You can often save money by buying a used bike, but there are some important things to remember when you buy one.

If you buy an overhauled, used bike from a bike shop or a bicyclist who is a mechanic, and the bike has a guarantee, you can be fairly sure that the bike is as good as new. It won't look new, but the quality of bike shop overhauls, or overhauls by experienced bicyclists, is often better than that of factory assembly of new bikes. Not only that, but you may be able to order a bike with the equipment you need. Since the bike is being overhauled anyway, it's no great additional trouble to mix and match equipment and give you what you need.

Buying a used bike without a guarantee is another story. You may get a good deal, but usually only if the price is low enough so that you can afford to have the bike overhauled. Many people never take care of their bikes or decide to sell bikes because the bikes are in bad shape. You can tell something about the condition of a bike by looking at the outside. If the chain, sprockets, and cables are worn and rusty, the rims beat up, and spokes loose, you know you're in for some work on the bike. If you do the tests suggested in Chapter 15, you can get a better idea of the condition of the bike. It also helps to take along a friend who knows bikes. Still, without taking the bike apart, there's no way to tell how much work it needs.

But often you can buy a used bike very cheaply, and if you do, it may be a good deal. Then you can take it in to a bike shop and have it fixed up just right for you. So consider the yard sales, flea markets, and classified ads. Your bike may be waiting for you.

RECYCLE A BICYCLE

Many people throw away a bike when something on it breaks. They think that a bike is like a washing machine or a car, that after a few years, it will be difficult to get parts.

These people overlook one important point; bike manufacturers do not make their own parts, such as brakes, rims, and saddles. They all buy these parts from outside. Everybody's parts have to fit everybody's bikes for this system to work. There can be no yearly model changes, except for details. As long as two bikes are of the same general type, most parts can be switched.

So if you see a bike lying in a neighbor's trash pile with a bent front wheel, and another lying in the town dump with a bent back wheel, you may have just found yourself a deal. Certainly, though, as with any used bike, take it in to a bike shop for a safety check and overhaul.

It pays to collect spare parts for your bike, too. And you should never throw a whole bike away. There are always parts you can save to sell or use on your next bike.

WHAT TO LOOK FOR IN A COMMUTING BIKE

Here are some features that provide ruggedness and comfort:

. . . Lugged or forge-welded frame joints. Avoid frames with spot-welded joints. The angles between the tubes are points of high stress and often come apart unless properly reinforced or smoothed.

. . . Rugged wheels, with thick spokes and relatively wide rims and tires. The wheels have to take what the road dishes out. A racer rides carefully selected routes. A recreational rider wanders at leisure. You may have to take the shortest, most convenient route, even if the pavement is not the best.

. . . Properly shaped handlebars. There are many shapes of handlebars adapted to different uses. Dropped handlebars should have a position above the brake levers on which to rest your hands.

. . . Brakes which work smoothly. Brakes which buzz, catch, or squeal loudly are one of the most sensitive signs of poor design or assembly in a bicycle.

Your bicycle must be suited to the type of riding you plan to do. Since you will be using your bicycle for daily transportation, it must be rugged and reliable. It should also be a pleasure to ride.

These requirements do not point to any one kind of bicycle which is best for everyone. Rather, they point to different kinds, depending on where you ride and what you use the bike for. A bike for shopping is ideally set up a bit differently than one for point-to-point commuting to work; a bike for clear, fast streets in the suburbs would be a bit different than one for city traffic jams.

TYPES OF BIKES

The price of a bicycle depends on how complicated it is, so a ten-speed is more expensive, as a rule, than a three-speed, and a three-speed is more expensive than a one-speed. But the price also depends on the quality, which refers to the frame construction, the components attached to the frame, and the care in assembly. Finally, price depends on who sells you the bicycle. As we've noted, a bike shop must charge a little bit extra because it supports a mechanic to check over your bicycle and carries spare parts to service the guarantee. But you get more than your money's worth.

Each type of bicycle, then, has its price range, and as a rule, you're better off buying a well-assembled, less complicated bicycle of good quality, than a fancier one of dubious quality, poorly assembled, with a poor guarantee service. Don't buy a bicycle at the bottom of the price range for its type.

Here are some general price ranges:

One-speeds:	$50 – $150
Three-speeds:	$75 – $200
Ten-speeds:	$90 – $500

For best results, aim toward the middle of the price range, or slightly above, for each type of bicycle.

Generally, you buy a more rugged and less complicated bicycle for shopping and city riding; a lighter, faster one with more gears for longer distance commuting. Take your choice among the following major types of bikes.

A CRUISER OR TANK BIKE

Don't be fooled; this bike is not fancy or fast. But it is a utility bike, perfectly practical for short trips to the store for shopping, for newspaper delivery work, and for riding on bad roads. It is relatively unpopular with thieves. The frame is strong and reinforced, and has curved tubes for a soft ride. Wide tires give comfort, huge load-carrying ability for shopping, and good traction on bad surfaces. Its coaster brake works in wet weather, and it is equipped with fenders. You don't have to concern yourself about shifting gears, because there's only one gear. So this bike is best in flat places, though the same bike can be bought with a three-speed hub. Then it's fine for hilly country, too.

A THREE-SPEED UTILITY BIKE

This is actually designed as a utility bike, a bike for transportation, not sport. It comes with relatively wide, rugged rims and tires; fenders for riding in the rain; and the trouble-free and weatherproof three-speed hub. This hub is available with a built-in drum brake or coaster brake, giving you brakes which work in the rain.

For most short-trip travel, especially in cities, this bike is a good choice, far better than a bottom-of-the-line ten-speed at the same price. While a derailleur-equipped bike can present a bewildering variety of problems to its new owner, a three-speed bike will be relatively reliable even to a person who doesn't know how to care for a bike.

A DERAILLEUR-GEARED ("TEN-SPEED") BIKE

If you have a bike, this is probably the type you own already; it's the most popular bike sold to adults today. Usually, this bike is a well-built machine which will last a long time with proper care.

Its derailleur gears are the best for touring in the country, or for open-road commuting. But they're not good in traffic because they won't shift at a stop, the way a three-speed will. You must learn to shift before you come to a stop.

The lower-priced version of this bike is usually sold without fenders and with brakes that don't work in the rain. Manufacturers assume it will be used for fair weather pleasure riding. So that's what it gets used for!

Sometimes, this bike is sold with tires too narrow and fragile for reliable commuting.

Any problems you have while shifting can be lived with. As you gain skill as a rider, you will learn to shift down before stopping as a matter of course. Other problems can be dealt with either by choosing the right model of bicycle, or by having your bike shop reequip the bicycle to suit your needs.

The derailleur-equipped bicycle which

is most easily adapted for commuting is the one which was designed for long-distance touring. This has wide, rugged aluminum rims, rugged tires, heavy-gauge spokes, and often a wider gear range than the lower-priced derailleur-geared bicycles. A rear rack for load carrying, as well as fenders for bad weather, may be standard equipment. If not, the bicycle is designed to take them, and its rugged construction is designed to carry loads. While the long-distance touring bicycle is too expensive and impressive looking for locking outdoors in a high-theft area while you go shopping, it is almost ideal for home-to-work commuting.

You can buy a bicycle that's too expensive and too fancy even for home-to-work commuting, that is, a true racing bicycle or one which is more or less a true racing bicycle. This is designed for low weight and high performance at the expense of reliability. It is not made to carry loads or fenders.

Wheels are lightweight and may not last long. These problems do not matter to the racer. One race lost in ten because the bike broke down is no serious problem. A race lost by seconds because the bicycle is too heavy is a problem. For you, the opposite is true. You can always start out for work 2 minutes earlier to compensate for your heavy bicycle, but it's a problem if you're 15 minutes late because you had to call a taxi!

A FOLDING BIKE

This has an overwhelming advantage; you can carry it with you wherever you go. You can ride it to work in the morning even if you need to catch a ride home in a car at night. You can take the bike with you by bus, subway, train, or plane, using it as the connecting link at the end of your trip. You can also store a folding bike easily in any closet or corner.

Properly equipped, the folding bike can be a good performer, too. It's almost as fast as a bike with bigger wheels, but its smaller wheels make it more maneuverable. With its low center of gravity, this bike can carry enormous loads comfortably.

Most folding bikes are adjustable to fit riders of different sizes, an advantage if a bike is shared.

Folding bikes vary much more widely in design than conventional bikes. The one to buy depends on the way you will use it. Light weight and compactness make the bike easier to carry, but a heavier, sturdier bike usually rides better. If you ride one mile to the train station and ten miles on the train, you would want an easy-to-carry bike. If you ride the bike most of the time and only carry it once in a while, you would want a nice-riding bike at the expense of its being harder to carry.

Here are some folding bikes presently on the market:

. . . The Bickerton Portable. Equipped with a three-speed hub, it weighs 23 pounds. The Bickerton is sold with its own carrying bag, which doubles as a large handlebar bag when the bike is unfolded. The bike is an excellent choice for a small person, or for a person who rides the bike a short distance to public transportation. The Bickerton is not well suited to hard riding because its frame is too flexible.

. . . An intermediate class of folding bikes is made mostly in central Europe (Italy, Yugoslavia, Germany). They weigh about 30 pounds as sold, complete with fenders, lights, and a rack. They are sturdier than the Bickerton, but still flex a bit under hard pedaling. They are much less expensive than the Bickerton.

. . . Finally, the workhorse folding bikes, which

are as sturdy and stiff as conventional bikes, and sometimes heavier! Their riding qualities are impressive. Three examples are the Raleigh, the Dawes, and the Peugeot. If you are large, if you ride most of the time and only transport the bike infrequently, or if you carry heavy loads, these bikes are the best.

Some manufacturers make a small-wheeled town bike, similar to a folding bike, except that it doesn't fold. It has the same advantages in load carrying and adjustability. But if you're buying a small-wheeled bike, buy one that folds. A small-wheeled bike that doesn't fold is like a cake without frosting.

BIKES FOR KIDS

Your children's bicycling may save you many hours of driving. But, just like anyone else, children need the right bikes, and there are some special things to look out for.

The first thing to remember is that kids are very hard on bikes. Most kids will ride up and down stairs, over rocks, into curbs, anything. They love to explore backwoods paths, so they need tough bikes.

Also, there are some special safety problems to look out for. We'll start with one, talking about trikes for small kids.

The classic upright child's tricycle is a very dangerous machine. It is top-heavy and it doesn't have brakes. On downhill runs, the pedals get going too fast to follow; then the trike either topples over or keeps on going, perhaps out into a street.

The plastic Big Wheel trike is much safer. It still doesn't have brakes, but its center of gravity is low. It will skid around turns before it can tip over, so it can usually be stopped by turning it. The Big Wheel trike does not last very long, but it's inexpensive.

A small sidewalk bicycle for a child is best equipped with a coaster brake. This is easiest for the child to operate. Do not buy one without a brake. It's very dangerous, for the same reason the upright trike is. A child's first bike should have wide, deep balloon tires so it takes curbs well. Do not buy training wheels, but teach your child to ride without them as described in Chapter 5.

A larger child who still rides mostly on sidewalks and paths is best off with a BMX (bicycle motocross) or high-riser bike. These two types of bikes have wide tires which take abuse well. They are also adjustable as your child grows. A coaster brake is best until you can instruct your child how to operate a front hand brake safely. Then you can add the hand brake and give the child permission to ride faster and to take to the streets more.

Small three-speed and ten-speed bikes are available. These are best if your child is becoming a serious young cyclist. They are less rugged than the BMX and high-riser bikes, but they go faster in the street. Your example as a responsible and careful adult cyclist will make the biggest difference when your child is ready to ride a street bike. Most of your child's friends will have bad riding habits which you must overcome. When your child is ready to ride a bike without damaging it and has learned to ride well in the street (generally between the ages of 10 to 14), a good street bike will expand the child's horizons and allow you to go on family bike outings without slowing down so much.

Never buy a bike with handlebars higher than the child's chest. Though these are popular, they make the bike hard to control. Many types of bikes sold are adjustable to fit a child from age seven to eight onward. So your child will probably go through four machines: a trike, a sidewalk bike, a high-riser or BMX bike, and a street bike.

ADULT TRIKES

A trike is excellent for heavy load carrying (see Chapter 11). And if you are elderly and have to worry about fragile bones, a trike may spare you the worry about falling. A trike is also right for many people with handicaps.

Trikes come in heavy-duty, middleweight, and lightweight versions. The ones most commonly available in this country are the heavy-duty ones, the three-wheeled equivalent of the tank bike. Others are available on special order; many are made in England.

Advantages and disadvantages of the trike may not be clear at first; let's set the record straight.

Only as long as you take it easy on the corners is a trike stable and safe. At high speeds, and when cornering, a bike is safer because it leans; a trike does not lean, so it can tip over without warning. You must beware of this and slow down for turns. (The Oxtrike is an exception to this.)

Rough or slippery surfaces pose a hazard to a trike; a bike is less stable, but its wheels are one behind the other. You can pick one path on a bike, but on a trike you have to pick three at once. When a trike gets stuck, it's harder to push and carry. The only place a trike outranks a bike is on a flat lake bed or river ice surface, where stability is much more important than traction. On ordinary, snow-covered streets, the bike is far better.

You'll squeeze through the traffic jams better on a bike, because a trike is clumsier in traffic than a bike.

ADAPT BICYCLES FOR COMMUTING

There is certain equipment which every commuting bicycle needs. Since few bicycles are sold expressly as commuting bicycles, your bicycle may come with more or less of this equipment. Your bicycle needs:

1. Fenders, for wet weather.
2. Brakes which work in wet weather.
3. Lights for night riding.
4. A rack to carry loads.
5. A set of tools for on-the-road repairs.

All of these subjects are covered in detail in other sections of this book. In this chapter we'll discuss how changes relate to each type of bicycle.

A CRUISER OR TANK BIKE

The single-speed gear of a tank bike can be raised or lowered, and often should be. Its coaster brake works in the rain, but install dual hand brakes as well for panic stops and downhill runs.

Saddles, handlebars, and pedals are set up for an upright riding position when the bike is sold. You can switch them for a more efficient crouched position, just as on any bicycle. Since the crank fittings for the pedals on most tank bikes are of an unusual size, you will have to use bicycle motocross pedals, rather than the usual road racing pedals, if you wish to install toe clips.

A THREE-SPEED UTILITY BIKE

Three-speed hubs with built-in coaster or hand-operated hub brakes are available to solve your wet-weather braking problems. You may buy a wheel with one of these hubs as original equipment on a new bicycle, or switch wheels on an older bicycle. Used three-speed coaster brake wheels are fairly easy to obtain. Or you might choose another wet-weather braking option such as Fibrax or Kool Stop brake pads, a front drum brake, or aluminum rims.

The three-speed's frame fittings for the saddle, handlebar stem, and pedals are identical to those of ten-speed bicycles, so there's no trouble switching to a more efficient riding position.

Most three-speed bicycles are geared too high, but improving the gear range is a simple matter of replacing a $2 sprocket.

A DERAILLEUR-GEARED ("TEN-SPEED") BIKE

Beyond the addition of equipment for wet weather, night riding, and load carrying, the chief improvements you can make to the derailleur-geared bike are:

. . . Switch to wider tires, particularly if your bike has very narrow ones and you will be using it in the city or to carry loads.

. . . Consider improving the gear ratios. The versatility of derailleur gearing gives you a wider choice right from the start, but you may want a lower low gear, better spacing in the midrange, or a more convenient shift pattern. All of these goals are achievable at very little expense.

. . . Improve the fit of the bike. Remove "safety" brake levers and replace stem shifters, get a more comfortable saddle, and add toe clips and straps. Switch from dropped to upright handlebars or use a taller handlebar stem if they're what you need because of an arthritic neck or infrequent riding.

A FOLDING BIKE

Like any other bike, a folding bike needs to be equipped right for transportation use.

That means the lights, fenders, rack, and brakes must work in the rain. Note that a hub brake will be more effective on the small wheel of a folding bike than on a conventional wheel.

To make best use of the bike's "folding," here are some suggestions:

. . . Carrying bags are absolute musts. Many public transportation lines still prohibit bikes, even folded ones unless in a bag. If your bike does not come with a bag, you can have a local awning maker sew one up for you. An old mail bag or laundry bag may work fine, too.

. . . All parts of the bike must either be small and easy to carry with you or must be secured to prevent theft. This is especially true of the quick-adjust seat and handlebars. A locking cable looped over a U-bolt lock can secure all removable parts.

. . . Ruggedness is of the greatest importance. An internally geared hub is preferred over derailleur gears on a folding bike. All parts must be rugged enough to withstand the treatment that only baggage handlers seem to know how to give a bike.

Some folding bikes such as the Bickerton have unusual handlebar and wheel sizes. But most use the very common 20-inch wheel size and can be adapted for dropped handlebars. To improve riding qualities:

. . . Improve the riding position and pedaling efficiency with dropped handlebars, metal pedals, toe clips and straps, and a better seat.

. . . Make the switch to aluminum rims. These are now available in 16- and 20-inch sizes.

. . . If your folding bike has narrow (16 or 20 × 1⅜ inch) rims and tires, consider switching to wider ones. With the smaller wheel diameter, narrow tires give a skittish, bumpy ride. Wider tires slow you down just a little, give you more control, let you ride on dirt roads, and let you carry enormous loads safely. Bicycle motocross cement track tires are the best; they are wide, but take high pressure for lower rolling resistance.

. . . 500A (French 22-inch) tires used on the Peugeot are available in various widths. Get the widest ones, labeled ballon, French for balloon.

CHAPTER TWO

ACCESSORIES FOR COMMUTING

If you just took your bike out for slow, easy rides on quiet streets and paths, in daylight, and in good weather, then you wouldn't have to buy much beside the bike itself. But if you are going to use the bike for reliable, all-weather transportation, day and night, you need some additional pieces of equipment for your safety and comfort. These items are as essential as the bike itself.

CLOTHING

. . . Wool and cotton are nicest for bicycling, because they "breathe." Cotton undergarments are best. Trousers and shirts should have at least 50 percent cotton or wool for the greatest comfort. Wool is best for outer garments in the cold and damp — it is warm even when wet. Wool socks are best, hot or cold. Synthetics like polyester are fine in blends with cotton or wool — they wear better, wash better, and have permanent-press qualities. But synthetics alone can be clammy. They get soaked easily, because they don't absorb water. And they hold odors such as perspiration and exhaust fumes.

. . . Be prepared in case you have to make an on-the-road repair on your bike. A light pair of cotton work gloves will keep your hands clean as you fix a flat tire. Use facial tissue, leaves, or newspaper to hold a dirty chain as you lift it back onto the sprockets. Drape your rain cape over yourself as an apron.

. . . A large, touring saddlebag is best for carrying clothes. Or you can fold them neatly around a sheet of cardboard, wrap them in a plastic trash bag, and strap them to your bike's rear carrier.

. . . Either pick your outer clothes for high visibility, or wear visibility aids over your clothing. Any windbreaker you buy for bicycling should be bright orange or yellow — preferably day-glo. If you're wearing an ordinary jacket or shirt, wear a runner's safety vest over it. The safety vest will have reflective stripes for night riding. Add reflective material or tape to a windbreaker, and wear reflective trouser bands to add to your night visibility.

. . . Clothes should be compact for minimum air resistance and for safety. Don't wear anything that flaps in the wind, that might get caught in the bike's wheels or chain, or that might fly into your face and cover your eyes.

Bicycle racers wear tight-fitting jerseys and special shorts with no seams to chafe them. Bicycle tourists sometimes wear these racing clothes, but more often wear ordinary tough, outdoor clothing. The tough, outdoor clothing is probably best for you, if you're going shopping or anywhere else where you don't have to look spiffy. But if you're going to work where you have to wear dressy clothes, you'll probably want to change at least some of your clothes at the end of your ride. The trick, again, is to strike a balance for your convenience. So here are some tricks of the trade.

Trousers take the hardest use in bicycling. The right cuff can get dirty from the chain. A leather bicycle saddle can stain trousers, and any seat will wear them out quicker than you've been used to. A plastic saddle or a saddle cover prevents stains.

Tough trousers with good anti-wrinkle qualities are best — corduroy is good, and is presentable with a jacket and tie. Cotton-polyester permanent-press blends work well too. Dark colors hide chain dirt and saddle stains. Avoid lightweight or sheer fabrics, common in women's dress trousers, and avoid knits — woven cloth is much more durable. There are plenty of good-looking trousers for both men and women which work well for bicycling. You've just got to be a little more choosy.

Some commuters will sew a bicycle racer's chamois seat inside the seat of the trousers they wear to work, or they'll wear racing shorts inside their trousers. This isn't a bad idea for someone who commutes longer distances, though it's not really needed for most commuting trips.

Trouser bands never keep your cuff perfectly clean from the chain, but they keep it from getting snagged. The reflective cloth and plastic trouser bands are best. If your cuff has to be truly clean, wear long socks. Tuck the cuffs of the trousers into them. Then when you get to your destination, put the socks inside. Special gaiters are also sold which protect your cuffs.

A woman who wears a skirt at work can wear the skirt for a short commute if the bike has a saddle with a shortened front. If the skirt is long enough to get caught in the rear wheel, the bike needs skirt guards. Fenders, plus the plastic guards that come with child seats, work well.

Wear trousers of some sort under the skirt for your ride for the warmth when necessary and to keep chain dirt off your leg. Black tights are OK for riding and at work, but nylons or bare legs risk becoming unpresentable.

Shirts and jackets are not much to worry about while bicycling. In warm weather, you carry your jacket with you or keep it at work. You might want to change your shirt, too, and you certainly won't want to wear a necktie while riding. In cool weather, you'd probably just change from a windbreaker jacket to your dress jacket when you get to work.

GLOVES

You'll wear gloves in cold weather. In warm weather, too, you'll do well to wear special bicycling gloves. These have padded leather palms, cool mesh backs, and no fingers. They have three purposes: to cushion your hands on the handlebars, to let you wipe the tires clean of glass while riding, and to save you a skinned palm if you put a hand down on the road to break a fall. Since you're more likely to fall when you first take up riding, get gloves right away if you're just starting.

Bicycling gloves should fit tightly; you should have to turn them inside out to get them off. Most bicycling gloves will go on either right side out or inside out, saving you the trouble of turning them right side out after you take them off.

If you don't want to spend $10 to $15 for bicycling gloves, you can cut the fingers off an old pair of leather gloves and punch a few holes in the backs of them for ventilation.

Most casual riders don't use gloves. For short trips, they are a minor inconvenience, and the cushioning isn't terribly important. But we'd suggest that you not wait to get gloves until after your first fall.

HELMET

Buy a good helmet right away. It might cost $35 or $40, but what's your head worth?

Even if you're a beginner, you need the helmet from the start. You're more likely to fall when you're still unfamiliar with your bike and inexperienced with riding. Between 50 and 75 percent of all deaths and permanent disabilities in bike accidents are caused by head injuries, and a good helmet will protect your head in most accidents.

We can recommend:

1. The Bell Biker helmet: good protection, and the best ventilated for hot weather.

2. The MSR helmet: protection comparable with the Bell's, though a bit less well ventilated.

3. The Pro-Tec helmet: This provides reasonable protection, but is not well venti-

lated. Its greatest advantage is that it is available in small sizes for children; it is the helmet to buy for a child who rides in a child seat.

Other helmets, such as motorcycle helmets, hockey helmets, climbing helmets, and some sold as bicycle helmets, do not provide adequate protection or ventilation, are uncomfortably heavy, or cover your ears so you can't hear well.

A good helmet protects you if you have an accident, and its visibility may also prevent you from having an accident. Also, a helmet identifies you as a responsible bicyclist. Motorists often treat you with more respect if you wear a helmet.

Usually, you don't have to follow special rules to wear a helmet; just put it on and wear it. The instructions with the helmet will tell you how to adjust the fit. But there are a few tricks besides:

. . . In rainy weather, a helmet cover will keep rain out of the ventilating holes. It's hardly necessary, however, except in a downpour.
. . . In cold weather, a stocking cap under the helmet will keep your head and ears warm. Most helmets have some way of adjusting the fit enough so a stocking cap will fit.
. . . In hot weather, if your helmet, like the Bell, has movable foam pads, arrange them so air can get in all around the edges. Some helmet instructions suggest that you set one of the longer pads sideways at the front as a sweatband, but you'll end up sweating more this way, canceling the sweatband's effect. Use a separate sweatband below the helmet, if you need one.
. . . Shorter hair, and water squirted into the helmet's top ventilating hole from your water bottle, also help keep you cool.
. . . Helmets reduce ventilation, but they also keep out the hot sun. The Bell is comfortable for even the hottest weather, as long as air is

blowing through it. For a very long, slow climb, you may sensibly take the helmet off. You're going slowly enough that you're unlikely to have a serious accident.

. . . When wearing a sweatband, stocking cap, or filter mask with a helmet, put the helmet on first and slide it down on the back of your neck with the strap around your throat. Then put on the other equipment and lift the helmet back onto your head.

. . . If you are bald, you have the least to worry about keeping a cool head under a helmet. But don't forget the sunscreen lotion — since you can get a suntan through the ventilating holes.

EYEWEAR

You may or may not need eyeglasses to see clearly. Still, when riding a bike, it's often good to wear them to protect your eyes from flying insects, wind, dust, and bright sunlight. Some kinds of glasses have special advantages for riding.

Metal frames have several important advantages. The rims are narrow, blocking your vision less than those of plastic frames. The nosepieces and temples can be bent to hold the glasses securely in place. When metal frames are abused, they usually bend rather than break. And if they break, they can be repaired simply and cheaply by soldering. The best metal frames have a double top bar for extra strength.

Your glasses need to stay on securely even on bumpy roads when your face is wet with perspiration. Cable temples, the kind that curve all the way around the backs of the ears, are best, or use an eyeglass strap. Like a good bicycle saddle, cable temples are often uncomfortable at first. But get them adjusted

carefully, give them a chance, and they'll win you over.

Thin wire temple pieces obstruct side vision less, but hold the glasses poorly, and won't hold an eyeglass-mounted rearview mirror steady. Wider temple pieces are better for mirrors and are stiff enough to keep the glasses on straight. Wide metal temples about $3/16$ inch will do the job.

You need a wide field of vision. When you look as high and as far to the sides as you can, you should still be looking through the lenses of your glasses. Aviator style frames are excellent. Special shooters' frames, standard on many sunglasses, have extra coverage at the top, and are good for use with dropped handlebars. Frames with *wide,* rectangular lenses cover as well at the top as aviator style frames but don't go as low at the bottom, an advantage if you need heavy, thick lenses.

Consider tempered glass lenses, rather than plastic. Especially in summer, when sweat drips salt onto your glasses, you'll have to clean them frequently. Plastic ones will scratch, though they are lighter and a bit safer. There's little chance, though, that you'll land on your glasses if you wear a hardshell helmet.

If you are nearsighted, your glasses make things look smaller, so there will be a ring around the edges which you see twice. Also, you don't have to look so high when riding with dropped handlebars. But the view outside the frames will be blurry when you turn to glance behind you — a rearview mirror helps. If you are farsighted, your lenses magnify. There is a ring which you don't see at all, and you have to look higher to see ahead of you when using dropped handlebars. Prism lenses of 15 to 20 diopter strength, mounted base up, can help you see without straining your neck. Fresnel prism lenses are lighter than solid ones, though they may give you less clear vision. If you are very farsighted, contact lenses may be preferable to glasses. With contact lenses, you'll not have the magnification problems.

Soft contact lenses are acceptable for riding. Hard contact lenses are not — too many problems with dust getting underneath them. It is best to wear plain lenses such as sunglasses, safety glasses, or goggles over contact lenses while riding.

If you wear bifocals, use them for riding (you'll need them for map reading). If you use a wrist or handlebar rearview mirror with a convex surface, you'll also need bifocals to see clearly in it.

High-quality prescription sunglasses or other good sunglasses are recommended for bright days, especially when you are riding on into the evening. They'll allow your eyes to adapt to darkness quicker. The most effective sunglasses are of a neutral gray or green tone, with infrared and ultraviolet filtering. Polarized sunglasses cut down road glare. When riding with sunglasses, always carry a pair of clear glasses for use when it gets dark. Photosun and Photogray glasses don't become completely clear.

Reflections off the back of your glasses may be annoying or even give you a headache when you ride in a crouched position. The worst are flashing reflections of the sun through tree leaves. For a very moderate charge, your optician can have your lenses anti-reflection coated like camera lenses, greatly reducing reflection problems. It is especially helpful to coat sunglasses, since the reflection off them will be brighter in proportion to the view through them. Dime-store sunglasses aren't coated, though, and aren't worth coating. Clip-on sunglasses give you double reflection problems — four surfaces

to send light back instead of just two — unless you can mount them behind your normal lenses.

Safety glasses with wire screens at the sides are best for riding where insects fill the air. The screens also cut out low-angle light which would reflect off the lenses. Goggles keep out insects, cold air, and rain too — you only have to wipe off the front surface. But goggles may steam up, so make sure yours are well ventilated. They are best in cold, wet weather.

MIRRORS

A rearview mirror is a valuable aid in traffic. Many traffic techniques are easier with a mirror. The best mirrors mount to your helmet or eyeglasses, or to your wrist. These are a relatively new idea; traditional handlebar-mounted mirrors were clumsy, often broke, and vibrated too wildly to give you a clear view.

We recommend a helmet-mounted mirror with a reflecting surface at least ⅞ inch across and a bendable wire stem for adjustments. One advantage of a helmet mirror is the simple fact it stays with the helmet and is less likely to get lost. It also won't adversely affect the balance of your glasses' frames, or chew them up, which is a problem with some mirrors and some glasses. In any case, take your helmet or glasses with you when you buy a mirror, to make sure they agree with each other.

Don't point the mirror stem back toward your eye; it should pass to the side of your head. The mirror should sit about 3½ inches in front of your eye. You must aim it carefully for it to work well. If you have good vision in your left eye and the patience to learn to use the mirror, the helmet or eyeglass mirror can be very effective. (You can also wear this sort of mirror on the right side if vision is weak in your left eye or if you go touring in a country where traffic keeps to the left.)

Wrist-mounted mirrors are also effective, though you must shift your eyes farther from the road ahead. Some riders find a wrist-mounted mirror easier to use.

Try one kind of mirror. If it works, fine. If not, try the other kind. Mirrors are cheap, so you can afford to experiment.

ADJUSTING A REARVIEW MIRROR

First, get your hair out of the way. Nothing should stick out farther than your ear. Tie your hair back, or trim it.

Put the mirror on so that its reflecting surface is about 3½ inches ahead of your eye. Now bend the base of the mirror stem, where it attaches to the helmet or glasses, to move the mirror as far up and to the left as you can while looking in it comfortably. Make sure you can look "through" the mirror with your right eye; don't move the mirror so far up and to the left that it covers things you see only with your left eye. If you wear glasses, the upper left corner of the mirror should point the same way from your left eye as the upper left corner of your right glasses' lens does from your right eye.

Once you've adjusted the mirror's position, sit on your bicycle and adjust the mirror's angle by bending the stem at the outer end near the mirror glass. Sitting in the lowest crouched position on your bike, you should see your ear at the right side of the mirror, and your shoulder should come about one-third of the way up from the bottom. It's important to have your ear and shoulder in the picture;

they're points of reference, so you know which way you're looking.

Check the adjustments again, then try riding your bike. The mirror should give you a view back down the traffic lane just to the left of you. By turning your head slightly, you should be able to look farther to the left or right.

Readjust the mirror occasionally. Once you are used to the adjustments, you can do them in a few seconds.

SHOES

Many walking, jogging, and tennis shoes are fine for the kind of bicycling described in this book. But there are some things to look for in shoes, and some things to avoid.

It's best to wear shoes which lace up, with the laces going most of the way to the toe because these give the best support. The best shoes are low at the ankle and have relatively thin but stiff soles. Rubber soles give you the best grip on the pedals and the pavement, as long as they are stiff enough. Check by flexing the shoes between your hands.

Leather or suede tops last longest and stretch to a comfortable fit, but may eventually stretch until the shoes no longer support your feet well. Leather breathes well, especially in hot weather. Canvas and nylon do not stretch much, so the shoes must fit from the start. Nylon frays quickly under toe strap buckles, so make sure the shoes are reinforced with rubber or leather where these fall.

Many dressier shoes are acceptable for riding, as long as you stay within reasonable guidelines. Your main concern has to be whether the dusting and wear you'll give the shoes by riding in them will be acceptable where you are going. Toe clip booties help (these lace to the toe clips to shield your shoes — available at better bike shops) or you may wish to use pedals without toe clips if you're using your bike for short hops between business meetings. Rubber block pedals give a better grip when you're riding without toe clips.

On the other hand, sporty shoes like jogging shoes are becoming better accepted in many work situations. They're more comfortable, and it's hard to fight comfort. Or you may decide to ride in comfortable shoes and carry your dress shoes with you.

Avoid riding in shoes with heavy block soles, like Earth Shoes and clogs. They won't fit toe clips, and they'll make your bike's seat adjustment wrong for you. Also, avoid high-heeled shoes because the heels will drag on the ground as you go around corners. Ripple soles and Vibram hiking boot soles can trap your feet in the toe clips, so avoid them. Unventilated plastic, rubber, and patent leather shoes and boots will steam up your feet. Many kinds of boots and galoshes with high ankles can give you blisters. Avoid them, except for leather lace-up work boots. These can fit well, and are best for slushy weather.

For longer rides, you may wish to use special bicycling shoes. Bicycle touring shoes, like the Bata Biker and the Avocet, have stiff soles, fit better in toe clips than ordinary shoes, and are reasonably good for walking. Bicycle racing shoes are another story. Slotted cleats lock them to the pedals. Fine for pedaling, bicycle racing shoes are not good for walking. They're suitable for long commuting trips. But if you want to try them out, get good advice from someone who uses them regularly — you must install cleats carefully for them to work well, and you need special skills to ride safely with them.

SAFETY FLAGS

For a child or a very short adult who rides in traffic, a safety flag is a good idea.

For the average rider, a safety flag's advantages and disadvantages come about even. The average adult on a bike is already high enough to see over the tops of cars, and for the drivers to see the bicyclist's head. A bright-colored helmet with reflective tape completes the image.

At higher speeds, the safety flag's flexible staff is likely to whip down until it is as low as the rider's head in any case.

Any safety flag can poke into the face of another rider on a group ride, and can snag on a passing car or overhanging branches. So a safety flag is not for group rides and must always have a breakaway mount so it doesn't throw the rider if it snags. It is useful for solitary rides on hilly country roads.

Motorists can be kept from overtaking too close on the left by using a safety spacer. It is a flag on a flexible mount, sticking out from the left side of the bike behind the saddle.

One potential hazard of a safety spacer — and to a lesser extent a safety flag — is that the rider expects to be safe because of it. No item of visibility equipment, even essential equipment like lights, substitutes for good riding techniques. These flags and spacers are not as essential.

Remember that you're taking more things onto your bike that make it clumsier — the safety flag has to come off when your bike goes into a car. Consider the advantages and disadvantages. Your riding technique is your most important safety item.

E

THE
YOU

n more important
ride. It's just the
hoes — you can
y all have to fit. If
e that doesn't fit,
missing.
s a bike must fit.
e frame.

FRAME

and over the frame
e. For most people,
ight height can be
But there are some
t and tall people.
"mixte" or "ladies"
o tube is alright for
y not be possible to
enough for efficient
ious pitfall for a be-
ften like to start with

their handlebars high, but prefer to lower them as they gain experience riding. It should be possible to put the top of the handlebars as low as the top of the saddle, or lower.

Also, if you have short arms, a frame may be too long for you, or if you have long arms, too short. A good rule of thumb: put your elbow against the front of the seatpost. The back of the head tube should be between 2 and 6 inches from your fingertips.

The frame must allow you to use cranks of the correct length. Tall people do best with extra-long cranks, but many tall frames are made for standard cranks.

ADJUST YOUR
BIKE TO FIT YOU

Once you have chosen the right parts, you adjust them to fit you. Learn the adjustments even if a bike shop has set them up for

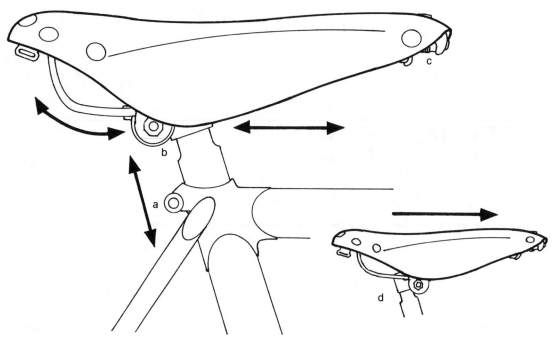

Adjustable parts of the bicycle.

Saddle
Height: *loosen seatpost clamp bolt a), raise or lower seatpost. (Note: remove fully before raising; at least 2 inches must be inside the bike.)*
Front-Back: *loosen saddle clamp b), slide saddle forward or back. Many saddle clamps can be flipped over for an additional range of adjustment.*
Tilt: *loosen saddle clamp b), and rotate saddle.*
Tension: *(leather saddles) adjust nose bolt c). A special wrench, bought at a bike shop, may be needed.*

Handlebars
Height: *loosen bolt at top of stem a) and tap it down with a hammer and wood block. Grip stem and twist to raise or lower. (Note: remove fully before raising; at least 2 inches must be inside the bike.)*
Stem Extension b): *replace stem.*
Handlebar Width c), Reach d), Drop e): *replace handlebars.*
Handlebar Tilt: *loosen bolt at front of stem, turn handlebars f).*
Brake Lever Size: *replace brake levers.*
Brake Lever Position g): *loosen bolt inside brake lever hood (visible if you squeeze the lever).*

Pedals
Crank Length a): *replace cranks.*
Pedal Width b): *replace pedals.*
Toe Clip Length c): *replace toe clips or add washers under bolts.*

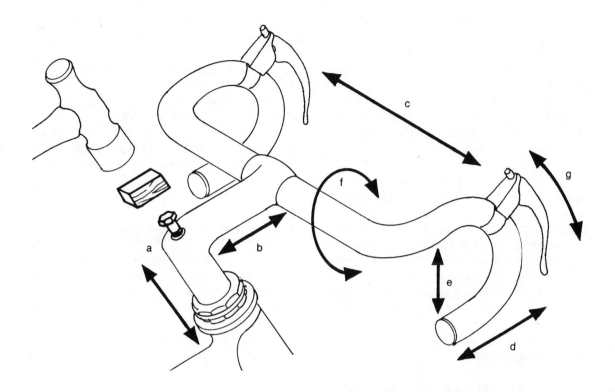

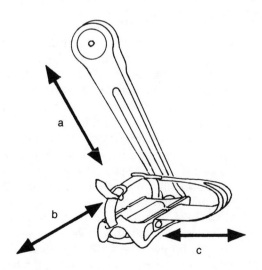

you. The only way you can be sure the adjustments are right is to ride the bike for a while, and to experiment with them.

You adjust your bike in the following order.

SADDLE HEIGHT

Wear your usual riding shoes, and sit on the bike. Look in a mirror to your side, or have a friend describe your position to you. Pedal backward until one pedal is in bottom position. With the ball of the foot on the pedal — *not the arch or heel* — the toes should point down just slightly. The knee should be slightly bent, not locked. Pull the knee back until the leg is straight. It should pull back about 2 inches.

If the saddle is too high, you will have to reach for the pedals, risking ankle strain. If the saddle is too low, you will not be able to get full power from your legs. Note that many beginning riders think that it is safe to keep the saddle low so they can put both feet on the ground. It only makes sense to keep the saddle this low for the first couple of days of learning to ride. After that, you stop the bike with the brakes, not shoe leather.

To adjust the saddle height, loosen the seatpost clamp bolt. Twist the saddle sideways to loosen it as you push or pull on it. If you are raising the saddle, pull it all the way out first. Make sure that at least 2 inches of seatpost will be inside the frame. Any bike shop can sell you a longer seatpost. Take the old one with you, because seatposts come in different diameters. You can shim an undersized one, but never force in an oversized one. When you're done adjusting, tighten the seatpost clamp bolt.

SADDLE FRONT-TO-BACK

Sit on the bike and backpedal until one crank faces straight forward. Hang a string or bungee cord down next to your leg. For a first try, the center of the knee joint should be directly over the pedal axle. Later, you'll readjust by feel.

You'll know if the saddle is not adjusted properly — if the saddle is too far back, you will find yourself sliding forward on it to get over the pedals when you push hard. On the other hand, if it is too far forward, pedaling will push you forward into the handlebars, and you may feel cramped because your arms can't extend enough.

To adjust it, loosen the saddle clamp. Now you can slide the saddle forward or backward on its rails. If the saddle clamp is separate from the seatpost, you can flip it from the front to the back of the seatpost to increase the range of adjustment.

Note that big changes in forward-to-back position can change saddle height adjustment, so check height again if you have to.

The saddle clamp also allows adjustment of saddle tilt. Adjust for pedaling efficiency and comfort. For men, the front of the saddle should tilt up slightly or the saddle should be level; for women, the front should generally tilt down slightly.

SADDLE TENSION

All leather saddles and a few plastic ones have a tension adjustment underneath the front. Adjust this so the saddle doesn't sag. For comfort, it should be tight, though not drumhead-tight. Remember that leather stretches, so check the adjustment frequently.

HANDLEBAR HEIGHT AND DISTANCE

For efficient pedaling, the top of the handlebars should be about 1½ to 2 inches below the top of the saddle. If you aren't comfortable holding your head up, you can set the handlebars higher or use flat handlebars. But think about lowering the handlebars as you get more used to riding. Dropped handlebars give you more control over the bike and more efficient pedaling, once you are used to them.

The bolt at the top of the stem pulls a wedge against the bottom end of the stem, inside the bike frame. To adjust handlebar height, loosen this bolt about five turns — no more, or you might lose the wedge down inside the frame. The head of the bolt at the top will rise up out of the stem. With a hammer

This most common type of saddle clamp not only slides along the saddle rails but also flips completely over to provide a further range of adjustment. Note that it has been flipped forward in the second picture, while the saddle has been slid back on it to provide a more moderate change in position.

cushioned by a wooden block, tap the bolt down to break the wedge loose. Then stand in front of the bike, grasping the front wheel between your knees. Push or pull on the handlebars; first pull the stem all the way out to make sure there will be a safe 2 inches of it inside the frame when you're done. You can buy a longer stem if you need one.

When you're finished adjusting handlebar height, tighten the bolt at the top of the stem. Get it good and snug, but do not tighten it with all of your strength, because you may damage the frame. It's all right if you can still twist the handlebars, grasping the front wheel between your legs. You never use this much force when steering.

Remember that the correct handlebar position is not written in stone. If you're just starting riding, you may want to raise the handlebars. If you have dropped handlebars which are large for you, you'll want the center closer to you so the brake levers are at the right distance. If you're in good shape and like to ride fast, you may want to buy a longer stem to put the handlebars farther away from you.

You can change the distance to the handlebars by raising or lowering them, or by moving the saddle forward or backward. This is helpful for minor adjustments, but you've already made these adjustments for their own purposes, not for the purpose of changing handlebar distance. It's better to buy the right stem.

If you're using flat (upright position) handlebars, test handlebar distance by putting your back at the angle that feels right for you, and lifting your hands to the handgrips. Note that the stem usually sold with English three-speed bikes has almost no forward extension. In almost every case, you will find it more comfortable to use a stem with a longer extension, turn the handlebars upside down, or both. Even a slight forward tilt of your back is much more comfortable than a bolt-upright position.

HANDLEBAR TILT

Sit on the bike and put your hands on the handlebars — in low position with dropped handlebars. Take your hands off the handlebars, relax your wrists, and put your hands on again. You should not have to flex your wrists. They must be straight, so you can put weight on them without using muscle power to keep them from collapsing. The ends of the handlebars will point downward a bit. The forward part at the top of dropped handlebars should slope slightly downward toward the front.

Don't put your handlebars at a strange angle. Some people turn dropped handlebars upside down. Then it's hard to control the brakes, because braking throws you against the levers. Some people twist handlebars upward, to raise them. They lose most of the comfortable hand positions. If your bike is not comfortable with handlebars in normal position, you need different handlebars, a different stem, a different saddle, or maybe just the patience to develop your neck muscles until you're used to holding your head up.

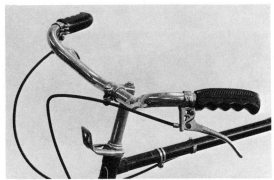

These are North Road bend handlebars, slightly raised and swept back at the ends.

ADJUSTING BRAKE LEVERS

Brake levers should be on the upper part of the curve of dropped handlebars. The lever bodies should point upward at about a 35 degree angle. The levers should follow the curve of the handlebars. If levers are either too high or too low, you'll lose the top braking position. Sit on the bike and check this position. Also check whether you can comfortably reach your hands around the brake levers in the bottom position. If you've bought brake levers of the right size, this should not be a problem.

To adjust brake lever position, loosen the lever attachment bolt and slide the lever along the handlebar. You may have to replace handlebar tape. If you're not sure how to do this, take your bike to a bike shop.

With flat handlebars, brake lever adjustment is simpler. You loosen the bolt on the lever body and move the lever until it is in a comfortable position under the handgrip — it's usually best angled outward a bit. If the bike is a three-speed with a trigger control,

"Bent knees" handlebars have no comfortable hand position over the brake hoods.

put this just ahead of the brake lever body. Then, you can operate the brake and the shift at the same time.

PEDAL ADJUSTMENTS

If you aren't using toe clips, there's nothing to adjust. If the seat is adjusted right, you'll automatically pedal with the ball of the foot, as you should.

If you use toe clips, check that they place the ball of the foot over the pedal axle.

Too-short toe clips invite ankle and knee problems. Buy longer ones, or put stacks of washers under attachment bolts. Most toe clips can slide sideways to set toe-in.

And that's it for fit. Once you've adjusted your bike, try it out. It will probably feel better to ride, though it may feel strange if you're not used to normal seat and handlebar positions. The positions we give here are tried and tested. If they feel strange, live with them for a while. They will probably feel better in time. If they feel worse instead, try to figure out what is wrong and correct it. Ask the advice of an experienced bicyclist, who may be able to pinpoint the problem.

Also remember that these adjustments aren't sacred. Handlebar positions, especially, may vary widely. You may decide to keep two or three handlebar stems, graduating to the longer ones as you get into shape. You can test that you're ready for a longer stem by reaching forward to grasp the brake levers as if they were the handlebars, or with flat bars, by bending your elbows and crouching down. If these positions feel better than the one you're using, try a longer stem. Also, experiment with slight changes in saddle height; they may make a surprising difference. Only by experimentation will you find the riding position that's truly best for you.

Think about your position as you ride. With dropped bars, switch hand positions — low for speed, high for looking around. Keep your back arched so its natural spring will absorb road shock.

FITTING THE BIKE TO YOU

	ADJUST-MENT	HOW AD-JUSTED	INTER-AC-TIONS	ADJUSTING/LOCKING DEVICE	TOO LITTLE	JUST RIGHT	TOO MUCH
S A D D L E	**Width X**	Choice of saddle.	4	. . . .	Crotch pain.	Maximum comfort, wide for women: upright position.	Chafed legs.
	Springi-ness	Choice of saddle; nose bolt.	4	Nose bolt (leather saddle).	Sore pos-terior.	Best com-promise.	Inefficient pedaling: poor control.
	Height	Seat post height.	1,5	Seat post clamp bolt.	Inefficient pedaling.	Leg almost straight at bottom.	Ankle prob-lems: saddle may come off.
	Front-back	Seat rails in clamp.	1,2	Seat clamp nuts.	Back: Makes you "twiddle" pedals.	Knee over pedal with crank forward.	Front: Makes you push hard.
	Tilt	Seat clamp rotation.	3	Seat clamp nuts.	Crotch pain.	Balanced.	Arm strain: weight on arms.
H A N D L E B A R S	**Shape X**	Choice of handlebars.	4	. . . .	Flat bars: only one position. OK with long stem.	Dropped bars unless: neck prob-lems, ride infrequently.	Too deep drop: hard to reach.
	Width X	Choice of handlebars.	. . . .	. . . .	Harder to breathe, less control.	Breathing control, speed of steering.	Slow steer-ing.
	Front-back X	Choice of stem.	2,5	. . . .	Inefficient pedaling.	35° body lean.	Can't reach brake levers.

X — Buy the right part. Not adjustable   3 — Body tilt
1 — Affects leg extension   4 — Crouch/upright
2 — Affects saddle-handlebar distance   5 — Frame—limited

FITTING THE BIKE TO YOU—*Continued*

	ADJUST-MENT	HOW AD-JUSTED	INTER-AC-TIONS	ADJUSTING/LOCKING DEVICE	TOO LITTLE	JUST RIGHT	TOO MUCH
H A N D L E B A R S	**Height**	Stem insertion.	3	Stem expander bolt top down.	Severe crotch pain. Back problems, can't see.	0"-2" below saddle top.	Inefficient pedaling. Can come loose.
	Tilt	Rotate handlebars in stem.	3	Stem handle-bar clamp.	Sore wrists: lose hand position.	Can use all hand positions.	Sore wrists, lose hand position.
	Brake Lever Position	Move along handlebars.	....	Brake lever attachment bolts.	Too low: lose top braking.	Can use all hand positions.	Too high: hard to reach.
P E D A L S	**Crank Length X**	Choice of cranks.	1	....	Inefficient "twiddling".	Full power.	Knee problems: crank interference.
	Pedal Surface X	Choice of pedals.	4	....	....	Rubber; without toe clips. Metal; with toe clips.	....
	Pedal Width X	Choice of pedals.	....	....	Foot pain.	Optimum compromise.	Cornering problems.
	Front-back	Toe clip length.	1	....	Ankle problems.	Ball of foot over axle.	Inefficient pedaling on arch.
	Toe in/out	Toe clip position, cleat angle.	....	Toe clip bolts; reflec-tor bolts.	Toe out: inefficient, hit cranks.	Slight toe-in.	Toe-in: possible joint problems.

CHAPTER FOUR

UNDERSTANDING GEARING AND CADENCE

Pedaling a bike is much different from walking or running. Because you have used your legs primarily for walking and running, you must understand this difference and teach yourself to pedal the right way.

To understand the difference, start by standing on one leg. Swing the other leg back and forth. It is a pendulum, hinged in the middle so you can lift your foot between steps. Your leg swings naturally at a rate just over once per second, sixty times per minute. As you walk, the natural swing of your leg saves you from using extra energy to push your leg back and forth. Children step faster because their legs are shorter pendulums.

But when you ride your bike, your leg is no longer a pendulum. Your foot does not swing freely. It is guided all the way around by the bike's pedal and crank. Your leg is like the connecting rod and piston of a steam locomotive or a car's engine.

Since they are guided, a piston and connecting rod assembly do not have to travel at any special speed. The steam locomotive

can go fast or slow, and the connecting rods will just follow the driving wheel's crank pins. It is the same with your feet on the pedals of your bicycle. You can spin your legs much faster than when walking.

When you walk or run, your legs are nearly straight. They not only move you along, they also carry your weight. Your knees carry your weight when they're straight or nearly straight, but when you pedal a bicycle, you are pushing down on bent knees. You are putting a strain on your knees and on the muscles and tendons around them. Over and over again: more than 2,000 times in a half-hour ride.

Now we get back to the idea of your leg as a connecting rod and piston. We've noted that you can pedal either slow or fast. You can put out the same amount of power by pedaling slowly and pushing hard or by pedaling fast and pushing lightly. Pedaling fast and pushing lightly is the right way, because it doesn't strain your knees.

Work toward developing a smooth, even,

pedal stroke. Your feet should point straight ahead on the pedals and your knees should point straight ahead, too. Riding in your practice area or where there's no traffic, look down at your legs — remember to check that they're straight ahead. See that they don't wobble out to the sides during parts of the pedal stroke. Your knees aren't made to handle sideways forces — even small forces can hurt over thousands of pedal strokes.

Keep your legs warm because muscles and joints are happier when they're warm. In cool weather, keep your legs clothed and control your warmth by removing clothing from your upper body. Be especially careful of refrigerating your legs when coasting down long hills.

Listen to what your legs are telling you. To a certain degree, muscle ache is normal as you strengthen. But any small ache or pain in a joint or tendon is your early warning that you're overstraining. Ease off, or correct your technique before the pain flares up and sidelines you.

Without a conscious effort to learn to pedal right, many people get trapped in a stair-climbing style of pedaling. They pedal this way until knee trouble catches up with them. Quite often, they also find it hard to travel long distances on a bike. Hard pushing means sore, aching muscles.

So you should make an effort to learn to pedal fast. Look at racers and experienced tourists. See how they pedal. They know how to keep going all day long, through tens of thousands of pedal strokes, without getting tired. They know how to make their knees last through a lifetime of riding. After a while, you will want to pedal their way — without thinking — because it will feel right.

But for now, do it even if it feels strange at first.

Pedal fast and easy, like turning on an eggbeater crank. Practice spinning your legs by using lower gears that feel right.

Toe clips and straps help immensely in pedaling — obviously, it is impossible to pull up on the pedals without them. But their advantages go far beyond this. Once you've learned to handle the bike confidently, it's time to install them.

With toe clips you can pull back at the bottom, up at the rear, and forward at the top of the pedal stroke. Avoid pushing down hard at the bottom of the stroke — the pedal is moving back, not down. As you ride, consciously give more emphasis at different times to different parts of the pedal stroke, so you will get used to using the different muscles. Usually, you use your pushing muscles most. When you're tired, you can relieve them by using your pulling muscles instead for a while. Work into this easily, though — don't pull up hard until you've strengthened your legs.

YOUR GEARS AND HOW TO USE THEM

Whether your bike has 1 speed or 15, using your gears well is very important to your riding. Correct pedaling style and gearshifting technique make every trip easier, and increase your speed and the distance you can comfortably travel.

ONE-SPEEDS

The most common one-speed rear hub is the *coaster brake* hub, suitable for around-town use in relatively flat places. The brake is waterproof, a great advantage in the rain.

A coaster brake must always be used along with a hand brake on the front wheel. A rear wheel brake has only half the stopping power of a front brake, so it is unsafe for panic

Front Chainwheel Size	Rear Wheel Size							
	28	**27***	**26**	**24**	**22**	**20**	**16**	
40	17	17	16	15	. . .	. . .	. . .	
42	18	17	17	16	14	. . .	. . .	
44	19	18	18	16	15	14	. . .	Rear
46	20	19	18	17	16	14	. . .	Sprocket
48	21	20	19	18	16	15	. . .	Teeth
50	22	21	20	19	17	15	. . .	
52	. . .	22	21	19	18	16	13	

*Note: includes 700c sometimes called 28 × 1 5/8 inches.

HOW FAST IS FAST PEDALING?

Here's a trick to remind you. Use music.

That's how the Army does it, marching — like the *Stars and Stripes Forever:*
"Be **kind** to your **Web**-footed **friends**
For **one** may be **some**body's **mo- ther**."

But actually, that's too slow — marching is walking, and a walking pace, as we've pointed out, is too slow on a bicycle for anything but lazy ambling.

So we need some better examples. Here are some, drawn from different styles of music, so at least one will be familiar to you.

. . . *Beethoven's Fifth Symphony, first movement* (the first few notes where it keeps stopping are so you can get your feet into the toe clips).
. . . Johnny Cash:
  "**Because** you're **mine (pause) (pause)**, I **toe** the **line**. . ."
. . . Bob Dylan, *Subterranean Homesick Blues:*
  "You **don't** need a **weath**erman to **know** which way the **wind** blows."
. . . And my own:
  "A Solid **boogie woogie eight** to the **bar**."

These pieces all have a cadence of about 80 per minute — a good average pedaling speed.

stops. Also, a coaster brake is not useful for long downhill runs; it will overheat until the grease boils out from inside. If your riding includes long downhills, install two hand brakes in addition to the coaster brake, and use the hand brakes on downhills.

A coaster brake prevents you from back-pedaling, so you must work harder on pedal technique to start, stop, and corner.

The right gear for a one-speed will vary with the terrain, but the ones we list are about right, on the average. Lower than the cruising gear on a multi-geared bike, they are for climbing hills. Where your riding is mostly uphill and downhill, use a lower gear. Make sure that the gear on your one-speed is right. When you have only one gear, it's even more important that it be the best possible gear. Fortunately, the gear can be changed easily by replacing the sprocket. The above sprocket combinations will give you a good compromise gear for your one-speed.

As much as possible, you use technique, training, and judgment when riding a one-speed, to compensate for its limitations. Push harder going up hills and take it easier going down, maintaining a steadier pace. Stand up more in the pedals, for starts and climbs. Get off and walk *before* you begin to hurt on long climbs.

Riding a one-speed is not the grueling

Front Chainwheel Size	Rear Wheel Size							
	28	**27***	**26**	**24**	**22**	**20**	**16**	
40	20	19	18	17	16	15	. . .	
42	21	20	19	18	16	15	. . .	
44	22	21	20	19	17	16	13	Rear
46	. . .	22	21	19	18	17	14	Sprocket
48	. . .	. . .	22	20	19	17	14	Teeth
50	. . .	. . .	22	21	20	18	15	
52	. . .	. . .	. . .	22	21	19	15	

*Note: includes 700c sometimes called 28 × 1 5/8 inches.

ordeal it may seem from this description. Most people think of a one-speed as a heavy clunker. Yet, because it does not use double chainwheels, a heavy multiple freewheel, or derailleurs, a one-speed bicycle can in fact be the lightest and most efficient of all bicycles when built on a lightweight frame. It is mechanically simple, nimble to steer, and an unusual pleasure to ride, except for prolonged climbs.

INTERNAL HUB GEARS

Three- and five-speed internal hub gears have many important advantages for city riding, and few disadvantages. They're rugged, foolproof, weatherproof, and less attractive to thieves. You might go just a little slower sometimes than with derailleurs, but sometimes you'll go faster, too, especially after you've kicked the hub into low gear at a stoplight while the ten-speed bicyclist next to you is still struggling to get started in high. A three-speed hub is available with either a coaster brake or a drum brake, both neat solutions to wet-weather braking problems.

The Sturmey-Archer five-speed hub gear is not available with the coaster or drum brake, but otherwise it has all of the advantages of the three-speed hub and more. It has

a higher high gear and a lower low gear, and the gears in between are more closely spaced. For stop-and-go city riding, a five-speed hub has as many gears as you'd use on a ten-speed, plus instant shifting, whether or not your bicycle is moving. The five-speed hub gear is just now reentering the market after a lapse of several years. Unless you are buying a new bicycle, you will have to install this hub as a replacement part. It will fit into a three-speed rear wheel, replacing the internal parts of the Sturmey-Archer three-speed hub.

For an internal hub gear to serve you well, it is more important to use the right sprocket than with derailleur gears. With derailleur gears, if one gear is wrong, you usually have another close to it. With internal hub gears, you have only one gear in the cruising range. The other gears are far away. Your cruising gear is top gear with a three-speed hub, and fourth with a five-speed. Most internally geared bikes are geared way too high, with the idea that the middle gear is the normal cruising gear. Then the top gear is of little use, and you're missing the nice low climbing and starting gears you'll get if you change sprockets.

Needs vary somewhat, but you won't be far off if you use the sprocket sizes shown in this chart. These are appropriate for either the three- or five-speed hub.

With the sprocket shown in the chart, the top gear of the three-speed hub and the fourth of the five-speed should be an easy-spinning gear for level-ground riding.

Note that Sturmey-Archer makes all of the sprocket sizes shown except 21 teeth. Shimano makes a 21-teeth sprocket which fits the Sturmey-Archer hub. If you can't get a Shimano sprocket, you'll have to use a 20- or 22-teeth sprocket or change chainwheels. The gears shown here are a starting point. However, if the cruising gear makes you push too hard, lower it by using a larger sprocket. If, as is less likely, you spin out in this gear, use a smaller sprocket.

USING INTERNAL HUB GEARS

Internally geared hubs are almost foolproof. Still, it takes a bit of practice to shift one well. The trigger shifter control for a three-speed hub has click stops for the three positions. When you want to shift, you ease off pressure from the pedals, but you keep pedaling forward as you move the shift lever. When you've completed the shift, you push the pedals again.

There are a couple of tricks behind this technique. If you're upshifting, you can preselect the next gear. You move the shift lever, say from first to second, but you don't release pressure on the pedals. Then, when you want to shift, you release pressure. This way, you can move the lever when convenient and then move your hand away. The hub will not preselect a downshift. If you try to shift down without releasing pressure on the pedals, the hub simply will not shift. But you can pull on the lever and then release pressure on the pedals momentarily for a quick downshift.

The five-speed hub is a little more com-

plicated. It will preselect up into third, fourth, and fifth gears, but it will preselect *down* into first — the left side shift lever that selects first and fifth gears works backward for first. Sometimes you have to coax the five-speed into gear by pedaling forward rapidly after you've released pressure.

An internal hub gear sometimes needs a little help from the pedals to shift at a stop. As you move the shift lever, rock the pedals and roll the bike back and forth slightly. A five-speed hub will not shift easily into first gear unless it is already in second — so pull down the right lever first.

Since the speeds are farther apart on internal hub gears, shift down a little sooner and up a little later. It's better to spin than to strain.

USING DERAILLEUR GEARING

Derailleur gearing is more efficient, gives you more gears, and allows you to use a quick-release rear wheel, making it easier to transport your bike and replace tires. These are important advantages if the use you make of your bicycle requires them. But it takes more skill to use derailleur gears well.

A bike with only a rear derailleur is the simplest. All of the gears are in order as you shift the chain across the sprockets. But there are some things to learn about the way it shifts. Whether your bike has a rear derailleur alone or a front one as well, lift the rear wheel and have a look at how the rear derailleur works. (Have a friend hold the rear wheel up, or hang the bike up. Do not turn the bike upside down — if it has dropped handlebars you will damage the brake cables.)

First, try to move the shift lever back and forth without turning the crank. Don't pull the lever too hard because you might break the cable. If the wheel is not turning, the chain can't shift. The derailleur can't move, so there is no reason to shift if the wheel is not turning.

Now turn the cranks forward with one hand while operating the shift lever with the other. See how the chain hops from one rear sprocket to another. Notice how the spring-

Avoid this crisscross gear — small inner front chainwheel to small outer rear sprocket. It will wear out the chainwheel, the sprocket, and the chain rapidly.

loaded roller cage of the rear derailleur moves back and forth to keep tension on the chain. Note that the shift lever has no click stops at each gear. You have to shift by feel and by sound. As you shift, listen to the sound the chain makes. Get it on a middle sprocket, then pull the lever back a little. The chain will start to make a clanking noise as it tries to climb up onto the next larger sprocket. Now move the lever forward a little and hear the clanking noise go away as the chain centers over the sprocket. If you move the lever forward a little further, you will hear a rubbing noise. The chain is trying to jump off onto the next smaller sprocket.

You adjust the lever for the quietest sound, once you've shifted. When the chain is quietest, the derailleur pulleys are directly below the sprocket, so the chain is running straight up from the derailleur pulleys. Practice shifting back and forth — you may have to overshift slightly and then backtrack, but you should be able to get the chain onto each sprocket in order. If the chain will only shift two sprockets at a time, won't reach a sprocket, or jumps completely off the sprockets, something needs adjusting. It's not your problem; it's the bike's.

A bent or poorly adjusted derailleur will turn your ten-speed bike into a one-, two-, or three-speed bike. Don't let this happen to you.

Notice that the shift lever has a little wing nut on the side, or a big screwdriver slot that you can turn with a dime. The cable pulls against the shift lever, and the wing nut adjusts the friction in the lever. If there is too little friction, the lever will slip and the bike will shift by itself. Once this happens — and it will — you just tighten the wing nut a bit. Not too much, or it'll be hard to shift.

If your bike has a front derailleur, have a look at it now. With the chain on a middle sprocket in the back, shift the front derailleur.

The chain runs quietly and smoothly when the derailleur is adjusted so its pulleys are directly under one of the rear sprockets.

The chain makes a rubbing noise and may unexpectedly jump off onto the next sprocket, because the derailleur pulleys are between sprockets.

Notice how the chain jumps between chainwheels. With the chain on the large chainwheel, now shift the rear derailleur. As you shift the rear derailleur, note that the chain moves at the front derailleur. You may now have to adjust the front derailleur so the chain doesn't rub against the sides of the front derailleur chain cage. Learn to recognize the rattling noise when the chain rubs, so you'll know to correct it as you ride. If you can't stop the noise or the chain keeps falling off, the front derailleur needs adjusting or fixing.

Now, try turning the cranks backward. If both derailleurs are set right for the sprockets the chain is on, the chain will behave well. But try shifting the rear derailleur as you turn the cranks backward; note how the chain hangs up. You need to turn the cranks backward sometimes to get the pedals into starting position, but you must be careful that the derailleurs are set right. Never backpedal hard. Push, lightly, and if the chain hangs up, stop backpedaling and adjust the derailleur lever position. Backpedaling hard onto a poorly adjusted rear derailleur can bend it into a pretzel.

Now, think about how the sprockets and chainwheels give you high and low gears. Attached to the crank are a larger and a smaller chainwheel. With each turn of the crank, the large chainwheel pulls the chain faster, so the large chainwheel gives you a higher gear for going faster.

On the rear wheel, however, the smaller sprocket gives you the higher gear for faster riding because the same length of chain turns the rear wheel around more times on the smaller sprocket. One easy way to remember is that the higher gears are toward the outside of the bike. Shift from low to high gear as you turn the crank by hand, see which are which, and feel the rear wheel pick up speed.

Finally, before you get onto the bike, look down at the chain from above as you shift. Note that it sometimes goes from front to back at an angle. When the chain must cross all of the way between inside and outside, the angle is largest. The chain will probably make more noise in the two extreme combinations. When going from the small, inside chainwheel to the small, outside sprocket, the chain may drag on the large chainwheel. Because both the chainwheel and the sprocket are small, the rear derailleur may not be able to keep tension on the chain, and it may sag. These conditions don't mean anything is wrong with the bike as long as everything else works right. It's a bad idea to use this gear anyway. Either of the extreme combinations, large-large or small-small, put extra wear on the chain, chainwheels, and sprockets. The small-small combination is the worst, because it spreads the load among a smaller number of teeth on the chainwheel and sprocket, wearing them — and the chain — quickly.

Shift the bike into low gear and take it down from its stand. Now you'll try out the gears while riding.

Get onto the bike and get moving in low gear. It shouldn't be long before you're pedaling fast — low gear is easy. When you decide to shift, release pressure on the pedals but keep turning them. Get a good grip on the rear (right) shift lever. Hold it with the palm of your hand so you can swivel your wrist to operate it. Don't just hold the lever with your fingertips — they give you nothing to brace against. Rotate your wrist slowly, bit by bit, as you keep pedaling. Listen to the chain begin to make noise, then clatter and get quiet again. You'll probably feel a little shock through your feet as the chain jumps to another sprocket. When the shift is complete, start pedaling again. If the chain hangs up, release pressure from the pedals and stop the bicycle, and check out what went wrong.

Try this routine until you're used to it. Shift up and down, using the front and rear derailleurs. Use the same hand to shift both, except with bar-end shift levers. Remember to avoid the extreme combinations. Of course, this means that as you go up or down through the gears you will shift the front derailleur when the chain is on one of the middle sprockets in the rear. If the front derailleur makes a big jump in crank speed because the two chainwheels are of very different sizes, you may want to shift the rear derailleur back one step after shifting to the front, so the jump is smaller.

In your parking lot practice area, look down at the chain as you practice shifting at first. See how it works, but listen to it and feel it too. When you're riding on the road, you'll have more important things to look at than the chain. Practice until you can shift without looking. Remember to downshift before you stop, or you won't be able to start again in low gear.

Now, we'll work on finding the right gear for the speed you're riding at.

There's one thing to remember before everything else: you don't shift into top gear and stay there, the way you do in a car. Top gear on a ten-speed bicycle is an overdrive, only for going down hills or riding with a very stiff tail wind. If you use top gear much, you'll get sore legs for sure.

Actually, you shift your bike much more like an 18-wheeler semitrailer truck than like a car. Your 2-wheeler and that 18-wheeler have one important thing in common: a heavy load compared to the power of the engine. The 18-wheeler has ten gears, like your bike! You've listened to the truck drivers shifting over and over again as they go up and down hills. You shift your bike very much the same way, because you shift often.

Like the truck's engine, your engine, which is your legs, works best over a small range of speeds. If you go too slowly, it strains. Too fast, and it spins out, using up more of its power just to keep itself running.

As you shift up out of low gear, you keep the pedaling speed and effort constant. When you get to a cruising gear that lets you maintain a comfortable level of speed and effort, you leave the bike there. You don't automatically go up to high gear. But when you notice that the bike is getting harder or easier to pedal, you shift. Even very slight changes in slope or wind will make a shift worthwhile. You may not even notice why you feel like shifting, but your legs will tell you when it's time.

Much of the time, on level ground, you will ride with the chain on the large front chainwheel and one of the middle rear sprockets. That's a good cruising gear range on most bikes, for most people. You have smaller rear sprockets left for higher gears on downhills, or for tail winds. You'll use the second smallest sprocket a fair amount — the smallest rear sprocket rarely. It gives you a top gear.

Your shift sequence is what we men-

tioned before — straight across the sprockets at the rear, shifting the front chainwheels somewhere in the middle. But there are some variations.

HOW NOT TO DAMAGE DERAILLEURS

1. Check the adjustment of your derailleurs. Make sure the limit screws are adjusted correctly and the derailleurs aren't bent so they won't shift the chain off the sprockets.

2. Keep your chain well lubricated.

3. Do not shift unless the bicycle is moving forward.

4. When shifting, release pressure but keep the pedals turning. Without pressure on the pedals, *feel* the derailleurs working through your feet. If you feel the chain begin to snag or go completely loose, stop pedaling and stop the bicycle.

5. After shifting, apply force slowly, building it up to check if things are working right. The pedals should turn smoothly. If they turn bumpily or not at all, stop pedaling and stop the bike — the chain is coming off. If you pedal hard and the chain has gone off, you may snag it in between the sprockets and the frame, or spokes. You got it in there with your feet, and you have to get it out with your hands. Your feet are stronger than your hands.

6. Once you have shifted, listen to the derailleurs and adjust them until they're quiet and in line with the sprockets. If you hear rubbing, you're wasting your energy and wearing out your derailleur.

7. Backpedaling is an important technique to get a pedal in the right position for a start. But backpedal only after you have adjusted the derailleurs to be in line with the sprockets. Otherwise the chain will catch as you backpedal, and could bend the derailleur into a pretzel. If you feel the tension increasing like a spring as you backpedal, stop backpedaling immediately.

Your low gear may be lower than it has to be for a good start. This is usually true when the bike has a large, touring freewheel with the largest sprocket over 28 teeth. In this case, it's easiest to shift only partway down, to a middle gear. In traffic, you might just shift the rear derailleur down, and forget about the front derailleur — leave the chain on the large chainwheel. For a couple of seconds as you start, it's all right to use the large-large gear combination. Then you'll ride your bike as a five-speed. You only have to deal with one shift lever — easier in traffic. But when you're climbing a long hill, don't use the large-large combination; shift to the small front chainwheel instead.

Sometimes, you may find it best to skip over gears. Particularly when you start, you may pick up speed so quickly that you'll spend most of your time shifting if you want to use every sprocket. It's fine to skip gears then. But when you reach cruising speed, be choosier. If you're going to be cruising at the same speed for any length of time, it's worth the trouble to get the bike into the right gear, even if this takes tricky shifting. Such is the case if you're going up a long hill. The right gear will let you go the farthest, the fastest, with the least effort. Sometimes the gears using the smaller chainwheel are between those using the larger one, giving you a finer choice. Again, if your bike's gears don't serve your needs, they can easily be changed.

Learn to think ahead about shifting. Especially when you're about to go up a hill, shift early. It's much easier to spin a little fast for a second or two as you lose speed than to shift the bike into a lower gear after you've already lost speed.

Practice using your gears, listening for the shift, and going through the gears. Feel the vibration of the chain. Find your favorite sequences and your favorite gears for different conditions. Learn to shift smoothly and quickly — one good way is to shift back and forth between two gears next to each other when you're just cruising along and don't need top power.

CHAPTER FIVE

BASIC RIDING SKILLS

Let's get to the point. Being able to ride confidently, efficiently, and safely is a learned skill. Not a difficult skill to master, but a skill nonetheless. Unfortunately, too many people think they can just hop on a bike and ride off into the sunset.

Because many people see cycling as an activity first and foremost engaged in by children, they naturally assume that cycling is "kidstuff", a sport without a discernible set of skills. Nothing could be further from the truth.

In fact, because cycling involves a subtle biomechanical relationship between man and machine, because it is comprised of so many variables, adjustments, and positions, this sport is indeed a very complex activity. Paradoxically, the same people who would rush to the tennis instructor to solve a bad case of "running around their backhand" would never think of going to any authority for instruction in cycling skills.

In a *Bicycling* magazine editorial, James C. McCullagh discussed the experiences of Pittsburgh Pirate catcher Ed Ott who, on a bike ride for charity, had trouble getting used to the toe clips. Ott remarked that "I'm not used to pedaling a bicycle with toe clips. I never gave a thought at getting my feet out and then stopping."

Overall, Ott thought that the most difficult skill to master was simply riding the bike. "We were like country-boy bicyclists," he said. "We had no style whatsoever."

After two weeks on the road Ott had this advice for newcomers to the sport. "Definitely learn your equipment. A bicycle is fairly simple, but there are a lot of things that you might not take into consideration. Like the toe clips, for instance."

Most people, like Ed Ott, discover their bicycling mistakes the hard way. They fall off again and again. If that doesn't discourage them so much that they give up, they've still gone through much unnecessary suffering.

With this chapter, you'll learn the easy way, through controlled, safe practice sessions. Your learning will be filled with the pleasure of discovery, not the pain of landing on the ground. Oh, yes, you can expect to fall off a few times, especially when you're just beginning (not as often as Ed Ott did, though!). But then we'll also show you how to fall off so you're unlikely to hurt yourself. That's just one more part of our program. It's all here for you.

YOUR LEARNING BIKE

If you've never ridden before or haven't ridden in a long while, or if you're not confident that you can handle basic balancing, turning, and braking, then the best bike to learn on is not the same as the easiest one to ride on once you've learned.

The best bike to start on is a classic English utility bike, with a three-speed hub, upright handlebars, and rubber block pedals without toe clips. Derailleur gears, dropped handlebars, and toe clips take a little extra trouble to learn. You can put them off until later.

You can learn on another kind of bike; it's just a little harder. But we suggest that you borrow or rent a three-speed at the start, unless you have one already. You can learn before you sink any money into a bike, and you'll give yourself more time to think about the type you want or whether bicycling is for you. We think that it will be, but you'll probably feel better finding this out for yourself.

Your instructional bike should have at least one hand brake, and it helps if you can lower the saddle until you can put both feet flat on the ground. To get the saddle this low, the frame has to be an inch or so smaller than would be normal for you — though a frame of the correct size for you is still reasonably good — you'll just have to tiptoe a bit.

We also suggest that you wear tough, out-door clothing — wear either work gloves, bicycling gloves, or old leather gloves. A helmet of some kind should be worn; even a football or motorcycle helmet will do. Even if you've never ridden before, you won't have to fall off to learn the way we show you. But you do have more of a chance of falling when you're just starting. It's best to be prepared and spare yourself possible scrapes and bruises.

HOW TO BALANCE AND STEER

Here's how you can learn, or teach a child to ride without falling off. You'll need an adjustable wrench to prepare the bike. Lower the seat. Remove the pedals (remember that the left one unscrews clockwise). Find a stretch of pavement without traffic and a gentle slope such as a supermarket parking lot on a Sunday or a church parking lot on a weekday. We've recommended a hand brake, because a coaster brake doesn't work without pedals. If the bike doesn't have a hand brake, make sure that the slope is gentle enough to stop the bike easily by dragging your feet.

Sit on the bike and paddle down the slope with your feet. While still going slowly, test the brake. Squeeze the brake lever slowly and gently for an easy stop. Practice this several times, so you won't be tempted to grab it hard.

Go down the slope, again and again. Keep paddling along and steering the bike. Start lifting your feet off the ground. If the bike starts to lean to one side, steer into the lean. Think of balancing a yardstick on the end of your finger. Let yourself wander off course if you have to in order to keep your balance. You'll learn to keep your balance, then you'll learn to steer a straight course.

Poor form — the stiff, straight arms and back transmit road shock and result in soreness after a few short miles.

Sooner or later you will discover to your amazement that you don't have to put your feet down anymore. Congratulations — you've made it! But practice a little while longer. Practice holding a straight course and using the brake to come gently to a stop. Notice that you have put a foot down when you stop — you can't balance unless you're moving.

Once you feel confident about using the brake, put the pedals back on the bike. First, just coast with one foot, then both, on the pedals. Then, with the seat still lowered, practice pedaling. It's a little harder to balance while you're pedaling, but no real problem. For now, don't use toe clips if the bike has them. Ride with the pedals upside down or take the toe clips off.

Start a good pedaling technique right away. Don't pedal slow and hard, like climbing stairs. Keep the bike in a low gear. Pedal faster and lighter. Note that it's easier to balance the bike if you're not pushing down hard and throwing your weight around. Be steady and relaxed on the bike. Hold the handlebars — don't clench them.

Practice getting started. Sit on the bike. Keep your hands on the brakes, so the bike won't roll. Pull the left pedal around backward with your foot, to the ten o'clock position. Or with a coaster brake, scoot the bike backward while pushing down on the forward pedal. Your right foot will be on the ground, ahead of the other pedal. Look where your foot is; remember to keep it outboard or behind the pedal, so your leg doesn't bang the pedal as you start. Let go of the brakes, push down with your left foot, and lift your right foot all at once. As the right pedal comes up to the top, lift your foot onto it. If you begin to lean and lose your balance, just put a foot down. Practice getting started first on level ground, and then uphill, which is harder. Don't start by "scootering" along with one foot on the ground. It's slower and wobblier, and it doesn't work well uphill.

Once you can pedal steadily, practice stopping. As you stop, let the left pedal come all the way around to the bottom position (with a coaster brake, brake with the left foot). Just as you have come to a complete stop, stand

With the seat lowered and the pedals removed from the bicycle, it is possible to scoot along and learn to balance without danger of falling.

up on the left pedal and put your right foot down. Don't put your weight on the ground before you stop. With your weight off the bike, the brakes suddenly have an easier job, so you may tip painfully forward onto the handlebars. Practice stopping now, because you need to know the right technique before you've put the saddle up to its right height.

When you've stopped, lean on your right foot and try looking over your left shoulder. This is how you'll look back at traffic once you're riding in the street.

Practice starting, braking, and stopping until you feel confident. Then call it a day, or raise the saddle up to the right height for you and go on to the next step.

GETTING ON THE BIKE

Now raise the saddle to the right height for you. You may also wish to raise the handlebars to match the saddle. Pull the seatpost and handlebar stem all the way out before putting them back in, to make sure at least 2 inches are still inside the bike. If not, you could buy longer ones, but if the bike is a borrowed one, it may be time to switch bikes.

With the saddle at the right height, you can no longer put both feet on the ground, so it becomes a bit harder to get onto the bike. Don't keep the saddle too low; you can still lean the bike to put one foot down easily when the saddle is at the right height for you. If the saddle is too low, the bike will be very hard to pedal. Your legs only work well if they can straighten out.

Getting onto the bicycle. The cowboy mount —the cyclist throws one leg over the bicycle as if it were a horse. Since she makes no use of the pedals, this technique is slow. Since she throws her body weight completely across the bicycle, it's wobbly, too.

The shuffle mount — a slow start, which makes no use of the pedals. Neither this nor the cowboy mount is satisfactory in traffic.

The step mount — the right way, fast, and steady. The cyclist climbs over the bicycle.

First the bicyclist puts one foot on a raised pedal. Then she pushes down on the pedal — at the same time starting her going and lifting her onto the saddle. When stopping in traffic, it is necessary to remove only one foot from the toe clip.

So you raise the saddle. And the next step is to learn to get onto the bike. Here's how. Hold the handlebars and swing your leg over the back so you're standing over the bike in front of the saddle. If there's a child seat or something else big on the rear rack, you either tilt the bike and lift your leg over, or if you're limber, hold the saddle and swing your leg over the handlebars instead. Or roll the bike next to a curb and use the curb as a footstool.

Now you get on. Hold the bike steady with your hands on the brakes. Get one pedal into the forward position, as you've learned.

Here's your leap of faith, but since you already can balance it's easy. Let go of the brakes and at the same time stand up on the forward pedal, using it as a step to raise you onto the saddle. If the pedals have toe clips, forget about them for now. Just put your foot on the upside down pedal. As the pedal starts to go down, the bike will begin to move. Put your other foot on the other pedal as it comes up, and you're off. Keep your bike in low gear for now.

GETTING OFF THE BIKE

To get off the bike you slow down with the brakes, gently. As you come to a stop, you put one pedal in down position — preferably the left pedal — put your weight on it, and use it as a step to slide yourself forward off the saddle. Then you put your other foot on the ground. Remember not to put the foot down till you've stopped completely. Keep your hands on the brakes so the bike can't roll. You don't have to put both feet on the ground. If you keep one on the pedal, you can get started again quicker. While you're stopped, take the foot that's still on the pedal, hook it underneath the pedal, and hoist the pedal back around to your ten o'clock starting position. With toe clips, you will be able to pull the pedal around without taking your foot off it. If the bike has a coaster brake, switch feet so you have a foot on the front pedal.

Now, you're in a position to get going again quickly. You just step up onto the saddle the way we showed you before.

RIDING IN A STRAIGHT LINE

In your parking lot practice area, you can wander in all directions, but in the street you have to keep going in a straight line. You can probably already do this when there are no distractions. Now, we'll make it harder to ride straight to improve your skill.

First, practice riding straight when looking behind you. You will need to do this whenever you are preparing to make a turn across traffic. In your practice area, find a straight, painted line to ride down. Ride steadily in a

Learn to ride in a straight line by practicing looking back while riding in a straight line — an invaluable skill for traffic riding.

The cyclist practices riding straight while both signalling and looking back at the same time.

low gear. Look over your shoulder. Look ahead again. You've probably swerved to the left, because you've leaned your body to the left. Try again. Turn just your neck. This way, you'll keep your hands steady on the handlebars so you can feel if you're turning them, and you'll keep your body weight centered over the bike. Keep practicing until you can ride straight. Then practice some more, but lean your body. Learn to keep going straight by leaning the bike the opposite way.

When you've mastered looking behind you, practice riding with one hand on the handlebars. Pretend you're making a turn signal, which is a primary reason to ride one-handed. Wave your free arm around and feel how it affects your balance. If you start to wobble, try using your arm to help keep your balance, like a bronco rider.

Practice making a turn signal and looking behind you at the same time, since you often do both at once.

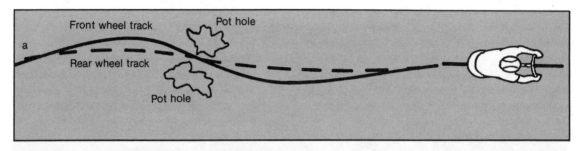

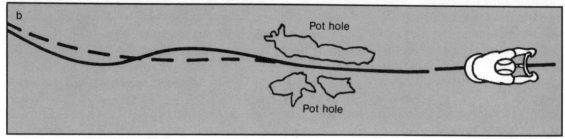

a) Technique for avoiding two small side-by-side obstacles at an angle to your path. b) Technique for aligning your bike to pass through a narrow corridor with the rear wheel directly behind the front.

Practice reaching for the shift lever, pushing up your glasses, adjusting your clothing — all of the things which you will do with one hand while riding.

Finally, practice aiming your bike's front wheel. It is easiest to do this during actual rides. Find a pebble, 15 or 20 feet ahead of you. It should be big enough for you to feel but not big enough to damage the tires. Ride straight at it and try to get the wheel to roll over it. Keep your eyes on the pebble as long as possible, though you won't see it as it goes under your wheel. Practice a few times on each ride until you almost always hit the pebble. As you get better, practice doing this while you look away. This skill will be very valuable to you in threading your way between bumps, potholes, and other road hazards.

Also practice riding down a painted line. You'll find this harder than aiming for a pebble, because you can't swerve. You have to go

steady all the way. It's hardest if you're going slowly, so practice this.

Riding in a straight line is fine training for balance, but also a valuable exercise for riding in traffic. If you can just creep forward while waiting for a stop sign or traffic light, you get started quicker and surer than if you have to stop and put a foot down.

Some people learn to keep the bike balanced while standing absolutely still. The trick is to turn the front wheel sideways so it's facing up a slope. Then you pedal forward and let the bike roll backward to balance.

RIDING WITHOUT HANDS

This is something you rarely do when actually traveling somewhere. But it is excellent practice for balance and relaxation. It is the most sensitive test of your bike's steering. And when you change hand positions you release both hands from the handlebars. If you feel comfortable riding without hands, you can get smoothly from one position to another instead of groping along the handlebars.

Start learning to ride without hands during your daily riding by relaxing your grip on the handlebars. The bike steers itself. Your hands are light feathers on the handlebars, just sensing, not steering. By relaxing your hands and arms, you have more energy left for pedaling, and you'll save yourself aches and pains after riding. You'll also be able to feel your balance better if you're not holding the handlebars in a tight grip.

Once you've learned to relax, practice riding without hands: go to a parking lot or an empty street with smooth, clean pavement. Get yourself moving fairly fast. It's harder to ride without hands slowly, because your bike's self-steering works better at higher speeds. A slight downhill is good, so you won't have to pedal. With your hands on the top of the handlebars, lift one off. With one hand still on the handlebar, relax your grip and feel how the bike steers itself. Now stop pedaling and coast while you lift your hand off bit by bit. Finally, you will have only your index finger on the handlebar. By this time, the bike is steering itself. You can't turn the handlebars with one finger but you can feel how the handlebars are turning.

Finally, lift the finger off — you're riding without hands.

If you can't do it the first time, try again. But if several tries don't bring success, don't blame yourself. Your bike could be at fault. Riding without hands while coasting is not much harder than normal riding. But worn headset bearings can make it completely impossible. And if the front fork of your bike is bent, you'll find that you have to lean to one side to keep the bike going straight. Have someone test your bike who can already ride without hands. If the problem is with the bike, have it fixed. Even if you don't ride without hands, worn bearings make it harder to steer precisely. And a bent front fork will give you an aching shoulder from pushing on one handlebar more than the other.

When you've learned to coast without hands, practice pedaling without hands. This is harder, because pedaling motions disturb your balance. You must pedal smoothly, lightly, and fast. Pedaling without hands is good practice to eliminate wasted motions in your legs.

Practice shifting your hands between handlebar positions. Once you can ride without hands, this is easy. With dropped bars, practice getting from each of the other positions into braking position. Learn to do this quickly, without thinking. With flat bars, practice switching from the middle to the ends.

Changing your hand positions is your main use for riding without hands. But once in a while, on a long trip, you can take your hands off the handlebars, sit up straight, and stretch your back. It's refreshing, and it's safe as long as the pavement is smooth and there's no traffic around you.

TURNS

Up to now, you've been doing moderate turns in your practice riding. Now, we'll take you through some techniques so you'll learn how to take more severe turns.

Before you get on the bike, here are three experiments you can do to learn some basic things about how your bike turns.

First, stand next to the bike. Put one pedal in bottom position and lean the bike over until that pedal hits the ground. If the bike has toe clips, turn the pedal right side up. How the pedal hits the ground sets your limit on turning while you are pedaling.

Now, turn the pedal up and lean the bike farther, pressing down on it in line with the frame and wheels. See how far it will lean before the tires begin to skid out. Tire skidding sets the absolute limit on turning. Tire skidding will happen at different angles on different surfaces — about 45 degrees on hard pavement down to almost nothing on snow and ice.

Also, you've noted that your bike steers itself when going straight. But turn the front wheel sideways a bit and push the bike. Note

For maximum stability in turns, the cyclist keeps her body in line with the bicycle.

that the wheel turns sideways farther. The bike only steers itself when the front wheel is close to straight. At normal speeds, it will be. But at very slow speeds, you can turn sharply enough so the front wheel will steer itself farther to the side. So at very slow speeds, turning sharply, you must be more careful about turning.

Your bike steers by leaning, more like an airplane than like a car. That's another reason it turns steadier at higher speeds. Think again of balancing a yardstick on your finger; before you can make it go sideways, you must lean it. The bike and the airplane both steer like the yardstick. It's no wonder that the Wright brothers, who were bicyclists and bicycle mechanics, succeeded with the first airplane. They already had practice in steering. (Their interest in aerodynamics was not limited to airplanes, either — they invented dropped handlebars, too!)

In your practice area, try some turns. First, pedal around in large circles. Keeping the size of the circles the same, note how you must lean more as you speed up. Try circles in both directions. Get used to the idea of the whole world being tilted while you feel like you're right side up. Raise the inside pedal and coast as you lean sharply — remember about catching the pedal as you lean.

Pretend there's a patch of sand or oil somewhere ahead of you as you turn. Practice straightening out momentarily to avoid a skid, then getting back into your turn after you've passed the slippery place.

While turning, practice looking in different directions.

Now, try small, tight turns at low speeds. Note how wobbly the bike is. Try the slowest, tightest curves you can make. They are good practice for balance, and sometimes in tight places, you have to make turns like this.

Now, try a little experiment. Ride along

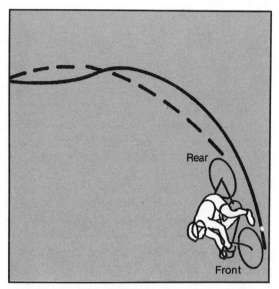

In order to turn sharply to the right, turn the handlebars to the left first to start a lean to the right.

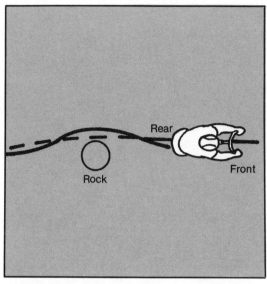

A quick turn of the handlebars also gets you by small obstacles. You turn the opposite way afterward to regain a straight course.

Practice slaloms to get the sense of how to start and finish turns quickly. Take the dotted line if you can't see around the curve; the solid line if you can.

straight at medium speed and then turn the handlebars momentarily to one side without leaning. Doing this will upset your balance, and you'll have to swerve to keep from falling. But which way will you swerve, and why?

If you turn the handlebars to the right, you will end up swerving to the left — and vice versa. Why? When you turn the handlebars to the right, the bike steers to the right under you. Then you are leaning to the left. Once you are leaning to the left, you must steer to the left to keep your balance. It's the yardstick example again. If you move the bottom of the yardstick to the right, the yardstick will lean to the left and then you must chase it to the left to keep it from dropping. The same thing happens if you steer your bike to the right under you.

Steering without leaning is how you start and end every turn. If you do it slowly, you probably won't even notice it. But if you do it fast, you can start a turn fast — and sometimes you have to do this.

Now practice a slalom. Make large, easy turns at first. Then make them tighter. Notice how you use steering without leaning to cross over from one turn to the next. You actually steer sharper to the right at the end of your right turn, so you can lean into your left turn. Practice raising one pedal and then the other as it comes to the inside of the turns.

Once you're used to the steering without leaning, here are two ways you can use it to swerve quickly. Swerving is your most important way to avoid accidents. Since your bike is narrow and can turn quickly, swerving works better than braking many times.

Practice a quick weave by laying a bean bag or sponge on the pavement. Ride toward it and at the last moment steer to one side. You

do this without leaning, so you will have to steer the other way right afterward. Your bike goes first to one side and then to the other under you — two back to back turns — but your body keeps on going in a straight line. This is how you avoid an obstacle like a rock or pothole without swerving out into traffic.

To make a quick turn, move your front wheel to one side without leaning. This way, you quickly get yourself started turning in the other direction. The quick turn will be especially useful if a car pulls past you on the left and then cuts a right turn in front of you. Instead of running into the car, you turn with it. Practice with the sponge again, but pretend it is a car.

Now let's consider the best way to go through a corner at speed.

Your bike can lean the same amount regardless of speed — but at higher speeds

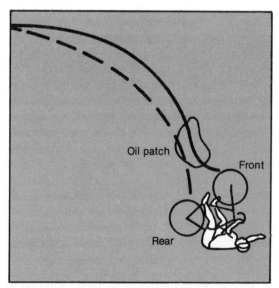

Aerial view of front wheel skid. In a typical scenario, the front wheel plows ahead and the rider turns more sharply to keep balance — and subsequently falls.

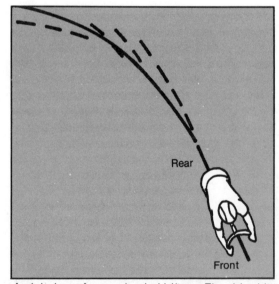

Aerial view of rear wheel skid/turn. The rider hits the rear brake and the rear wheel slides to the outside. The rider turns less sharply and keeps balance.

the same lean gets you a less sharp turn. The more sharply you turn, the more you must slow down. So the fastest way to go through a turn is to make the turn as gradually as possible. Suppose you're going around a right turn — you move from the left side of your traffic lane to the right, and then to the left again. This is what you do if there's no traffic — clearly, you wouldn't do this if a car were next to you! But on a downhill run, for example, when you're going as fast as the cars anyway, you keep up your speed by choosing your line through a turn.

Depending on how sharply you turn, you may or may not have to lift the inner pedal. In level riding, there are few turns too sharp to pedal through, except sharp right turns onto cross streets. Develop your sense of when a pedal is getting close to the pavement. Racers lean the bike outward so they can pedal through sharp turns, but for general riding, it makes good sense to keep the bike in line with you for stability and raise the inner pedal. Practice riding around in small circles, pedaling faster until you actually hit a pedal lightly. It's relatively risk free if you build up your speed gradually, and you should get used to the feeling and know the limit. The front wheel may jump outward a bit, and then you will recover balance.

More about turning and braking in the next section on braking which follows, and in the section on downhill riding. More about turning on bad surfaces in the section on riding on ice and snow.

HOW TO USE THE BRAKES

The front and rear brakes on a bike do not work the same. It is best if you use your stronger, more sensitive hand to operate the front brake. Unless you already have learned to use the brake levers the opposite way, have them switched before you study braking.

Do an experiment to see how the brakes work differently. Stand next to the bike and roll it along. Squeeze the rear brake lever.

The rear wheel will skid. This is because the bike tries to keep moving forward after you apply the brake. Since the bike is high above the ground, weight lifts off the rear wheel.

Now try the same experiment but squeeze the front brake lever instead.

The bike will stop much more quickly, but if you brake too hard, the rear wheel will lift off the ground.

Because the front wheel will not skid, the front brake will stop you most quickly. But if you apply the front brake too hard, the rear wheel will lift, and you'll go flying over the handlebars. To get the quickest possible stop, you have to understand the front brake and how to control it. With a little practice, you can learn how to do this reliably and safely.

Now you know that the two brakes work differently, and you've tested them and decided which to use with which hand. Next, you'll get the feel of them through practice.

You'll use your paved practice area. But also find another area with a hard, smooth dirt surface — or in winter, smooth, packed snow. You'll be skidding the bike a little, and it's best to do this where you won't wear out the tires so quickly.

Practice getting in the right position for braking. Crouch down low and slide back on the saddle with your arms reaching straight forward to the brake levers. You get low and far back on the bike so you can brake harder without going over the handlebars. Try this a few times, braking moderately as you have already been doing. You don't have to get into this extreme braking position for moderate braking, but it's good to learn right at the start.

If your bike still has "safety" levers, don't use them. We've recommended that you remove them. It is not possible to use the proper braking technique and position with "safety" levers. If you can't reach the normal levers on dropped handlebars, that's because the handlebar stem is too long. Replace it with one that fits you.

On the dirt surface, practice using the rear brake. Travel straight at a moderate speed and apply the rear brake, squeezing the lever slowly and gently. Make several runs. Each time, squeeze the lever a little bit harder. As you squeeze the lever harder, the rear tire will make a grating noise. When you hear this noise, release pressure on the brake lever slightly — the tire is just beginning to skid. Practice taking the tire near the skid point several times.

This bicycle is equipped with "safety" levers and stem shifters, hazardous devices.

Practice rear-wheel braking some more on the dirt surface, but get into the braking position now. Notice that you can apply the brake harder before the rear wheel grates.

Finally, practice rear-wheel braking, increasing force on the brake lever until the rear wheel actually skids. Notice that you can still control the bike. The rear end of the bike will slide around a bit, but you can still steer, since the front wheel is not skidding. Practice releasing the brake lever quickly as soon as the rear wheel begins to skid. Your properly trained reaction to skidding is to release the brakes. A too common panic reaction is to grab them harder — with predictable results.

Now, move to your paved practice area.

Practice moderate braking. On the paved practice area, use the front and rear brakes together. At first, apply both brakes equally hard. Listen to the rear tire. When it begins to make a grating noise, reduce force on both brake levers.

Now, practice braking harder. Make sure the pavement ahead of you is free of sand, gravel, and bumps. Get going faster. When you start to brake, crouch down into braking

As this experiment shows, a strong application of the front brake will result in a short stop as the rear wheel lifts off the ground.

position. Apply the two brakes together, but apply the front brake two or three times as hard as the rear brake. First, try this with moderate pressure on the front brake. After a couple of runs, increase front brake pressure until the rear wheel begins to make noise, then, back off. Just as you are about to stop, release force so the brakes can't grab. This is important. Friction between the brake shoes and rims is less as long as they are sliding past each other. When they stop, they will

grab unless you release force. Either you will lurch to a stop, or you may go over the handlebars.

Now, practice full panic stop technique. In the crouched position, apply the front brake three times as hard as the rear brake. Apply the brakes quickly partway — still within safe limits — then slowly increase force until the rear tire begins to grate. For this exercise it helps to have a friend call out when to hit the brakes, so you'll have practice doing it with-

If you are going too fast on a downhill turn and are drifting off the road, steer straight momentarily to allow you to lean further.

out thinking about it first. Note that you can get a very sharp stop this way. In an actual panic situation, you rarely come to a complete stop. You usually slow, but keep going so you can still steer or swerve.

While still on the paved surface, practice braking with your front brake only. Remember how hard you were braking when practicing panic stops. As long as you keep well below this range and the road surface is hard and clean, it is safest to use the front brake alone. As long as you're going straight (not leaning), the front wheel will never skid, and if you don't use the rear brake, neither will the rear wheel. So, braking with your front brake gives you the best control for moderate stops on good, dry pavement. Also, your rear tire will last much longer. Too many people wear out rear tires like rubber pencil erasers. But as you practice braking with only the front brake, learn to keep your eyes on the pavement ahead. Bumpy, loose, soft, or wet surfaces are not for braking with only the front brake. Next, you will practice what to do on them.

Go back to your dirt surface. First, use the rear brake alone. Then practice looking carefully at the surface ahead of you. If it looks reasonably good and if you can apply the rear brake reasonably hard before the tire skids, apply the front brake lightly, too. Remember, you must be very careful with the front brake on a bad surface. But as you develop judgment, you will learn to apply the front brake safely for extra stopping power.

Practice taking the front brake to the limit on a bad surface. If your dirt surface is hard, try something softer and slipperier — mud, sand, or gravel. Just go very slowly. Be ready to put a foot down.

Make several runs. Apply the front brake harder each time. Listen to the front tire and feel it through the handlebars. As it reaches its limit, it will begin to make a grating

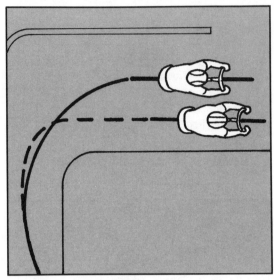

The fastest line through a high-speed turn is the one in which you turn least sharply. Take the solid line if you can see around the curve; the dash line if you can't.

noise — or on a soft surface like mud, it will sink in and feel "mushy." If this starts to happen, release the brake.

Finally, apply the front brake too hard. You'll find you can't steer the bike. As soon as the front wheel stops turning, it will just plow along. It doesn't matter which way you steer because the front wheel will go sideways as easily as it will go straight. You will have to release the brake quickly or put a foot down.

On the dirt surface, practice braking while turning. You use the dirt surface so you can see what happens at low speeds, under easy conditions.

First, practice applying the rear brake lightly as you turn. Go slowly! Note that the rear wheel will tend to skid out. If it does, release the brake — you may have to put a foot down.

Then try the front brake — note that you will definitely have to put a foot down as the front wheel plows straight ahead.

At a higher speed, you would fall. A front wheel skid will almost certainly result in a fall; a rear wheel skid less certainly. Turning and braking don't mix well. Your tires have only a certain amount of traction — more on good surfaces, less on bad. The better the surface, the more you can lean. The more you're leaning into a turn, and the worse the surface, the less braking you can do.

Brake only lightly, favoring the rear brake, when leaning much at all. When leaning hard, don't brake at all. Again, remember to straighten out in the middle of a turn if you come to a slippery place, or if you must brake. On a long slippery or gravelly stretch, you alternate turning with braking.

Finally, practice a controlled skid turn or "brodie," using the rear brake. Kids do this all the time on their coaster brake bikes. You don't want to do it a lot if you value your rear tire, but it's one more way to know how to control your bike. It's useful at times to avoid falls and accidents. Start the bike into a turn, then jab the rear brake. Notice that you can swing the rear end of the bike out as it skids, making for a very sharp turn. Practice until you're comfortable with the technique.

ONE-HANDED BRAKING

Ride at a moderate speed with your hands in the braking position. Take your rear brake hand off the handlebars. Hold it just next to the brake lever in case you need to reach for the handlebar. One-handed braking is difficult at first.

Stop pedaling and apply the brake slowly and lightly with the hand that is still on the handlebar. Notice that you will have to shift your balance. If anything scary starts to happen, release the brake. After you've slowed down, turn around, ride up and down through your practice area, and practice one-handed braking until you feel confident. Try it with the other hand, too. As you brake harder, turn the pedals so the leg on the side with the hand off the handlebars is in the forward position. Brace this leg against the bike's top tube. Your momentum, through your arm, tries to push the handlebar away from you. When you press on the top tube, you can push forward on the pedal instead of your hand.

Learn to balance braking forces so you keep riding in a straight line. Keep applying the brake harder, bit by bit, until you can't keep the bike going straight. Get a feeling for how hard you are applying the brake. This is as hard as you can without bringing the other hand to the handlebar.

Practice waving your free arm around to see how it affects your balance.

We've suggested using the front brake hand, because one-handed braking works best with the front brake. Since the front wheel won't skid, you have better control of the bike — and in any case, you can't brake hard enough one-handed to be in danger of going over the handlebars. On bad pavement, you'd have to use the rear brake, but you wouldn't be riding one-handed. Still, practice braking again with each hand as you make a turn signal with the other.

If your bike has derailleur gears, practice one-handed braking while you reach for the shift levers. With down-tube shifters, you shift both levers with one hand. It's best to use the right hand, as you need more control for the right, rear derailleur shifter. But if you are right-handed, you might see if you can shift with the left, to keep your more sensitive right hand on the brake lever. You must work handlebar-end shifters one at a time while braking, but then they're closer to the brake levers. Stem shifters are clumsy, no matter how you try to use them. We strongly recommend that you replace them with handlebar-end or down-tube shifters.

Now, brake one-handed again and imagine that a pedestrian suddenly walks out in front of you. Practice reaching for the handlebar with your free hand — try it with each hand. Use a smooth, sweeping motion. Practice until you can reach accurately for the brake lever to make a panic stop.

ADVANCED BRAKING

Here's how you take your brakes closer to the panic-stop limit without going over the front of the bike. Also, here's how you can use the front brake more to give you better control in normal braking.

Make sure your brakes are in top condition. Everything should be tight and adjusted properly, the cables should be greased, and the rims should be free of bulges and dents. Aluminum rims usually work better, though steel rims in good condition are fine. Your brakes should work smoothly, without buzzing or grabbing, and little squealing, if any. You should be able to modulate brake pressure smoothly, not just in jerks.

Take your bike out to a parking lot or empty street practice area. Wear thick clothing, helmet and gloves! There's a bit of calculated risk here.

First, try out the panic-stop technique you've been using. Apply the front brake harder than the rear brake, increasing force until the rear wheel begins to skid. Try this several times. Get a sense of how hard you are applying the front brake and how quickly you are slowing down. Each time, hold the rear brake lever more lightly, so you're braking harder before the rear wheel begins to

skid. Remember to let some pressure off the front brake lever just before you stop because the front brake is most likely to grab the wheel when it's barely turning.

Now practice moderate to heavy braking using the front brake alone. Never apply it quite as hard as you did when you used the rear brake as a gauge. But notice that you can get a very solid stop out of the brake.

You can keep your front brake hand on the brake lever all the time in heavy traffic, while your other hand is free to operate the shift levers and make hand signals. In case you have to stop quickly, you will grab for the handlebars with your other hand, but you needn't get that hand to the brake lever.

For a controlled panic stop from the high downhill speed, you will still want to use the rear wheel as a gauge for the front. But at more moderate speeds, you will rarely have to stop this quickly. You know how hard you can use the front brake before you're in any danger of spilling, and you stay just short of this.

Finally, practice going beyond the limit of front braking. Do this at a very slow speed — two or three miles per hour — for safety. Grab the front brake and instantly let it go. Practice this several times. Then start grabbing the lever a little harder, bit by bit, until you're actually lifting the rear wheel off the ground. Get the feeling of this technique so that your reflexes are trained for lightning response. Then, if you ever do lift the rear wheel off the ground in actual braking, you'll have a fighting chance of getting it back down again. We've done it successfully in actual panic situations.

We end this section with the same comments we made at the beginning: you want your brakes to be in top shape. Look at it this way. A small bulge in your front rim means that you can use the front brake only *half* as hard, doubling your stopping distance. A big difference, when you really need your brakes.

A STRAIGHT, QUICK START

Starting straight and quick is one of your most important skills for riding in traffic. You'll move out much sooner from a stop sign, because you won't have to wait for such a long break in the traffic. And at a traffic light, a good start makes the difference between moving out smartly in the traffic flow or holding up drivers behind you while you fumble around in a cloud of exhaust smoke.

There are four ways people commonly get onto bicycles. Only one of these ways gets you started quickly. Examine which way you use, and then learn the right way.

1. The cowboy mount. You push down on the pedal on your side of the bike as you throw yourself over. Fast, but wobbly, and no use once you're already straddling the bike.

2. The scootering mount. You run along next to the bicycle and hop onto it while it is moving. This looks flashy, but works poorly, especially with toe clips. You have to put both of your feet into the toe clips while you are moving. Also, you are likely to wobble as you hop onto the bicycle.

3. The shuffle mount. You stand over the bicycle with one foot on its pedal, but the pedal is in the down position where you can't push it. You shuffle along with your other foot on the ground until you've built up some speed, then lift up that foot and push down on the other pedal. This is a very slow way to get started.

4. The step mount. This is the best way to mount, which is the one we've described.

A properly threaded toe strap is twisted under the pedal so it doesn't slip around, and is adjustable while riding.

To get started quickly, you use the step mount, and then:

1. You must be able to ride your bike in a straight line as it speeds up. A bicycle is not very steady at low speeds, especially when you're adjusting your balance just after you've climbed onto it. It takes a bit of practice until you can start straight every time.

2. You must be able to use your gears correctly to get the most power as you gain speed. You've got to have the bike in a low gear before you start, and you have to know how to shift it quickly and smoothly up through the gears as you gain speed.

You've practiced the different parts of starting technique already — mounting, riding straight, and shifting. Now put them together, practicing with a series of starts and stops. You also get to practice your braking technique. With derailleur gears, remember to shift down before you stop. And when you stop, take only one foot out of the toe clip — you only need to put one foot down. If you take the other foot out, you'll just have to put it back in again before you start.

Now you're ready to tackle hills.

UPHILL RIDING

"How can I climb that?" you may ask.

And we'll answer: "On your bike," — and depending on how you do it, you can make it easier than walking, or you can pace yourself for maximum effort and the fastest possible time up the hill. Then you can rest going down the other side.

Now is the time to shift down — before the hill begins.

Hills will be harder when you're just starting. It takes time to build up your strength, though you'll have a good head start if you've practiced another endurance activity like running or swimming.

But even if you're out of shape, you can climb almost any hill if you have a low enough gear on your bike and if you use good technique. So this section is mostly about technique. Strength and endurance will develop by themselves, through your riding.

The basic technique in hill climbing is pacing yourself. The most common mistake beginners make is to work too hard at the beginning of a hill and get tired out before the top. This almost always goes along with trying to climb the hill in too high a gear, standing up on the pedals.

Beginners often unconsciously think of hills as flights of stairs, and push harder on the pedals to climb, like climbing stairs. But how many flights of stairs can you climb before you're worn out?

You'll be climbing hills much taller than five-story buildings, so a different technique is in order. Follow the instructions below.

Shift down, again and again, before you have to. Get your bike in a low enough gear that you're not tiring out. Push a little harder than on level ground but keep the pedals spinning just as fast. As you slow down, you shift gears, but your pedal speed stays the same. Stay sitting down on the bike; get into a low crouch. Stand up to push hard only if you're in bottom gear and losing speed or on a very steep hill where the bike is tilted so far back you can't push down effectively. If you have to stand up and push frequently on hills, even after you've been riding regularly for a month or two, you need a lower gear on your bike.

After you've reached the top of each hill, think about how you've climbed it. If you had some endurance left over, you know that you can start up it faster next time. And if you've had to walk, you'll take the hill slower next time. Develop your judgment, and plan each climb in advance. Best to misjudge on the side of caution, though. It's nice to take the first part of a hill too slowly and have some energy left to go charging over the top. For the final burst of acceleration, go ahead and stand up on the pedals. It's a welcome change of pace. The extra speed will stay with you as you go down the other side.

At first, you may get tired and have to get off and walk on hills even if you've been using the best technique. It's probably not worth the trouble to put very low gears on your bike if you'll be building up strength quickly. Though there are some places, like San Francisco, where hills are steep enough that very low gears make sense even for strong riders. The same thing applies if you're going to be pulling a trailer with your bike. In general, it's good to have the low gears available in case you need them, and our advice on buying and adapting bikes has reflected this opinion.

DOWNHILL RIDING

How to go down a hill depends on what you want out of it. There are many ways, and different hills demand different styles.

Be sure to always keep within the limits of control. Those limits will depend on many things, such as the steepness of the hill, the pavement, the curves, how far you can see, and the possibility of crossing and entering traffic. Riding downhill is one situation in which you can go very fast. Gravity gives you several horsepower on a steep hill, compared with the ½ horsepower in your legs. Speeds up to 50 mph are not uncommon on long, steep hills. And your bike was made for comfort and pedaling ease at lower speeds, not

Standing up out of the saddle is useful for a short burst of power to gain speed at the top of a hill.

for its best handling at very high speeds.

Unlike a car or a motorcycle, your bike has a high center of gravity, hard narrow tires, and no spring suspension. Tire contact with the road becomes less certain as you bounce over bumps at high speeds, and there is an increased possibility of your skidding or tipping over forward. When you're going down a hill, you're already partly tipped over forward.

Beginners commonly get caught up in the excitement of fast downhill runs, and crash by misjudging a curve at the bottom of a hill and running off the road. And a high-speed downhill accident is much more dangerous than one at normal speeds, so be warned! If you're not really sure, take it easy.

Subject to these cautions, here are some techniques for descending hills:

. . . For moderate downslopes, you just keep pedaling. You shift into higher gears so the pedals don't outrun you. (Bicyclists call it "spinning out" when they can't keep up with the pedals.) Toe clips and straps help you keep your feet on the pedals at high rpms.

. . . Even on a moderate downslope, there is a point at which you will go faster if you coast than if you pedal. This point is actually one gear below the highest gear on most ten-speed bicycles if you use correct coasting technique. You can prove this to yourself on group rides. If you coast well, you will sail right past people who are still pedaling, to everyone's amazement. When you coast, you can tuck in like a skier to cut your air resistance. You squeeze your legs together against the bike's top tube for stability, with one knee above the top tube and one below, so the legs are mostly in line with each other. Crouch down low, so your upper body is nearly horizontal. Lift slightly off the seat, still grasping the top tube between your thighs — spring with your hands and feet — arms bent — and keep your head up. Again, toe clips will help you keep control.

. . . Sprinting for top speed is not your only good choice, even when you could go down the hill at top speed safely. In hot weather, it is pleasant to cool yourself on the downhill by sitting up to let the air breeze by you. You can, up to a point, control your speed by how upright you sit. With dropped handlebars, keep your hands at the outer ends as you sit upright, for control. You can use the brakes lightly from over the tops to slow your speed. Remember, though, that you have less control when you are sitting up. Moderate your speed as you approach turns.

. . . On your downhill run keep pedaling in cold weather. When you stop pedaling, your legs cool down. Not only are you producing less heat, but muscle action helps squeeze blood through your legs, and when you stop pedaling, this action stops. In hot weather, on the other hand, spinning your overheated legs after you've gone past the top of the hill will help the blood cool them. You don't have to push, just spin idly.

. . . As you reach the bottom of a hill you've been coasting down, start pedaling lightly before you have to. Put the bike in top gear and start spinning. As you slow down, the free-wheel will "catch up" with you and you will move smoothly into pedaling for power. Do not push hard if you've been coasting. Pedal lightly till your legs warm up, shifting down as necessary to keep your feet spinning. Hard pedaling on cold legs is very bad for your knees. Many a knee injury has occurred as a rider reached the bottom of a hill and began to charge up the next hill on stiff, refrigerated legs.

. . . To slow or stop on a hill, you must use more care than on level ground. You must maintain a longer safety distance. It takes longer to slow or stop, both because of the slope and because you will tip over easier if you use your front brake hard. On a steep hill, it is safest to use both brakes evenly, or in extreme cases favor the rear brake. At high speeds, you must be especially careful that sand, gravel, bumps, and pebbles don't cause the front wheel to skid while braking. It is especially important that your brakes work smoothly.

. . . Beware of brake fade. A coaster brake is nice in wet weather but not suitable for downhills because it will overheat. In addition to a coaster brake, install rim brakes on both wheels. If you can go down a hill without using the brakes, you can count on them for a good, solid stop even from high speed. If you go down slowly, braking, you're all right too. The worst situation is where a hill is steep enough that you must use the brakes constantly but straight enough that you can still go quite fast. Then your brakes will be generating a lot of heat. The brake shoe rubber may soften. The brakes may have reduced friction if you need to apply them harder to stop. Test them occasionally by applying the rear brake harder.

Since rims can get very hot, use both brakes equally to keep heat buildup down. Excess heat may expand the air in a tire and pop it off the rim. Apply the rear brake a little harder to make up for cable friction.

. . . One problem on fast downhills is that your bike's front wheel and fork may begin to shake. This happens when the rotation of the wheels matches a natural vibration of the frame. Loose headset or wheel bearings, poor frame alignment, poorly fastened handlebar bags and front racks, wheel imbalances caused by spoke reflectors, loose spokes, or poor truing can all help to feed a shake. Keep after these problems. Test your bike for its shake — you do this at low speeds by shaking the handlebars back and forth. If they tend to keep going by themselves, your bike may shake at high speeds. A very rapid shake is rarely a problem. A slower, wobbly shake is the one to watch out for. Remember how it feels. If you clamp the top tube between your knees and hold the handlebars at the outer ends, you will usually keep a shake from starting. You use your arms and your knees to stabilize the frame. But if a shake starts to build up, hold the handlebars tighter — keep your arms slightly bent, but stiffen your arm and leg muscles to act as shock absorbers. Brake to reduce your speed. Use the rear brake mostly, but use the front brake lightly, too, because it will clamp the front wheel and help increase stability.

. . . Hills with turns require special care. When banking steeply, keep the bike in line with you for the best control. When you must brake, do it well before you come to the turns. The faster you are going, the more you lean in a turn and the more you lean, the less traction is left for braking. So brake first, then turn. It is easy to misjudge turns — if you are taking a turn too fast, your instinct will be to lean less. But then you'll run off the road or into traffic. It's better to lean deeper into the turn and stay in your traffic lane. Your tires probably have much more traction than you expect, and if the tires do skid out and you fall, your lean has already shortened your fall. So it's better to lose traction and skid along on your rear end than to run off the road and go flying. Practice momentarily turning the front wheel straighter, steering without leaning to increase a lean. This takes nerve at high speeds.

On hills with turns, be ultra careful of the road surface. Your tires are pressing straight down under you, but straight down to you is sideways to the road. Even a small bump or pebble can make the bike jump sideways. So take downhill turns at high speed only when you can be sure that the surface is smooth, hard, and dry. When leaning hard, stay out of the very middle of the traffic lane if cars have left an oil film. When you must pass through a slippery area, straighten up momentarily. When you can, follow car wheel tracks, where they sweep the surface clean.

. . . You can be freer about downhills on a route which you use repeatedly. Then you learn all of the little peculiarities of the road surface and work carefully toward your limits day by day. But remember that surprises like oil patches and potholes can appear overnight.

. . . Practice downhill riding. Practice pedaling downhill and coasting. On group rides, compare yourself with other riders downhill to see what strategy works best. On downhills along your daily route, practice all of the techniques we've listed here but especially practice developing your judgment. As you practice downhill riding, there's an added advantage. You'll also get to practice your uphill riding!

KNOW THE SIZE OF YOUR BIKE

Here's a common situation for a beginner. You're crossing a street, riding, and head for a curb cut, the kind that gets put in for wheelchairs. You get halfway up the curb cut onto the sidewalk when the bike lurches to a stop with a huge clank underneath you, and you fall off. When you pick yourself up, you look at the bike and notice that a pedal is bent. What happened?

You were at the right side of the curb cut. As you came up to it, the pedal was down. It caught on the curb at the edge of the curb cut.

You weren't thinking about the size and shape of your bike. The pedals are the hardest part to think about. They fool you the most because they move up and down. Catching a pedal is a common problem for a beginner, though it is rare for an experienced rider. An experienced rider feels the bike as a part of himself or herself. With experience you will actually feel when parts of the bike are coming close to parts of the landscape. But it takes practice to develop a sixth sense about your pedals. Try coasting along close to a curb on a quiet street. First, do it with the right pedal down. The pedal must clear the curb. Then put the right pedal up and see how you can get closer.

You also have to think about the pedals when you turn since they can hit the ground or the front wheel on some bikes. This problem is covered in the section on turning.

Think also of the handlebars, and of wide loads on your rear rack. At both low and high speeds, practice riding through narrow spaces, close to trees, posts, and walls, so you can aim the handlebars to just clear them.

Remember that your bicycle's back wheel swings to the inside as you turn. When you're clearing a pothole, rock, or other obstruction, swing a little wide with the front wheel so the rear wheel clears.

To get both wheels through the same narrow opening, swing wide first so the path of the rear wheel crosses the path of the front one at the opening. Then straighten out or turn the other way. If you make a symmetrical S-curve (swinging the front wheel) from one side to the other when the front wheel is directly over the narrow opening, the rear wheel will go over exactly the same place.

And if you need to pull both wheels into a line to go down a narrow, straight path, make an S-curve first so your bike is completely straightened out.

BUMPS AND POTHOLES

The smallest bumps just make you a little bit uncomfortable. You keep pedaling, but you might relax your arms and bend your elbows a bit more as you go over them. It's more comfortable to ride in the low position so the bumps don't go up your spine. Dropped handlebars make this easier, but you can crouch down over flat bars too. You can ride over a long stretch of rough pavement this way. If it just gets too annoying, slow down.

The larger bumps shake you up a bit. You decide when they're going to be too uncomfortable. Stop pedaling, set the pedals horizontal, and lift your weight off the saddle. Your bent arms and legs become leaf springs for the rest of you. Some toe clips help you keep your feet on the pedals.

See how high your bike's tires are above the rim. When you run straight into a bump, the tire will squash down, since it is just a bag of air. If the bump is not as high as the tire, it can't squash the tire all the way to the rim. If it is as high or higher, it can. Then the rim will begin to bend. The bumped part will push in toward the hub, and the sidewalls will spread apart. The bump will feel not only bigger, but sharper, because you're riding on metal. If you hit hard enough, the rim may cut through the tire and tube. Then you could have a blowout or you could have one later, when the weakened tire lets go. And the next time you use the brakes, you'll discover that they catch each time around on the spread sidewalls of the rim.

To keep this from happening, you watch carefully for bumps this big. Round-topped bumps like cobblestones or speed bumps are less likely to damage your wheels, because your wheels rise up onto them gradually. Bumps with sharp, step-shaped front edges are the worst. Be very careful with any bumps which are higher than your tires, including raised manhole covers, pavement edges, and curbs.

When you approach a bump like this, slow down. (But release the brakes before you hit, to decrease strain on the fork and frame.) If the bump is less than about twice as high as the tire, you can safely ride over it, slowly, as long as your tires are properly inflated. As you come to the bump, stop pedaling, put your hands in low position, and spring your weight up on your bent elbows and knees. Then only

the weight of the bike itself is connected tightly to the tires. Yank up on the handlebars to help the front wheel over. Then, just before the rear wheel hits, yank your feet up. It's harder to lift the rear wheel, but at least get your weight off it. It's easier to jump the rear wheel with toe clips and harder if you've got a load on the rear rack.

If the bump is big enough that you're not sure you'll make it safely, get off and walk. Save your rims!

The front edge of a pothole doesn't do anything — the bike just falls over it. The rear edge is a bump like any other bump. It's easier to jump your bike over a pothole, though. Sometimes at high speed you can jump completely over one.

There's another way to deal with bumps. Use it whenever you can; simply ride around them. This may seem obvious, but some rims we've seen make it clear that many people never think of it. It's easy to do this on a bike, because the wheels are one behind the other. As you ride more, you will learn to do this

When riding over bumps, rise off the saddle, flexing the elbows and knees to absorb shock. From this position, it is possible to yank up on the handlebars — and with toe clips on the pedals — to jump the bicycle if necessary.

automatically. You wander a little bit, just to be comfortable. Your practice at avoiding pebbles comes in handy here. On the road, it's safer to wander a little with a rearview mirror to check on traffic behind you. When there is traffic, you must take it into account — sometimes riding straight through bumps, sometimes claiming more space so you can wander safely.

Practice popping pebbles again, and then practice picking your way along a bumpy stretch of road. Take your bike over a few low edges and potholes, just to get the feel of it. But most of your learning about bumps will be out on the road. It's best to ride a bike with fat tires or "disposable" rims until you're good at dealing with bumps. Everybody damages one or two rims in the first year or two of riding. When you stop hitting bumps hard, think about getting lighter wheels.

If you're looking away, you will first feel a bump through the handlebars. Learn to relax your body and lift your weight off the seat quickly when this happens. Unless you're going very fast, you can still make things easier for the rear wheel and your rear end. Practice taking bumps while looking away. Use small enough bumps that they won't damage the wheels.

When you're riding down a hill at a good speed, even relatively small bumps can be uncomfortable. To make your ride more comfortable, set the pedals horizontal and lift yourself off the seat. Just as when going over a bump on level ground, keep your elbows and knees bent to absorb the bumps. Clasp the seat between your legs for stability. Use mostly the back brake to hold your speed down — the wheels may not be holding the ground too well because of the bumps.

"Floating" will help the wheels hold the ground better though because the springiness in your arms and legs will push the wheels down into dips in the road so they're not just skimming the surface. The bike will bounce up and down under you and take the stiffness right out of your arms and legs. It's not entirely unenjoyable.

Try it out a few times so you're used to it.

THE ROLE YOUR TIRES PLAY

When you first start riding, you may find that a bike is rather bumpy, not at all like a Cadillac, or even a Volkswagen. But with time, as air seeps out of the tires, the bike will become more comfortable to ride. Many beginners let this happen, and welcome the seeming improvement.

But bike tires are deliberately hard. When they are hard, the bike is easier to pedal. But more importantly, one job of the tires is to protect the rims from damage. As you ride over bumps, the air in the tire compresses, and the tire "swallows" the bumps without damaging the rims.

So keep your tires correctly inflated. Check them every day with your thumb before you go out riding, to make sure they haven't gone flat overnight. Top off the pressure and check it with your tire gauge once a week. Bike tires have more surface area in relation to the amount of air inside than car tires do, so you have to top off the pressure more often.

DEVELOP SENSITIVITY TO THE ROAD SURFACE

When you walk, you can tell whether the surface under you is hard or soft, smooth or rough, tight or loose, grippy or slippery. You feel the ground through your feet and test it by sliding your feet over it as you put them down.

On a bike, it's a little harder to get a feel for the road surface, but you can do it.

You look. We stress looking because it's what will tell you about a patch of road before you get there. With experience, you will judge every foot of road before you get to it. Sometimes you need to do no more than give the road a glance every few seconds. Sometimes, you must keep your eyes glued to it constantly. But you look enough to be aware of all of the potential trouble spots.

You should also listen to the sound of the road under your tires. Every surface has its own sound — learn it. When you're braking or turning, learn the sounds the tires make as they begin to slip. You'll learn to ease back on the brakes or the turn when you hear these sounds.

You should feel the bumpiness of the surface, the rolling resistance, which increases on a soft surface as your bike digs in and plows along, and the mushiness in the steering as the front tire digs in on a soft surface. You should also feel the tires skittering sideways as you go over bumps or gravel in a turn; the rear tire fishtailing, skittering, and scraping as it skids from too much rear braking.

You test the road surface by applying the rear brake until the wheel skids. On a soft surface, especially, you use this technique to get an idea how much traction you have to work with.

Another test is waving the handlebars slightly from side to side while riding straight at a low speed. On soft, slippery surfaces like gravel, sand, snow, and mud, you can judge the traction by whether the front wheel steers or just plows along. You do this test leading into a turn, to judge whether you can ride the turn or whether you will have to put a foot down.

THINGS THAT TRY TO STEER YOUR BIKE

Paving edges, breaks, cracks, and railroad tracks have long, narrow edges. As long as they are straight across your path, they're just like any other bumps. But if they are at an angle or parallel to your path, they're a much more serious problem.

When your bike's front tire nudges up next to the edge of a raised piece of pavement, or gets trapped in a railroad track slot or other crack, the tire will slide sideways. Since you have to steer to keep the bike under you, you will almost certainly fall. Any edge more than about half the height of your bike's front tire can catch it this way. To make things worse, sand, water, and mud often accumulate under paving edges, and railroad

The edge of a pothole compresses the air in this tire. Unless the tire is squeezed completely flat against the rim, no damage is done.

tracks are made of slippery metal, making it easier for your tire to skid. To avoid a fall:

. . . Look out for edges and cracks. If you are riding parallel to one, keep a foot or two clear of it so you won't have to go into it if a gust of wind blows you sideways or if you have to steer around a stone.

. . . When you have to cross an edge or crack, turn to go straight across. If you have to cut across the road to do this, look for traffic and wait if necessary. Look for a place in the edge where it's easier to climb: a joint between sections of pavement, or a place where the railroad track is more level with the road. Remember, the slower you are going, the sharper you can turn. If you ride to six or eight

miles per hour, you need only flip the front wheel sideways and back straight in a quick double turn. The rear wheel will follow, since it will still be angled after the front wheel has straightened out. As you turn, lift your weight off the saddle to make it easier for the wheels to climb the edge. When crossing, hold the handlebars very firmly by their widest points — the edge may try to turn your wheel to trap it. Brace your arms so the bars can't be twisted out from your control.

. . . If you see an edge or crack too late to turn, steer into it as much as you can and yank on the handlebars to jump the front wheel over it. At the same time, you go up on your toes to take your weight off the rear wheel. The rear wheel may slide along the edge sideways, but you can usually still control the bike, as with any rear wheel skid. The more the rear wheel skids, the bigger the angle it will make with the edge. After a long moment, it will climb over.

Practice the double turn to get over an edge. Also, once you've learned to jump the front wheel, practice taking some small (1 inch) paving edges diagonally. Jump the front wheel and feel the rear wheel come over. Check out your skill on railroad tracks as you ride. If there's a trolley track or railroad track near you that runs down the middle of a street, practice cutting back and forth across one of the rails sometime when there's no traffic.

A railroad track can steer your front wheel out from under you, causing a fall.

SEWER GRATES AND EXPANSION JOINTS

These have slots parallel to your path of travel, like railroad tracks. To a car or truck, they're nothing. But your bike's narrow wheels can sink into them.

Watch out for them. Sewer grates are primarily at the sides of streets, though not al-

This rim has suffered an impact from a bump or pothole too big for the tire to swallow. The rim has spread, making the brakes grab; spokes have been loosened and will eventually break if this damage is not repaired.

ways. Expansion joints go all the way across every large bridge. Some are alright, and some aren't. Keep your eyes open. Newer designs are safe for bicycles, and many older ones can easily be made safe. Often no more is involved than turning a sewer grate at right angles. Get after your community to remove these hazards. If you fall into one, the community is probably legally liable, especially if you've notified the appropriate agency of the hazard.

MAKING ACCIDENTS LESS SEVERE

If you haven't already, sooner or later you are going to fall off your bike. We want you to be prepared for when you fall off your bike. And that's why we include the following sec-

tions. They're about how to protect yourself from injury when you fall or crash. Not just by wearing a helmet, but by taking action to protect yourself as you crash.

By the way, the very large majority of falls from bikes don't result in serious injury. But we'd like to cut down the number that do, and make even the minor injuries less serious. Even bruises and scrapes are painful.

THINGS YOU RIDE NEXT TO

We'll start with trolley tracks and curbs. Parallel to your path, these can dump you, though with proper technique you can deal with them.

Higher things will certainly dump you. If you drift into anything between about 6 inches

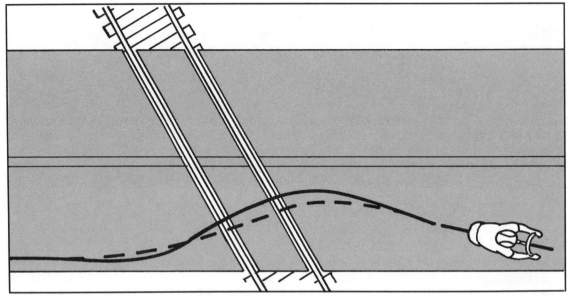

Cross railroad tracks at right angles to avoid trapping the rear wheel. If you must move farther into traffic, be sure to look back, signal, and yield if necessary.

and 4 feet high, definitely you're going over it headfirst. Be especially careful of low bridge railings. Stay far enough away from them that you'll be inside them if you fall.

Anything high enough that your shoulder rubs it is a different matter. If it is smooth enough that it doesn't catch you, you can bounce off it at a low angle, and keep riding in another direction. As long as that other direction doesn't take you into danger, you'll be all right. Examples of high objects are walls, high bridge railings, and the mid-section of car sides.

Practice riding slowly at a low angle toward a smooth surface, like the side of a van. Bounce off while still riding. Lead with your shoulder, so it hits, rather than the pedal. After you've had to swerve, in real riding, you might have to bounce off a car, tree, or telephone pole. You might even be able to control which way you're headed afterwards, like a human billiard ball — it could be useful.

IF YOU ARE HEADED FOR A CRASH

You have somehow lost control of your bike. You've run into an unexpected slippery place on a turn. Or you've had to swerve to avoid a pedestrian, and you're headed for a curb. Or any of a thousand different things. Every crash is a little different.

But in many crashes, you have a choice where to go and how you'll fall. The choice is not whether or not you will crash — you will, or probably will. But there is often an interval of time when you can still steer the bike and choose the least of several evils.

Rules don't always hold true, but it's usually better just to fall to the ground than to run into something (snowbanks and hedges are clear exceptions). It's usually better to fall toward the inside on a turn than the outside — you just fall, you don't flip — and it's better to run into a stationary object than a moving one such as a car or another bike, especially if the moving object is coming toward you. Aside from the increased impact force, moving objects can swerve toward you.

Set your priorities and think about them before you get into a crash situation. Priorities go like this: save your life, save your bones and flesh, save your skin, save your bike. If you're about to run into a pedestrian or bicyclist, try to save the other person, too. Try to run into a car or something else that doesn't feel pain.

Practice priorities by imagining what you'd do if any accident situation came up as you ride. Here's an example: you suddenly see a patch of broken glass ahead of you. Swerving to avoid it, you run out in front of a car. Time after time, you have been training yourself to swerve around glass to avoid flat tires. But if you can't be sure that you have a clear path as you swerve, it's better to ride right through the glass and risk the flat tire. So practice. And every time you take evasive action to avoid a lesser hazard, like glass, check that you're not creating a greater one, like swerving in front of a car.

We've already very strongly recommended gloves and a helmet. Some falls happen so quickly that they're over before you know it. You may bang your head, and you will almost certainly instinctively put out a hand. Both parts of you deserve protection.

Many falls, though, happen slowly enough that you can plan how you are going to land. Gloves and a helmet are invaluable here, too. If you know that you can put out a hand painlessly, you are much less likely to draw it back and bang your elbow instead. And if your head is protected, you can relax much more as you fall.

The most common type of fall is to the side, usually caused by loss of tire traction. There are two approaches to reducing the impact of this type of fall. 1) If you are coming off the bike put a hand down, and with your arm slightly bent in front of you, push hard as the arm collapses to absorb the impact. Use the arm to swing you over to land on your rear end and the side of your back, below the shoulder blade. This way, you spare the bony parts that get hurt most easily. 2) The other way to fall sideways, if you are still on the bike, is to hold the handlebars in the middle to protect your hands, and turn your hips so you land on your rear end behind the hip bone. You and the bike go down together. This technique is one you use more often with toe clips. Your feet can stay in the clips with the bike sliding in front of you. When the bike slides into a curb or whatever, you can cushion the impact just as you do riding over a pothole.

The other common fall is to the front, or more commonly to the side and front, over the handlebars. It happens when the bike stops too quickly, from running into something or from excessive braking. The bike will tilt up, and your feet will be yanked off the pedals, even with toe clips.

The technique for this type of fall is to put both hands out and push as your arms collapse to absorb most of the impact. Meanwhile, roll yourself up to do a somersault. It is better to roll along the road than to pancake full length onto your back — or your front. Try to land on the area below and inside the shoulder, but not flat on the spine; twist a little to one side or the other. If your back lands flat, slap your hands to the pavement as your back comes down. If the object you ran into is high enough that you will hit it with your body and not just the bike, aim a hand or hands for it and slow yourself. Try to turn your head sideways and make it land on the helmet or against the back of one hand. If you run into something, there may be two impacts. The second impact occurs as you fall to the ground. If you've handled the first impact well, you may be able to control the second one.

When you can, avoid an over-the-handlebars crash by turning it into a less serious sideways crash or fall. Use a controlled rear-wheel skid to turn the bike sideways just before you hit a high obstacle. If you're headed for a low obstacle (one which would stop the bicycle but which you would go over), do the skid turn and then hit both brakes to drop the bicycle to the ground.

Falls happen quickly. All of this advice may make you say "But I'll never think to do it in time." This is true, but then, you don't think, you use your reflexes. If you train your reflexes, they will work with lightning speed and in most cases you will be able to protect yourself. Gymnasts and people who do judo train themselves in techniques for falling. So can you. A little training goes a long way.

Training prevents panic. If you have no idea what to do when you start to fall, you will probably panic. You may tense up and even close your eyes, or grab the brakes hard. Then chances are much greater that you will get hurt. If you have trained yourself for falling, you will probably keep calm, keep your eyes open, and protect yourself.

After you've taken a fall, think about it. Make every fall a learning experience. Think about what led to the fall, so you can avoid making the same mistake in the future. Think about how you took the fall, so you can improve your technique to protect yourself.

NONRIDING SKILLS

Like an airplane, a bike is graceful when it's flying, but it can be a clumsy lunk when it's taxiing. It's worth the time to give some conscious thought to how you maneuver your bike when you're not riding it. Here are some ideas.

WALKING AND CARRYING YOUR BIKE

There's a little more to this than meets the eye. Here are some pointers. Stand on the left side of your bike, where the chain can't dirty your leg or your clothing. If you're walking on level ground or uphill, you can hold the handlebars at the center with your right hand. This way, you can balance, steer, and push one-handed, leaving the other hand free. If you're going downhill, it's easiest to slow the bike with the brakes. Grasp the left brake lever with your left hand and the saddle with your right hand. If you have the front brake on the right, put both hands on the handlebars.

From the braking position, you easily shift to the carrying position with your left hand still on the handlebars at the brake lever, and your right hand down the right side of the seat tube

The cyclist stands on the left side — the clean side — of the bicycle and carries it by the top tube with one hand and the shoulder, steering the handlebars with the other hand. This technique is most useful when carrying the bicycle over high obstacles and for longer distances.

It is easy to roll the bicycle through tight places by rearing it up on its back wheel like a horse. This lifts the width of the pedals well clear of the ground and makes it easy to take the bicycle around tight corners. You walk behind the bicycle, not beside it.

The bicycle may be carried lower down by grasping the seat tube with one hand — best for shorter distances.

When walking your bicycle down a hill, it is easiest to control its speed by using the brakes.

Another way to carry a bicycle.

to pick up the bike at its center of gravity. This position works for a short carry. For a longer carry, it is easier to put the top tube over your right shoulder. If you must carry the bike through narrow halls and stairwells, steer the front wheel around corners with your left hand.

To get through a doorway easily, step to the side of the bicycle which is closest to the door's hinges. Then you can hold the bicycle with one hand and the door handle with the other. It is sometimes easiest to get through a spring-closed door by rolling the bicycle back wheel first. Or hold the door open with your foot until the bicycle clears it.

If your bike is heavily loaded, it's usually easier to roll it, even up stairs, than to carry it. Push the center of the handlebars with your left hand, lifting the front wheel if you're going up stairs. Hold the seatpost with your right hand to steady the bike. For obstacles the bike won't roll over, reach your right hand down and lift the bike by the seat tube.

SCOOTERING

To scooter you stand on the left side of the bike with your right foot on the left pedal and your hands on the handlebars. You push yourself and the bike along with your left foot. You can coast by lifting your left foot.

Scootering helps you move your bike through crowds of people. It's faster than walking, but you can stop and pick up the bike quicker than if you were riding.

It's a little harder to balance the bike and ride straight when you're scootering than when you're riding, because the bike is leaning away from you. So scootering is a good way to practice balance — and practicing balance is a good way to learn scootering! Try to keep the bike as upright as possible — if you lean it too much, you may collapse your wheels!

ELEVATORS AND ESCALATORS

In an elevator, you want to be out of the way as much as possible, but close to the door so you don't have to roll the bike past other people.

If the elevator is small or crowded, stand the bike up on its back wheel and walk in backward, rolling the bike in against the wall next to the door. Stand between the bike and the other people in the elevator, so it can't soil their clothes. When you get off, roll the bike out, still standing on its back wheel, and keep yourself between it and the other people getting on and off.

On an escalator, you roll the bike on and then turn the front wheel sideways so it can't roll. Turn the wheel straight just before it reaches the end of the escalator, so it can roll out onto the floor.

The technique of standing a bike up on its rear wheel like a rearing horse is often useful for maneuvering through very tight spaces. You push the bike while standing directly behind it. This raises the pedals clear of low obstructions and can get you through gaps almost too narrow to walk through.

The rear brake is very useful in this maneuver.

This usually can't be done conveniently if you have a full length rear fender.

TRICKS FOR LEANING YOUR BIKE

As you've probably discovered, your bike is as unsteady as a drunken sailor when you try to lean it against something. We don't recommend kickstands, so it's only fair if we point out a few alternatives.

. . . Lock your bike. Use the lock to stabilize it.
. . . It's steadier resting against a wall, which will keep the front wheel from turning, than against a post.

. . . You can roll the bike backward until one pedal rests on a curb. The curb will also keep the front wheel from steering. As long as the bike is pointed uphill, it's steady.

. . . Make one brake into a parking brake by stuffing something, like one of your gloves, under one of the brake cables to jam the brake shoes against one of the wheels. Or adjust a brake quick-release so it works backward — normal braking in the open position and parking brake in the closed position. By using two quick-releases, on the brake lever (Weinmann) and one at the caliper or cable hanger, you can have the parking brake and a normal quick-release, too.

. . . The Flickstand is a clever little device that installs under the bike's down tube, keeping the bike from steering or rolling. It's great, but it can't be used on a bike with fenders.

. . . You can also steady the front wheel with a toe strap or bungee cord wrapped between it and the down tube.

NOW THAT YOU'VE LEARNED THE BASICS

You know how to ride a bike! You don't know everything about traffic, but you know more about bike handling than many people ever learn. Especially, you have learned the limits of your bike's braking, steering, and maneuvering performance. Since you know the limits, you know how to stay safely inside these limits. You can be appropriately careful without limiting your riding with unnecessary fear.

To stay inside the limits, you will hold your speed down in certain situations. That's only normal, the same as you would do while driving a car or even while walking across a room cluttered with furniture. A little extra caution is a good idea at first, but on the other hand, don't scare yourself into just plodding along. You'll miss most of the fun and the exercise — and you'll probably avoid falling once or twice. All good things have their risks. So wear your helmet and gloves, and keep learning.

Probably the best questions you can ask yourself while riding are: "Do I know what's going on now? Do I feel in control?" If things are happening which catch you by surprise, or if you have a blank feeling that you don't know what might happen next, take it easy. Think about it later, and keep using safe, controlled practice sessions to expand your riding knowledge.

At this point, consider yourself ready to go out on easy rides on quiet streets and bikepaths. But first begin reading the next chapter. At least get to know the basic rules of the road and traffic techniques. They apply to the street and to the bikepath too. You'll probably want to stay on quiet streets until you've built a little confidence, and that's alright. But keep going and keep growing.

CHAPTER SIX

DRIVER TRAINING

If you are going to use your bicycle for transportation, you are going to have to ride it in traffic. There's no way around that. Sidewalk and bikepath riding is slow. Often, there isn't a sidewalk or bikepath convenient to where you want to go. But the streets go everywhere.

Still, if you're like most people, you're not comfortable riding in the street, in traffic.

Then you will be pleasantly surprised to find out that riding in traffic is safe. Even for the average bicyclist, it is per mile, safer than walking, and safer than sidewalk riding. For you, after you've studied the riding techniques in this chapter, bicycling in traffic will become even safer.

DISPENSE WITH YOUR FEARS

We can tell you that bicycling is safe, based on accident statistics. But cold facts

don't melt fears. To be comfortable riding in traffic, you must *feel* safe. And if you are like most people, you have to undo some old ideas about bicycling before you will feel safe. These ideas are leftover from your childhood bicycling.

When you were a child, your coordination and judgment were not as well developed as they are now. Your parents told you to ride on the sidewalks and to walk your bike across streets.

Later, perhaps, you moved out onto the streets when sidewalk riding began to frustrate you. But if you're like most people, you never overcame the first impression you were given — the street was not a good place for a bicycle. And you never learned the best way to ride because nobody ever showed you.

You learned to ride a bicycle as a child, but later you took up driving a car as part of becoming an adult. You found teachers who showed you the right way to drive. At first, you found driving scary, just like riding your bi-

75

cycle. Yet you accepted the idea of driving along a two-lane highway at 55 mph with cars coming at you at the same speed. It was clear that your protection in this situation was not the car but your skill and judgment, and that of other drivers. You knew that driving was something grownups do successfully. So you didn't let your fear keep you from learning to drive. Instead, you gained experience and as your skills improved, your fears faded into simple caution and watchfulness.

That is what will happen when you learn to ride a bicycle the way we will show you here — not as a child but as a grownup. You can now apply your adult coordination and judgment — and as an extra benefit, your adult car-driving skills — to riding a bicycle.

To further demolish your fears, let's look at the myths many people believe.

MYTH #1
MOST BICYCLE ACCIDENTS ARE CAUSED BY CARS

Only about one serious bicycle accident in five is a collision with a car. Most are single-bike collisions — falls, or running into things.

You are only about 1¼ times as likely to have an accident on a street with traffic as on a street without traffic. But if you try to avoid traffic by riding on a bikepath or sidewalk, then you're going to increase your chances of an accident much more. Bikepaths have 2.6 times the accident rate of streets, and sidewalks are much worse than that. We've pointed out how car-bike collisions are more likely if you ride from the sidewalk to the road. Falls, bike-bike collisions, and bike-pedestrian collisions are more likely, too. The same is true on bikepaths which in most cases are little better than sidewalks.

MYTH #2
CRAZY DRIVERS

It can be disturbing to look out into the street and see drivers cutting in front of other traffic or squealing tires as they turn, brake, and accelerate.

From the sidewalk, the noise and apparent frenzy of traffic look formidable.

But neither statistics nor experience bear out these observations. Accident rates aren't significantly higher in places where drivers have a reputation for being aggressive.

Of course, drivers don't always respect your rights automatically. But they're not out to *get you;* they're just out to *get somewhere.* Driving is, after all, frustrating in a crowded city. Drivers will sometimes try to inch out from stop signs or make other bluffing moves. Many bicyclists take these moves as proof that traffic is dangerous. Such is not the case.

Usually, a bicyclist's style of riding invites accidents. It's a vicious circle. A bicyclist who is afraid of traffic rides in a way that increases risks, and that makes the bicyclist even more afraid. The way to solve the problem is to *drive your bike.* The more you ride like a driver, the better the motorists will understand you and the more they will respect you. If cars can't pass in your lane without skinning your elbow, you don't cringe along at the far right and invite them to. You pull out so they have to pass you in the next lane as if you were driving a car. If a driver is inching out from a stop sign, you keep right on moving. Long before you reach the point where you'd have to stop, the driver will stop.

Where drivers are aggressive you, too, must be a bit aggressive. The collaborators for this book speak from experience. We live in Boston, which is the aggressive driving capital of the United States. We ride there successfully. The main difference between the motorists and us is that they drive aggressively trying to set their rights ahead of ours, while we are only aggressively standing up for our rights. This isn't a crusade for us, by the way. It's just that it's the fastest and safest way to ride.

MYTH #3
CARS AND BIKES DON'T MIX

Motorists worry about hitting bicyclists and about having to slow down for them. Bicyclists worry about being hit, and about getting stuck in difficult traffic situations along their routes.

Myths, myths, myths! Every bicycle on the road makes life easier for motorists by freeing up road space, parking space, and fuel. Car-bike collisions are not frequent enough to be worth constant worry and are usually caused by unskilled bicyclists violating traffic law. With the easy-to-learn techniques in this chapter, bicyclists can confidently handle any traffic situation, with very few exceptions. Cars and bikes do mix.

MYTH #4
REAR-END COLLISIONS

Beginning bicyclists fear rear-end collisions. So let's cite some cold, hard statistics.

Only about 4 percent of all collisions between bicycles and cars are rear-end collisions. And of these, at least half are caused by simple mistakes by bicyclists, such as swerving abruptly out in front of cars.

Startling? Then think about it for a minute. Rear-end collisions are rare because as you ride along the street you are exactly where drivers expect you to be.

On the other hand, about 90 percent of collisions between cars and bicycles are turn-ing and crossing collisions. These are more common, because turning and crossing interrupt the normal flow of traffic. There's more of a chance that people will make mistakes.

And, while some bicyclists take to the sidewalks to feel safe, *riding on the sidewalk greatly increases the probability of turning and crossing collisions* — much more than it decreases rear-end collisions. Why? If you ride on the sidewalk, drivers still cut across your path at every intersection and driveway. But on the sidewalk and crosswalk, you are where drivers can't see you and have no reason to expect someone to be traveling at your speed.

SAFER THAN WALKING

According to accident statistics in the *Bicycling and Air Quality Information Document, Final Report* (Environmental Protection Agency, 1979.), compiled by Marda Fortmann Mayo, walking is responsible for about three times as many deaths as bicycling per mile of travel.

That's assuming you're an average bicyclist, which isn't assuming much. The average bicyclist learned to cycle as a child, has had no driver training, makes many elementary mistakes which lead to accidents, and does not use a helmet or other important safety equipment. You will do far, far better than average after you have read this chapter.

In comparison with this average bicyclist, the average motorist is about three to ten times less likely to have a fatal accident per mile of travel.

Consider that. You feel safe driving, and driving is fairly safe, at least compared with the average bicyclist's record. But you also feel safe walking, though walking is more dangerous than bicycling. You ought to be more afraid of walking than of bicycling, but your childhood fear of bicycling in traffic has overpowered your reason. Now, having overcome fear with reason, let's look at the statistics in another way.

Let's look at walking, bicycling, and driving in terms of lifetime risk. Assuming more or less typical American travel habits (1,000 miles per year walking, 3,000 bicycling and 10,000 driving, typical for people who use these modes), the risk for all three modes is approximately *equal*, if you're only slightly better than the average bicyclist. But you can become far better than average.

HOW TO MAKE CYCLING SAFER

Half of all collisions between bicycles and cars result directly from bicyclists violating the traffic law. So, obey traffic laws.

You will learn traffic riding techniques from reading this chapter. These techniques go well beyond what the law requires. You will learn to move smoothly in traffic, to let drivers see you and react to you, and to test that drivers have seen you and reacted appropriately. And in case an accident is about to happen, you will learn how to take evasive action.

You will use a helmet, bright-colored clothing, lights at night, and other appropriate safety equipment. The helmet alone reduces your chance of death or permanent injury by half or more.

If bicycling is reasonably safe for the average rider, then it's going to be far safer yet for you, especially as a commuter.

COMMUTING: THE BEST RECORD

A 1975 survey of members of the League of American Wheelmen, the national bicyclists' organization, showed the effect of their greater than average riding skills in an accident rate about five times lower than that of the average bicyclist. But what was more surprising was that the accident rate for commuting was only 60 percent of the average for all trips.

The result is surprising, considering these factors:

. . . Commuters do not have the choice of routes that a recreational rider has.
. . . Commuters ride in bad weather and after dark, not just on fine, sunny days.
. . . Commuters often ride in heavy traffic.

Why, then, is commuting safer? Two reasons:

. . . Commuters ride the same route repeatedly, so they know the route well.
. . . Commuters regularly ride their bicycles for transportation. Regular commuting gives more experience and more opportunities to develop traffic skills, on the average, than any other type of riding. Skill, it turns out, is the single most important factor leading to a low accident rate. And it will be your key to safety. This book will start you out with a solid foundation of riding technique, and then your commuting will give you every opportunity to improve your skill. Your lifetime risk from bicycling will be no greater than from driving a car — maybe less.

RIDING ON THE ROAD

There are three keys to riding on the road:
1. *Rules of the Road.* These are the principles of how to move in traffic which apply to you on your bicycle and to everyone in traffic. Consider, for example, the rule that everyone travels on the right side of the road. The rules of the road are the same for all drivers of all types of vehicles. Because they are the same, everyone can know what to expect from everyone else, to create the safest, smoothest flow of traffic. Throughout this chapter, we will highlight the rules of the road as keys to safe riding.
2. *Traffic Techniques.* These go beyond simple understanding of and obedience to the rules. The rules tell you what to do and what not to do. Traffic techniques tell you *how* to travel in traffic, such as where to ride in a traffic lane depending on its width. By and large the traffic techniques refer to all material in this chapter, excluding the rules of the road and traffic tips.
3. *Traffic Tips.* While not essential to riding in traffic, the tips, such as how to time traffic lights, will help you go farther and faster, but in a safe manner. So consider the tips a refinement of traffic techniques.

AN EXPLANATION OF TRAFFIC TECHNIQUES

The following pages list all common traffic situations.

There is more than one way to deal with many of these situations depending on your experience, traffic conditions, and the loca-

RULE OF THE ROAD: YOUR RIGHT TO THE ROAD

Free travel is a basic Constitutional right, and the roads are a public space set aside for travel. Accordingly, the laws of all 50 states affirm the legal right of bicyclists to ride on the road. Whether you are driving a car, truck, moped, bicycle, motorcycle, bus, farm tractor, or horse and wagon, you have the right to use the roads properly for their intended purpose.

There are a few exceptions. Some roads prohibit bicyclists. In some places, as on freeways where other roads are available, the prohibition is of little importance and can be justified legally. In other places the prohibition is of importance and is an injustice because a road prohibiting bicycles may be the only road — or the only good road — to your destination. When the automobile was the only transportation people took seriously, car-only roads were built and no-bike laws were passed. Now, the trend is to recognize your rights and to open up access to bicycles everywhere.

tion. So we have set up three different ways to deal with each situation, which we call Level 1, Level 2, and Level 3.

All of these are legal and reasonably safe ways to handle traffic situations.

LEVEL 1 is the easiest if you're not used to riding a bicycle in traffic. At Level 1, you avoid difficult situations. This, in many cases, means walking the bicycle.

At **LEVEL 2** you make most maneuvers very much as if you were driving a car but you time them or ride lightly traveled roads, so you don't have to deal too much with traffic. You will make each maneuver at Level 2 when you have to deal with only one or two other vehicles at a time.

79

At **LEVEL 3** you mix right into the traffic. You do this so you don't have to slow and stop so often. You make maneuvers as if you were driving a car, but you also prepare the other drivers around you for your maneuvers by signalling to them and double-checking their reactions. Because you double-check, Level 3 is not only faster, but safer. Furthermore, it allows you to ride more places, under more traffic conditions.

Level 1, Level 2, and Level 3 apply to straight-road environments and to intersection environments differently.

In straight-road situations, there is no different way to ride depending on your level of experience. For each road and set of traffic conditions, there is one best way to ride, so your experience will determine not *how* you ride but *which roads* you use.

At intersections, you have a choice whether to go across as a driver (Level 2 or 3) or as a pedestrian. So for intersection riding, we will describe each situation at all three levels.

At any particular time as you ride, conditions may be more difficult, or they may be easier. Whether you are a beginning rider or an expert, or anywhere in between, you will find situations in which you will ride at each of the three levels. As a beginner, you will ride more at levels 1 and 2. You will choose routes which let you ride at these levels. Once you gain experience, you will use level 3 more and more. As you ride, think through each maneuver as you approach it, and then make the maneuver at the highest level at which you feel comfortable. That way, you'll be increasing your level of skill as you ride.

WHEN TO USE LEVEL 3

To use level 3 techniques, you must *make* space for yourself in traffic between one car and the next, not just *find* space. This difference is most crucial when you are changing lanes to make left turns or to avoid obstructions at the right side of the road like double-parked cars, stopped buses, and potholes.

Generally, you can succeed at making space every time when the average traffic speed is as much as 15 mph faster than you. So, if you can hold a traffic speed of 15 mph (easy after a month or two of riding), you can use level 3 technique in any normal 30 mph city traffic.

Where traffic goes faster than 30 mph, such as on city boulevards and on highways, you will sometimes have to retreat to level 2, timing yourself into an existing longer gap in the traffic. That's usually not hard, though, because traffic moves in convoys at higher speeds. In the city, traffic lights leave long gaps in the traffic. And when the speed limit is above 30 mph, the road will usually have wider, unobstructed lanes. You will be able to travel smoothly without moving into the traffic stream, unless you need to turn left.

Level 1

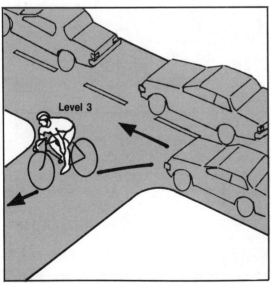

The three levels of traffic techniques: Level 1, be a pedestrian and avoid difficult maneuvers. Level 2, maneuver when there's no traffic. Level 3, mix right into traffic. Remember that you will likely be operating on all levels at different points in any one ride.

HOW TO ENTER TRAFFIC
(ALL LEVELS)

When you're about to ride in traffic, you must first enter the traffic flow, smoothly and safely. Here's how.

Look in every direction. No matter which direction you're going, look to the left and look to the right, too. In the city, pedestrians and wrong-way bicyclists come from the right; in the country, overtaking cars come from the right. Look across the street or road you are entering for opening car doors and pedestrians which might make drivers on the far side swerve toward you.

When entering a city street, look three times: once as you approach the sidewalk or shoulder for pedestrians and to see what you can. Look again when you can see the traffic lanes. If you're stopped at the crosswalk, look while you're waiting. Look a third time as you pull out past parked cars, for what you couldn't see before — principally, bicyclists and runners close to the parked cars.

Position yourself to see. When you position yourself to see, you also position yourself to be seen — important if anyone is about to enter the driveway where you are. Keep in the middle of a narrow driveway where you have the longest sight line in both directions for bicyclists and runners. Avoid stopping by putting your bike in your low, starting gear, and crawl forward with your feet on the pedals, if possible. Then you can make a quicker start, and fit into traffic more smoothly as you enter.

When entering a road with more than one lane in either direction, be aware that vehicles in nearer lanes may hide others farther back in more distant lanes. Be especially aware of motorcycles, which are small but fast, and sometimes quiet. No smart motorcyclist would ride in a blind spot, just as no smart bicyclist would, but some do.

Note that a driver on the road may have to slow down for you sooner or later, once you've entered traffic. That's all right. You don't have to wait till traffic is completely clear, but just long enough to give the driver behind you a safe length of time to see you and react — and a little extra for courtesy.

GOOD PLACES TO ENTER TRAFFIC
(ALL LEVELS)

On your bicycle you may enter traffic from a driveway or a small side street, or just from the side of the road. On major streets in the city, it's usually best to move into traffic with the help of a traffic light or pedestrian light.

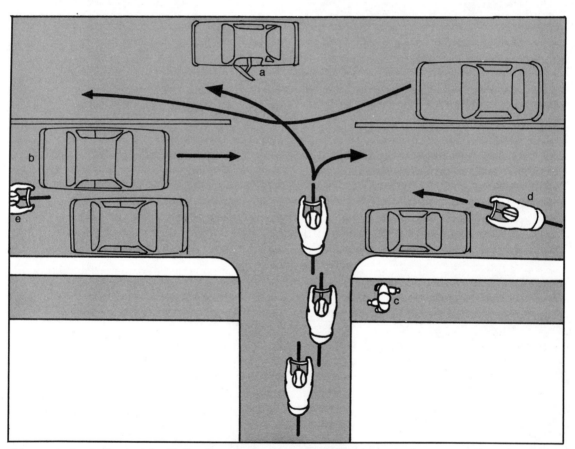

When entering traffic, look in all directions and anticipate possible hazards. Some examples: a) a car door opening on far side causing traffic to swerve toward cyclist, b) car on near side hidden behind parked car, c) pedestrian, d) wrong-way cyclist, and e) hidden motorcycle.

You pull out into the stopped traffic waiting for the light, or you pull out into the clear area past the light; or you start going out across a pedestrian walk on a walk signal, then turn to change from pedestrian to driver. It's best not to walk your bike out between parked cars in the middle of the block, unless there's no traffic or unless traffic is already stopped in the closest lane. If you're on foot there, you're jaywalking. A bike is clumsy to jaywalk with. But if there's an alley or driveway in midblock, or a long space between parked cars, you can ride out as a driver. This maneuver is legal, and it's easier to enter moving traffic when you're moving.

Entering traffic is one of the maneuvers which many bicyclists perform badly. They try to be half-pedestrian and half-driver, riding a little ways down the wrong side of the road before cutting across, or riding out from a sidewalk curb cut without yielding. Be a pedestrian and walk until you are in a good place to enter traffic. Then, decisively, become a driver.

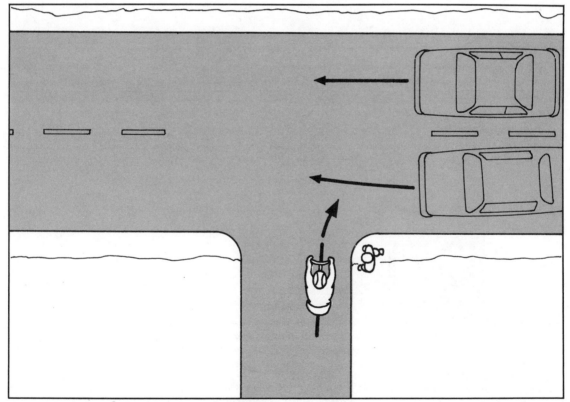

When entering a two-lane highway, look left but always look right as well for pedestrians and overtaking cars.

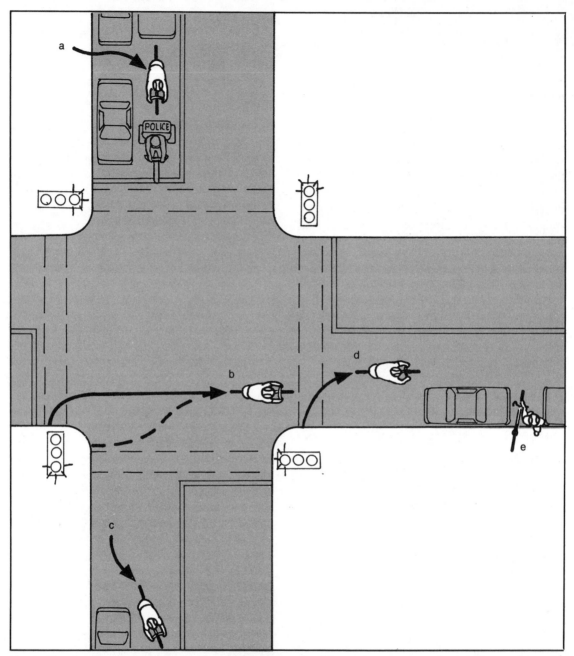

Use traffic signals and other aids to enter traffic in the city. Here are some scenarios: a) The cyclist walks or rides slowly out to a convenient starting place in traffic which is stopped for a red light. The cyclist is going to make a left turn. b) The cyclist waits at the pedestrian crossing, yielding to traffic, then turns at a right angle. Note the unsafe procedure shown with a dashed line: drifting sideways from a crosswalk into a parallel street. A cyclist starting this way is forced to look ahead and behind at the same time. c) The cyclist uses a gap between parked cars and the clear area downstream from a red light to change lanes out into traffic. d) The cyclist turns right from a pedestrian crosswalk, yielding to traffic. e) Avoid this — walking out between parked cars in the middle of the block. The cyclist here is jaywalking, and there's no way to get onto the bicycle and moving until already in the stream of traffic.

WHERE TO RIDE ON THE ROAD

The best place to ride on the road is where other drivers can see you and where other drivers can overtake you when it is safe.

Everyone tells you to ride on the right, but there's more to riding right than just riding on the right. Because your bicycle is narrow, you have a choice where to ride in the traffic lane. In the interest of your own safety, you make a different choice in each different traffic situation.

Sometimes the safest place to ride is near the edge of the road, and sometimes it is farther out in the road. Sometimes, you should let motorists overtake you, and sometimes you must prevent them from overtaking you.

Many bicyclists ride with traffic, but they sneak along at the edge of the road trying to make themselves as thin as possible. They duck into every available space between parked cars, trying to get as far away from traffic as they can. If bicyclists feel unsafe and uncomfortable riding this way, it is because

this style of riding *is* unsafe and uncomfortable. This behavior contributes to many close scrapes and accidents.

Read the next few pages carefully, and follow the reasoning. If you always ride at the very edge of the road, your close scrapes may have made you fearful. It may be hard for you to accept that the safe thing to do is exactly the opposite of what you expect: what seems even more dangerous. But, when you actually try riding the way we recommend, you will break loose from the vicious circle of fear which has made your riding unsafe. You will quickly come to the realization that you aren't having close scrapes any more, and that you don't have to be afraid. Read, then ride. If you have been afraid, words alone will not convince you. Only experience will.

RIDE WITH TRAFFIC
(ALL LEVELS)

You ride on the right not only because it's required by law, but because it's the safest place to ride.

Consider what happens at every intersection and driveway you cross. If you ride with traffic, drivers and pedestrians will be looking toward you. If you ride against traffic, they will be looking away from you. Sooner or later, you'll run into one.

Bicyclists who ride against traffic think they are safer because they can see the cars approaching them, but the reasoning is faulty. Even aside from the intersection problems, if you ride with traffic, a driver approaching you has only to slow down to your speed to avoid an accident. If you ride against traffic, *both* you and the driver of the car will have to come to a *complete stop* to avoid an accident. With traffic, *one* of you sees, then just has to slow. Against traffic, *both* of you have to see and both have to come to a complete stop. And you have to see each other much sooner, at a far greater distance. The odds aren't as good. If you hit each other, you hit each other at a far greater relative speed.

Bicyclists who ride the right way will be very annoyed with you if you ride the wrong way. That's because they are frequently hit by wrong-way riders who suddenly appear in front of them in the same space. If you consider yourself a bicyclist and want other bicyclists to be your friends, ride right!

If a driver hits you from behind when you're going the right way, the accident will be the driver's fault, and the driver's insurance will cover it. If you're going the wrong way, the best you'll get is no-fault minimum payments, because the accident is your fault. If you injure a pedestrian or another bicyclist when riding the wrong way, expect to lose a lawsuit.

Enough reasons?

If you're concerned about the drivers approaching from behind, do what all good

---

ON WIDE ONE-WAY STREETS YOU MAY STAY LEFT (ALL LEVELS)

On wide, one-way streets such as New York's avenues, it is sometimes most convenient and safe to ride on the left side. This is especially so when buses travel the right side of the street. On the left, you won't have to deal with them.

When a one-way street is several lanes wide, fast traffic travels in the middle, not at the edges — the left lane is used mostly by drivers about to turn left. There may be double-parked vehicles in it, but the technique for overtaking them is just a mirror image of your normal technique.

---

cyclists do: dress brightly, use lights and reflectors at night, and be extra-careful on the narrow highways when the sun is low and when the drunks are out — generally, Friday and Saturday nights. A rearview mirror helps at times when you want to check where the car behind you is.

And keep repeating the statistics to yourself: rear-end collisions are only 4 percent of all car-bike collisions; wrong-way collisions are 14 percent, even though relatively few bicyclists ride the wrong way.

KEEP CLEAR OF ROAD-EDGE HAZARDS
(ALL LEVELS)

Road-edge hazards include:

. . . Parked cars whose doors might open in front of you, or which might nose out to the edge of the traffic lane.

RULE OF THE ROAD: KEEP TO THE RIGHT EXCEPT TO OVERTAKE

You keep to the right side, and other drivers coming toward you from the opposite direction keep to theirs. That way, you can expect to come around a curve or over the top of a hill without finding someone headed straight at you.

To overtake a slower driver, drivers are permitted in some places to use the left side of the road — but then the overtaking driver must make sure that this is safe.

In England and some other countries, drivers keep to the left side. It doesn't matter which — right or left — as long as everyone keeps to the same side.

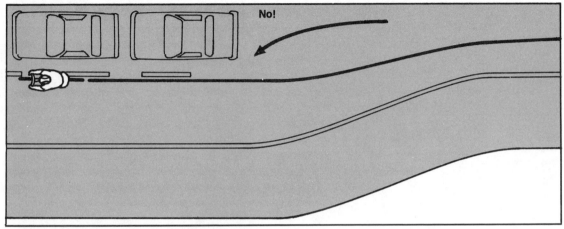

Follow the traffic lane, not the edge of the street.

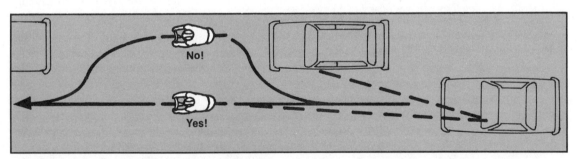

Don't duck in between parked cars, since you become invisible to motorists.

. . . Pedestrians stepping out from behind parked cars.

. . . Cars and bikes nosing out of side streets and driveways to where the drivers can see them at the edge of the traffic lane.

. . . Gravel, sand, and trash. The cars sweep these out of the traffic lane, leaving them piled up just to its right.

The traffic lane where you ride should begin just to the left of where these hazards end. Don't ride within range of the doors of parked cars. That's a danger zone. The driver of a parked car, and everyone else, assumes that nobody would be so foolish as to come along within range of the door. They're right, unless you are that foolish.

Many bicyclists ride in the danger zone because they're afraid of rear-end collisions. In fact, riding to the left of the danger zone does not increase the chance of rear-end collisions, because it puts you where you can be seen. Riding in the danger zone, on the other hand, you blend into the roadside scenery. Cars turning right are much more likely to run into you because their drivers did not see you. And that's aside from the risk of running into car doors and pedestrians or falling in gravel — a risk which is in any case many times as great as that of a rear-end collision.

IN A WIDE LANE, KEEP TO THE RIGHT OF CARS
(ALL LEVELS)

You always stay out of the range of parked car doors and other side-of-the-road hazards. Beyond this requirement, where to ride depends also on the width of the traffic lane in which you are riding.

If the lane is wide enough for you to share

RULE OF THE ROAD: VEHICLES MAY OVERTAKE WHEN SAFE

Sometimes you will overtake other vehicles; more often they will overtake you. Since you move slower than some of the other vehicles on the road, you have a special need to understand the overtaking rules.

First, let's make one thing clear.

There is nothing wrong with going slowly. You do not have fewer rights because you go slowly, and there are only speed limits on ordinary roads — no slow limits. (There can't be; nobody could stop!) But there are two special rules of the road about slow-moving vehicles when there are faster ones behind whose drivers want to overtake.

The overtaking rules are:
1. The driver of any vehicle following a slow-moving vehicle must *exercise caution* in overtaking, and
2. A slow-moving vehicle must allow a faster vehicle to overtake *when it is safe,* and must pull to the side of the road if causing the faster vehicle an *unreasonable delay.*

Rule #1 exists to protect the slower moving vehicle. The driver of the faster one

behind *must* be responsible for avoiding an accident, or the driver of the slower vehicle would have to have eyes in the back of his or her head.

Rule #2 comes *after* Rule #1. Rule #2 recognizes the right of the faster vehicle to get by the slower one *when it is safe.* Safety is more important than convenience. But if the slower-moving vehicle is holding up traffic for a long time — say a minute — it must pull over and let faster ones by *when this is safe.* In the real world, a bicyclist must do this rarely, because a bicycle is narrow. A bicyclist rarely has to delay a motorist more than a few seconds — a reasonable delay.

Note that the slow-moving vehicle rules don't make distinctions between different kinds of vehicles — such as bicycles, cars, or tractors. These rules only make distinctions between how fast vehicles are going. You will often be the slower-moving vehicle, but you will also often be the faster-moving one. In traffic jams, especially, or with other, slower bicyclists, you will be moving quite fast.

You have the *right of way* to the section of road where you are riding. If it is not safe for drivers behind you to overtake, you may ride far enough out in the road to prevent with cars side by side, then you keep just a comfortable distance to the right of where the cars go — about three feet. You allow the cars to overtake you because it is safe for them to.

Do *not* pull farther to the right than necessary to let the cars overtake you. You're already giving them enough room. You may be tempted to move right if the lane becomes very wide.

Keep just to the right of the cars:

. . . So you're where you'll be seen by drivers behind you, and also by drivers ahead of

you — in side streets or preparing to turn left across your path.

. . . So motorists won't be so likely to cut in front of you to make right turns — and if they do, you can avoid an accident by turning to the right.

. . . So you can continue in your straight line in traffic when the lane becomes narrow again.

. . . So you'll be to the left of the car, not directly in front of it, if a motorist overtakes illegally on the right in this wide lane.

If there are spaces between parked cars, don't duck in between them. Keep your

them from doing it. You don't have to let them skim by your elbow just because your bicycle is narrow enough that they might possibly

be able to overtake you.

Since the risk is yours, *you* have the right to decide when it is safe for them to overtake.

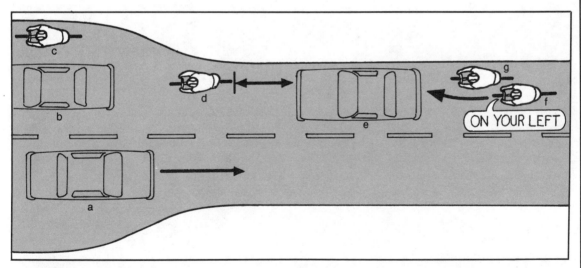

Rules for overtaking and being overtaken. Oncoming motorist a) prevents motorist e) from overtaking cyclist d). Where the road gets wider, motorist b) may safely overtake cyclist c), who is required to permit overtaking when it is safe. Motorist e) is responsible to slow down and to follow cyclist d) until it is safe to overtake. Cyclist d) may prevent overtaking when it is not safe. Cyclist g) is required to allow cyclist f) to overtake safely on the left. Cyclist g) may not swerve left without looking back and yielding.

Stay out of right turn lanes. The bicyclist has kept a straight course to the left of the right-turning traffic, and now proceeds out across the intersection in this wide lane.

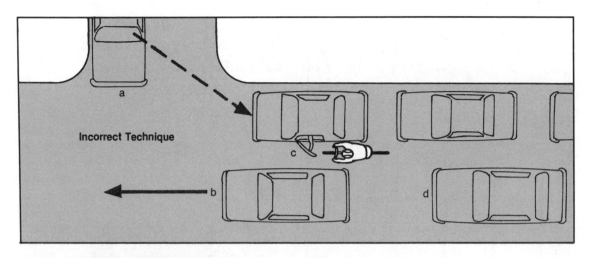

Incorrect Technique

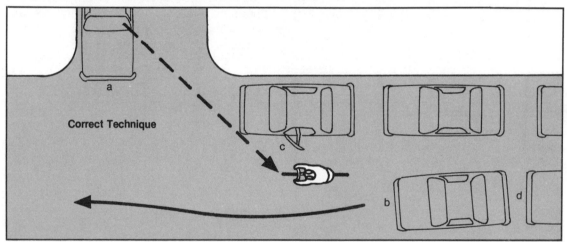

Correct Technique

By riding a safe distance out from roadside hazards, you increase your safety on all sides. At a), the motorist in the driveway sees you; you are not hidden behind parked cars. At b), the motorist overtaking you will not take the easy way out and skim by your elbow, but will change lanes for safe and proper overtaking. At c), the car door is no threat. At d), the motorist behind can see you — you don't blend into roadside scenery (or become completely hidden, as on curves to the right). Also, the lane changing of the motorist at b) announces your presence to the one at d).

straight line in traffic. Farther right, you'd often be hidden between parked cars. Drivers behind you may forget about you or may never have seen you. You will be a surprise to a driver who is about to pull into the empty parking space where you are riding. When you pull back out into traffic, the space in which you were riding has disappeared. You have legally and in fact lost your right of way. You must look back and yield to traffic behind you just as if you were entering traffic from a driveway.

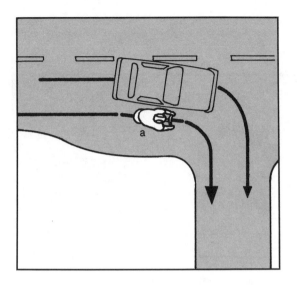

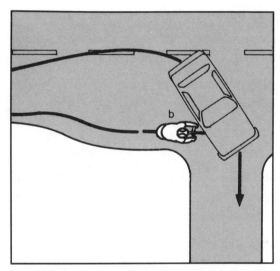

In a wide lane you are safer if you stay just to the right of cars. A car turning right in front of you is the second most common car-bike collision. a) In this position the driver is less likely to turn in front of you in the first place and you can turn to avoid an accident almost every time. b) In this position you are less visible and the car is going sideways before you can see it, so there's no way to avoid an accident.

IN A NARROW LANE, CLAIM YOUR SPACE
(ALL LEVELS)

Sometimes a lane is so narrow that you cannot safely share it with a car side by side.

Then you must pull far enough out into the lane so a driver will have to either follow you or move partway into the next lane to overtake. Ride about three feet out in the lane.

Be assertive and decisive. Give yourself the benefit of the doubt. If the lane is too narrow for overtaking, it is too narrow, and that's that. If you have to ride within range of parked car doors to let cars by you on the left, the lane is too narrow. When motorists cannot overtake you safely, you are safer if you do not let them.

Many riders stay a reasonable distance out in a narrow lane to keep away from the side-of-the-road hazards *until* they hear a car behind them. Then they cringe to the right. But to move to the right is to *invite* the driver behind to overtake just when it's unsafe. Claim your space; don't trap yourself between hell and high water.

MAKE ROOM FOR YOURSELF

Beginners commonly fear riding farther out in the street. They're especially afraid of falling and being run over by cars.

Now, clearly, if you are just beginning to ride and haven't learned to properly control the bike yet, it isn't a good idea to go out riding on a busy street. And it's also not a good idea to go out there if you haven't learned some traffic-riding techniques. You build up to riding the busier streets by studying, by riding quieter streets, or maybe by taking a League of American Wheelmen Effective Cycling course. You build your skill and you build your confidence.

But the fact is, even on the quieter streets you're safer riding farther out where pedestrians and drivers in side streets can see you and where you won't run into the doors of parked cars. Even if you're a beginner, that should be easy enough for you to accept. Since there are few cars overtaking you on these streets, clearly your main need is to be out of the way of the edge-of-the-road hazards.

But what about the big, busy streets? Why would you want to ride out farther there too? Isn't it better to accept an increased risk of running into a car door in order to decrease the risk of being hit from behind? In other words, aren't these streets much more dangerous to ride, and that's that?

These streets *are* more dangerous to ride if you accept the false compromise between riding too close to the parked cars and riding too far out in the street. In fact, you make these streets *safe* for yourself by riding farther out in traffic, as part of the correct traffic-riding technique.

By riding farther out in the street, you make more room for yourself. You make room to your right, because you're farther away from the parked cars. You make room to your left, because drivers won't try to squeeze by you in a too-narrow lane. You make room ahead of you, because people can see you from the side streets. And you make room behind you, because people can see you from there too and are moving out to overtake you instead of leaving a narrow passageway for you between them and the parked cars.

By riding farther out in traffic you create a safety space around yourself, on all sides. You do this on a quiet street and you do it on a busy street, too. You're much less likely to fall with the safety space, since you're clear of

road-edge hazards.

But if you *do* fall, you've left the drivers around you more room to get out of your way.

Accomplished traffic riders aren't worried very much about falling, because it doesn't happen very much.

Keep reading, keep trying out the traffic techniques, and keep building up to those bigger streets. Soon, you'll be riding them without thinking much of it.

**TRAFFIC TIP:
DO NOT CONFUSE
UNPLEASANTNESS WITH DANGER**

The noise and the exhaust fumes from cars are unpleasant. The noise, especially, seems threatening. But you must clearly distinguish between unpleasantness and danger.

If you ride to get away from the unpleasantness, by moving far to the right of the road, you increase your danger in many situations. No matter how heavy the traffic, ride in the correct position on the road.

If you want to ride in a place that is more pleasant, then ride on another road with less traffic, or on a bikepath. But also, understand the special dangers of these places and ride accordingly. They are more pleasant, but often they are not less dangerous.

WHEN YOU CAN EXTEND COURTESY

In a wide lane, it never makes sense to duck into a space between parked cars: drivers behind you can overtake you anyway. But in a narrow lane — especially in a one-way, one-lane street — you may occasionally pull aside as a courtesy to a following driver. Do this only when there's a long space between parked cars, and just one car behind you. This car has to be able to get by before you reach the end of the empty parking spaces. Pull decisively aside and wave the car by. Once it's ahead of you, look back to make sure another hasn't pulled in behind it, then move back out into the traffic lane.

If you pull aside when there's a string of cars behind you, they'll *all* speed up and you'll just have to stop and wait until they've all gone by. Don't give up your right of way when you aren't reasonably sure you'll get it back, unless it is required by law and common courtesy. But, as we've noted, you'll rarely need to do this.

There are other maneuvers as well in which you can be courteous — for example, move to the left of right-turning traffic. By all means, take the opportunity.

WHEN TO RIDE THE MIDDLE OF THE LANE
(LEVEL 3)

You will often go just as fast as the cars either because you're going fast down a hill or because they're going slowly in crowded city traffic.

In either case, you are safest in the middle of the lane. You make space for yourself and the driver behind falls back to make room for you. You are free either to move left to overtake if the car ahead slows down, or to move right if it speeds up. The rules of the road for overtaking don't force you to the right. Since the drivers behind you couldn't go any faster even if you weren't there, you have a

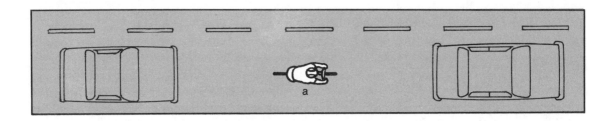

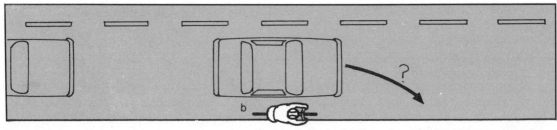

When going as fast as the cars, you're much safer if you ride in the flow of traffic. In a) you can be almost certain that the driver behind you has seen you. In b) the driver next to you very likely has not seen you and could very well turn right.

perfect right to be in the middle of the lane just like a car.

On fast downhills, keep in the middle of the right lane even if the cars might go faster than you, though you'll usually take downhills as fast or faster than they. You need lots of room at high speed to make turns and avoid pavement irregularities. Make a driver use the entire next lane to overtake. Keep your distance from the car ahead. Cars don't lean like bikes, so they often brake sharply and take turns slower than you.

If it seems bold to be in the middle of the lane, consider the alternative. If you stay on the right, with cars going as fast as you, you'll often be next to a car in the driver's blind spot. The driver could swerve right to clear oncoming traffic, or make a right turn without ever having seen you.

WHEN TO RIDE THE MIDDLE OF THE RIGHT LANE
(ALL LEVELS)

When there are not any cars behind you, the danger zone of roadside hazards grows. Pedestrians expect to hear cars, and if they don't hear any they will often walk out into the street without looking. Drivers in side streets look for cars, and often do not look over to the side of the street where you normally ride. Drivers in side streets may not be able to see you at all, if a parked car blocks the view.

For these reasons, when there are no cars behind you, move out to the middle of the right lane. Then the drivers in the side streets will see you as soon as they would see a car. The pedestrians may still walk out — but you'll be where you see them before you could run into them.

You can almost always hear a car approaching from behind when it is the only one around, but glance back once in a while to see whether there is a car. As the car approaches from behind, move back to your normal position in the traffic lane. With the car clearing the way for you now, you no longer need to be out in the middle of the lane to be safe.

But be warned! This information is not applicable on high-speed highways, especially in passing zones. In any case, these highways always have clear shoulders and road-edge hazards are minimal. On the highway, stay to the right to avoid the hazard of a head-on collision.

KEEP A STRAIGHT LINE IN TRAFFIC
(ALL LEVELS)

In any of the correct positions in the lane which we've described, you *keep a straight line*. You have the right of way as long as you keep going straight, and you are a known quantity to other drivers. They can overtake you in confidence that you will not swerve across their path.

Since your bicycle is narrow, keeping a straight line means not only staying in the same lane but also staying in the same place in the lane. You determine this place according to the usable width of the lane as you enter.

Sometimes, all of the lanes in a street will move over to one side while the street goes straight. For example, they may move left to make room for parking. Follow the *lane,* not the side of the road. All of the other drivers follow the lane, and if you follow the side of the road, you're going to cross paths with someone who doesn't expect you.

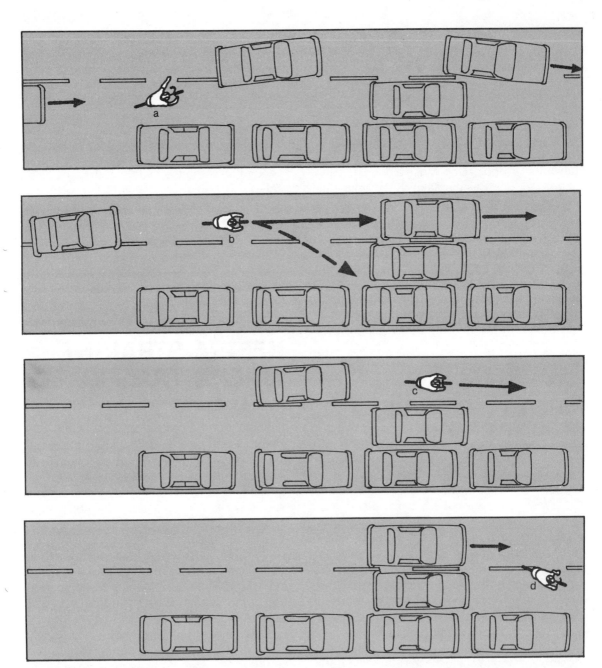

Look back, signal and yield (if necessary) when moving farther out into the traffic lane. a) Signal, look back and move into the traffic stream when there's plenty of time for the next driver to react. b) Double-check that the driver behind you has slowed or moved aside while you still have your escape route. c) Overtake the double-parked car. Leave plenty of room for the car door to open or for a jaywalker or a wrong-way rider. d) When it's safe, pull aside and let the driver overtake you. If it's safe to take your hand off the handlebars, acknowledge with a wave-by.

HOW TO MOVE FROM ONE POSITION IN THE LANE TO ANOTHER

(ALL LEVELS)

When the traffic lane narrows, you must move farther into the lane.

Other drivers cannot predict or expect that you will move sideways. You are taking the initiative, so you must take the responsibility. You do this whenever you move farther into the lane, for whatever reason — even when you're just moving sideways a few inches.

HOW TO MOVE SIDEWAYS IN THE LANE

(ALL LEVELS)

If the lane becomes wide enough so you can change position in it, there's no great

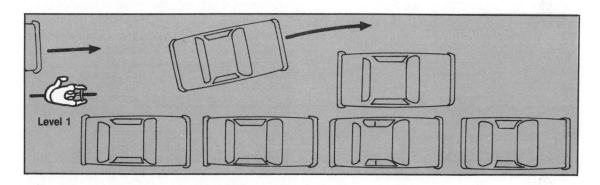

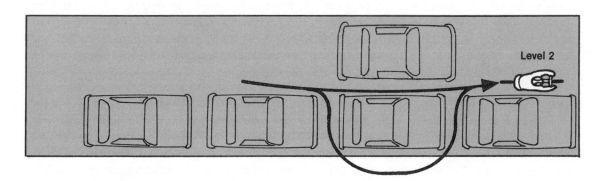

Alternatives to changing lanes and merging into traffic. Level 1, slow or stop and look. Problems: Since you must accelerate from a stop, you'll need a greater gap in traffic. It will take you more time to get around parked cars. It's better to stop well back from the double-parked car so you can pick up speed before overtaking it. Level 2, walk or ride slowly past the curb side of the car, since you could be hit by a car door from either side or by a jaywalker. This is a safe procedure as long as there's no place into which the car could turn right. Yield when entering traffic.

RULE OF THE ROAD: SIGNAL AND YIELD FOR TURNS

Other drivers must be able to assume that you will not move to one side or the other without warning. Without this rule, every driver behind you would have to *stay* behind you, because no driver would ever know whether you were about to move to the side.

When you are about to move to the side and it might affect another driver, you are required to let that driver know what you are about to do. So you make a turn signal, even for a partial lane change.

In practice, on a bicycle, you sometimes must keep your hands on the handle-bars — mostly, in tight traffic situations where the drivers are close to you and you can signal with a turn of the head; or where you're already in the middle of a lane of traffic and can move your whole bike to one side or another as a signal.

The law recognizes that you can't always make hand signals, and does not require you to when your safety would be affected. But in practice, it's no problem because you can signal so many ways.

problem. You just ease over toward the right with perhaps a quick glance back in case a cyclist is about to overtake you there.

Here's how you move to the left when the lane narrows. You have more to do.

Look ahead and give yourself plenty of time. Don't wait until the last moment before you get to the narrow place, and then look back. Then, if there's a car just behind you, you'll have to stop.

As soon as you see the narrow place ahead, look back. Then:

LEVEL 1

If the traffic behind you looks too much for

you to deal with, get off and walk, or ride past the narrow place slowly on the sidewalk. If the obstruction is a double-parked car, you can ride by on the right, *slowly,* as long as there's nobody in it to open a door. But *never* pass a bus or long truck on the right. The bus may discharge passengers at you, and either a bus or truck might make a right turn catching you underneath. If you're overtaking on the right, get all the way onto the sidewalk and walk around.

And remember, when you pull back into traffic, *look back* for the vehicles coming around past the narrow place. You are entering traffic and must yield to them.

Lane changing. The cyclist is moving from right to left in preparation for a left turn. Signalling, looking, and yielding, he makes his way across two lanes of heavy traffic.

LEVEL 2

Go ahead and pull out if there's no traffic, or slow down and wait for the traffic behind you to clear. Then speed up and move left into the narrow place, keeping well away from the obstruction on your right, out of its danger zone. If the obstruction is something like a car or bus that might begin to move, keep even further clear to give you more room and so the driver will see you when looking back to pull out.

LEVEL 3

You have the right of way, and you can use it!

So do you have to stop and wait till traffic has cleared, just because a lane goes from wide to narrow, and there's a car behind you? Definitely not!

The requirement to yield is not the same as the requirement to stop, and in any case you are already in the *same lane* as the car. You have the right of way over that car as long as the driver has a safe distance to slow or move over for you. We repeat: *You* have the right of way, being in the same lane. You are required to let drivers overtake only as long as they can do it safely. The driver of the car *must* slow or move over for you, but you *must* give the driver enough warning that you are about to pull to the left. So you signal and look, and pull to the left if it's safe.

Usually, a lane gets narrow because of something that stays put for a while, such as a bridge or a double-parked car. But you can see the narrow place ahead of time, so you look back as soon as you see it.

Consider this example.

You are riding along a wide two-lane street. There is room for the cars to go by you on the left. Traffic is moderately heavy and moving faster than you — about 30 mph to your 20. Up ahead of you, you notice a double-parked car. It's still several hundred feet ahead. To keep moving, you're going to have to mix into the stream of cars on your left.

You wait until the car on your left has *just* gone by you, well before you come to the double-parked car. You speed up a little, put out your left arm for a turn signal, and look back just to be sure no new cars have entered traffic ahead of the next one you know is behind you. Then you begin to move over to the left. At this time, you still can pull back to the right if the car behind you does not slow down, and the driver of the next car has plenty of time to react to you. This driver has been keeping a safe following distance from the one ahead, a great enough distance to avoid hitting the car ahead even if its driver came to a panic stop. But you are not coming to a panic stop; you are moving along at a good speed. You look back again to check that the driver has slowed to follow, before you reach around the double-parked car. You give this car plenty of clearance in case the door

The cyclist signals a lane change to overtake a row of double-parked vehicles. Note that the cyclist is keeping well clear of these vehicles in case a door opens or a pedestrian walks out.

Having overtaken the double-parked vehicles, the cyclist waves by the car following him.

opens. Once by the double-parked car, you pull to the right and give a hand signal that the driver behind you may overtake.

How do you do it, again? How do you make it safe?

. . . You start with a look back as soon as you see the problem ahead of you.

. . . You use a naturally occurring safety zone in the traffic. Here, a gap created by a safe following distance.

. . . You use your legal right. Here, you have a right to pull into the stream of traffic as long as you leave the driver behind you a safe time to react.

. . . You signal your intentions.

. . . You check the safety zone as you move into it, just to make sure someone else didn't move into it before you did.

. . . You leave yourself an escape plan (here, to pull in behind the double-parked car and stop) and you make your move soon enough that you have time and room to carry out your escape plan.

. . . You double-check that the driver behind you has slowed down and made room for you.

By using these techniques, you keep yourself moving rather than constantly slowing down and stopping. By the way, it is *safer* to keep moving in most situations, riding at Level 3. If you're always slowing down and stopping, you're disrupting the flow of traffic unnecessarily. Traffic is safest when it flows smoothly. You are safer merging in ahead of that car behind you than you would be if you pulled from behind the double-parked car from a stop.

**TRAFFIC TIP:
OVERTAKING A BUS**

The stopped or slow bus is one of the terrors of the traffic-shy cyclist. Walk around on the sidewalk? Stay behind the bus and get bathed in diesel smoke? No — there's a better way.

Signal and change lanes to the left well in advance. Take the *entire* lane to the left of the bus. Ride right out in its middle. The first slowed car behind you will protect you from other traffic. Also, you want to be out far enough so that you'll be in the bus driver's rearview mirror where a car would be. The bus driver will almost certainly not pull to the left if you're where you can be seen, and even if the bus does begin to move forward and pull to the left, just stay in the middle of the lane, and drop back. No driver behind the bus is going to pull directly out at you if you are where a car might be. When the bus pulls ahead of you, signal and change lanes back to the right.

DEVELOP A FLUID SENSE ON THE ROAD

We've been stating rules. They are good rules, but they are only a foundation on which you build your judgment.

The width of the danger zone at the right varies. Where there are parked cars, it extends as far as an open car door. On the other hand, a country road may have a gravel shoulder and a right lane just wide enough for cars to overtake safely. Then you can safely ride close to the edge of the lane, so cars can overtake. If you suddenly see a rock on the pavement and have to swerve onto the shoulder, you'll be able to keep your balance and stop, even though the shoulder isn't good

for riding. And drivers on side roads can see you, because the shoulder is unobstructed.

How far out in the lane to ride depends to a considerable extent on your speed, too. The faster you go, the farther out in the lane you must place yourself. Then drivers in side streets ahead will see you sooner and you have more room to maneuver. Fortunately, at almost any time when you must place yourself in line with the cars, you're not going to interfere with them anyway.

Your position in the lane depends on pavement conditions. On rough pavement, you need more room to avoid the bad spots. It's best to place yourself consistently a bit further to the left and make your little swerves to the right, though a rearview mirror will let you know whether it's clear to swerve a foot or

---

**TRAFFIC TIP:
ANTICIPATE DRIVER BEHAVIOR**

You do very well just by holding the correct position in your lane, depending on its width. But by making conscious decisions about whether to allow motorists to overtake you in a narrow lane, you can both increase your safety and be more courteous to motorists.

Make it very clear that motorists are not to overtake you when it is unsafe. Use your position on the road and a slow signal to indicate that they must follow you.

On the other hand, there are times when a cautious motorist hesitates unnecessarily or continues to follow you after overtaking has become safe. Wave the motorist by.

To some degree, whether a motorist can overtake you safely depends on the size of the vehicle. A Corvette can overtake you where a Winnebago can't. A rearview mirror helps you to decide early whom to wave by and whom to block, and allows you to be more courteous to the drivers of small vehicles.

---

two to the left without your having to take your eyes off the potholes in front of you.

Once you've had some experience riding according to the rules we've given, the right choice of position will become second nature to you.

RIDING THROUGH INTERSECTIONS

Again, as with the section on straight road riding, read carefully. The way many bicyclists ride through intersections is far from the safest.

You must particularly avoid the temptation to pull to the right of cars which are turning right.

You often have to change lanes to ride properly through an intersection as a "driver". So we'll describe lane changes first.

Intersection collisions are the most common type caused by wrong-way riding, which is dangerous and illegal.

CHANGING LANES

You change lanes to get to the correct starting position to make left turns; to ride around obstructions; to go left when a lane narrows or ends; and to position yourself at a ramp, union, or separation.

LEVEL 1: No lane changes. Walk across at an intersection.

LEVEL 2: Wait for a gap in the traffic. Preferably, move across all of the lanes at once. This is what you must do in high-speed traffic.

LEVEL 3: The level 3 lane change is the big question for most beginners. "How could I possibly compete with the cars?" they — maybe you — ask. It takes courage the first time to stick your arm out and expect a driver to slow down and let you pass across in front; but try it — you'll see that it works.

You can change lanes with nearly complete freedom in traffic going as much as 15 mph faster than you — up to that difference in speed, rarely exceeded in city traffic, the drivers will have plenty of time to slow down and let you into their lane.

Actually, we've pulled a surprise on you: you've already learned the most difficult part of lane change — the partial lane change which gets you from the right side of a lane further toward the middle. You can use this lane change to build your confidence. You always have an escape route back to the right side of the road if you time the partial lane change early enough.

You complete your full left lane change with a second partial lane change — from the left side of the old lane to the right side of the new one. Remember, as long as you're in the old lane, the driver behind you has already slowed. You maintain your right of way ahead of this driver until you have established your right of way in the new lane. So every lane change in wide lanes is actually two — one which gets you into a lane and one which gets you across it.

Level 3 lane changing is easiest, once you get the hang of it, because you always control a car in one lane behind you; or in wide lanes, with the lane line as a refuge, you can let cars go by on both sides till one driver lets you in. If you fail to get all the way over to the left to make a left turn in time, you just ride up to the next cross street and turn left there instead.

At level 2, you can use the lane lines, but you don't control the drivers behind you.

APPROACHING AN INTERSECTION IN STOPPED TRAFFIC

(ALL LEVELS)

As you approach an intersection in stopped traffic, place yourself on the lane line

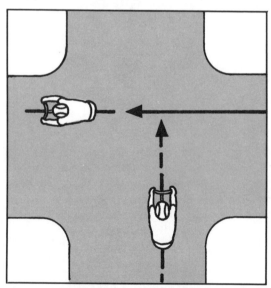

At an unsignalled intersection or a four-way stop, the driver on the right has the right-of-way if two drivers arrive at the same time.

appropriate for where you are going: to the right of the right side straight-through lane to go straight; to the right of the left lane to turn left. Pull up behind the bumper of the first car in that lane. Don't pull up next to that car, because you don't know for sure whether it might turn toward you, or whether the driver can see you.

Now look back to the second car, the one just behind you. See which way it is going. Make a hand signal for the way you are turning. If it isn't clear from a turn blinker and the car's position which way the car is going, ask the driver with gestures, if you have time. Then make a signal for the side you want the car to pass you on. You can have a useful conversation waiting for the light to change, and set up your plan for the intersection.

As traffic starts, pull slightly in front of the car so you lead it out. When you're going forward, the car will drop away to the side, behind you. When you're both going the same way, the car will follow you, and overtake you when there's room.

APPROACHING AN INTERSECTION IN MOVING TRAFFIC

If you're going straight through an intersection, at level 2 or 3 as a driver, you need to get to the left of the cars which are turning right. To do this, you may have to change lanes to the left.

LEVEL 2 AND LEVEL 3

If there's a separated right turn lane to your right, keep going straight and station yourself in your normal position to the left of the right-turning lane. Otherwise, move until you're in the first lane to the left of any lane which is in fact a right turn lane. Often, parked or double-parked cars past the intersection will block the right lane beyond the intersection. Then it is a right turn lane. Also look for turn blinkers on cars ahead, and with right turn on red, look for turn lanes clearing while lanes to their left are filling with cars stopped for the red light. You may even see arrows on the pavement.

BE WARY OF RIGHT TURN LANES

Once you enter a right turn lane, the law requires you to turn right. If you go into a right turn lane, you will have to cross in front of all of the right-turning cars to go straight. The drivers will be looking left at the traffic in the cross street, not toward you.

It is much safer, and legal, to hold your straight line in the straight-through lane. Drivers are required to yield to you to move into the right turn lane, and most will. Even if one doesn't, an accident is unlikely because all you have to do is follow the car around to the right. It helps if you make a left turn signal so the drivers can be sure you're not going right.

If you are not confident about riding through an intersection in the through lane, don't cut in front of the cars in the right turn lane. Pull to the right and wait for the pedestrian lights. It's acceptable for you to be a pedestrian, but not to cut in front of the right-turning cars.

Where there is no formal right turn lane, note that a right turn lane is any lane where the cars around you are turning right. There may even be two lanes on the right of a multilane street where cars turn right. If so, you should be to the left of both of them. As you approach an intersection, you may have to change lanes to the left to get to the left of the right-turning cars. If a lane is carrying both right-turning and straight-through traffic, look back, yield, and pull far enough to its left to keep right-turning drivers from cutting around your left side. Changing lanes is perfectly safe once you're used to it. Going straight through on the right side of right-turning cars is anything but safe.

RULE OF THE ROAD: USE PROPER LANE WHEN APPROACHING AN INTERSECTION

A driver is required to get into a lane at the right for a right turn and at the center for a left turn. When going straight, a driver must keep out of special turn lanes.

If drivers were permitted to turn in any direction from any lane, they would run into each other when pulling out into intersections. If drivers were permitted to go straight after entering special turn lanes, they'd have to squeeze back into the flow of traffic in the middle of the intersection. And a narrow vehicle like your bicycle would be even worse off, cutting across turning traffic as well.

By putting yourself in the correct position when approaching an intersection, you can set up the way the motorists will deal with you as you leave the intersection.

A RIGHT TURN ON RED

Right turn on red is the dread of novice bicyclists who pull to the right curb at every intersection.

Don't do that, unless you're going to walk across.

On a multilane street, get to the left of turning cars as we've advised.

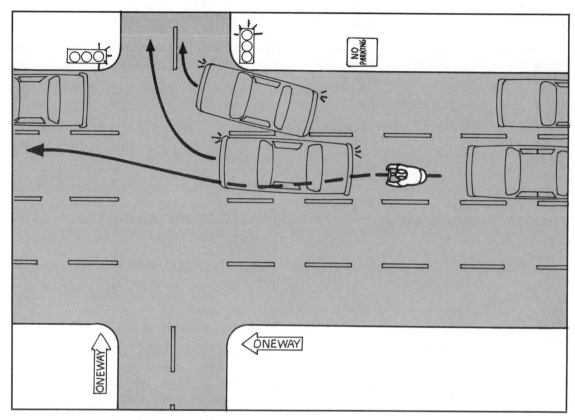

Keep behind or to the left of right-turning traffic as you ride through an intersection. Do not go to the right of traffic unless you are turning right.

On a street with only one lane in your direction, let the motorist by on your right if you can do it safely. This is usually possible where parking spaces at the right stop before the intersection, leaving more room. As the light changes, you are first in line. Make a slow signal on your right side, look back, and pull back to your normal position in the lane.

You may sometimes have to block a car from turning right on red. It's your right.

MAKING A RIGHT TURN

LEVEL 1: Hold your line in traffic. Look for pedestrians on the corner as you approach. Signal if any driver ahead needs to know that you are turning. Yield or stop for pedestrians — even if they're crossing against the light! — though you can usually pass behind them. At a stop sign or at an unsignalled intersection, slow down and check the street to the left for traffic; also check the street ahead for left-turning drivers, and time your turn into the street to the right to fall in between them. With right turn on red, look to the left for pedestrians. In general, look all around the intersection no matter which directions are supposed to be safe. Obey traffic signals. Once you've pulled into the intersection, look past the parked cars ahead of you for jaywalkers and wrong-way bicyclists.

LEVEL 2: This is the high-speed right turn, which you can use only if you can see all around the intersection before you get to it, and nobody is going to cross your path. Usually, you turn this way when you've been coming downhill.

As you approach the intersection, you are already in the middle of the right lane, going as fast as the car behind you or faster. You pull further to the left of the lane, then cut smoothly across the lane, passing close to the curb on the corner, and back out to the middle of the lane in the street to the right. This is what you would call a sweeping turn, used to avoid having to brake and lose speed.

LEVEL 3: A level 3 right turn is a traffic right turn, exactly like a level 1 turn, except that you first make a partial lane change to the left to pull ahead of the next car behind you. You do this if the right lane in the cross street is narrow, or if for any reason the driver may come too far to the right as you take the corner—for example, if there is a long truck behind you whose back wheels will swing far to the right as it turns.

MAKING A LEFT TURN

Make a left turn either like a driver, or like a pedestrian. Do not hesitate or cross to the left side of the street before making the turn, and do not go to the far side of the intersection, and turn left from the right lane. These fudge maneuvers are dangerous, and illegal.

LEVEL 1: Pull to the right side of the road before the intersection and walk your bike around two sides of the intersection. Then get back on and ride. You are entering traffic. Look back and yield.

LEVEL 1-2: *Ride* your bike straight across the intersection. Stop at the far corner

(do not swerve into traffic without stopping!). Now as a pedestrian, turn your bike to the left. Wait for the light to change or for traffic to clear, then go. Wait either on the sidewalk or, if the crosswalk is on pedestrian sequence, wait on the crosswalk to the left of where right-turning cars go. If you're on the sidewalk, start out on the pedestrian light, look back and yield.

Note: Level 1-2 is not just for left turns you find difficult. It is how you make a left turn legally when there's a "no left turn" sign.

LEVEL 2: With no cars about to cross your path, move to this position: the *left* side of the rightmost left-and-through lane, or if there is a left turn only lane without a left-and-through lane to its right, the right side of the left turn lane.

In other words, you want to be on the appropriate side of the rightmost lane from which vehicles turn left, so you can easily get to the right side of the street you are turning into.

Continue around to the left. If a left-turning car is coming in the opposite direction, pass it right side to right side.

LEVEL 3: Level 3 is like Level 2, except you prepare the turn in traffic. Where you station yourself to begin the turn depends on where the cars around you are going. Move to the same place as for Level 2. Signal and change lanes as we've described.

If you are at the head of a left-and-through lane waiting for a traffic light or for cross traffic, claim the entire lane until you know which way the driver behind you is going. Depending on which way most of the traffic in this lane goes, you will be at its left making a slow signal, at its right making a left turn signal, or if the lane is too narrow to share, blocking it.

If you are pulling up between lanes in stopped traffic, notice whether the second car

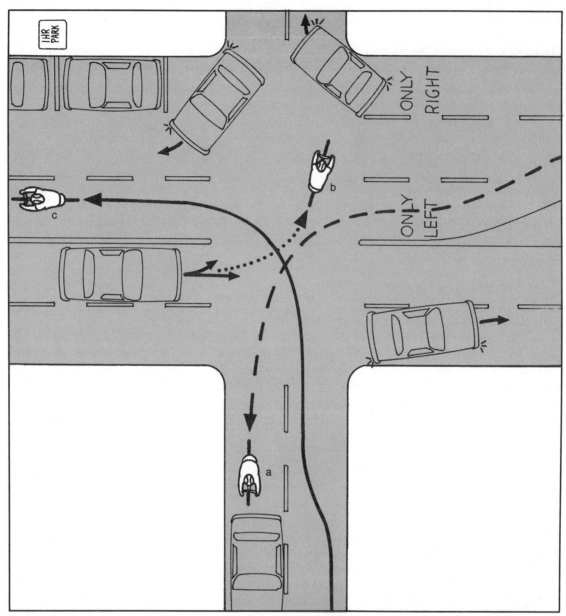

Correct paths for left turns. a) The cyclist has changed lanes into a left turn lane, keeping to its right, as there is no conflict with traffic going straight in this lane. The cyclist proceeds across the intersection, keeping to the right of or in line with the left-turning cars. b) The cyclist turns left from a combined left and through lane. Wait for a traffic light at the center of such a lane unless you have determined which way the car behind you is going. The cyclist must yield to right-turning traffic from the opposite direction. c) The cyclist changes lanes, overtaking a right-turning car, and makes the left turn into the center lane of the cross street, avoiding the need to yield to right-turning traffic in this four-lane street.

has its turn blinker on. Then position yourself accordingly ahead of this car near one side or the other. While you wait, show the driver what you are going to do with hand signals.

In moving traffic, you will usually be changing lanes from the right, ahead of a car. Watch for the car's turn signal. If the lane from which you will turn is for through traffic as well as right-turning traffic, hold the middle of the lane unless you're sure the car is going straight — then pull farther left.

If there isn't a special left turn sequence that gives you a clear path, move slowly out toward the middle of the intersection as soon as you have the green light. Make your turn as soon as traffic clears to your left. If the light has turned red, you still have the right of way, and the middle of the intersection is the safest place to start your turn. You're well ahead of cross-street traffic.

Always, as you enter the intersection, look for traffic from the left and the right, and for the traffic coming toward you. Pass a left-turning car from the opposite direction right side to right side. Watch for a right-turning car from the opposite direction. You must yield to this car.

One-way streets give you extra choices. Turning from a two-way street to a one-way street, start in the same place as if turning into a two-way street, and go to the right side of the one-way street. Or from the centerline of the two-way street, move to the left side of the one-way street.

Turning from a one-way street to a one-way street, you may make the turn from the left side to the left side. Or you may make the turn just like a left turn on two-way streets, from the rightmost place you can turn left to the right side of the cross street.

Turning from a one-way street to a two-way street, don't make the turn from the left side if there is left-turning traffic behind you.

Make the turn the same way you would from a two-way street, so you end up on the right side of the cross street, not pushed over the center.

DIAGONAL INTERSECTIONS

A diagonal intersection is just like a right-angled intersection, except drivers will have a harder time seeing vehicles approaching them on the cross street close to their side, especially on the right side. Many vehicles have a blind spot there. Be especially careful of vans without windows on the right side. Time yourself ahead of them or behind them — not next to them, even if you have the right of way.

Drivers making left turns into a street almost straight ahead of them will not have to slow down as much, and may be more inclined to pull out to the left before turning. They can see farther into the cross street, and if there is no traffic, they may cut wide. Dodge right so the left-turning driver second in line can see you.

TECHNIQUES FOR ON- AND OFF-RAMPS
WHEN THEY'RE ON THE RIGHT

If entering by the on-ramp or leaving by the off-ramp, just follow it around until it merges into the road. Yield to through traffic when entering.

LEVEL 1: If going straight through with a ramp on your right, either get off before the on-ramp, or ride down the off-ramp. Walk your bike across. Yield to through traffic, and to traffic already on the ramp. Or you may ride all the way across a cloverleaf intersection by way of the ramps, if the cross road is easy to get across.

LEVEL 2: Keep your line in traffic. Ride straight across the end of the ramp. Do not duck into the ramp.

LEVEL 3: Same as level 2, except when necessary use a preventive technique: slow signal, turn signal, or partial lane change, to insure that motorists overtake you on the right side as they enter the ramp. See the section on preventive riding in this chapter.

WHEN THEY'RE ON THE LEFT

To enter by a ramp from the left, ride down the right side of the ramp, then:

LEVEL 1: Walk across the main road.

LEVEL 2: Find a gap in the traffic long enough so you can cut all the way across to the right side of the main road.

LEVEL 3: Change lanes one by one across to the right side of the main road.

WHEN EXITING BY A RAMP ON THE LEFT

LEVEL 1: Ride past the ramp, or to a pedestrian crosswalk, then walk across and ride up the right side of the ramp.

LEVEL 2: As you approach the ramp, find a gap in the traffic long enough to cut all the way across, then ride to the left of the ramp. Ride up the ramp, then change lanes across to its right.

LEVEL 3: Move to approach on the left of the ramp, then ride up the ramp and to the right.

UNIONS AND SEPARATIONS

These are like on-ramps and off-ramps,

except that the total number of lanes does not change.

For example, a two-lane, one-way street may separate into two one-lane, one-way streets.

When entering a union from the right or a separation to the right, just hold your line in traffic. When entering a union from the left, ride on the right side, then:

LEVEL 1: Walk across to the right side of the lanes which join on the right.

LEVEL 2: Time yourself into a gap in the traffic long enough so you can get all the way across the lanes to your right. Note that it is helpful to slow before you come to the union, so you can speed up before your enter it and cross quicker.

LEVEL 3: Move across to the right of the lanes on your right.

When positioning yourself in the left lanes at a separation:

LEVEL 1: Ride past the separation, then walk across the right lanes. Yield as you re-enter traffic.

LEVEL 2: Find a gap in the traffic long enough to cut across all of the lanes going right. Ride into the right side of the lanes going left.

LEVEL 3: Move across to the lane line between the two sets of lanes. Then go up the right side of the rightmost lane that separates to the left.

ROTARY INTERSECTIONS

LEVEL 1: Make a right turn into the rotary. Get off and walk at each cross street. Be especially careful to look behind you and to the left before you cross each street; that is where the traffic comes from. With heavy traffic, and no pedestrian lights, or in the country, where the pedestrian rule is to walk on the left facing traffic, you're safest walking around the circle clockwise. Then the drivers in the rotary are looking at you as you cross each street. But walk, don't ride — wrong way riding is wrong way riding, even in a rotary.

LEVEL 2: If there are no cars in the rotary in your path, ride across or around, pulling to the outside of the inner lane and then back out. Glance back to your right before you pull to the right to cross the right lane.

LEVEL 3: If traffic is jammed up and moving slowly, you move through a rotary with two lane changes. You can begin the first lane change before you enter the rotary, placing yourself in line with the right (or only) lane of entering cars. As you enter, pull in between the inner and outer lanes and ride just behind the right rear corner of a car in the inner lane. When you've passed the last exit before yours, change lanes to the right and then pull out into your exit.

If traffic is light enough to be moving briskly in the rotary, move left before you enter the rotary. Move to the left middle of the right lane if you are entering in a single lane of traffic, and to the right side of the inner lane if you are entering with two or more lanes. Remember, all traffic turns right; but you want to get to the inner lane of the rotary, so you move left.

Now ride around at the right side of the inner lane, behind the right rear corner of a car. If there is a car ahead, keep back and be prepared to brake, because centrifugal force in the rotary affects the motorist stronger than it affects you.

Begin making a left turn signal as soon as you enter the rotary. This is to let drivers know that you wish to get to the inner lane. Once you are in the inner lane, hold its outer edge even if there's no car directly behind you, and continue making your left turn signal. You don't want cars overtaking on the left, because they

The cyclist uses a "straight-ahead" signal to let the motorist on the right know that he wants to leave the inner lane of the rotary. The cyclist speeds up slightly, the motorist slows slightly, and they switch places.

will exit sooner or later, and centrifugal force will throw them outward. You need the entire width of the inner lane to yourself. You let traffic enter and exit freely in the outer lane, and by holding the outer edge of the inner lane, you make yourself visible to drivers around the center island. In the interests of civic beauty, some center islands are planted with tall bushes or decorated with bulky monuments, making visibility difficult.

Just after passing the last exit before

[*Continued on page 115*]

RULE OF THE ROAD: FOR ROTARY TRAFFIC

Vehicles in the inside lane in a rotary have the right of way. All rotary traffic has the right of way over entering traffic. Without this rule, entering traffic would block exiting traffic and everything would jam up. This rule is not widely known, so it is usually enforced with a stop or yield sign at entrances.

A NOTE ON UNIONS AND SEPARATIONS

Level 1 riding is often not useful here, because there are no pedestrian crosswalks. The idea of unions and separations, and on- and off-ramps, is to keep traffic moving. Accordingly, they are built in places where crosswalks do not stop the traffic. There are many places you can safely cross at level 2 or 3 but not at all at level 1 — or with serious danger.

If you are not confident of getting through one of these at level 2 or level 3 — say if the only ramp is to the left across several lanes of heavy, fast traffic — you may have to take the next exit. If you are entering a union on the left with several lanes of heavy, fast traffic on the right, you may have to walk back. But you can usually safely get across a one-lane on-ramp or off-ramp at level 1.

But even at high speeds, level 2 and level 3 are far safer than they appear — safer than level 1. Remember, if you hold your line, the driver always has at least one choice where to go — to your right or to your left. This isn't so when you're walking across a ramp! The faster the highway, the longer the merging strip for the on-ramp or off-ramp, so Level 3 works with right-side ramps even at highway speed.

Union and separation (here and facing page). *The cyclist moves from left to right across two lanes of a union and separation.*

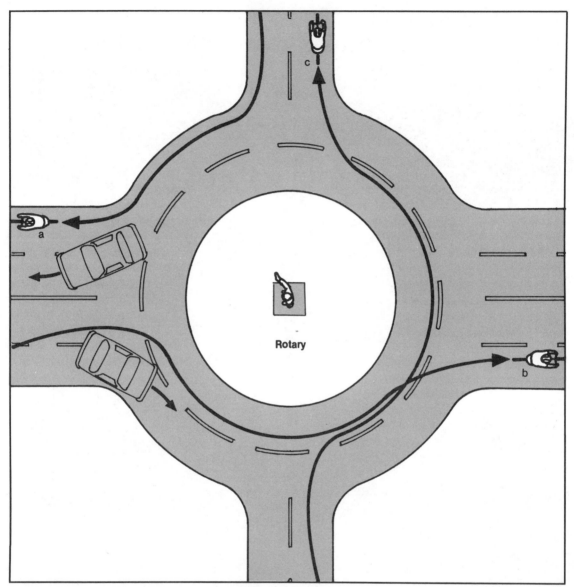

Paths through a rotary intersection. a) From one entrance to the next, just make two right turns. b) When entering from a four-lane street, change to the right side of the center lane before reaching the rotary. Ride around at the right side of the center lane of the rotary, making a change back to the right lane after leaving the rotary if traffic is heavy at your exit. c) When entering from a two-lane street, change lanes to the left side before reaching the rotary. Change lanes back to the right before exiting into a two-lane street.

yours, shift to a right turn signal and change lanes to the right; then exit.

A rotary is usually the last kind of intersection a rider tackles with confidence, but it really isn't that bad. The cars in the inner lane have to go slowly because of the constant turn, and won't likely catch up with you.

ON-THE-ROAD ENVIRONMENTS

The rules of the road and the straight road traffic techniques we've talked about apply everywhere. But riding environments can be very different. City traffic, suburban streets, country back roads, or highways — each of these environments requires special attention to different parts of your riding technique. Some are easier and some are more difficult.

Except for the wide-to-narrow move, which isn't really straight riding, there is no beginning, intermediate, or advanced way to ride each straight road environment. The best and safest way is the same, regardless of your level of experience. The way you'll ride will depend on your speed, but not as much as you might think. It's better to choose where to ride based on your speed. There is a best range of speeds for each environment. If you're less experienced or weaker, choose places where you can ride slower so you don't outrun the limits of your bike-handling technique. Your main focus at first has to be on handling the bike. Once you can do that, you begin to move out into the more demanding traffic situations.

If you're experienced and want to get somewhere fast, you're safer out on the wide, main streets. So, as you ride, you'll choose your route according to your needs at the time. That'll depend on your skill, how fast you want to go, and the traffic conditions. We'll show you the techniques and you make the choices.

BACK STREETS AND ROADS
(LEVELS 1, 2)

Old through streets and newer residential streets often connect into a network on which you can almost entirely avoid heavy traffic and exhaust fumes, though it will take you some exploring to find all of the routes you need to get around town. On back streets, you usually travel slower than on main streets, because you will run into more stop signs and red lights — the lights will be green longer for the main streets. Back streets are less hectic than main streets, but they have special problems you must be aware of. They are usually narrower; when there is traffic, you often must block cars from passing you when it is unsafe. Pedestrians and other bicyclists are less cautious, so you have to ride more toward the middle when there are no cars around. And back streets often cross main streets without traffic lights. You must either choose your route to avoid unsignalled intersections or take extra care when crossing the main streets.

Sometimes you will find a real gem of a road, wide but with little traffic. More often, back streets and roads will be narrow, more winding and hillier than the main roads, and the pavement won't be as good. If traffic is even moderately heavy on a narrow back street, riding becomes more hectic than it is on a wide main street.

MAIN CITY STREETS
(LEVEL 3)

Generally, the larger streets with traffic lights let you ride faster than the smaller ones with stop signs. On main streets not every block will have a light; side streets will have stop signs which give you the clear right of way. The bigger streets are safer if you want to ride fast. Though there's more traffic, there's more room for you than on the back streets. With the level 3 techniques, on main streets you move fast and safe. To minimize delays caused by traffic lights, look for routes which border railroad lines, freeways, rivers, or industrial areas. These routes often will have less traffic than other streets since they're not in the middle of things.

TIMING
TRAFFIC LIGHTS

If all of the streets are two-way, street light synchronization will have to be more or less random. Use the pedestrian interval to your advantage, if it's separate from the green light for the cars. In many places, you are allowed to ride on a pedestrian crosswalk. You don't have to walk as long as you take care and yield to pedestrians. Remember to look before reentering traffic.

Where streets are one-way in a gridwork, usually the lights are synchronized to 30 mph. Cars will move steadily, and the drivers will never see a red light. Red lights will catch up with you every few blocks. But at 20 mph — you will go a half-mile at a stretch. Then, you'll wait 45 seconds, go a half-mile and wait again. In times of light traffic, increase your span between red lights by slowing in midblock and accelerating just as the cars begin to move at the intersection behind you. Then the light ahead will turn green just as you reach it.

A similar trick is to slow or wait at the top of a hill for a red light at the bottom. If you've got the light timed, you use the power of the hill to get you going instead of wasting it braking at the bottom.

Look at the traffic signal for the cross street, if you can see it. If it's yellow, you'll have a green light before you get to the intersection. If you're stopped, you use the side street signals as your clue to get into the toe clips and moving before your light turns green. Pedestrian signals change before the yellow comes on, giving you earlier notice.

If you get caught on a yellow light, you must either get through the intersection or stop before it. Since some lights, especially on very wide streets, have yellows too short for bicyclists to get through, you need to have a plan.

If the light's turned yellow and you can't stop before the intersection, speed up. You've been staying below your top cruising speed, so you'll have a reserve of power for situations like this. Now you put on extra power, and usually you get across. Glance back, then move out toward the left so the drivers on both sides ahead can see you. If the traffic starts to move, go ahead of it. Usually, you'll be to the far lane so you'll turn left. If there's a lane divider in the center of the street that is wider than your bike is long, you might seek its shelter.

This scheme works except for delayed green lights — you'll have to time these by experience over several trips.

YOUR BEST SPEED
IN TRAFFIC

There's a best traffic speed for you. This speed is brisk, to give you plenty of time to deal with the drivers coming up from behind. But it is just a bit below your top cruising speed, so you'll have a reserve of power for acceleration. You time your interactions with other drivers sometimes by slowing down and sometimes by speeding up. If you're already going at top speed, you'll always have to slow down to time a merge into a line of traffic, often using the brakes. Using the brakes wastes your energy. At the best traffic speed you want to usually slow down gently so you won't have to brake, though you often accelerate quickly.

If you're going too slowly in traffic, you'll more often lose the chance to enter lanes where the cars are going faster than you. You'll lose more time with your slow pace than you would where there's no traffic.

The best traffic speed is different for every person, depending on strength and endurance, but it follows these same guidelines.

RULE OF THE ROAD: RIGHT OF WAY AT INTERSECTIONS

The rules are different according to the signs or signals installed at the intersection. Where two lightly traveled roads cross, with no signs or signals, the first vehicle to arrive at an intersection has the right of way. On these roads, traffic must travel slowly. It is understood that anyone may have to wait at an intersection, even without a stop sign.

When two vehicles arrive at an intersection at the same time, the one on the right has the right of way. That's because the one on the left has more room to stop — half the width of the cross road.

Where a main road crosses a less important one, stop signs on the less important one give traffic on the main one the right of way. That way, through traffic on the main road can travel without having to slow at every intersection.

Where traffic is heavy on both roads at an intersection, traffic lights prevent confusion by requiring drivers on the two roads to enter the intersection at different times.

TRAFFIC TIP: IF THE LIGHT NEVER TURNS GREEN

This usually happens when you're alone on a small street which crosses a larger one. The light probably is tripped by an electronic coil buried in the pavement, which is not sensitive enough to respond to your bicycle. You may see patterns of lines in squares on the pavement where the sensor is buried. If a car is approaching behind you, it will trigger the sensor. Or if there's a pedestrian walk button, use it. But remember, when you do, you may be out of the correct lane position. Look for turning traffic.

If there's no button, wait for a gap in the traffic and go across on the red. No judge can convict you for doing this, when the light won't turn green.

Whoever installed the electronic coil is who actually violated a law — the law giving you the rights and responsibilities of a driver.

HOW TO RIDE NARROW FOUR-LANE ROADS
(LEVEL 3)

To a rider inexperienced with them, roads with four or more narrow lanes look too formidable. Certainly they don't let you be highly relaxed while riding. If there's traffic, you have to keep your attention focused. But as long as you do, there's rarely any actual safety problem.

You don't have to give as much attention to oncoming traffic as on a two-lane road. The only oncoming traffic that crosses your path is making left turns, and it has an extra lane to cross before it gets to you. And traffic from behind you is easy to handle, too.

The novice's idea of safety is to keep as far right as possible here. That's the worst

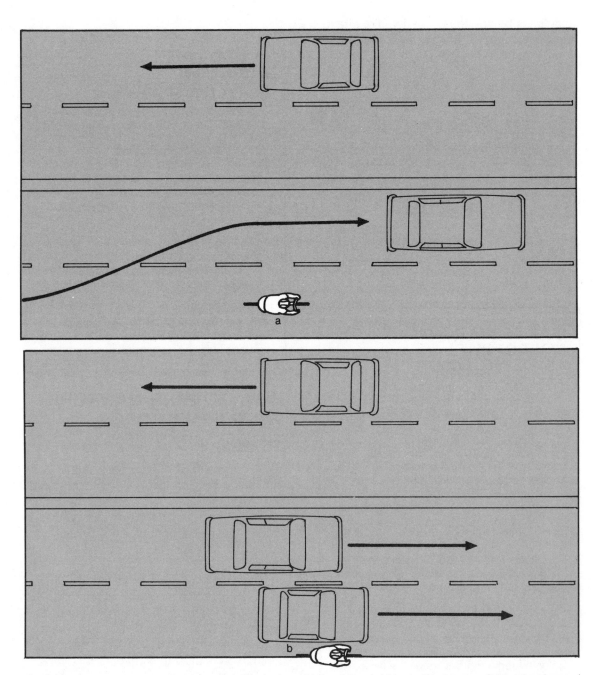

On a four-lane road with narrow lanes, a) ride in the middle of the right lane. If not, you might get squeezed out b), especially if you hug the edge.

thing to do. It exposes you to the *double-decker squeeze.*

The squeeze comes when two cars are stacked up next to you, one in each lane. The driver in the far lane may never have seen you. As the driver in the far lane pulls past, the one in the near lane gets squeezed, and you get squeezed in turn. You can get squeezed again and again!

Avoid being squeezed by riding out in the middle of the right lane. Just as if you were driving a slow-moving car, you make each driver behind you move to the passing lane.

We recommend a rearview mirror for peace of mind when riding in this position, though none of us has yet had a near rear-end collision doing it.

As long as you stay in the middle of the right lane, each driver will move left in plenty of time to avoid having to slow down. Usually, traffic is light enough on this sort of road that all of the cars can easily fit into the left lane. Often, on a multilane one-way city street like this, there will be few cars in the right lane anyway — it's too close to the parked cars. With four or five lanes to the left, the drivers hardly miss the one you're using. If traffic actually does begin to jam up, it won't be because of you. Maximum load-carrying capacity of any traffic lane is reached at 22 mph. If you're the kind of rider who prefers this sort of street in the first place, you can go nearly that fast. Most likely, you'll be moving out to the center lane to overtake cars if the traffic gets really heavy.

NARROW TWO-LANE COUNTRY ROADS

(LEVEL 3)

Two-lane roads and secondary highways are favorite places for group rides, and fine routes for your utility riding as well.

But when a narrow highway has fast, heavy traffic, it necessitates very demanding riding. Cars tend to bunch up into convoys, often behind large trucks. The drivers behind the first vehicle may have trouble seeing you.

As a convoy overtakes you from behind, the first vehicle will have to slow for you if there is oncoming traffic, a blind curve, or a hilltop. Drivers behind are required by law to follow the first vehicle — and it is very unwise for them to overtake. For all they know, if they don't see you, the first driver might be slowing to turn either right or left. Still, an occasional aggressive driver may attempt to overtake either on the right or on the left. If the shoulder is narrow or soft as it is on most of these roads, usually they'll overtake on the left. Particularly if the overtaking driver did not see you before pulling out, you may be squeezed right as the car pulls back into line.

Drivers ahead of you also may miss seeing you and pull out to overtake. On the narrow highway with its unpaved shoulders, you will be riding in the traffic lane rather than just to its right. You must not let your attention wander from the oncoming traffic.

When there is a string of cars catching up behind you and oncoming traffic as well, nobody will be trying to overtake from either direction. But the drivers behind you will be guiding on the oncoming traffic. They will be more likely to miss seeing you, and they will be farther to the right in any case.

When you stay on the pavement and let a convoy overtake you, the helmet or eyeglass mirror is best to judge the clearance of each car as it overtakes. You can glance into this mirror and still keep your attention on the pavement ahead, to hold a steady line near the right edge.

In difficult situations, especially with both following and oncoming traffic, you may decide to swallow your rights and move off the

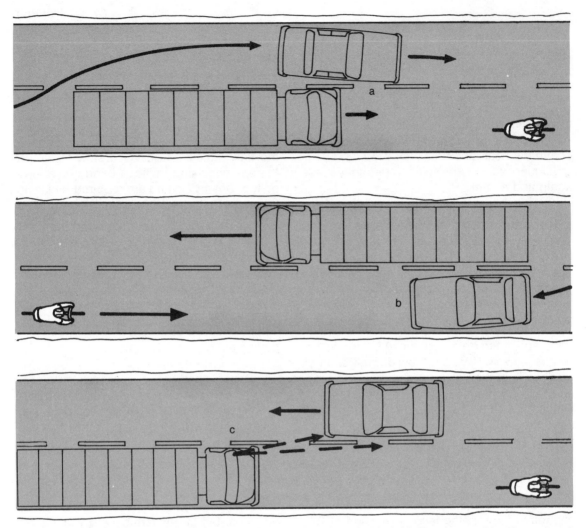

Narrow two-lane highway difficulties. a) Unsafe overtaking from behind. b) Illegal overtaking from ahead. c) Attention of drivers behind diverted by oncoming traffic.

pavement. You do not do this for the convenience of the motorists, but for your own safety. It's best to move off the pavement before the following vehicles have to begin to slow down. That way, they continue to move smoothly. Since the traffic moves in convoys when it's heavy on a high-speed road, you will pull off the pavement only every once in awhile — a small part of the time.

Though this sort of highway may not have paved shoulders, it at least doesn't have any curbs. The shoulder next to you is usually ridable at least as an escape route. Keep track of the shoulder next to you, and if you decide to use it, pull off onto it decisively. Once on the shoulder, slow down carefully — brake lightly, and avoid turning if the surface is bad. At least, since the shoulder is bad, you have little to worry about from cars pulling off onto it. Your main problem is in getting back up onto the pavement after the cars have overtaken you. Be very careful of the pavement edge, which is usually higher than a soft shoulder. From some angles you can't see the steplike edge parallel to your path.

Avoid this sort of highway during heavy traffic periods if you can — there are usually parallel routes. With caution, attention, high-visibility clothing, and a rearview mirror, you can ride this sort of highway safely.

Highways like this are usually found in rural areas becoming suburbs. They were usually built many years ago and are not up to handling heavy traffic volumes from increased population. Either the traffic volume or the speed limit is too high. But the speed limit was set long ago when traffic could tolerate it, and if the highway is still the only route through an area, there will be pressure from some motorists to keep the speed limit high. A narrow two-lane highway holds extra risks for motorists, too, by the way, not just bicyclists.

WIDE TWO-LANE COUNTRY HIGHWAYS
(LEVEL 2)

On wider highways, the motorists have ample room to overtake you. Some of these highways have wide lanes, and others have wide, paved shoulders you can ride on.

Here, you follow the wide-lane rule, keeping to the right of the cars. On a road with wide lanes, you generally ride a foot or so inside the right edge of the pavement. With wide shoulders, you ride just outside the shoulder stripe. Some highways have shoulders which are paved, but rougher than the travel lanes. Then you ride just inside the right lane when there is no traffic behind you. Be careful in case there's a step or crack between the shoulder and the travel lane. Often, the shoulder is lower — almost never higher.

On a wider highway, unsafe overtaking from behind is no problem. Unsafe overtaking from ahead is less of a problem than it is on a narrow highway, but watch for it. Your primary problems are drivers making right turns around your front, and to a lesser degree drivers attempting to overtake on the right, assuming the shoulder is wide enough for this. To make a right turn in front of you, a car must slow down from highway speed, so keep an eye and ear out for slow cars on your left as you approach intersections and driveways. Overtaking on the shoulder usually happens when a car has slowed or stopped in the right lane to make a left turn. When a car slows behind you just after you've passed an intersection, keep on the stripe between the shoulder and the traffic lane so any illegal overtaker can get by you.

Wide two-lane country highways are quite safe, though often unpleasant to ride on because of noise and exhaust if the traffic is heavy.

MULTILANE WITH WIDE RIGHT LANE
(LEVEL 2)

This is your typical freeway or city boulevard.

You ride just to the right of the cars, the same as you would on any road with a wide right lane. You do not have to worry about oncoming traffic much — or at all. Either the road is divided, or there are two lanes between you and the oncoming traffic.

It's easy riding, though sometimes noisy.

OTHER RIDING ENVIRONMENTS
(ALL LEVELS)

In some riding environments, the standard rules of the road are modified, or other rules apply. These environments are stopped traffic, the sidewalk, the bikepath, and all situations in which there is heavy bicycle traffic.

STOPPED TRAFFIC

You can safely move ahead through stopped traffic, though there are certain things to watch out for, and ways to do it. Here are the main points:

1. Ride *slowly,* because

. . . other bicyclists and pedestrians will take advantage of stopped traffic, just the same as you. They often don't expect you, and you can't always see them around the stopped cars.

. . . people in cars will open doors in front of you from either side, in any lane. They don't expect you, so you must be able to stop. Be especially wary of a single car which stops in the street for no apparent reason. Overtake it on the left with plenty of clearance or wait for it.

2. Know the danger and safety zones around stopped cars, and deal with them, and remember

. . . next to a rear wheel of a car, you're quite safe because that part of the car can only move backward or forward, not sideways — also, the driver of the next car behind can see you.

. . . as you come up toward the front end of a car, be wary. Look whether the front wheels are straight or turned and listen in case the engine speeds up. If you notice these signs, stay by the back end of the car.

You're safest where the drivers don't have anywhere to turn. Watch out for driveways or parking spaces on the right side of stopped traffic. Move slowly but keep moving, look for the turned wheel, pull away

slightly to the side, into the open space, and glance back as you pull ahead of the car's windshield to check that the driver has seen you. Sometimes it helps to knock on the window, just to let the driver know you're there.

. . . sometimes you must cut across in front of a stopped car to change traffic lanes. First make eye contact with its driver. Look to the car ahead now to see whether there is any reason it might back up. Usually, there isn't, but don't cut across on a steep uphill just as the light is changing (manual transmission cars roll back as they start!), and don't cut behind a car that's rolled too far out into an intersection. Watch for backup lights. When you've checked these things, cut across. Look back down the lane line on the far side of the car behind you. Another bicyclist might be coming up it.

. . . when overtaking in a clear lane next to a line of stopped cars — in a right turn lane, for example — give them plenty of clearance in case one turns toward you. Look ahead for the turned front wheels. Never overtake a stopped bus or truck on the right when it's in the curb lane, where passengers might get off. When overtaking a stopped bus on the left, pull clear or slow down in case a jaywalking passenger is coming around the front. And for any long vehicle, make sure it is really stuck in traffic with no place to turn toward you before you overtake close to its side.

Subject to these cautions, stopped traffic is quite safe. Much of the time, the cars have no place to move to, and then you have only the jaywalkers, car doors, and other bicyclists to watch for. To your advantage in stopped traffic, you are very close to the drivers. You can see what they are doing inside the cars, and communicate with them easily.

RIDING IN VERY SLOW TRAFFIC
(ALL LEVELS)

If traffic is moving at 2 or 3 mph, you can still move through it, just as through stopped traffic. But be more careful. Move only between cars that are clearly going straight and have nowhere to turn into. Keep an extra sharp eye out for turning front wheels — brake and fall back to the rear corner of a car if you see them. Be especially careful of long vehicles that might be turning. Halfway back along the right side of a bus is not a place to be when it's about to pull into a bus stop; you'll end up by the door next to the passengers. If the bus pulls right over to the curb, you might have to climb up on the sidewalk!

WHEN STOPPED TRAFFIC PICKS UP SPEED
(ALL LEVELS)

You're riding in midblock, up toward a traffic light in stopped or slow-moving traffic. The light changes, and the cars start to pull out. What do you do?

Put yourself next to the end of the rear bumper of the next car ahead, where the driver of the one behind can see you. Don't overtake that next car ahead — you're going to be in the driver's blind spot as you come up beside it, and you'd be going too fast to get out of the way if the driver began to turn toward you. If the lane is wide and you're on the right, stay next to the cars as they pick up speed and begin to go by. If it's narrow, or if you have to change lanes either left or right, pull in between cars. Glance back at the

driver behind you and make a signal to turn.

The cars are only beginning to move, so there's little danger. Wait till the driver behind responds to your signal by making room for you — then pull into line.

If the driver won't drop back, be obstinate. Move over a little closer and glance back again — or make a vigorous, jabbing hand signal. Once you're in the lane you want to be in, you move to the position in it that is appropriate to its width, your destination, and the behavior of the driver behind you.

SIDEWALK RIDING
(LEVEL 1)

In the very early stages of riding, you may feel safest on the sidewalk. But remember, a pedestrian can stop almost instantly. You can't, unless you are going as slowly as the pedestrian. Also, you have a wheel sticking out in front of you. A car, bicycle, or a pedestrian could come out of a driveway, path, or door onto the sidewalk without warning. Don't let your speed build up going downhill on a sidewalk.

Most sidewalk crossings at intersections are not protected from right-turning cars. A driver can see a pedestrian waiting on the corner, but may not see you coming up from behind on your bicycle. So you must stop and look, like the pedestrian.

This is how you must ride, and this is how you must teach your children to ride if they ride on the sidewalk.

Sidewalk riding is not much faster than walking. If you try to make it faster, it becomes very dangerous. Because it keeps you from using your bike to get anywhere at a reasonable speed, it is limiting. Sidewalk riding will always be useful to you to get around street obstructions, across long bridges with narrow

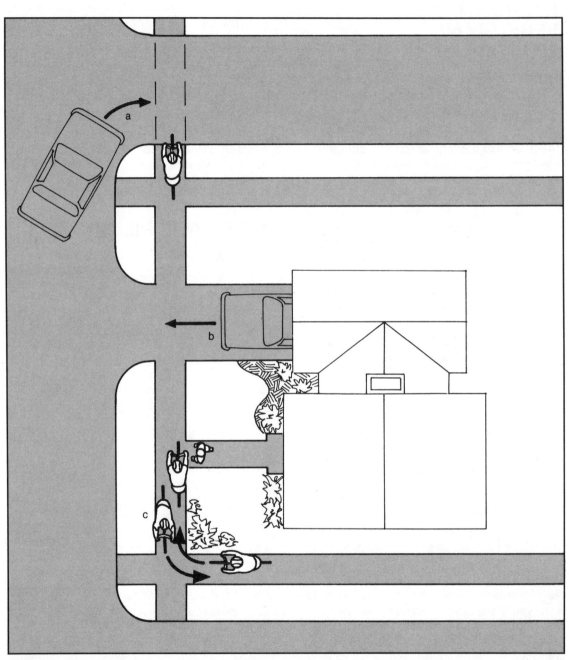

Sidewalk riding is hazardous, so ride at a walking pace. At a), the cyclist rides faster than normal sidewalk traffic and may surprise the motorist turning right. At b), a car exiting a driveway moves into the path of the cyclist. At c), a narrow corner and shrubbery create hazards for cyclists and pedestrians.

traffic lanes, and up the driveway to your garage. But as soon as you can, begin to practice street riding. Study the traffic techniques. Start your street riding on quiet streets where you have time to think in between the times you have to deal with other drivers. Your confidence will build along with your skill.

Many bicyclists switch from sidewalk to street riding in desperation, because the sidewalk is slow. They know they can go fast in the street, but they think that they are paying for speed with danger. It isn't so — the street is safer as well as faster.

Laws on sidewalk riding vary. Usually, you may legally ride outside business districts, but may have to walk in business districts. Check if in doubt, but above all, use common sense.

RIDING IN BIKE TRAFFIC
(ALL LEVELS)

Bicyclists must obey the rules of the road while riding with other bicyclists, not just with cars. Take special care on very wide, empty streets. A 6-lane car street becomes more or less an 18-lane bicycle street, but there are lane markings only every 3 lanes across. That makes it harder to follow the lanes, so give other bicyclists plenty of clearance to the side. Where you'd stay three feet out from a parked car, stay three feet out from a bicycle.

Do not swerve without looking around.

When riding in a large group, stay at the same speed and position in the group, unless you have plenty of room to pull clear and overtake. When you do, give a warning.

Don't follow too closely. Above all, avoid getting your front wheel next to someone else's rear wheel. If the two wheels touch, you'll be unable to steer or balance, and you'll fall while the other rider rides on ahead.

Always overtake another bicyclist on the left, never on the right except when entering a right turn lane. Never force another bicyclist to swerve into traffic, or cut off another bicyclist's escape route to the right.

Where there is a lot of bicycle traffic and also fairly heavy motor traffic, the best practice varies according to conditions. On main streets with more than one lane in your direction, bicyclists travel best double file in the right lane, overtaking on the left, and allowing motorists to merge in to make right turns. Occasionally, very fast bicyclists will move to the left edge of the right lane or into the second lane to overtake both files of bicyclists. Two bicyclists can ride along side by side in the same lane steadily, holding a conversation while riding. As long as there's a lane available to the left in which motorists can overtake without jamming up, this is reasonable. But avoid riding three abreast in one lane except if the bicyclist on the left is actively overtaking — the bicyclist in the middle is trapped if it's necessary to single up. On streets with only one lane in your direction, pull into single file when cars are behind unless there is simply no room. If heavy bicycle traffic fills a lane entirely so it would jam up by pulling into single file, then use the whole lane, even if motorists could use more room. Singling up would only worsen the traffic jam by making the bicyclists take more space.

The more bicyclists on the road, the more they can help each other maintain right of way. In Dutch cities, some bicyclists move in informal units, using the whole right lane and moving out from traffic lights together.

BIKEPATH RIDING
(ALL LEVELS)

Bikepaths may connect parts of a back-street network, or provide alternate, scenic

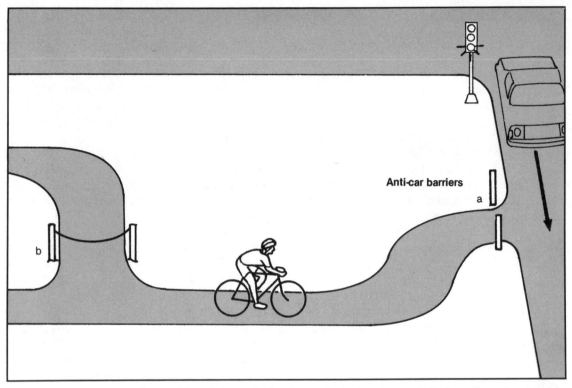

Bikepath hazards are similar to sidewalk hazards, but be on the look out especially for anti-car barriers b), and unprotected street crossings a).

routes, free of noise and pollution, but most are less safe than riding in the street. Bikepaths are very popular, and not only with bicyclists. In pleasant weather, they often become clogged with joggers, roller skaters, lovers walking arm in arm, people with dogs on leashes, tiny tots on tricycles, and mothers pushing baby buggies — among other users! Bikepaths usually are not designed as well as streets, and have unsafe sharp turns and blind spots. They are rarely maintained as well as the streets are, so they may be covered with gravel, sand, or glass, and in the winter, snow and ice, long after the streets have been cleared.

Bikepaths often cross streets without the protection of a traffic light or stop sign. Since

A bikepath hazard — watch your head!

Can you see the chain?

A bikepath crosses the end of a busy bridge. No traffic light, no stop sign.

A smooth barrier for the cars, sharp edges for the bicyclists.

about 90 percent of bicycle accidents are crossing and turning accidents, the hazard of crossing streets is greatly increased on bike-paths. For safety, you must stop, or slow to a crawl, and yield just as you would when crossing any street away from an intersection. If you have children who ride, be especially careful to point this out to them; otherwise, they may think that a bikepath is a safe place just because it is labeled as one.

BIKELANE RIDING

(ALL LEVELS)

On a long stretch of road without cross traffic, like a bridge, a bikelane conclusively separates you from the motor traffic, putting you under less pressure. It is, in effect, the same thing as a wide highway shoulder. It may allow you to cross a bridge where high speed and narrow lanes previously frightened bicyclists away.

But on normal streets, a bikelane frequently creates more dangers than it removes. The bikelane is not a haven of safety because someone put down a stripe of paint on the pavement. Traffic moves the same way with or without the bikelane. If the bikelane makes you ride too close to parked cars, or pulls to the curb side of turning cars, change lanes out of it. Obey the straight road rules instead.

Bikelanes cause conflicts. a) A bicyclist going straight is in the blind spot of a motorist turning right. b) A bicyclist is encouraged by a bikelane to make a left turn from the right side of the street, which is a very dangerous practice. c) This bicyclist has taken the safest course for either a left turn or straight-through riding, but note that the bikelane narrows the street, forcing this cyclist to slow for a right-turning car.

A bikelane that makes you ride on the wrong side of the street will put you in conflict with crossing traffic. Bikelane or no bikelane, you're riding the wrong way.

A bikelane behind parked cars hides you from drivers out in the street. You are a sitting duck at every intersection and driveway. Slow to pedestrian speed, or ride another street.

If other people — police included — are concerned that you're not in the bikelane, or honk horns at you, your safety is still more important than their mistaken idea of justice.

On balance, then, riding in traffic is safer than riding on a typical bikepath, bikelane, or sidewalk.

Except where there isn't any cross traffic nor parked cars, bikelane riding is a distorted situation in which both bicyclists and motorists are asked to do impossible or impractical things in order to keep from running into each other.

PREVENTIVE RIDING

You know that:

. . . The right of way rules are the same for everybody.

. . . A car, or any vehicle, may overtake a bicyclist only when it is safe.

. . . A bicyclist going straight is required to keep to the right only when it is safe for vehicles to overtake. If it is not safe, the bicyclist may, or must, pull to the middle of the traffic lane to prevent overtaking.

. . . A car, or any vehicle, is required to slow and follow a bicycle unless the car can overtake the bicycle without the bicyclist's slowing or stopping.

. . . A bicycle typically travels at 15 to 25 mph in traffic and faster downhill.

But many motorists believe that:

. . . A car always has the right to overtake a bicycle. A car always has the right of way; even if a bicyclist must stop at every corner.

. . . A car always overtakes a bicyclist on the left, even to make a right turn.

. . . A bicycle moves very slowly, like a pedestrian, so there is plenty of room to swing around to the left before making a right turn.

Motorists believe these things because:

. . . When they rode bicycles as children, they rode this way.

. . . Today, many bicyclists still ride this way, making motorists think that this second-class behavior is proper, necessary, or safe.

. . . Some motorists are selfish, seeing bicyclists as annoyances and as people who can or ought to be traveling some other way.

. . . Many motorists do not know the law.

You can make the motorists obey the law and keep a safe distance from you by using special preventive riding techniques — no matter what they believe.

Many of these techniques require your delaying traffic slightly more than might otherwise be necessary. But these techniques are justifiable to guarantee you a clear path through an intersection even when dealing with the least understanding and most aggressive drivers.

WHEN IT IS UNSAFE FOR DRIVERS TO OVERTAKE

When you are occupying a narrow lane with a blind curve, hilltop, or other obstruction or blind spot just ahead, ride the middle of the lane in order not to lead drivers behind you into temptation.

Your chief danger if you pull to the right with a blind spot ahead is that a driver may attempt to overtake you and then have to swerve toward you in the face of oncoming traffic. The driver is gambling that there won't be any oncoming traffic — but you bear the risk, so you have a right to prevent the situation from occurring.

Also ride in the middle of a narrow one-way, one-lane street. Don't let motorists squeeze by you. Fortunately, motorists will not feel comfortable driving much faster than you can ride on a street like this.

SLOWING DOWN A DRIVER DIRECTLY BEHIND YOU

When a driver is approaching you from behind in a lane unsafe to share and is still a safe distance behind you, pull to the middle of the lane (if you're not there already). Then before the driver gets too close for safety, glance back to make sure the driver has slowed down. This technique works best with a rear-view mirror. Used with the mirror, it is perfectly safe. Without the mirror, it is not always safe because you may not be able to look back when you need to.

This is the same technique you use when entering traffic or changing lanes. You move over far enough in advance so the driver behind has plenty of time to react, and so you have an escape route. Then you look back again, to check.

Sometimes, make a driver give you more room even in a lane wide enough to share. For example, when you're about to go over the top of a hill and don't know what's beyond, move left a few inches, then move back to the right to let the driver by. If you move back to the right too late for the driver to take advantage of the extra space, you've created extra room for yourself on both sides.

CONTROL A DRIVER WHEN NECESSARY

You do this as you approach intersections or off-ramps where drivers might turn right and you want to go straight. On a multi-lane road with light traffic, take the entire right lane; you're delaying no one.

Check each car just after the previous one has overtaken you, to give yourself the most time. If you suspect a driver wants to turn right, look for the right turn blinker.

If you see it, and the car is in your lane, immediately make a left turn signal.

Pull further toward the middle of the lane to usher the driver by on the right. Speed up to give yourself more time. If there's a right turn lane, wave the driver by on the right. If not, hold the center.

Check that the driver is slowing or pulling right. If necessary, take evasive action to the right.

If you do not see the turn signal, use your preventive technique anyway if the driver behind you is slowing down for no apparent reason — or speeding up in an attempt to overtake you before the intersection. After a while, you can sense drivers who want to pull around your left by the way their cars move. Don't get squeezed into the right turn lane where you didn't want to go. By pulling to the left, you recondition the driver to expect correct and considerate behavior from bicyclists. By moving left, you are not only avoiding delay and danger, but also clearly going out of your way to make things easier for the driver.

If drivers behind you are preparing to turn right in moderately heavy traffic which fills the lane to the left of a freeway off-ramp, make it clear that they are to go to your right by looking back, making a left turn signal, and pulling slightly to the left into the through lane.

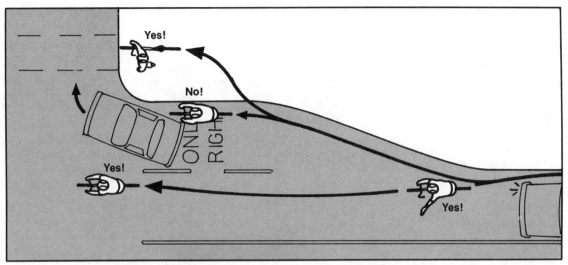

When riding to the left of a right turn lane, make a left turn signal and move slightly left if necessary to convince right-turning motorists to pass to your right. If you are not comfortable doing this, then go to the right side of the right turn lane and walk across the intersection.

This works safely even on a freeway.

As you pass an on-ramp, use a right turn signal or right side slow signal as necessary to get motorists to go to your left.

WHEN WAITING IN AN INTERSECTION

Your main need for preventive technique when waiting occurs in a lane which serves both right-turning and through traffic. This may be the only lane in your direction on a narrow street, or the second lane from the right where multilane streets cross.

If you're first in line at a stop sign or red light in a right-and-through lane, pull a little to the left — just far enough left so right-turning cars can go by you on the right, if you can do this safely. But don't be at the very left of the lane or too far ahead, especially on a two-lane street where left-turning cars from the right may cut wide toward you. If necessary, block the lane to keep right-turning drivers from cutting around your left side.

Where there can be no left-turning cars, as at an intersection with a one-way street, you may pull forward further, onto the pedestrian crosswalk if necessary, to let right-turning cars by. It's not strictly legal, but then if the cars can be turning right, it's because there are no pedestrians for you to block.

Get into the toe clips and start rolling on the yellow light in the cross street or anticipate when traffic is about to clear if waiting for a stop sign. Then move out smartly and pull back to your normal position into your lane as you cross the intersection. Glance to the right and make a forcible right turn signal if necessary to discourage the rare driver who might attempt to overtake you on the right. As you start, you are safely ahead of this driver.

CROSS-TRAFFIC PREVENTIVE TECHNIQUES

You know the maddening situation, when there's no car near you to keep the motorist, usually on your right, from inching out and trying to get you to stop.

Here's what to do.

When you're still well ahead of the intersection, speed up. Look back, and having verified that there's no car behind you, pull to the left middle of your lane. That's so you're sure to be seen; also, to give you more room to maneuver and so you look as though you're going faster. Your angle will be changing quicker as the driver in the side street sees you.

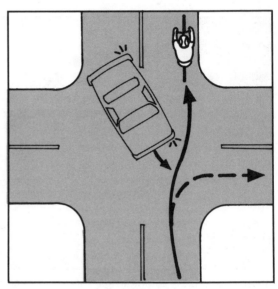

To call the bluff on a driver threatening to make a left turn from the opposite direction, drift left well before entering the intersection to make yourself more visible; then drift right to prepare an escape and increase your apparent speed.

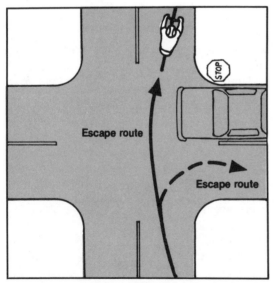

To call the bluff on a motorist inching out from a stop sign on your right, look back for traffic (there usually isn't any, or the motorist would stop), then put on speed and drift left, signalling your apparent speed to the motorist and gaining extra room for an escape if necessary. If the motorist does not stop, make your escape.

Yell, establish eye contact, and keep your hands on the brakes. You know that you have good brakes. The motorist doesn't.

When the car conclusively stops — and 9,999 times out of 10,000 it will — just keep moving.

You use a similar technique with a driver who's trying to start a left turn in front of you — only you're more cautious because you can't establish eye contact. Pull left well before the intersection, then move right just as you approach it to look as though you're going faster.

MAKING A RIGHT TURN

Wait in the middle of the lane if you're first in line in a narrow lane. Don't let a motorist squeeze in next to you at a stop sign or traffic light. Make a right turn signal so the motorist knows you'll be moving out once it's safe to turn right. As you turn the corner, position yourself according to the width of the right lane in the cross street.

If you're back in line, wait behind a car, not to the right of one. As you approach the intersection, note whether the car behind you is going straight. If so, you may courteously pull to the right a bit sooner to let it go by.

Preventive technique is necessary for a right turn only when lanes are narrow. You use it to prevent motorists from squeezing you as the back ends of their cars swing to the right in the turn, and to establish your right of way in the cross street. You won't, by the way, delay the cars — you can move out in a right turn as fast as they.

MAKING A LEFT TURN

If you're first in line in a lane which is both for left turns and for going straight through, approach the turn in the middle of the lane. You are not blocking traffic, because you are waiting for a red light or a stop sign, just as the car behind you. But if you do not know which way the car is going, you must not let it get next to you.

And on a two-way street without a center divider, you do not want to be all of the way in the middle where left-turning cars from your right might cut wide toward you.

When cross traffic clears, or the light changes, move out to the middle of the inter-section, pulling toward the left so a motorist behind you going straight can clear you on the right. A motorist behind you turning left

The cyclist follows a car through a level 3 left turn. The cyclist's path is behind the right side of the car to enter the cross street in normal lane position. Note that the cyclist is keeping pace with the car in the intersection — cars do not accelerate fast while turning.

will remain behind you rather than pull past you on the right into the path of cars turning left from the opposite direction. When straight-through traffic from the opposite direction clears, complete your turn.

If you're second in line or farther back in moving traffic, change lanes from the right to the middle of the left-and-through lane shortly before you reach the intersection, and complete the turn as described above. If you can determine for sure that the car behind you is turning left, you can be freer in allowing it to overtake you on your left as you enter the intersection.

If the intersection has little left-turning traffic and the road has a center divider, pull to the centerline. Then drivers can continue to overtake you on the right to go straight. But move out to the center of the intersection at the first opportunity to avoid being squeezed left to the wrong side of the cross street by a left-turning car.

A lane for only left turns is easier to handle. Simply maintain your normal position at its right. Pull only far enough into the lane to assure that motorists don't force you to the right of a too-narrow right lane in the cross street.

AVOIDING ACCIDENTS

Know which accidents are common, so you'll know what to look out for. And learn to avoid accidents through evasive maneuvers.

First, note that most accidents are single-bike accidents — mostly falls. Avoid these by improving riding technique and taking extra care where space is tight or the road surface is bad.

Most falls are not serious, and neither are most other accidents, whether caused by collisions with dogs, pedestrians, or other bicyclists. Counting serious accidents — those resulting in the need for medical treatment or in damage to the bicycle — about half are falls, about 20 percent are collisions with cars, and the rest divide up among collisions with dogs, pedestrians, and other bicyclists. Percentages vary according to location and type of riding done.

The following figures on the most common causes of car-bicycle collisions come from *A Study of Bicycle/Motor Vehicle Accidents* (U.S. Department of Transportation, 1978), written by Kenneth Cross.

1. Bicyclist on wrong side of street	14%
2. Motorist turns left in front of bicyclist	13%
3. Motorist turns right from left side of bicyclist	11%
4. Bicyclist turns left from right side of road	11%
5. Bicyclist exits driveway without yielding	9%
6. Bicyclist runs stop sign or signal	8%
7. Motorist runs stop sign or signal	8%
8. Motorist opens car door	7%
9. Motorist exits driveway without yielding	6%
10. Motorist hits bicyclist from the rear	4%

Accidents one (1), four (4), and six (6) are avoided simply by obeying the rules of the road. These are common children's accidents — much rarer for adult bicyclists.

The remaining accidents are to be avoided by proper riding technique and by evasive maneuvers.

Three (3) is much more common than it seems. However, because evasion is so easy, three usually does not cause an accident at all.

Eight (8) is a common beginner's accident, caused by excessive fear of overtaking traffic. The remedy is simple. Stay clear of the car doors.

Two (2), seven (7), and nine (9) may not only be prevented by good technique; they may also be effectively avoided.

Ten (10) is rare, though it is the accident beginners fear most.

Here are techniques for avoiding collisions with cars, pedestrians, and bicyclists.

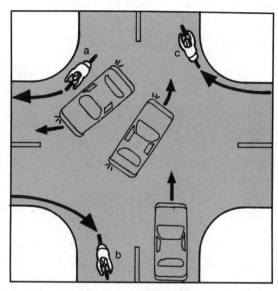

Accident avoidance. a) Quick turn to the right of a right-turning car. b) Quick turn to avoid a car running a stop sign. c) Quick turn ahead of a left-turning car.

MOTORIST LEFT TURN IN FRONT OF BICYCLIST

Your first line of defense against this type of collision is to maintain the correct position in the traffic lane. Not only are you more visible in the correct position, but you can begin evasive maneuvers quickly.

Watch the situation around you. Note when you are about to pass a street or driveway into which a car might turn, and look at the oncoming traffic to see whether a driver is slowing to turn. Be especially wary on streets where oncoming cars are already moving slowly enough to turn left without slowing down first. Watch for turn blinkers, but don't trust drivers to use them.

There's little danger from a driver who is stopped or has slowed and is merely trying to

outbluff you; use your preventive techniques. The real danger is from a driver who turns left suddenly, without warning. If one does, make a quick turn to the right, ahead of the car or next to it. Don't brake, except to give yourself more time to turn — more often than not, braking will only stop you directly in front of the car. If you're going too fast to make a full right angle turn, you will cross the street into which the car is turning; but the car wouldn't likely be turning if anything were coming fast up the far lane of that street, so the risk is small.

In a diagonal intersection where the cross street goes from 11 o'clock to 5 o'clock, it is sometimes easier to swerve to the left; but only do this when you can get across to the far side before the left-turning car or another car could reach you. Remember, the driver of the left-turning car may swerve back into a straight path after finally seeing you.

MOTORIST RIGHT TURN FROM LEFT SIDE OF BICYCLIST

Keep to the left of right-turning traffic on multilane streets, and use your preventive techniques at right turn lanes, off-ramps, and intersections on streets with only one lane in your direction.

If you are caught off-guard by a motorist making a right turn from your left side, brake if there's time, then quickly turn into the side street with the car. This evasion is so easy and sure that motorist right turn accidents need rarely be a serious problem. Remember, though, that the quick turn only works if you are close to the car. If you wander off to the far right of a wide lane, you not only won't see the car begin the turn as soon but also will be unable to turn quickly enough — the car will already be going sideways before it reaches you.

MOTORIST COMING OUT FROM A SIDE STREET

Just as with motorists making left turns from ahead of you, the danger here is not with the ones who are merely bluffing. Staying visible works with most motorists, and your preventive techniques work with the bluffing ones.

Real danger comes from the motorists who don't stop at all, or who stop, look as though they've seen you, and then start again as you pull into the intersection. It rarely happens, but it happens.

When it happens, brake if you have time, then quickly turn to the right, into the side street. Just as with the left-turning motorist ahead of you, don't brake so you end up in front of the car.

If you only see the car coming from the right at the very last moment, you may have to quickly turn to the left instead of the right. Don't do this unless it's so late that a quick turn to the right would put you into the side or front of the car.

AVOIDING REAR-END COLLISIONS

Choose low-risk routes. When possible, avoid high-speed, narrow routes with heavy traffic, especially after dark and when the drunks are out. Be visible, and keep a steady course. In tight quarters, a rearview mirror helps you check the size of vehicles behind you. Be especially wary of rental trucks and motor homes, whose drivers may not have much experience with them. Extension mirrors on cars with trailers are a special hazard; so are vehicles which are wider at the rear than at the front. You decide whether it is safe to be overtaken when the road is narrow. In case the driver behind you decides to overtake unsafely before you've given your go-ahead, keep your ears tuned in to the engine.

Most overtaking collisions are sideswipes. The vehicle is next to you before it threatens you. Usually, the driver has misjudged your speed and is pulling back to the right to avoid oncoming traffic. Hit the brakes and then if necessary pull off to the right side of the road. It is relatively easy to do this. Remember, the driver may be preparing to make a right turn, so do not come to a stop until the car is ahead of you. If the vehicle is a long truck or bus, hitting the brakes won't get you behind it quickly — so pull to the right instead.

There's no way to avoid a rear-end collision ahead of time except by using an escape route, though in a low-speed rear end collision you may have time to react after the car hits you. Stay up on the bike if you can; it is better to go over the car than under it. Try to steer out of the way. If you go over the car, tuck and roll to protect yourself as you land.

When stopping in traffic, as for a traffic light, glance back — a rearview mirror helps. Shift down before you've completely slowed down, and as you stop, keep one foot in starting position on its pedal. If a car approaches too close behind, ride your bicycle out of the way. That's faster than trying to scramble off the bicycle.

HOW TO RUN INTO A CAR

Stay up on the bicycle. If you are going at a low angle nearly parallel to the car, hit it in the middle, where you'll bounce off — maybe still riding — rather than the front or back where you'll go over. But if the car is turning toward you, remember that the back, behind the rear wheels, moves away as it passes. So aim farther back if caught on the inside of a turning car. If headed straight at the side of a car, turn down your face and put up your hands to shield you from the window glass.

If you have a choice, try to be going the same way as the car when you hit it. Our evasive maneuvers have stressed this principle.

AVOIDING COLLISIONS WITH PEDESTRIANS

Stay clear from the side of the road when there are no cars around, keep clear of parked cars, ride slowly in stopped traffic and on sidewalks and bikepaths with bad sight lines — in any of these situations a pedestrian could suddenly appear in front of you

unless you take the proper preventive measures. When children are playing in a quiet street, warn them with your voice or a bell before you reach them. Remember, there may be children whom you don't see at the sides of the street, so keep clear.

On a sidewalk or bikepath, warn pedestrians with a bell; the bell attracts attention best, because your voice just sounds like another pedestrian. Once you've got attention say "bicycle passing left"—or right, if the pedestrian is stubbornly on the left. Many runners keep to the left on bikepaths, because they are used to doing this in the streets. Do not overtake until the pedestrian has reacted to you.

Ride slowly when a pedestrian is approaching you, at least until you have established eye contact. Be especially careful of children; rollerskaters, whose legs move out to the side; skateboarders, who have little control; and anyone playing a radio or wearing earphones.

More often than a motorist, you can keep moving while crossing the path of a pedestrian in the street, since your bike is narrow. Still, give a warning and slow down if you are going to come within several feet of a pedestrian. If possible, pass behind the pedestrian; it's easier and safer to have the pedestrian moving away from you.

Where a constant flow of pedestrians crosses your path, slow way down or get off and walk as necessary. Remember, you are usually at fault if you run into pedestrians.

BEWARE OF UNSKILLED BICYCLISTS

It's a sad fact that you can trust the average American motorist a lot further than the average American bicyclist.

Watch out for wrong-way riders — one more reason to stay clear of parked cars. A wrong-way rider on your side of the road will usually expect you to pass on the traffic side like the cars, forcing you to assume the risk of swerving into traffic. If you can't get clear, the wrong-way rider will usually duck in between parked cars or go up on the sidewalk, but it may be you who has to do this.

A rider on the other side of a narrow street, going the same direction as you, forces motorists on the other side to swerve toward you. If there are motorists behind you on your side, the problem becomes more serious, both for you and for everyone else. You may have to leave the road or make a slow signal and compel the motorists on your side to follow you. The one advantage of the wrong-way rider's position is that you have time to express yourself — to the tune of "ride right or get off the road."

Be especially careful of wrong-way riders when entering the traffic stream or crossing a street. Keep clear of parked cars and trucks on your right so you can see around them.

When overtaking other bicyclists, take extra care. Use your bell and voice and wait for them to react, just as with pedestrians, unless you are well clear. Beware of overtaking bicyclists who may zoom by inches from your handlebar end. Do not make even minor swerves on a bikepath without glancing back. On the street, a bicyclist may overtake you on the right if you are riding a safe distance out from the edge. Be especially careful if you are about to make a right turn.

As with pedestrians, be careful of bicyclists who listen but do not look before crossing in front of you.

Even when these actions do not affect you directly, be careful when a bicyclist is cutting across the street at an odd angle. This bicyclist disturbs the flow of traffic and may draw drivers' attention away from you when you need it.

At night, be extra wary. Don't ride on bike-paths, especially where car headlight glare hides unlighted bicyclists. Ride streets with bright overhead lighting.

Note that all of the hazards created by unskilled bicyclists involve violations of traffic law. The cure for these hazards is education and law enforcement.

AVOIDING DOGS

A dog has superb hearing but poor eyesight. From a distance, a dog can't see your wheels, but hears whirring noises and no footfalls. With your arms sticking out like a huge beak and your legs flapping under you like wings, you might look like a huge bird of prey swooping down on children and puppies.

Usually, the dog will chase behind you. Then let the dog know you're human. "Bad dog, go home" is good, delivered in stern tones. Outrun the dog if you can, or slalom, traffic permitting, to confuse the dog. A squirt of liquid red pepper (Halt) dog repellent is effective and educational. A squirt of water from a water bottle or a hand raised threateningly may be. Don't use your pump — it may break or get caught in the spokes.

If the dog gets close, there are two dangers: bites and collisions. Collisions are far more serious, so brake quickly and dismount on the far side of the bike. The dog will probably lose interest, once you become a normal human being.

Most dogs know enough not to ambush you from the front, but a few don't. Usually, these are dogs who lack street wisdom because they have spent most of their lives tied up. Most dogs will warn you with barking. Slow down and be prepared to stop if you hear a hidden dog ahead of you. But even a friendly, tail-wagging dog can get under your wheels and may have no caution running out into the street — so keep clear, and wear your helmet.

Most dogs are not vicious — only confused, and protective of their territory. But if a dog attacks, you must attack back. Rocks and sticks put you at an advantage — dogs can't throw things or swing them around. Keep the dog away from you if possible. If it gets close, trap it under the bicycle, or lift a stick or your pump for the dog to grab. Then kick it in the ribs or the belly.

The owner is legally responsible for the dog's actions. If the dog gets you into an accident, you can sue for damages. If you are bitten, even lightly, be sure to identify the dog so it can be quarantined; otherwise, you may have to take a series of rabies shots.

Dogs are mostly a rural problem. City and suburban dogs usually understand bicycles, and vicious or unruly dogs do not last long where people must be close neighbors.

LEARN FROM ACCIDENTS AND CLOSE SCRAPES

There is a reason for every accident and every close scrape. Close scrapes are many times more common than accidents, and are good ways of determining what parts of your riding need to be improved.

As your riding improves, the number of close scrapes will decrease. Good riders have them down to two or three per year, counting only times when an accident was prevented only by chance, not by riding technique or evasive action.

CHAPTER SEVEN

ON-ROAD COMMUNICATION

As a bicyclist, you are by far the most communicative driver on the road. Out in the open with no engine, you can hear. No other driver can hear so well. You also can see much better than anyone inside a car. There's no hood in front of you. You can come right up to corners at intersections to look into the side streets, and you can look right down at the pavement for bumps. There aren't any door pillars, glass with glaring reflections, nor flashing chrome to distort your view. You can use new types of rearview mirrors which give you a better view than car mirrors. Perhaps more importantly, you can feel the road surface through your bike.

That's what you can take in. You can also put out much more than other drivers. Because you are out in the open, you can use your voice as a warning, and you can use a variety of hand signals which make the stop and turn lights of a car look pathetic in comparison. Since your bike is narrow, you can show where you want to go in traffic much more clearly by your position on the road.

Learn to use your ability to communicate. It's one of your most important safety factors on the road, and one of the things that keeps you moving.

USE YOUR EARS

Since your bicycle is quiet and unenclosed, you can hear all the sounds around you. On quiet roads and paths, listening is one of bicycling's great pleasures. In traffic, it is an important safety factor that you can hear the sounds of motor vehicles around you.

You listen to your bike. Any rattle or squeak is an early warning of mechanical trouble. You listen to what the tires tell you about the road surface, but you also listen to traffic. To use your ears best, you must be aware of what they can and cannot tell you about traffic.

On a quiet street or road, your ears will

often, though not always, warn you of vehicles behind you and of stopped vehicles about to pull out into traffic. If there's only one vehicle, you will hear it unless wind noise masks the sound. Many newer cars with catalytic-converter exhaust systems are very quiet. So don't trust your hearing if there's a head wind making noise in your ears. If you turn your head sideways for a moment, your ears will face into and away from the wind, cutting wind noise.

If there's more than one vehicle, you may only hear the loudest one. So, if there's a car ahead of you which you hear, take extra care to glance behind you for another which you don't. If you hear one vehicle behind you, glance back to see whether there's another with it.

In heavier traffic, your ears no longer give you an early warning, but they help greatly in telling you what drivers around you are about to do.

Brakes squeak sometimes, or the car's tires make a rushing sound as they rub against the pavement. A turning car's tires make the same rushing sound or may squeal. Listen for braking and turning sounds; also for the rising sound of acceleration. Any of these sounds deserve your special attention.

Different sorts of cars make different sounds, though you can't always trust your judgment. Sometimes the smallest cars are the loudest. But learn the different sounds which cars with automatic and manual transmissions make as they accelerate. With an automatic transmission, the musical pitch of the exhaust sound will rise or fall quickly in proportion to the power the engine is putting out. With a manual transmission, the pitch will rise slower in proportion to the car's increasing speed, falling back with each shift. With a manual transmission, the loudness of the exhaust sound will change quickly as a driver starts to accelerate.

Assuming that you have normal hearing in both ears, you can hear which direction sounds come from, though not accurately enough to tell how much clearance a car will give you as it overtakes. Riding on narrow roads, especially with high speed limits, you hear a car and then look back to plan your strategy (decide whether to prevent overtaking, or allow overtaking, for instance). Again, a rearview mirror helps in assessing the situation quickly.

When things are straight ahead and straight behind, sound takes the same length of time to get to each ear. Since your ears use timing to tell which way sounds are coming from, they can confuse these two directions. If you hear a car ahead of you coming over the top of a hill and it's not there when you look up, it's behind you. You can eliminate the confusion with a slight sideways turn of the head.

As an overtaking car comes closer to you, listen carefully. Normally, the engine sound will stay steady or rise slightly as the car accelerates past you. Go on alert if the car slows down next to you or races past you just before an intersection or driveway. The car may be about to make a right turn. Listen—the giveaway that a car is about to turn right is when you hear the brakes.

You can't hear a bicycle. Never pull out into traffic or cross an intersection just because you can't hear anything coming.

City traffic sounds sometimes are loud enough to cause slow damage to your hearing. Not as loud by any means as a rock concert or a steel mill, but loud enough to take some of the high-end sparkle off your hearing if you ride in heavy traffic for several years. It is unfortunate but true that we have allowed our city streets to fill with noises that can be safely endured only by people sheltered inside buildings and automobiles.

If you ride — or walk — where there is noisy traffic, protect yourself with a wad of absorbent cotton or Kleenex stuffed loosely in each ear. These will cut down the sound enough to protect your ears reasonably well, but not enough to keep you from hearing the cars around you.

In noisy traffic, it is hard to hear the chain rubbing to adjust your shifters. "Positive shift" or self-adjusting derailleurs and internally geared hubs solve this problem.

Some riders attach radios or other noise-makers to their bikes. Don't! Not only may other people around you have different tastes in music from yours, but it's really more important to hear that car or dog behind you.

AUDIBLE SIGNALLING

Your voice is the most convenient and quickest instrument to use. With practice, it can be very loud, and a voice in traffic attracts attention instantly. It also has more than one message. Some audible signals you need to know are:

. . . A loud, sharp yell — HEY! to warn motorists. Yell as *loudly* as possible. Your riding helps develop breath support. Yelling loudly once in a while, by the way, is good for you!

Spoken warnings and instructions for other bicyclists and pedestrians are also helpful and have been covered in the traffic chapter.

. . . A bell is best for bikepath riding and other situations in which you must warn pedestrians and other bicyclists. It isn't annoyingly loud — not loud enough to hear inside a car — but it instantly identifies you as a bicyclist to other bicyclists and pedestrians. You mount a bell close to the brake lever, where you can use it in or near braking position on the handlebars.

. . . A horn makes sense sometimes if it is *loud*. One good choice is a marine compressed air horn, available at a marine supply store. A large, curled-up oriental bulb horn is heavy but works well, too. We know of one bicyclist who mounted one so he could squeeze the bulb between his knees. Remember, a horn must be loud enough to be heard inside a running car with the windows up. Most horns sold for bicyclists are useless! A loud horn is a bit bulky, but mount it near braking position on the handlebars if possible — or between your knees — for quick action.

. . . A whistle of the type used by police and gym instructors is common in some cities and unknown in others. It is loud, and you can keep it in your mouth when riding through a difficult traffic situation, so you can keep your hands on the handlebars. But then it keeps you from opening your mouth to breathe hard. And if it's hanging by its lanyard, it's clumsy to use. Also, a whistle is illegal in many places, since it is a police warning signal. It promotes an uncooperative style of riding, clearing an entire intersection so you can go through.

Should you use a horn, bell, whistle, or your voice? Bell and voice work fine for most situations. But when in Rome, do as the Romans do. If motorists where you ride behave appropriately because you use a horn, use one. We prefer a loud horn to the police whistle, for reasons of legality.

Remember, an audible warning is to alert other people to give you your legal right of way. Don't use it to take away theirs. Courtesy leads to courtesy, and abuse leads to still more abuse.

Also, be aware that you can't always count on an audible warning to someone inside a car. Some cars' engines are loud enough inside to drown your horn out. The warning is to alert the driver; look and test whether the driver is responding to you.

DEVELOP WIDESCREEN VISION

Your eyes give you one small patch of sharp vision surrounded by a much larger area of blurry vision — blurrier toward the edges.

Some people use their entire visual field consciously. You must, if you're good at sports like football, basketball, lacrosse, or hockey. In any of these sports you need widescreen vision. The same is true if you are good at picking up dance steps, or drive a car well. For these activities, and to ride a bicycle well in traffic, you need to see things at the edges. Things look blurry, but you *see* them without actually looking toward them. You keep track of everything at once, everywhere in your visual field.

But if you have used your eyes primarily to read books or watch television, you may have tunnel vision. You see only one thing at a time. You use the blurry part of your vision only *unconsciously,* just to guide the small sharp part to the next thing you'll look at.

You can retrain your eyes from tunnel vision to widescreen vision. Start working on widescreen vision outside traffic. Start with simple exercises:

. . . Stare straight ahead while you move both hands out to the sides and concentrate on seeing both of them at once.

. . . When you think of it, look in one direction while looking at something in another direction. Don't do this to your friends, though when you're talking with them, or they may think you're hiding something!

. . . Have some fun; practice at the movies. Sit up front, and keep your eyes pointed at the middle of the screen while you *see* what is going on at the edges. Choose movies with a lot of visual detail. Movies with group dance numbers, Chinese martial arts movies, or the Beatles' *Yellow Submarine* are good.

. . . Look at large buildings, trees, or doorways which fill most of your visual field. See them as a whole, not just in bits and pieces. Watch the surroundings expand and disappear at the edges as you walk or ride through them.

It takes time to get results, as you are opening up connections in your brain which have never been used. But after a few weeks, you'll begin to get results. For example, when riding your bike, you'll suddenly notice that you've seen a four-way intersection full of cars all *at once.*

Next, you'll learn to keep track of different people doing different things at one time in different parts of your widescreen picture.

With this stage of training your eyes, you outgrow widescreen movies and start looking at the widescreen world.

Usually, all of the things going on at once in a movie picture are related to each other. In the real world, different people's actions just might have something to do with each other, or they might not.

Sit in a place with several people all doing different things — a hotel lobby, public transit station, or public beach area. Start by not looking at any one particular person. Look at the wall or sky somewhere, so all of the people are in the blurry part of your vision. Watch them move around you — see how some of them have something to do with each other and some do not. Keep track of more than one at the same time, at first two, then all.

Then try aiming your clear vision at one person while you keep track of others in your blurry vision. If you can't keep the person in your clear vision from taking all of your attention, go back temporarily to looking between people.

When you've overcome this, go on to the next stage: you become part of the picture yourself.

Up to now you've been making yourself quiet to concentrate on seeing. Now that you've learned to see more things at once, you move out among them again. It isn't really a picture you're looking at, after all!

As you move through groups of people, notice all of the people at the same time. When walking with a friend in a public place, notice the other people around, all at once.

Team sports are excellent training, giving you many opportunities to make judgments based on what you see all around you, and the actions of several people at once.

Riding your bike does, too. Now is when you really begin to feel the effects of your training on your riding.

KEEP YOUR EYES MOVING

There are certain things you need to see sharply: the piece of glass on the road surface in front of you, the eyes of a driver waiting at a stop sign to make sure the driver is looking at you, or the car 300 feet back in your rearview mirror. If you don't see these sharply, you won't see them at all! There are other things, like the car overtaking you on the left, which you don't need to see sharply.

And there are certain actions which you take without looking at all, such as adjusting

your gears and toe clips. You have enough to look at without these.

As you ride, you judge what is most important to see next. You must often do this consciously, at least at first. It is easy to stare at one thing, but if you do, you're missing something else. Don't look at any one thing longer than necessary. You want to keep several things going at once. Seeing on a bike is like juggling. You catch one thing and then throw it aside as soon as possible so you can catch the next. But you haven't forgotten about that first thing. You know you'll have to catch it again, and you know how soon.

You keep your eyes circulating among the things you must see sharply. You look at the pavement ahead of you only until you're sure you've seen enough. You also judge how soon you're going to have to look at the pavement again, and file the reminder away while you shift your glance to the driver in the side street or the car in the rearview mirror. Then,

Be careful of people in whose direction you cast a long shadow.

when it's time, you look at the pavement again. Some things you'll look at more often and longer than others. It's not just a round-robin rotation of the eyes. You leave a little extra time to sweep your eyes around and look for new things you'll need to keep track of. And all the time, you keep your widescreen vision going.

Decide whether you are seeing enough. If you are, you can confidently keep riding at the same speed, go faster, or allow your eyes short vacations to look around at the scenery. But if your glances don't cover everything, you'll be looking at one thing and knowing that you need to be looking at something else at the same time. Then you know you're going too fast — you need to slow down just to give your eyes more time to do their job. The feeling of being out of control in traffic often comes straight out of the sense of not seeing enough. Depending on how well you've learned to use your eyes, you can be in control at higher speeds and in more difficult situations — and safer at any time. That's why you train your eyes.

Speaking of what you don't see, let's consider blind spots.

ANTICIPATE YOUR BLIND SPOTS

Blind spots are areas along the road which are hidden behind something: a curve, a hill, or a parked car.

You know that you can't ride safely into a forward blind spot around a curve. So, as you're going down a hill around a curve, you slow in case there's a patch of gravel or a stopped car. The blind spot constantly moves away from you, but you never ride so fast that you couldn't stop before you get to where it is.

If things could come toward you in the blind spot, you'd have to go much slower. That's why the rules of the road require you and the other drivers to keep to the right side. You have the right of way into the forward blind spot, and you don't expect to find another vehicle in it coming toward you.

Your biggest blind spot is behind you. You have the right of way there, too — other drivers behind you yield to you as long as you keep your line in traffic. And you have blind spots in side streets, driveways, and crosswalks, where other drivers and pedestrians must yield to you. You aren't required to yield or stop for anyone who's hidden from your view. It's common sense, and it's written into the rules of the road.

That's the theory. In practice, though, certain blind spots have danger zones extending outward from them. Beyond a parked car is a danger zone, because a pedestrian might walk out before you could stop. You should stay out of these danger zones. You know that the pedestrian doesn't expect traffic there, within range of opening car doors. When you get good at it, you can feel a pedestrian or wrong-way bicyclist coming out from in front of every parked car, and you keep clear of the danger zone.

On bikepaths and sidewalks, you do not effectively have the right of way. A danger zone extends outward from every doorway, from around the corner of every building, and from behind every bush. Ride slowly there! What you don't see can hurt you!

OTHER PEOPLE'S BLIND SPOTS

Other drivers have the same blind spots that you do. Ordinarily, you keep out of these blind spots if you obey the rules of the road.

But because your bicycle is narrow, you

can fit into someone's blind spot when a car couldn't. So you sometimes have to position yourself outside the blind spot, deliberately. Here's an example.

Let's say you're overtaking a car. You're moving right along, and the car is crawling along at 5 mph at the right side of the street. The driver is trying to read an address on a house.

You know that the car's door is not going to open, because the car is moving. And the driver has to look back to the left before pulling out into traffic. So do you whiz close by the side of the car?

Not a good idea. The driver will look back, not wanting to risk a big dent in the left side of the car. But the driver will look off to the left where other cars would be — not right next to the car. You have to pull wide to overtake, so you'll be where another car would be. Before you reach that crawling car, you signal, move left, and into the middle of the next lane. Then, you can be sure the driver will see you. You have kept out of that driver's blind spot.

RIDE WHERE DRIVERS CAN SEE YOU

There are several ways to ride where drivers can see you, depending on the particular situation:

. . . First, and common to all situations, you put yourself where you will be seen by drivers whose paths you might cross.

. . . In many situations, you ride out toward the middle of your lane to avoid disappearing into the roadside scenery. We dealt with these situations in detail in the section on straight road riding techniques.

. . . If you're just behind a car going straight through, take extra care to be seen by motorists about to make left turns from the opposite direction. Problems occur often when a traffic light has just turned green and you're second in line, or whenever you're last in a steady stream of slow traffic preventing a car from turning left in an intersection. Check behind you, then pull far enough to the left and behind the car leading you that the driver of the approaching car will see you.

. . . If the second car in line coming toward you is flashing a left turn blinker, you might then dodge a little to the right just as you enter the intersection to put yourself in view of the driver.

HOW TO BE SEEN

It's easy to think of being seen as a passive act; you just sit there, and people see you. But it isn't so. If it were, we wouldn't have an advertising industry, and the boxes on our supermarket shelves wouldn't be decked out in day-glo colors.

You can become like the supermarket boxes, with your bright-colored clothes, lights, and reflectors. You can position yourself, but you can go even further. You use active techniques to test that people have seen you.

One way you test is with eye contact.

MAKE EYE CONTACT

In your personal relationships, eye contact is a sign of trust. People who won't look you in the eyes are generally looking for a way to escape your reactions to them.

When you're in traffic, eye contact has fewer deep psychological meanings, but it's still very useful. When you make eye contact with another driver, you can both be fairly sure you've seen each other.

Eye contact is especially useful with drivers who are waiting to pull out into traffic from the right side. As you get to the point where you're going to have to know the driver will wait for you, you look straight at the driver. If the driver's eyes are pointed toward you, that's one powerful clue that the driver will wait. If the driver is looking in another direction, *always* yell to draw attention, and be prepared to get out of the way if the driver's eyes don't turn toward you in time.

You also use eye contact when you are about to pull into line in front of a driver who is going slowly. Your turn of the head to look at the driver is at once a request and a check that the driver has seen you. And you use eye contact with pedestrians who might be about to cross your path.

Eye contact is not as useful with drivers about to make left turns toward you, because their slanted windshields drown out their faces with the sky. You must often rely on other clues. Eye contact often doesn't work at night, though under streetlights you can often see well enough into the cars to use it. You draw attention to yourself at night by flashing your headlight at people.

You also check whether a driver has seen you by watching the motion of the car.

WATCH THE MOTION OF THE CAR

Watching the car's motion works whether or not you can make eye contact, and no matter which direction the car is coming from.

A driver about to enter the road from right or left is going to slow down in order to look up and down the road and in order to make the turn into the road. Position yourself to be seen as soon as a car could be. When you see a car coming in from the side, give it your attention. Watch for it to slow down more than it would

have to if you weren't there. Before you reach the point where you'd have to brake, the car should have stopped. You have the most assurance that a car will stay stopped if the driver stopped it just for you. You look for a sudden little nose dive and quick stop. If a car is already stopped and waiting as you approach it, you can't run this test. Use eye contact if you can, or flash your headlight at the driver's window at night. Pull wide to make yourself visible and to give yourself room in case the car moves out.

A driver approaching you from the front and about to make a left turn will have to slow, except when already going slowly on a narrow street. Look for the car to stop, just as for cars entering from the sides. On narrow, slow streets, take extra care.

On the road, you are just one more thing the driver has to get past. There's no reason the driver should hit you any more than any of the other things. You have advantages, because:

. . . You are traveling away from the driver, and reducing your closing speed for drivers approaching from behind.

. . . You are a human being, and drivers take your safety more seriously than they do that of a parking meter or traffic island.

. . . You can control the driver's decision about when and where to overtake you.

. . . You take evasive action if necessary.

Think of the driver. Think of reaction time, braking distance and sight lines, and getting answers to your signals. When you need a driver to do something, signal your need and give the driver time to respond to you — check his response. Riding in traffic involves a steady series of signalled conversations. That's what makes you safe. Remember, you're dealing with a human being, not a metal hulk.

TRAFFIC TIP:
THINK OF THE DRIVER,
AND THE CAR

When you think of a car, you are thinking about a mindless metal hulk bearing down on you. That's how most people think of moving cars, unless they're inside them.

But a car is not just a metal hulk. It is under the control of the driver, a human being. The driver has to steer that car every inch of the way, to stay on the road and to avoid obstructions and other vehicles. Drivers generally do this successfully, otherwise they wouldn't be driving long.

HAVE YOU BEEN SEEN? RULES OF THUMB

. . . If you haven't seen a car, the driver hasn't seen you. But if you're not riding into that car's right of way, you have little to worry about. The driver is concerned that something much bigger, heavier, and faster than you might be coming along.

. . . If you have seen the car, the driver probably has seen you, as long as you're riding where traffic habitually goes.

. . . If you have tested that the driver has seen you and you've gotten a response, you know that the driver has seen you.

WILL THE CAR STAY STOPPED?

Yes, if:

. . . The driver stopped just for you — that is, the driver wouldn't have stopped if you weren't there.

. . . The driver stopped for a car which is with you, or for another car.

. . . The driver has stopped for a traffic light.

. . . There is no driver, or the car is otherwise inactive — parked with wheels parallel to the curb, or the engine not running.

Maybe, if:

. . . The driver stopped for no particular reason you can figure out. Watch cars stopped in the middle of the street. They often turn right or left, or discharge passengers. A passenger will feel safe opening a car door on the right into a space too narrow for a car to drive through — but this space is not too narrow for you to ride through. Go slowly, or overtake on the left, giving plenty of clearance there, too.

. . . The driver stopped for a stop sign but has not looked your way.

. . . The car is parked but the engine is running, there is someone in the driver's seat, lights are on, or the wheels are turned toward traffic.

Whenever the answer is "maybe," give the car extra clearance. Position yourself where the driver can see you and use an audible warning.

SUN CAN BLIND DRIVERS

Take extra care when the sun is low. When the sun is directly behind you, drivers ahead may not see you. Be particularly on the lookout for cars slowing to make left turns, or those about to enter from side streets and driveways. When you have a long shadow, be careful of anyone it points to.

When the sun is shining directly into a side street, watch out. Though the sun glare doesn't come from your direction, a driver may be blinded from having stared into it before approaching the intersection.

The worst conditions are low sun and water on the roads. Then the glare comes from both above and below.

When the sun is ahead of you, pick a route that's not facing it. Sun angles and times of sunrise and sunset change gradually with the seasons — so if you're commuting regularly, you have plenty of time to plan. You have the best choice if you live in a place where streets aren't all parallel to each other. If your city has east-west streets, the sun will glare down the full length of these streets around March 21 at 6 A.M. and 6 P.M., and September 21 at 7 A.M and 7 P.M. daylight savings time. Consider shifting your schedule if it would require riding at these hours.

A driver behind may not see you against sun glare, so pay special attention whenever there is or might be a car behind you. Ride far right or pull out of traffic if you're not sure the driver has seen you.

As long as it's bright enough for you to see colors intensely, the blue light of the sky will help make your fluorescent material visible. After that time, white is the most visible color. Turn your lights on early — as soon as they're visible. As it becomes darker, they will become more visible, and when the car headlights come on, so will your reflectors.

TACTICS FOR BEING SEEN

Just after you've gone over a sharp hilltop, drivers approaching from behind won't be able to see you. Before you've gone over the top, it helps to glance back and see whether there are any vehicles approaching fast from behind. If so, make yourself visible *before* you go over the hilltop. Also, gauge when the vehicle is going to overtake you. After you've gone over the hilltop, though, don't trust that there isn't another vehicle

ahead of the one you saw. So pull well to the right until there's a reasonable safety distance behind you.

Your height is to your advantage. If you sit up straight after cresting a hill, you'll be visible sooner. And if you stand up on the pedals to build up speed, you'll build a safety distance quicker too. A bright-colored helmet will be the first thing a driver behind you sees — additional fluorescent and reflective material on the helmet isn't a bad idea if you ride much in hilly country. Just check it to make sure it works at the angle at which the helmet normally rests.

On a right curve with a wall, building, or some vegetation blocking the view behind, prepare yourself just as you did for the hilltop, by scouting what's behind you.

If the right lane is wide, pull well over to the right so drivers behind will be able to go by. If the right lane is narrow, pull far enough to the *left* side of it so drivers behind can see you.

In all situations in which a driver can't see well from behind, it is that driver's responsibility to drive carefully to avoid running into you. But some drivers do not expect anything smaller or slower than a car on the road, so you must take precautions.

Fog, dust, smoke, and to a smaller degree rain, make it harder for a driver behind to see you. Use the same tactics as with low sun. Fluorescent (day-glo) clothing is especially effective during daytime in foggy and rainy weather. Turn your lights on sooner if it's foggy and dark.

These situations are one of the strongest arguments for a rearview mirror. With one, you can give yourself more room and ride with greater safety and confidence. In these situations, you will glance frequently back into the mirror and test whether each approaching driver has seen you. Then you will only have to pull aside for the occasional one who hasn't.

WHEN TO LOOK BACK

Here's when to look back. *Always* look back:

. . . Whenever you are going to change your line toward traffic, even when you are moving just slightly sideways in the same lane, you must look back. The procedure is covered in the traffic chapter.

. . . You also look back and *to the side* when you are about to make a turn across traffic, merge, or full lane change.

. . . You look back sometimes just to keep track of what is going on behind you, especially if it has changed or might have changed.

HOW TO LOOK BACK

In upright position, you just "swivel" your neck and twist your body sideways. You can look as far around as directly behind you with your sharp vision.

Learn to take in all the information you need in one glance, sweeping your eyes from back to left as you turn your head forward again. Get used to seeing the world sideways as you glance back from a crouch.

SHOULD YOU USE A REARVIEW MIRROR?

We think that you should at least try one.

Much of the time you can make any of the traffic maneuvers we describe in this book without a rearview mirror. A glance over the shoulder will tell you what you need to know. And there are times when a mirror will *not* tell you; only a glance over the shoulder can tell you enough.

There are riders who have developed an advanced ability to turn their heads, and who ride in the most difficult traffic without mirrors. Their heads spin like tops as they look back and then ahead. But many riders can't look back so fast — and the feeling of the road ahead as one huge blind spot headed for your front wheel can be very disturbing.

If you have an arthritic neck or otherwise have trouble turning your head, you certainly should use a mirror. If you're nearsighted enough so the area outside your glasses frames is very blurry, or if you're farsighted so there's a ring you don't see at the edge of the frames, a mirror is advisable.

Even if you don't have any of these problems, a mirror helps in traffic. There are many situations in which you will be able to maneuver more effectively if you use a mirror. There are many situations in which you can't safely glance over your shoulder. And at the same time, your decision what to do must depend on what is behind you. One good example is when a driver is inching out from a driveway or stop sign, trying to bluff you into stopping. You can't let that driver's car out of your sight, yet you're more comfortable pulling out to the left a bit to get past the front of the car. A glance in the mirror will tell you if there's a car catching up on you from behind, and allow you to use the whole lane in front of you if there's not. Without the mirror, you'd be more likely to have to stop.

A mirror is most useful in making decisions about your position in the traffic lane, or when making minor swerves to avoid potholes. It usually shows enough in these situations. It has a blind spot to the left, but any car in the blind spot will be well off to your left side. For cutting across traffic to make turns, a mirror is no substitute for a look over the shoulder. But time after time, a mirror will allow you to keep riding when caution would force you to slow or stop without one. And a mirror will allow you to ride in the middle of the right lane with complete safety and confidence. We highly recommend that you use one as you learn to ride in traffic situations. Just work to be aware of what the mirror can and can't show you. Soon, you will know without thinking whether you have seen enough in the mirror or whether you must glance back.

There is one and only one good reason *not* to use a mirror: if you are terrified of the traffic from behind, stare into the mirror, and run into things in front! If you find that the mirror hypnotizes you, take it off until you've developed the confidence to ride without it. Then try it again.

WHEN TO USE (AND NOT USE) THE MIRROR

A properly positioned and aimed helmet or eyeglass mirror will give you a view back down the traffic lane just to your left. You should not have to turn your head, though you may have to tilt it up slightly when riding in a deep crouch. Your ear and shoulder at the side and bottom of the mirror provide points of reference so you know which way you are looking. You position your head so the mirror is pointed in the direction you want. Then you can hold your head steady, and glance between the mirror and the road ahead without having to aim the mirror again.

The helmet or eyeglass mirror has a limited field of view. It is most useful when aimed down the lane behind you to the left. That's the farthest place you have to turn your head around to look, and it's where the most things happen behind you that you have to keep track of. By turning your head slightly to the left, you see directly behind you or slightly to the right. The mirror is useful for these directions, too.

But this mirror leaves you a blind spot out to the left side. You could turn your head right to cover the blind spot with this mirror but it's easier and you see more if you turn your head left to look directly to the side. You look back in the mirror and then turn your head to look to the side. Because of the mirror, you don't have to turn your head as far. It's quicker, and you're less likely to swerve.

So you use the helmet or eyeglass mirror to keep track of traffic in the lane behind you. With practice, you will get so you can trust it to make partial lane changes: you look in the mirror while the next car is still well behind, signal and make the partial lane change, then look again to see that the driver has slowed to follow or moved over a lane.

When you are occupying a whole lane, you also trust the mirror to show you that drivers are slowing or that they're giving you enough clearance as they overtake.

But you cannot trust this mirror when making left turns or full lane changes. A car can creep up on your left without your noticing, and if you just look back in the mirror, you might make a left turn in front of the car. If you're going straight, or making a partial lane change, a car in the blind spot of the mirror is no problem. It'll surprise you, but it will be well off to the left as it overtakes.

The convex wrist or handlebar mirror's reduced size image gives you less detail. The mirror will tell you whether a car is behind you, but isn't so useful in judging overtaking clearance. The wider field of vision that goes with the reduced image leaves a smaller blind spot, but you still can't trust this mirror when you're making full lane changes or left turns. The wrist mirror is less useful in the inner hand position. Neither the wrist mirror nor the handlebar mirror lets you look behind you to the right, as the helmet or eyeglass mirror does.

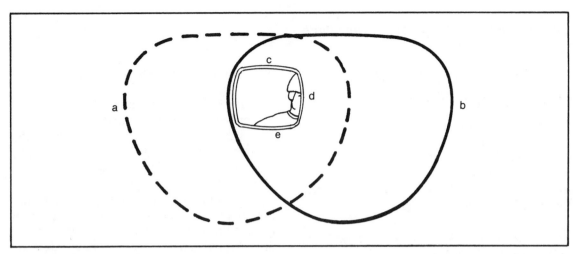

Position the mirror correctly in your field of vision — high and to the left. You can see "through" the mirror if your right eye sees the area the mirror covers in the field of vision of your left eye. Aim it to look down the traffic lane just to your left. Your ear and shoulder should be in the picture as points of reference. a) Limit of field of vision of left eyeglass lens. b) Limit of field of vision of right eyeglass lens. c) Mirror position. d) Image of ear in mirror. e) Image of shoulder in mirror.

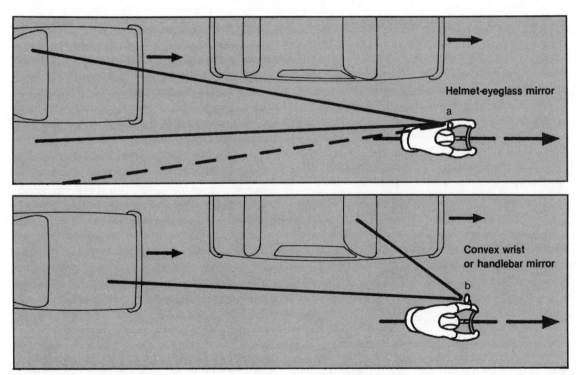

Mirror field of view, detail and blind spot. a) Helmet-eyeglass mirror: full-size image, clear enough to judge overtaking clearance. Field of vision too narrow to pick up a car just behind you on the left. You can reaim the mirror to the right behind you by turning your head. b) Convex wrist or handlebar mirror: wider field of vision, though the reduced image has less detail. Your body or the bicycle may keep the mirror from looking directly back.

WHEN TO LOOK BACK TO YOUR RIGHT

Usually, you look back to the left. That's why a rearview mirror is aimed down the lane to your left. There, it is most useful. But sometimes you have to look back to the right. Some of these times are fairly obvious, but others are not. The obvious ones are:

. . . When you're making a lane change from left to right.

. . . When you're riding the left side of a one-way street, or the center line of a two-way street — you'd look back to the left when riding on the right side.

. . . When you're keeping safely out from the curb and there's another bicyclist behind you, especially if you're preparing to make a right turn. This bicyclist may attempt to overtake you on the curb side. You must look back and firmly warn the bicyclist not to do this.

. . . On a bikepath, where bicyclists may try to overtake you on either side.

. . . When you're pulling through an intersection with an unseparated right turn lane behind you. Make sure that the next car behind you is actually turning right. If the driver wants to go straight, either get out ahead in time, or drop back and let the car go by you.

KNOW YOUR SAFETY ZONES

Every vehicle or pedestrian moving in traffic creates safety zones, places into which other vehicles or pedestrians cannot or will not move from certain directions. You don't always trust these, but you take advantage of them and use them in emergencies.

Ahead of it, every motor vehicle creates a safety zone into which people will not move.

If a vehicle approaching you crosses an intersection at the same time you do, or just before, you can be reasonably sure that there isn't any traffic about to cross the intersection at right angles to your path.

Just after a vehicle approaches and passes you in the other direction on a narrow road, you can be fairly sure there is no vehicle on your left headed in your direction.

A left-turning motor vehicle creates two important safety zones. If you are making a left turn along with this vehicle, you are reasonably shielded on its right rear corner. Here the vehicle is moving away from you and you will end up on the right side of the street you are turning into. But also, the turning vehicle clears the way for you as you cross the intersection.

Also, a driver preparing to make a left turn toward you will make sure that there is no traffic from the left, or that traffic is stopped. That's why your safest dodge if a car starts to make a left turn toward you is to make a quick turn to the right, ahead of the car. If there's any traffic on the far side of the street you turn into, you can be sure it's stopped or moving very slowly.

A pedestrian standing or walking, or a stopped vehicle in the middle of a traffic lane, assures that vehicles are approaching slowly in that lane, and clears the lane beyond (except, perhaps, for bicycles).

Using these safety zones takes timing; they appear and disappear quickly. But you can use them to help make space for you as you maneuver. And in an emergency, such as when a car makes a left turn at you, you can use these safety zones without looking, because that's the best choice you've got.

PREDICT WHAT THE DRIVERS WILL DO

We've told you to be predictable by riding according to the rules of the road. But you also want to predict what the other drivers will do. Our asking you to do this brings you full circle on the subject of communications — it's what we've been asking you to do all along as you test the other drivers' intentions and read their clues. The little motions of the cars, the eye contact, the turned wheels of a car about to pull out from the curb — these and many other clues will build your picture of what is happening around you as you become more experienced at riding in traffic.

Think about what is on a driver's mind. Is the driver moving along a clear lane? Is he following another vehicle? Or is he about to turn left, turn right, or change lanes? Look at all of the vehicles and see how they fit in with each other. The rules of the road make your predictions easier by shaping the drivers' behavior. See how you will make your way among the vehicles. When you know what's on the other players' minds, it's a lot easier to call some of the shots yourself. Be especially wary when you can't figure out what a driver is up to.

Your final goal is to make decisions based on timing of all the events which affect you — decisions like "I can get into the left lane before the car in it catches up, so I'll speed up because the light is green for a left turn and that car in the opposite direction will have just passed the intersection when I pull across the far side of the street." Fortunately, you don't have to think like this in words—only in your actions. That's easier.

EFFECTIVE SIGNALLING

Signals are not just a favor to other drivers, they are a powerful tool. If you learn to use them well, traffic problems will literally melt away around you. Remember, you don't use them just to inform other drivers. You use signals to clear your legal right of way. Motorists almost uniformly respond to your signals. Usually, all you have to do is to show them what you wish to do. If you don't show them, there is no way they will ever find out. If you do show them, they will almost always grant you your wishes.

The motorist, shut inside a glass shell, is limited to a very few signals: the turn signals and brake lights, and what can be communicated by the car's position on the road. Before turn signals and brake lights were required on cars, drivers used hand signals. These same hand signals for right, left, and stop are the ones you already know and are required to use when riding your bike.

But as a bicyclist, you can use signalling far more effectively than the motorist can.

Besides the driver's three traditional hand signals, there is another set of hand signals which every driver knows and understands. These are the signals used by police officers directing traffic: the hand language for pointing people in the right direction where verbal communication is not possible.

You will use these signals, but there's another important difference, too. You will use them in two-way communication. The motorist usually just switches on a signal to show the intention to turn, and leaves it to everyone else to figure out what to do about it. You will make signals and then watch how other drivers respond to them. Then, you will take the action which depends on their response. You will be making sure that drivers make room for you, and to a certain extent you will be directing traffic, just like a traffic cop.

Motorists are often confused about how to behave toward you on the road.

You can increase their confidence and

[Continued on page 158]

Glass, pothole — signal to a bicyclist following you.

Straight ahead signal.

Slow signal.

Right hand slow signal.

Jabbing left turn signal.

Crossing your path from right to left signal.

Right hand right turn signal, open hand (distance).

Right hand right turn signal, pointing finger (close).

Jabbing right turn signal.

Questioning a motorist as to his wishes.

Left turn signal, pointing finger (close).

Wave by from right to left.

make the situation go smoothly if you point the way to them. If you signal a motorist to overtake on the right in a right turn lane, the motorist has your go-ahead that you will not swerve right. A bicyclist leaving room on the right just does not make sense to a motorist who has lived in a world of bicyclists who don't leave the right side of the road.

Sometimes with your signals, you will be slowing motorists, and sometimes you will be giving them the go-ahead. It works both ways.

Motorists often underestimate your speed. They think of bicylists as they think of pedestrians. Understand the power of a turn signal or slow signal to a mistaken motorist behind you. Since the motorist thinks that you are going slower than you are, the car will slow *more* than is necessary to follow you. *You have completely turned the tables on a potentially hazardous situation.* Use a left turn signal for even the slightest partial lane change to the left — sometimes even when just going straight, to indicate that the entire lane to your left is yours and guide a driver into the proper path in the lane to your right.

SOME POINTERS ABOUT SIGNALLING

The left turn signal is the most common one, used for partial or full lane changes, and left turns.

The right turn signal is needed more rarely. Its main use is for lane changes to the right. Signal with your right hand. That makes the point much better and creates a "barricade" effect. In effect you become more visible to the right where you wish to go. You also remove your hand less far from the handlebars. The law of some states requires the left-handed "Saturday Night Fever" or "Toreador" right turn signal which motorists must use

because they're inside their cars. Still, we suggest the right-handed signal, because it really makes the point. Many drivers don't even know what the left-handed signal means anymore.

When drivers are far away from you, make turn signals with the out-stretched hand for more visibility. When close, a pointed finger is more emphatic. You can vary your signals. Jab repeatedly outward for more emphasis. Make your signals early — particularly when you are going to turn, so you can brake later with both hands on the handlebars. Alternating the use of your hands for signalling, braking, and control is one of the things you must learn through experience. You are not required by law to signal when you cannot safely remove your hands from the handlebars, but with proper practice you will have plenty of time for both signalling and braking. A long handlebar stem and/or dropped handlebars with your hand in braking position gives you the most stability for one-handed control, because your hand is far ahead of the steering axis. Just by shifting your weight sideways, you can keep the bike steering straight and still lean on the handlebars.

When you can't signal by hand because you are in close quarters (trying to move into a slow stream of traffic for instance), a turn of the head is effective both as a signal and to look for the driver's response through eye contact. With a rearview mirror, you can often signal and see the response without turning your head, but at close quarters it is better to turn your head anyway to reassure the driver that you've seen him or her.

You do not make the "slow" signal often. Usually, the reason you want someone to slow is so you can change lanes, so you're making a turn signal instead. The "slow" signal is primarily for use not when you're slowing down, but to discourage a driver from overtaking. Make the signal on the side on which the driver might overtake. Follow it by a "wave-by" as soon as it becomes safe to overtake.

When you are actually slowing down, you'll have both hands on the brake levers. But drivers can see by you and will usually be slowing down for the same reason as you. Besides, your stopped pedals are a signal that you are slowing.

You use hand signals when you move from your normal position in the traffic, but once you are out of your normal position, your new position itself becomes a signal. Since you're narrow and don't automatically take up a whole lane like a car, you are not only signalling which way you are about to go but also making it clear what other drivers are to do — go to your right, go to your left, or follow you. The position in which you put yourself to shape the drivers' behavior and the signal are one and the same.

A couple of legal notes. Though we recommend hand signals not completely in conformity with the law, we believe that it is more important to show your meaning clearly, obeying the spirit of the law, rather than to obey the letter of the law. The problem with the law is that it is written for motorists, not for bicyclists, who can communicate better.

A wave-by signal can get you into legal trouble if it gets the other driver into an accident. Be careful to use a wave-by only when you are sure that the other driver has a clear path. Clear cases for this signal are to direct a right-turning driver into a right turn lane, and to get a hesitating driver past you before the road narrows. Be sure not to make a wave-by when there's a chance that the driver will not be able to give *you* room.

At times, you will direct hesitating drivers in cross streets to cross in front of you when they have the right of way. This action is legally safer, since you are not potentially giving up your right of way. You just want to get a driver across an intersection when you have

the stop sign, so that you can safely move through the intersection. When you have the right of way, a "straight through" signal — a hand pointed directly forward — can be effective with a driver attempting to inch out of a side street.

When you extend your hand for a signal, don't point it directly toward a driver who needs to see it. Angle it around so the arm looks long. Hand signals are theater, so be demonstrative and emphatic.

A special signal to another bicyclist behind you is a finger waved at a pothole or patch of glass. This is not only a warning of the hazard but a warning to another bicyclist that you might swerve.

HOW MANY SIGNALS DO YOU USE?

We said it before: you use the signals for every turn, lane change, or partial lane change. Sometimes you use signals even when you're not changing lanes at all, just to show the drivers what you're *not* doing. (Especially, to show them that you're *not* going to follow the curb.) Sometimes you use several signals in a sequence to prepare one action, as when you're stopped at an intersection, showing which way you're going and asking the intentions of the driver behind you.

You use signals not just to show your intentions, the way you usually do in a car, but to ask questions such as: "Will you let me into your lane?" When you get the answer "Yes," then you take action.

It's very different from signalling in a car. How many signals do you use? Probably ten times as many. Think of yourself as directing traffic from your bike, because that's what you're doing.

PREVENTING DRIVERS' MISTAKES

So traffic will flow smoothly, and for the sake of everyone's safety, you anticipate situations where drivers make mistakes.

First, you make sure that you can see what you need to. You know where the vehicles around you are, and as much as possible which way the drivers want to go. Widescreen vision, a rearview mirror, and the traffic sense that comes with experience, all help you get the picture.

You know what the other drivers want to do and where they want to go. But sometimes you have to show them how to do it.

You make your lane changes, and partial lane changes, decisively, theatrically, with emphasis and aplomb. You use hand signals theatrically, too — not only to show what you are doing, but to show drivers the path to take.

As you do this, you sometimes are asking drivers to slow or wait, though only according to the rules of the road, which they understand. Often, you are showing them how to get where they want to go quicker than they thought they could. After all, it does work better for them, too, when you're riding according to the rules of the road. For example, where the driver is trying to turn right from your left, you pull to the left and wave the driver by on your right. Nobody has to slow down or stop. While if you stayed at the right side of the road and the driver tried to pass you on the left, you'd *both* slow or stop and wait, afraid of running into each other.

When you take control of the situation, you can often make things easier for a driver, just by riding according to the rules of the road, and showing the driver how to drive according to traffic. It's a wonderfully cheap courtesy to extend. You get to roll out the red carpet for the driver, and you get where you are going faster, too.

YOU CAN CONTROL TRAFFIC

Bonita Neff is Michigan's state bicycle coordinator. She commutes 11 miles each way every day by bicycle, pulling her two-year-old child in a bicycle trailer. She teaches the League of American Wheelmen Effective Cycling course. She was the first instructor. Talking about the course she says:

"When we come to doing left turns, some people literally shrink into themselves, pull their heads in and close their eyes. One woman who was a schoolteacher refused to make left turns except by walking on the crosswalk. She told me that, since she was teaching second graders, she could get by if she walked the left turn the way she would teach it to them.

"I told her: 'You teach second grade in school, but you don't use second grade math or speak in second grade English. If you are going to be in my class, you are not going to ride a bicycle like a second grader!'

"You can teach the kids to make turns by walking. But at some time, they're going to start riding in the street. And they have to know that there's a right way to do it, once they're ready. You don't hide it from them."

Bonita Neff stands just a bit over five feet tall and weighs about 90 pounds, and she speaks pleasantly and with a smile — with a conviction and authority that have nothing to do with her size or weight.

EXAMINE YOUR FEELINGS

Riding on the road with cars can bring out strong feelings ranging from unpleasantness to joy, from fear through confidence to overconfidence, and from excessive courtesy through courteous assertiveness to rudeness.

Fear is most common for beginners, and it leads to riding too close to the edge of the road. To overcome the fear, you must make room for yourself, both as you ride on the road, and to see yourself as a person with a right to be there.

YOUR RIGHT TO YOUR SPACE

You cooperate with everybody else on the road. You have a right to be there with your bike, and the motorists have a right to be there with their cars.

But just because their cars can go faster than you, you don't have to get out of their way to let them go by you all of the time. You cooperate by letting them go by when it's safe. When it's not safe to go by, they have to slow down behind you and that's that. The law is very clear about this and it's common sense, too. You can't be responsible for getting out of the way of drivers behind you, because you don't have eyes in the back of your head. *They* are responsible for overtaking only when safe.

And in a larger sense, the motorists have more to gain than to lose by sharing the road with you. You may delay a motorist for a few seconds now and then, but in fact your bike uses only about one-third the road space of a car. You don't tie up traffic with your delays: the intersections are what limit the flow of traffic, *not* the straightaways. (How often is there actually a string of cars behind you? And how often is there one at a traffic light?) By using your bike instead of a car, you make *more* room for the motorists in the intersections where it really counts. Not only that, you leave an extra parking place for someone somewhere, and you leave extra gasoline for someone else to use. The motorists ought to thank you!

And if there's some impatient buzzard behind you honking the horn and trying to get you to pull over, don't worry. You know for sure that's one driver who has seen you and has slowed down.

AVOID OVERCONFIDENCE

It's a pain in the neck to stop and have to start again, but once you've gained confidence that the drivers coming up behind you will overtake you safely, you may become overconfident in situations like this:

. . . A car slows to doublepark in front of you, and you decide that the cars behind will have to move left anyway. So you do too, without looking.

(But what if there's another car just behind you which is *also* pulling over to doublepark?)

. . . Another bicyclist ahead of you slows abruptly to make a right turn. To keep from hitting the other bicyclist, you pull to the left to go by — without looking back. You figure there's no car behind you anyway — the light's been green a long time and all of the cars have gone through. You saw the last car, five seconds before.

(You were following the other bicyclist too closely and forced yourself into a poor choice. You *don't* know for sure that there's no car behind. But if there is one, you *can* be sure that it's going good and fast, because the light's already green.)

. . . It's a quiet street. You don't hear anything, so it must be safe, and you swerve to the left to avoid a pothole.

(Suppose there's another *bicyclist* coming up behind you. Would you hear the bicycle? Probably not.)

. . . On a narrow street, you've just pulled to the right into a bus stop to let a car overtake you. There wasn't another car behind this car. After it overtakes you, you pull back out into your lane without looking.

(Suppose another car just pulled in out of a driveway, behind that first car that was following you. You don't know whether one did or not. But for sure if it did, it is close behind, because the first car was going slowly to follow you.)

So you *always* look when changing your line. You don't make lame assumptions or take gambles just to keep moving. But by looking ahead and preparing yourself to move sideways well ahead of time, you keep moving *safely, confidently,* and *legally* instead of *dangerously, fearfully,* and *illegally.*

OVERCOME PSYCHIC NUMBING

After riding in traffic for a while, sometimes you might feel that the traffic around you is not quite real. The phenomenon is called psychic numbing. It commonly affects people who are in situations they fear.

It is not possible to sustain the feeling of fear for any length of time. Fear as a natural reaction raises your adrenalin level and prepares you for action, whether it is to fight or flee. But after being in fear for too long when nothing happens, you get exhausted by the fear. You become numb to it, and may even become numb to actual danger.

Many riders who outwardly perform well in traffic still suffer from a residual traffic fear internalized as a kind of numbing. One way to explain the feeling is that the traffic around you looks just like a picture in which you do not have the sense of the physical size, speed, and momentum of the vehicles. You have lost that sense because at one time you were afraid of the large size, high speed, and

great momentum of the cars. Now you know on a functional level that you can move safely among the cars, but you have never overcome the numbing caused by their physical reality.

You may be jolted back into the reality if you have a near miss or an accident. Then, for a while, every car will seem distressingly real to you. But eventually, the numbing will return.

If you ride assertively and take control of the situation you can overcome the numbing without being afraid. If you are an active rather than a passive rider, the cars still move around you, but they are known quantities — tested realities. You do not have to be afraid of them, and you're confident that you don't have to be.

Certainly, a rearview mirror, well used, is one way to lower the level of traffic fear drastically. Rear-end accidents are rare. But the ability to see each car approaching from the rear and to check whether the driver has seen you goes far to build confidence, as well as to expand your freedom of movement in traffic. One of the primal fears is the fear of being sneaked up on from behind, even if the statistics don't bear it out.

Work on your sense of reality. Get to the point where, without being afraid, you know and sense that each car is big, and fast, and is pushing a danger zone in front of it. The more you sense this, the safer you are, because you know more acutely when you are in real danger and when you are not.

As we said before, think of the driver, not just the car. You are in real danger when you are in a car's danger zone and the driver has not seen you, or does not have time to react to you. If the driver has seen you and reacted, you're not in any significant danger. So you test when necessary, and you leave yourself an escape route until you're sure that the driver has reacted.

And slowly, your numbing will melt away. Then you will be able to save your fear for when you might really need it. And in your fear, you will have a heightened rather than a reduced ability to move quickly and decisively and avoid an accident.

BEING IN CONTROL

Yes, you really can call it being in control. It's an unusual and pleasing feeling. Here are some ways of looking at it.

It's like a high-level Oriental martial arts discipline, the kind in which you learn to be so on top of the situation that all you have to do is subtly redirect people's behavior. A sort of traffic tai chi, as you keep yourself moving and direct the other drivers how to move with you.

Then, it's a little like herding sheep, too, if you're dealing with drivers who come up behind you confused, and you show them the way. If you're dealing with drivers who are cooperative and understand you, it's like a team sports practice. Like basketball practice, let's say. Not like the game itself, where you have an opposing team. You and the drivers are all on the same team, with the same wishes: to play well, work smoothly with each other, and score goals. In traffic, the goals are to get through intersections or past each other. And on your bike, you get to be the captain of the team.

Redirecting people, even manipulating them a bit? Yes. You'll feel strange at times taking the responsibility. You put your arm out to signal a partial lane change, knowing that you are bluffing the drivers a bit. They don't know how far you are going to turn, and they give you more room than you need. That's manipulation.

But as long as your community has not taken it upon itself to educate its drivers to your rights, as long as you cannot trust substantially all drivers to be predictable and to obey the rules of the road, you have to take the responsibility for your safety and your rights a bit more into your own hands.

Fortunately, the only reason you are doing this is to stand up for your rights, not to take advantage of people. Since the safest way to ride a bicycle in traffic is according to the rules of the road, you are only directing people to do what they actually ought to be doing anyway. With your unparalleled ability to communicate with other drivers from your bicycle, you actually become an educative force. Every driver you direct to do the right thing becomes a little bit more aware of bicyclists as equal road users, rather than as rolling pedestrians cringing in the gutter or as pests who come riding at them on the wrong side of the road. If enough bicyclists ride well, good riding becomes the normal and accepted thing. So does good behavior by motorists toward bicyclists. When that happens, you can relax a bit in traffic.

Bicycling in traffic as a consciousness-raising activity, then? Yes, both for you and for your community. Bicycling is a way of taking control of a part of your life, of doing things in a simple, sensible way rather than paying other people large sums of your hard-earned money to do things in a wasteful, expensive way. But if you are going to take control of the transportation part of your life on the larger scale — by making the decision to use your bike rather than a car — you also have to take control in the moment-to-moment conduct of your alternative way of doing things. People who work to take control of their ways of living always find this to be true. If you want to take control of the transportation part of your life by riding a bicycle, then start with the nitty-gritty of actually riding the bike and doing it well. That's the greatest force for change, without which any planning for improved conditions for bicyclists is hardly more than empty theorizing. You need only read the warnings about bikepath riding in chapter six, or look at the unused bikes in your neighbors' garages, to understand what comes of empty theorizing.

But in a community where people like you get onto your bikes and begin using them well, meaningful, useful improvements will follow because there will be people who want them, need them, and know what to ask for. People like you who have taken control of your lives, right out there in the traffic.

Be assertive if you must. You are not being assertive to take advantage of anyone. You are being assertive because otherwise many motorists may not understand or respect your rights. You are assertive in that you are standing up for your rights and your safety. You are insisting, as long as you can do so with safety, that motorists treat you as an equal and not as a rolling pedestrian who must always give way to them. You insist because you know that you are right, because the law backs you up, because the motorists will respect the law when put to the test, and because this is the safest way to ride and the only way to get anywhere fast.

Many beginning bicyclists have trouble with the idea that assertiveness makes you safe. As pedestrians and as motorists, we have always learned — and properly so — to be cautious rather than assertive. Not to say that you aren't also cautious when you ride a bike. Certainly, you don't zoom through stop signs or change lanes without looking back. But you've got to switch mental gears when you get on a bike. Many times the safest thing to do is to move right out toward the front of a car and insist that the driver wait for you.

A side benefit: few activities in modern life offer so many opportunities as bicycling for constructive use of tension. Frustrated people, take heart. This is for you!

However, if you're not assertive, we respect that. Assertiveness is not a virtue in itself. It just gets you to certain places. And in the traffic of some of our American cities, it is what gets you through on a bicycle.

It may seem like a contradiction, because the bicycle is such a gentle way to travel. But the bicycle's strong points in the traffic mix (communicativeness, maneuverability, and compactness) are balanced by its weak points (vulnerability and people's lack of understanding of its place). So the way that you get around safely is to create your own secure space in which to ride.

If you're not assertive, you're looking for less hectic places to ride than the American main streets. We'd like to see such places, because we want everyone to be able to use the bike everywhere.

Unfortunately, misguided attempts to construct places to ride away from automobile traffic have created more dangers than they removed. The average American bikelane or bikepath is hazardous, all the worse for the nonassertive bicyclist who may look on it trustingly as a haven of safety.

But if you are content to ride relatively slowly, and if you understand the hazards, you can ride the bikepath reasonably safely (though usually not the bikelane). There are usually back street routes which, though less direct, will get you where you are going without dealing with heavy traffic.

What we would like to see for you would be a network of bicycle-preferred streets without through automobile traffic. Meanwhile, you do what you can. People have been known to become more assertive when there's something worth fighting for.

DEALING WITH THE POLICE

There are two instances in which you must deal with the police: when they enforce the traffic law, and if you have an accident.

Traffic law enforcement toward bicyclists varies widely. Police in some communities ignore bicyclists. In these communities, bicyclists have little to worry about from the police, but more from other lawbreaking bicyclists including wrong-way riders and night riders without lights. Many police do not understand that bicyclists must obey the law, though generally, where police ignore bicyclists, they do not enforce the law well against motorists, either. The police generally are overworked or have given up issuing traffic tickets because the courts don't deal effectively with violators.

Police may hassle you unfairly. Some police will apply the same standards to you that they do to their children. They want to get you off the road, supposedly in the interest of your own safety. For you the solution is to understand your rights. It's sometimes worth carrying a copy of your state traffic laws with you. Get this from the Department of Motor Vehicles. Remember, a police officer can't make you do anything which is not required by the law. Say: "Officer, I don't believe there's any law against what I'm doing — would you care to check?" Also make it clear that you *know* what you are doing and are perfectly confident as a bicyclist. Make it clear that the bicycle is your transportation, not a toy, and that you're on your way somewhere. If you're in a hurry, say so and ask either to be given a ticket or to be let go. Then overturn the ticket in court, if necessary.

If police issue unfair tickets, don't carry your driver's license. Keep them off your driving record.

Police may enforce the law correctly, but the law may be bad. The most common example is a law prohibiting bicyclists. For example, you know that you need to leave a bikelane for the sake of your own safety. But

the law may not recognize this need. If you choose to ride in a prohibited area, the officer has the right to issue a ticket. But do explain your problem, for the sake of education: "The bikelane is a deathtrap. Would you ride your motorcycle down the bikelane at my speed — 20 mph — and risk drivers making right turns at you from the left lane?" The officer may let you go. If not, and if you like crusading, fight your ticket in the courts and get bad laws overthrown. The League of American Wheelmen will be glad to provide a lawyer's advice.

Police may enforce good laws correctly. Then the police are some of your best friends, keeping reckless motorists and bicyclists from endangering you.

If you have an accident, the police will in almost all cases be helpful and sympathetic. But you must make sure that the police do what is necessary to protect your rights. They may not always understand what you need as a bicyclist. See the section "Reporting Accidents and Harassment," in this chapter.

If you have problems with police attitudes toward bicyclists or with restrictive local laws, the best thing for you to do in the long run is to get together with other bicyclists and talk with your local government officials. Group action and reasoned argument get things changed, in time. Remember, governmental officials are your civil servants, paid by your taxes and elected by your votes. It's just that you have to explain to them sometimes what bicyclists really need. If bicyclists don't explain that, there's nobody else who can or will.

BICYCLE LAW

Bicycle law in the United States is often confusing, contradictory, and poorly thought out. Some places have laws prohibiting bicyclists from riding streets when bikepaths are available or prohibiting the use of certain streets entirely. In some places police actually will give you a ticket for making a proper left turn.

No matter what the law says or where the paint stripes run, you are safer riding according to the rules and techniques we've presented in this book. Where the law contradicts the rules of the road, you are better off violating the law for the sake of your own safety than obeying it and having an accident; though where laws restricting bicyclists are enforced, bicyclists often simply have to use other routes or quit riding to avoid getting traffic tickets again and again. The best choice is to persuade your local government to overturn these laws.

DEALING WITH MISTAKEN DRIVERS

It is a frustrating and annoying situation in traffic to be faced with someone who is doing something wrong and dangerous, when that person thinks he or she is right. Typical examples are wrong-way bicyclists and motorists who've tried to make right turns on your left side, or who got behind you and honked their horns. Unfortunately, you don't have time to explain yourself. You're angry before anything else, and you know that the person you're facing has the entirely wrong approach. You'd have to go back to basics to set that person right, and you don't have time while the two of you are sitting side by side waiting for the traffic light to change.

Half of your anger probably is coming from frustration at not being able to say what you need to.

POLICE STORY

"I was riding up Commonwealth Avenue," said Ed Gross, an avid biker in Newton, "up past Boston College where it's two-lane and narrow. It was after dark. And in the beam of my headlight I just barely made out another bicyclist headed toward me on the wrong side of the road. It was a man wearing black clothing, riding an old black Raleigh with no lights and no reflectors. He passed by me. I was in a hurry and didn't have time to stop and talk with him.

"As I pulled up to the next traffic light, a police car pulled up next to me. I knocked on the window, and the officer rolled it down. 'Did you see that bicyclist back there?' I asked. 'Yes,' said the officer. 'That was really dangerous, the way he was riding — did you stop and talk with him?' 'No — what was the problem?' asked the officer. I explained the problem. 'That's against the law, you know,' I said. 'It is?' asked the officer. He really didn't know.

"And Newton is known all around the Boston area for having good police. Lieutenant Feeley of the Newton police started the first children's bicycle education program in the schools anywhere around Boston to have actual on-the-road training. But this officer didn't even know that bicyclists were expected to obey the traffic law.

"Believe me, I gave him a little lecture before the light turned green and we pulled away."

It helps a lot to carry information sheets targeted at the most common things you need to say. Then, you can just reach into your handlebar bag and pass the information sheet to the person. You've made a positive gesture, and there is some hope that this person will read the sheet and understand you.

YOU AND THE LAW

The law is how people have made sure, as much as possible, that drivers obey the rules of the road. The law is your protection. It protects you from unpredictable acts of other drivers, and if you obey the law, it protects you from lawsuit in case of an accident.

That's most of the time. Exceptions are the bad laws we've mentioned.

WHY OBEY THE LAW?

1. It is safer and more effective to obey the law. Rules of the road were worked out to make traffic flow as smoothly as possible, and to make the actions of each road user predictable to others. If you ride according to the rules of the road like other drivers, they will understand what you're doing — which is an important safety factor. And you will get where you are going quicker, because you go with the flow. When you maneuver in traffic according to the law, you are a participant in traffic. You often have the right to compel other drivers to slow or wait for you. If you ride any which way, you are an imposter. You always have to wait till the street is clear before you can make a turn or a lane change across traffic.

2. You foster respect for yourself and other bicyclists by riding according to the law. This respect not only has a long-term effect but also increases the courtesy which each individual driver shows to you in traffic.

3. If you obey the law, you're less likely to have an accident. But if you do run into someone, the law becomes very important to you. If the other person is at fault, you can sue for damages. If you are at fault, the other person can sue you. One or the other will be at fault. Make sure it's not you.

4. You could get a traffic ticket, too, if you are violating the law in a community where police take bicyclists seriously.

YOU MAY HAVE TO BREAK THE LAW

Breaking the law exposes you to penalties, disrespect, liability, and danger — all of the problems we've just described. Yet certain laws for bicyclists require you to ride unsafely or inconvenience yourself unreasonably, including: mandatory sidepath and bikelane laws and traffic signals operated by magnetic wire loops.

Timed traffic signals are a less clear-cut case. They will often make you wait while there's no cross traffic. However, you *are* legally at fault if you cross on the red.

Sometimes a traffic light will not give you a long enough green, and then you *must* move out into the intersection before the light changes. If you can demonstrate the problem, a court cannot reasonably convict you.

The solution to traffic light problems is presence detectors which *do* respond to bicycles. These never make you wait when there's no need to.

As we've said, it is unreasonable and not as safe to require you to come to a total stop at a stop sign. Slow to a crawl, so your feet are on the pedals and you can enter traffic smartly.

Many places have laws requiring you to ride "as far to the right as practicable." Don't misinterpret this law! As far to the right as "practicable" is not as far to the right as *possible,* but as far to the right as you can *safely* ride. You may have to educate a police officer or a judge who does not understand where it is safest for you to ride, but basically you're on good ground here. And remember, when you're making a left turn or overtaking, it's only practical to be to the *left* of other vehicles.

If you ever get into a dispute over the law in court, again, we recommend that you seek the advice of the League of American Wheelmen.

REPORTING ACCIDENTS AND HARASSMENT

Under the traffic law, you have a legal right to expect other drivers and pedestrians to conduct themselves safely toward you. If someone gets you into an accident, harasses or threatens you, here's what to do:

If your rights are violated, you must pursue them through legal channels. No-fault laws in many states provide a limited amount of compensation for your injuries in an accident involving a car through the car's insurance, without consideration as to whose fault the injury was. Otherwise, your conduct in riding your bike is as important as any negligence of the other driver (bicyclist included) or pedestrian in determining whether you will be compensated for your injuries. If you follow the law, you are less likely to be in an accident, and are more likely to be compensated if you are hurt. If you have an accident because of a road defect, you may be able to sue the agency responsible for maintaining the road. According to Peter Campagna, attorney, and Boston Area Bicycle Coalition member, you should follow these steps in case you are involved in an accident.

A. If you have or witness an accident:
　　1. See that anyone who is injured receives prompt medical care. If you are injured, you may have a friend or lawyer do the following steps, two through five.
　　2. Take down the names, addresses, phone numbers, and license numbers of all persons involved: driver, riders, victim, and witnesses.
　　3. Cooperate with the police if they are present. However, you do not have to give them a "statement."
　　4. A police report does have to be filed if anyone is injured, or if property damage is more than $100 (in Massachusetts — it may be different in other states). Be sure

to file one; it is your legal record of the accident, important in recovering damages as evidence of them at income tax time, if nothing more. Police may not consider it important to file a report if no car is involved or if you can't identify a hit-and-run driver, but do it anyway.
　　5. If you are a victim, it may be advisable to see a lawyer as soon as possible. The more serious the injury, the more you need a lawyer. Try to find a lawyer who is known to you or to a friend, one who is trusted and experienced in personal injury work. If necessary, call the lawyers' referral service of the Bar Association in your area.

B. If you are physically threatened by a motorist — or anyone else — or are physically harassed, and if you have reason to believe it was intentional:
　　1. Identification of the wrongdoer is most important. Note and write down the following: a car description, its driver and passengers, the license number, the time, and the scene of the incident.
　　2. Try to locate and identify witnesses, if any.
　　3. If you're injured, seek medical care and consult a lawyer.
　　4. Report the incident to the police and ask to swear out a complaint.
　　5. Be patient and persistent. The criminal justice system is slow, but the offense is serious, and you should see it through. Prosecution of such conduct will be a deterrent in the long run.

C. If you are verbally threatened or harassed, my best advice is just to smile back. More and more drivers are accepting the fact that bikes have a right to the road, so don't let a bad apple spoil your day. Bicycling can be safe, and if you follow the rules, the law will stand behind you.

CHAPTER EIGHT

TRIP PLANNING

In considering whether to make a trip by bicycle, you will have to weigh many factors, including distance and available time, routes and obstacles, loads to be carried, lighting and weather conditions, parking problems, and your skill in dealing with all of these. As your skill increases, you will confidently make more and more trips by bicycle. A good general rule is to use the bicycle whenever there doesn't seem to be a definite reason not to; and, when you can afford the time to experiment, to try out trips about which you have doubts. Don't overestimate your problems; most of them have solutions. You must sometimes actively seek out or invent the solutions that will make it possible for you to use the bicycle, but the fact is that in almost every situation there is a way to use the bicycle which gives you an advantage of convenience, speed, and economy over any other practical means of transportation. The key is to know your bike so well that you are never reluctant to use it when appropriate. With practice, this will be as easy as getting in your car.

TRIP PLANNING CHECKLIST

. . . Plan to get the most out of your trip by making it a multistop, multipurpose trip if possible. Because you do not have to park and walk, as with a car, or walk and wait, as with public transportation, the advantage of using the bicycle increases with the number of errands run in each trip. Keep a pocket calendar, and look through it for the errands which are in the general direction you are going. Do them in one trip.

. . . Look at your maps and plan your route.

. . . Figure out how long it will take you to get to points on your trip where you have fixed-time appointments. In case of delay, look through the errands on the way which you can bump to the return trip or to a later trip.

. . . Plan for parking. Call ahead, if necessary. If you are going to have to park your bicycle outdoors, you might decide to take your trashmo bicycle. Take your lock on all trips unless you are sure you'll only be parking your bicycle where you or your friends can watch it. . . . Besides the lock, make sure to take other items you may need: maps, weather equipment, night equipment, pump, tool kit, taxi money, things to leave off, and bike bags or containers for things you'll pick up.

. . . In case you're going to park your bicycle or take it on public transportation, be sure you can carry everything you need to. When parking, that's bike bags and removable accessories. On public transportation, that's the bicycle and baggage.

. . . Have a second plan in case something keeps you from completing the trip by bicycle. For example, if you stop at a store and find a special on 100-pound bags of potatoes, if you are taken ill, or if your bike breaks down, have a contingency plan. The most versatile second plan is to carry taxi money.

. . . Plan for the end of the day. Conditions for your return trip may be different from those for your outbound trip. Carry night and weather equipment in case of a delay or an unforeseen change in the weather. Use a folding bicycle or keep a car bike rack at work if a ride with someone in a car might separate you from your bicycle at the end of the day. Or keep two bicycles at home; then you can ride home with someone, use the other bicycle the next day, and bring the extra bicycle home at your convenience.

. . . Take a trip to the bathroom before you take a trip on your bicycle. It's a serious problem to have to look for a public rest room and a safe place to park your bicycle all at the same time. And exercise stimulates the bladder.

DISTANCES AND TIMES

For distances under five miles in the city, the bicycle is almost always faster than a car or public transportation, and more reliable, too. If traffic jams are bad, you'll outspeed a car for distances up to ten miles. Expect to average 8 to 12 mph if you're out of shape, 12 to 20 if you're in shape, depending on whether you're riding in traffic or on the open road.

For the longer distances, mixed mode transportation — bike to carpool or bike to public transportation — gives you speed and convenience.

EAT RIGHT

Long-distance bicycle tourists and racers plan their eating habits for the best performance while riding. For commuting trips, which are shorter, you needn't take such great care; but generally, avoid eating a very heavy meal just before riding — especially, avoid a meal high in fats, which your body must work harder to digest.

FATIGUE

There's more than one way to feel tired. The most common ways — morning doldrums and end-of-the-day fatigue — usually need not interfere with riding. The exercise of riding will wake you up. Also, the daily exercise of bicycling will give you more energy from one week to the next. Certainly, if you feel tired all of the time — if bicycling doesn't help you feel better — see your doctor. As you gain experience riding, you will become more and more able to gauge how you feel and anticipate how you will feel once you are riding.

For shopping and visiting friends close by, or for pleasure trips, you can hop on your bike without giving detailed thought to your plans. But when you use your bike to get to appointments and to work, you need to be confident that you will get where you are going on time.

You may have to build up to this confidence, unless your trip to work is an easy and short one. Before you begin commuting, you'll want to have ridden the bike enough to have faced and dealt with most of the things you'll have to learn.

The first step toward commuting is to go out riding when you're not under pressure. Check this book when questions arise. Talk with other bicyclists. Build up your skill until your rides are longer and harder than your commuting ride will be.

Then, when you decide you're ready for commuting, give yourself time to think and plan. You make your commuting trip every day, so you'll have plenty of time. Figure out in advance where you will park your bike. Ride over your route in your spare time, so you'll know it — explore a bit, so you'll know two or three alternate routes. Think about what traffic conditions will be like when you're actually commuting, and plan for them. The best route at one time may be a poor route at another.

Once you've prepared, you'll be ready for your first commuting trip.

YOUR FIRST COMMUTING TRIP

Make it easy for yourself. Wait for a day when the weather is good. Check the weather forecast so you'll be fairly sure the weather will be good for your return trip as well as your outbound one. Start when the days are long enough that you'll be riding home in daylight. Give yourself some extra time. And carry taxi money, or have a friend on call with a car to bail you out if necessary.

If you're well prepared, your first commuting trip will be easier than the trips you've already been taking.

Not every day will be the perfect day you picked for your first commuting trip by bike. Yet, on the average, your trip will become easier every day. Riding in itself will make you stronger. Your skills and confidence will build rapidly if you are commuting by bike even as little as once or twice per week. You will quickly feel ready to move on to deal with the more challenging stuff. There will be a day when you ride confidently to work, knowing that you will have to come home in the rain or in the dark. Congratulations — then you've arrived.

CHAPTER NINE

FINDING YOUR WAY

Good maps are your most important tool for finding your way. A map is an aerial picture of the area you ride in that permits you to see all of the streets and major landmarks. With a map, you not only have a much easier time finding your way, but you have a much better picture of the area through which you are traveling.

The next sections are about how to select the right maps, how to read them, and how to find your way by them.

MAPS YOU NEED IF YOU RIDE IN A CITY

As a bicyclist in the city, you need good maps. The best route for you may not be the main through route which motorists use, so your map must show every street — shortcut trails and paths, too. Your map must give every street name, so you can check your progress and know where you are during your trip. And it is very helpful for your map to show hills, so you can ride over them or around them as you choose. In the city, you will save much time if your map shows one-way streets.

The most useful map is often a special bicycle commuter's route map. Many areas have these maps now. Some are published by bicycling groups, some by governmental agencies, and some commercially. Some are in sheet form and some are bound into books.

Ask other bicyclists and ask at bike shops about these maps. If there is more than one available, see which serves your needs best. Some maps designed for tourists may show little information away from the routes they recommend. These routes may be useful to you, but you'll need another map besides. The most useful maps are bicycle commuter maps, which show routes between all parts of your area.

If your area already has a commuter map, you are lucky. Other bicyclists have already done most of your exploring for you. But if this map has contour lines to show hills, there's no room for all of the street names, so it's good to have another map too. The best contour line map is a United States Geological Survey topographic map or its equivalent in another country. This will show the hills and also the off-road paths. It will show all of the streets, but it will not give all of their names. As a survey map, it will have a large number of symbols for landmarks which will help you keep track of where you are.

You may buy a street guide map at a newsstand or at a gas station. Look through three or four maps, or ask another bicyclist's opinion before you buy one. Some are more useful than others. Look for one in book form with sheets you can tear out, or one that folds easily. If your city has a confusing traffic pattern with many one-way streets, look for a map which shows the direction of traffic. If you can't find a map which does, the traffic department of your city has this information. It's often worth a trip there to get it.

Every map has a legend showing the symbols it uses, a north arrow (so you know which way is which), and a distance scale. By the symbols, you can tell what features the map emphasizes. The distance scale is also useful in selecting a map. If it is more than 2 inches per mile in the city, and 1 inch in the country, you can expect it to show most or all roads.

MAPS FOR THE COUNTRY

If you live in the country or in a small town and use the bike to get around, a topographic map should be enough. It's best to buy two copies, one to carry with you and one to hang up. A county road map, too, may serve your needs. Most gas station maps and state highway maps do not show all of the roads, so they are much less useful.

If you are touring, it becomes expensive to buy topographic maps for your entire route, and it is usually not necessary. Many good touring routes have already been surveyed for bicycling and you can get maps from bicycle clubs or advice from other bicyclists. If you are touring away from a surveyed route, it is usually enough to carry a map from a gas station or state information booth and ask directions every once in a while. The map will give you the lay of the land and show major routes; the people you ask will fill in the missing links on scenic and traffic-free back roads.

State and county highway departments publish maps showing all roads; these are usually available only at the highway departments, but are often worth the trouble of a visit. These maps cover a larger area than the topographic maps.

MAP USE

One of your maps goes with you and one stays at home.

The topographic or highway department map stays at home. It goes on the wall near the door, where you can study it as you are about to leave. Besides being useful, it is a handsome wall decoration.

Take your street guide with you. The best place by far for it is the map case of a handlebar bag, where you can read it as you ride. The second best place is a box on the rear carrier, or a seat bag. Don't put it in a pocket in your clothing, where friction and perspiration will reduce it to mush. With your street guide, carry a waterproof and smudgeproof ballpoint pen to mark your new routes.

Now we look at the map. A map has the same layout as an aerial photograph, except that the photographic image has been replaced with a drawing. The map is much clearer, because it gives you symbols and labels for things you recognize from the street names, churches, schools, bodies of water, and parklands.

For the street pattern on the map to match the one where you ride, you turn the map the same way as the landscape, even if you have to read the labels upside down. To turn the map the right way, you lay it out or level with the ground. Then you line up the street you are on with the same one on the map. Or, you compare the position of the sun, stars, compass needle or landmarks with the map's north arrow. Map experts call this "orienting" a map. "Orient" means "east"; at the start of a day's travels, you turn the east side of a map to face the rising sun.

Once you have oriented the map, everything falls into place. The road you are traveling on takes the same turns as it does on the map. Landmarks are at the same angles. Intersections become recognizable by the angles of the streets coming into them.

You may have to read the labels on the map upside down, or turn it around to read them. Actually, they're upside down, but the map is right side up. Now as you ride, move yourself along through the map's miniature street pattern. The map will guide your way, showing which streets connect, how they turn, and which deadends you must avoid. But there are other clues to use along with the map to find your way. When you navigate, you are determining where you are, which way you are going, and how fast. Navigating includes map reading, but goes beyond just following the streets. You use landmarks, the sun, your shadow, and your wristwatch to help you navigate.

NAVIGATE BY LANDMARKS

Landmarks close by or along the road will tell you whether you are on the right road, and how far you have come. You see these on your map and check them off mentally as you pass them. These are buildings, hills, parks, river crossings, bodies of water, intersections, towns, and railroad lines.

Distant landmarks, such as hills, buildings, and radio towers, pinpoint your location on the map and the direction in which you are traveling. You orient the map. If you know what road you are on, you need to use only one landmark. Find it on the map and mentally draw a line from it to where it crosses the road. That is where you are. If you do not know what road you are on, you draw lines from two distant landmarks. They cross where you are. If you are lost and cannot orient the map to the sun because of cloudy weather, you can still find your location on the map from two distant landmarks, by noting the angle between them. Strictly speaking, you need three landmarks to do this, but two are usually enough — you estimate your distance to the landmarks from their apparent size and the haziness of the air.

Radio towers in a line and other landmarks which look different from different directions work especially well — you can tell what direction you are from them. On a clear night, flashing beacons from towers and tall buildings, stars, and sky glow from populated areas make it just as easy to navigate as by day. You'll feel, and sometimes wish, that you were in an airplane or boat which could take beeline routes.

NAVIGATE BY THE SUN

The sun is your compass; use it as a rough guide to your direction.

To use the sun in northern temperate latitudes, you need only to remember that it moves from the east through the south to the west every day. In summer it rises north of east and sets north of west, and winter it rises south of east and sets south of west. At noon it is directly south. To give you more light in the evening, daylight savings time makes the clock say 9 P.M. when it's actually 8, and 1 P.M. when it's actually noon. But the actual error in sun direction at noon due to daylight savings isn't very great.

USE YOUR SHADOW

To keep track of small changes of direction, use your shadow. As you look at your map, you will see which way you are headed. Look ahead on the map to see which way the road curves. Look at your shadow. Now, as you ride, small changes in the position of your shadow will tell you when you have turned slightly to the right or left, following the curves in the road shown on your map. You can keep track of where you are along the road, or whether you have made a turn onto the wrong road. This technique works as you ride up and down hills or among trees or buildings which shorten the length of roads you can see ahead and behind.

TWO MEASURING DEVICES

With a wristwatch, you not only tell time, but also tell how fast you are going. You can compare your trip time from day to day and get a very sensitive measure of the effect your physical condition, the weather, and the traffic all have on your riding.

A cyclometer is a small odometer which attaches to your front wheel hub. The best

kind is driven by a small rubber belt; others are driven by a "striker" attached to a spoke, which makes an annoying ticking noise with each turn of the wheel. With a cyclometer, you follow your progress on maps by looking for intersections and landmarks, as well as keeping track of your mileage.

HOW TO MEASURE YOUR SPEED AND DISTANCE

You easily measure distance with a cyclometer as you ride — it just adds distance up.

You measure distance with a map by comparing the length of the streets you've traveled with the distance scale in the map's legend. You can measure the streets with your finger, but it is more accurate to add up the length of the streets along the edge of a piece of paper and then compare the total with the scale of miles.

Knowing your commuting distance and time is as important as knowing the route. It helps to measure your speed a few times before you start commuting, just so you'll know how much time to allow.

The most direct way is to time yourself on a dry run over your commuting route. Otherwise, and for other routes, you can get a reasonable idea of your average speed and then measure routes on your wall map before you leave. Then check your time against your watch when you arrive.

To measure speed with a watch and a map, cyclometer, or roadside marker posts, see how long it takes to cover a mile or a kilometer. One divided by that time is your speed. For example, if you cover a mile in four minutes, you are going a quarter mile per minute or 15 mph.

Time other trips in proportion to distance, making allowances for traffic, obstacles, weather, and unfamiliarity with the route.

Some of this involves a little mental math, but it's not too hard to do while riding once you've done it a couple of times on paper. And it can help you figure whether you'll get where you're going on time.

ROUTE SELECTION AND EXPLORATION

You check your map to find routes that look good, and then you try them out. We'll give some hints and then take you on an imaginary trip so you can see how exploring is done.

A VARIETY OF ROUTES

Depending on the time of day, weather, traffic conditions, or just how you feel, different routes may suit you best. One of the advantages of bicycling is that you can use varied routes. Quiet back streets, traffic jams, and many outright obstacles which would slow or stop a car are no problem to you. You can take shortcuts through back alleys, parks, and courtyards, or across fields and railroad lines where roads don't cross. If you want a relaxed ride home after work, a slow back street or bikepath route may suit you best. If you need to get somewhere in a hurry, you wind yourself up and move out into the traffic on the main streets.

Explore different routes when you have time. Use them as it suits you, and learn the cross routes so you can sidestep in the middle of your trip if you feel like it.

AN IMAGINARY COMMUTING TRIP

Now, we'll take an imaginary commuting trip — a first day's trip, two-way, on two different routes. We'll assume that you have enough experience as a bicyclist to be reasonably comfortable in traffic, though you prefer to avoid heavy traffic when you can. But we'll also assume that you don't know the area and have to search out a new route.

Our exploration will center around the map you will use — a street guide of Cambridge, Massachusetts. See the following page.

Let's say you've just moved to Channing Street, off Mount Auburn Street in the western part of Cambridge. You have taken a job at MIT, which is at the other end of the city. You decide you'll commute by bike since it is only three miles, and you've been assured that you may park your bike in your office.

You've driven back and forth from MIT a couple of times, and you know that there's a bikepath along the Charles River. So you take down your bike one morning. You put the street guide in the handlebar bag, after a quick look at it to show you your route to the path: left on Mount Auburn Street, right on Hawthorne Street.

You quickly get to the path; unfortunately it's a bit slow. Furthermore, it's narrow in places, and it crosses the ends of three bridges without adequate traffic signal protection. In fact, the cars keep turning in front of you, and you have to scoot across in between them.

At Audrey Street, you cross Memorial Drive with a pedestrian signal. You took this route before in your car, because the parking garage is on Vassar Street. Vassar Street is a good route, as you discover — wide, and without cross traffic because of the playing fields on the right and the railroad tracks behind the buildings on your left.

You turn right on Massachusetts Avenue, and left at a mid-block pedestrian crossing which leads right to the front steps of MIT. Looking at your watch, you see it took 20
[*Continued on page 180*]

177

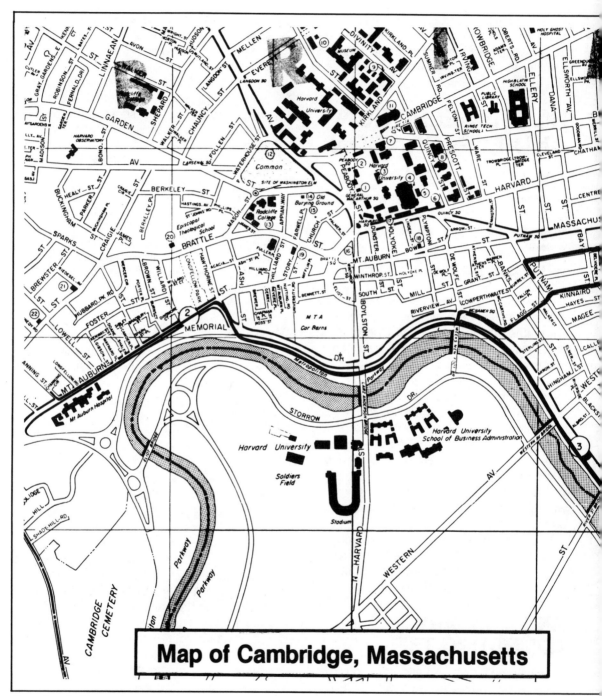

Map of Cambridge, Massachusetts

Reproduced with permission of copyright owner, Arrow Publishing Co., Inc.

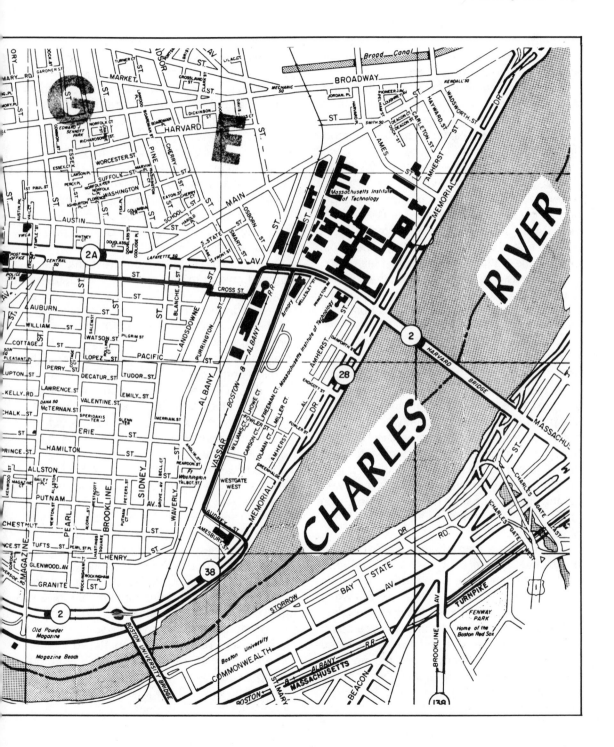

minutes, which is good time. It took you 25 minutes in your car, with the rush-hour traffic and the walk from the garage.

But you decide to take some time after work to look for a better route. You've noticed that the river bends, taking you out of your way. And you don't like those bridge intersections on the bikepath.

On the map, you notice that Massachusetts Avenue (or "Mass Ave." as you discover everyone here calls it) cuts almost straight across the bend in the river. Mass Ave. is a busy main street. But you're looking for a relaxed ride at the end of your day, away from most of the traffic. Just south of Mass Ave., you notice two parallel streets, Green Street and Franklin Street. They begin just past the railroad tracks, a couple of blocks from MIT, so you head for them.

You start your ride up Mass Ave. away from the river, and cross Vassar Street with the traffic light. You note the railroad tracks as you cross them, because you want to turn left onto the next cross street to get onto the back streets. There is a traffic signal where you will make your left turn, and it's green. But with the heavy rush-hour traffic, you decide to walk the left turn. You cross the intersection, pull to the right, turn your bike to the left, and wait for the light to change. When it does, you cross Mass Ave. and head down Albany Street.

You make a note on your map about Albany Street. Since it is next to the railroad tracks, it doesn't have cross traffic. It's in an industrial area, so traffic is light except when factories are opening and closing for the day. You imagine that there is some way you could walk your bike across the tracks between Vassar Street and Albany Street, too, and you make a note to investigate. If you were heading from MIT to visit a friend in Cambridgeport, this might be a good route to take.

But now, you take the first right turn off Albany Street, onto Cross Street. Cross Street ends after one block at Landsdowne Street. You stop and look. Half a block to your right, on the far side of Landsdowne Street, Green Street begins, and to your left, Franklin Street. Neither has a one-way sign, but you notice that the parked cars on Green Street face away from you and those on Franklin Street face toward you. So you take Green Street, even though you're doubling back a bit.

Your guess was right; Green Street is one-way. And it's a good find. It takes you almost a mile, arrow straight.

Most of the smaller side streets have stop signs. Looking to the left down these streets, you notice that Franklin Street has become one-way in the other direction. You take note of this since you may use Franklin Street for your trip to work tomorrow morning. At busy Central Square, you note that traffic signals protect both Franklin and Green Streets.

After Central Square, noting the back of the post office with the mail trucks on your right, you're sure you are on course. You make a left turn onto Putnam Avenue to jog sideways to the river.

But wait — this isn't Putnam Avenue. This ends at another street after two blocks. Where are you?

You trace along Green Street until you find a street that goes two blocks to the left and ends. There are two such streets — Bay Street and Hancock Street. You made the turn a block or two too soon. But you see that you can turn right here onto Kinnaird Street and get back to Putnam Avenue. No big problem.

Reaching Putnam Avenue, you find that it is busy and narrow. It was better to jog left where you did by mistake. Now you cut straight across Putnam Avenue to Flagg Street, one way in the right direction. Ahead of you is the river. This checks with your map.

You ride down to where Flagg Street ends at busy Memorial Drive. The bikepath is on the other side at Memorial Drive and there isn't any crossing signal. Looking to your right, you see that there is one at the next street. Memorial Drive has a wide sidewalk on this side. An iron fence separates the sidewalk from Harvard University dormitories on your right. Nobody will dart out onto this sidewalk unexpectedly, so you ride quickly up to the next street. Looking to your right, you note that Cowperthwaite Street is one way in the other direction. You'll use it for your inbound trip. You cross Memorial Drive at the pedestrian light.

Now you take the bikepath, over the end of the Boylston Street Bridge (there's a walk signal here, with a pushbutton actuator). You note the Harvard Stadium on your left across the river, double-checking that you're in the right place. From here, you'll retrace your inbound route. You continue along the bikepath, then cross Memorial Drive to Hawthorne Street. You ride one block, then signal and turn left onto Mount Auburn Street. This street is a bit busy, but wide — nice for easy riding. Then turn right onto Channing Street and you're home.

REVIEWING YOUR TRIP

Look back at the trip you just took. It's a good example of the different sorts of routes you might use on a bicycle, and of how to look for them. Main streets, back streets, a bikepath, and a sidewalk were all used during your trip. Some intersections you crossed as a driver and some as a pedestrian. You used your map-reading skills to find a good route, to recover yourself when you made a wrong turn, and to plot other routes besides the one you took. Especially, when you were on one-way streets, you took the trouble to look for your parallel route in the opposite direction.

As you hang your bike up, you decide that this was a good exploring ride. Because of the time you spent making notes on your map while riding, the three-mile ride took 25 minutes instead of 15. When you ride back in to MIT the next morning, you might give yourself 20 minutes, since you've already figured out most of your inbound route. You're glad you took the time, because now you won't be going out of the way on the bikepath anymore.

But there's one more thing you do now at home — you transfer your new route to your wall map.

Mark your route down on your wall map in pencil since you may change your mind about routes later. On the wall map, you see your new routes as part of the growing network of routes you have checked out. Also, in case you lose your street guide map while out riding, you won't have to do your exploring over again.

As you ride, you may meet other bicyclists and compare notes. At a bike club meeting or group ride, you may find other bicyclists who can use your routes or show you theirs. You may invite another bicyclist home to look at maps with you. By sharing route information, you can fill in your maps several times quicker than you could by yourselves.

If your area does not already have a bicycle commuter map, there may be a bicyclist's group working on one. If so, this group will be especially happy to use your routes, and will be a fine source of new routes for you. If nobody is working on such a map yet, just keep your routes handy, and keep your ears open. Sooner or later, someone will call on you to help; or you may decide to get a map project off the ground.

CHAPTER TEN

PARKING, STORAGE, AND SECURITY

If you know how to park your bicycle so it's safe from thieves and from the weather, you will feel more comfortable about using it for your transportation.

In some places, excellent parking arrangements are provided for bicycles. In many others, they are not. But with a little imagination, most parking problems can be solved. This chapter should be a spur to your imagination, a tool kit of the parking tactics used by experienced commuting bicyclists.

Protecting your bicycle against theft can use up a considerable amount of your time and energy, which is a minor price to pay compared with the expense of operating an automobile.

THEFT IS A SERIOUS PROBLEM

A bicycle is an excellent target for a thief. Almost one million are stolen each year.

An unprotected bicycle in a city will typically be stolen within a matter of minutes or hours — sometimes, seconds. A poorly locked bicycle may last its owner a few months. A properly locked bicycle is almost never stolen, though parts theft and vandalism may still be problems in some places.

Don't underrate the theft problem, or believe it can't strike you — or it will. You can relax your vigilance some in the country or the suburbs, compared with the city, but you should never leave an unlocked bicycle out of your sight, anywhere, if you expect to keep it.

Here are some things you do to make it less likely your bicycle will be stolen. You only have to do these things once, instead of every time you park the bicycle—so they take very little time in proportion to the benefits you gain from them.

KNOW YOUR COMMUNITY

The risk of theft varies greatly from one place to another. It doesn't make sense to waste your time and money on excessive precautions in a community where theft is rare any more than it makes sense to ignore security where theft is common.

Talk with other bicyclists. Learn about the theft problem in your community. Find out what sorts of theft are common, and where they are common. Learn especially about danger spots — where bicyclists are commonly stopped while riding, and their bicycles stolen. Avoid these or take extra precautions.

CHOOSE THE RIGHT BICYCLE

The appearance of your bicycle can help you. A time-worn bicycle is worth less to a thief. The bicycle does not have to work poorly — it may be in top mechanical shape. But the clean bearings and new grease are inside where the thief can't see them.

A bicycle with an internal hub gear or single-speed rear hub is much less likely to be stolen than a derailleur-equipped bicycle. And the one-, three-, or five-speed bicycle actually works better in many riding situations, especially in the city where theft is common.

A folding bicycle reduces the likelihood of theft, because you take it with you many places where you would have to leave a conventional bicycle outdoors.

Many people own *two* bicycles — a nice one for touring and point-to-point commuting, and a trashmo bike for errands.

MAKE IT UNATTRACTIVE

If you are willing to sacrifice the attractiveness of your bicycle, you can make it less susceptible to theft — and easier to recover.

Try a few splashes of odd-colored paint, or frame tubes wrapped like barber poles with reflective tape. Enjoy your bicycle longer by making it uglier on the outside.

Identification painted in large letters will give second thoughts to thieves who work in dark places or who might consider stealing the bicycle from under you as you ride.

ENGRAVE YOUR BIKE

Engraved identification on the frame and valuable parts makes a bicycle very dangerous as stolen property. Put engraving where it won't weaken the bicycle, but make it visible so it deters thieves.

Buy an engraving tool at a hardware store, or rent one from a tool rental outlet. In many communities you may get the use of an engraving tool for free — the police department or Chamber of Commerce has programs to lend them out. You mark your bicycle (and while you're at it, your other valuables) with a special code number. Police use this number to notify you if your property is recovered. Make sure this number works *outside* as well as inside your community. If it is based on your driver's license, it will. In case your bicycle is recovered (not by the police, but by a

Engraved identification discourages theft.

private party), it's good also to include your mailing address or telephone number.

Hidden identification may help you recover your bicycle if the visible identification has been removed. Put it inside the tires with a felt tip marker, engrave it on the rims under the rim tape, write it on adhesive tape wrapped around the steerer tube. Then an honest mechanic may someday retrieve your bicycle for you. Put one item of identification where nobody else will find it — inside a frame tube, for example. Then you will always be able to positively identify your bicycle to police.

SERIAL NUMBERS AND REGISTRATION

Keep a record of your bicycle's serial number, but remember that it cannot be traced to you like a police identification number or your address. If your community has a bicycle registration program, take advantage of it, but be aware that bicycle registration is not very effective in preventing theft. Relatively few bicycles are registered nationwide. An unregistered bicycle does not draw the attention of a police officer the way an unregistered car does.

MAKE IT HARDER TO REMOVE VALUABLE PARTS

Once you have the saddle angle properly adjusted, some epoxy glue on the seat clamp nuts will keep a wrench from turning them. The same for other nuts securing valuable parts and accessories. But ordinary paint remover will soften the epoxy when you need to turn the nuts. Just keep it away from the bicycle's paint!

An Allen-head binder bolt will make it harder to steal parts while still letting you adjust them. If you replace end nuts of hub axles with hub bearing cones turned bearing side out, the thief will need bearing cone wrenches to remove the wheel.

You may think of other, similar tricks. The more, the better.

CHOOSE ACCESSORIES TO DISCOURAGE THEFT

Lights and other accessories should be either firmly attached to the bicycle, so a thief needs tools to remove them, or they should be easy to attach and remove so you can take them with you. Bicycle bags should have easy attachment features so you can take them along, because you must protect their contents. A large, cloth, frameless backpack gives you a place to carry bags and accessories off the bicycle.

GET A GOOD LOCK

Generally, a U-bolt lock is the best. It is compact, relatively light, and secures your bicycle as well. Cables and chains can be as secure, but if they are, they are also heavy. The cable, chain links, and padlock shackle must be at least ⅜ inch thick and of hardened steel to resist thieves' tools. Cables and chains have no disadvantages if you leave one at each end of your commute. Then you don't have to carry any lock. The bicycle thieves' tool of choice, boltcutters, will cut a chain or padlock shackle quicker than it will cut a cable. So a cable with a built-in keylock is more secure for its size than one with a separate padlock.

For a child, a combination lock avoids

A strong cable wasted on a flimsy lock.

brackets do and some don't. It's quite convenient to carry a lock in a bike bag or strap it to the rear rack, so don't base your choice of a lock on the bracket.

Don't plan just to drape your lock over the bicycle's frame, as so many people do. It'll ruin the paint, disturb your road feel, and probably get in your way.

To lock your bicycle, find a sturdy, fixed object such as a parking meter or signpost to use as a hitchpost. Make sure your hitchpost can't be lifted out of the ground, and that the locked bicycle can't be lifted over the top of it. Avoid signposts with low signs that unbolt

the problem of lost keys. But buy a cable with a built-in combination lock, or a combination padlock with thumbwheels such as the "Sesamee." Most inexpensive dial-face combination padlocks are toys that can be smashed with a single hammer blow.

A light cable with loop ends, threaded through the shackle of a U-bolt lock, can secure a front wheel or an accessory such as a helmet.

A good U-bolt lock will cost you between $20 and $35. That may seem expensive, especially if your bicycle is a $30 second-hand clunker. But if you must rely on your bicycle for transportation, the distress and inconvenience of losing it is a greater cost than the replacement cost of the bicycle. So get a good lock.

Some U-bolt locks are sold with optional carrying brackets. Try one out before you buy it. Make sure there's a convenient and safe place to attach it. No part of the bracket or lock should protrude above the frame's top tube. Also make sure the bracket holds the lock securely, so it won't slip or rattle. Some

Properly locked, but the fence to which the bike is locked is not secure — its light-gauge links could be cut with a small boltcutter.

easily, or fences with flimsy top rails or chains that are easily undone or broken.

Pass the lock around your hitchpost and the bicycle's rear rim, inside the rear triangle of the frame — that is, above the chainstays, which go from the rear hub to the cranks, and below the seatstays, which go from the rear hub to the seat. Pass the lock around the seat tube, too, if it reaches. But note that the wheel has to be cut apart to get the frame even if the lock does not circle the seatpost. If you lock only the frame, a thief could ride away after

breaking the object to which the bicycle is secured. Also, many people lose their rear wheels because they secure only the frame. Secure at least the rear wheel and the frame, as described. If the front wheel has a quick-release hub, remove it and lock it next to the rear wheel. If not, secure it with a loop-end cable — or you may have installed wheel bearing cones as axle nuts as described earlier. Otherwise, you risk losing the front wheel — a relatively minor risk, since it is bolted in place. If locking to a parking

A cyclist buys a $30 lock for a $30 bicycle. The bicycle is his transportation, and its value is not measured by its purchase price.

meter or street sign, place the bicycle on the side away from the street so a car won't back into it.

Locking technique is similar with a chain or cable, but be especially careful to keep a chain up off the ground. A thief can apply extra pressure with boltcutters by bracing one handle against the ground.

If you are locking the bicycle in a public place, remove accessories and baggage and take them with you. Many helmets may be threaded onto the shackle of a U-bolt, by way of a ventilating hole. The saddle of a folding bicycle on its removable seatpost may be secured by passing the lock over one of the saddle rails.

This bicycle could be stolen completely by removing the front wheel and unscrewing two spokes. A lock is only as good as the way it is used.

WHERE TO PARK YOUR BICYCLE

Wherever you park your bicycle for long stretches of time — at work or at home — keep it under shelter from the weather, and in a protected space, such as:

. . . Your own private space: office, apartment, or house.

. . . An attended and guarded space: in sight of the attendant at a parking garage or just inside the front gate of your factory, in sight of the security guard.

. . . A locked space to which only you and other people you trust have keys — a locked storage room, for example.

. . . Any convenient wall or corner in an office complex or factory floor where people you know circulate frequently and where strangers would be noticed.

Lock the bicycle, too. A thief sees you take it in day after day to your home or office, and may be tempted to break in — or sneak in — to get it. But few thieves will hang around long enough to break your lock. Use a protected parking area to gain this added security and also so you can leave the accessories on your bicycle.

For short-term parking — like when you're shopping — lock your bicycle in a public place, where people are constantly walking by. Fortunately, shopping and other errands are usually done at times of peak hustle and bustle. Thieves don't like to be surprised at their work, so your bicycle is fairly safe. Remove the accessories, though.

Don't park your bicycle in an area which is concealed but also open to strangers — a dark street at night, the basement of a large apartment building, a bike rack concealed behind bushes, or any place a thief can work undisturbed. Your lock does not stop thieves, but only slows them down and makes it obvious what they are doing. The possibility of being caught is what stops a thief.

Sometimes, as when going to the theater, you have no choice but to park your bicycle on a dark street. That's the occasion to ride your trashmo bicycle, the one that probably won't get stolen, and if it does, no great loss.

INDOOR STORAGE IDEAS

It is safe and convenient to bring your bicycle into your own living space, or an adjoining locked porch, hallway, or garage. You won't have to unload your baggage all at once and carry it.

If you live at the top of a flight of stairs, a hook to hold your bicycle there is helpful so you'll have both hands free to unlock and open the door.

A spring-closed door can make it hard to get your bicycle in and out at the top of stairs. A door chock, or a hook and eye to hold the door open, is helpful.

If you live more than one flight of stairs above street level, you'll need an elevator to bring up a loaded bicycle. In a large apartment building, it's best to use the freight elevator and delivery entrance to minimize problems with other tenants.

Cleanliness can be a problem, especially on wet or snowy days. If you have to take your bicycle through a lobby or across a carpet, shake the bicycle and drop it a couple of inches to release loose water. Then towel off the tires all the way around — you might carry a towel with you for this purpose. Carry the bicycle if possible, rather than rolling it.

If cleanliness is important at your storage space, put down a plastic sheet or newspapers on the floor to catch the drips. Some sort of padding on the wall is helpful to prevent scratches, nicks, and rub marks from the handlebar end.

Bike shops sell hooks from which to hang your bicycle. Two hooks will hang a bicycle horizontally on a wall. One hook around the front rim will hang the bicycle vertically, cutting down on the space it takes — you can put a bicycle into a closet this way. Put the hook at just the right height to lift the rear wheel barely off the floor. Then you can roll the bicycle up to the hook on its rear wheel.

For day or night long-term storage, bringing the bicycle into a heated space in winter and an air-conditioned one in summer gives it a chance to dry out. For short-term parking, it's better not to bring the bicycle into the heated or air-conditioned space, because rapid temperature changes will temporarily cause water to condense inside the frame.

USING BIKE RACKS

Use a bike rack only if it is in a public place or a secured place. Do not break commonsense rules about where to park your bicycle in order to use a rack.

Use bike racks with caution. The conventional "dishdrainer" bike rack is an obsolete relic of an age when bicycle wheels were tougher and thieves weren't. Placed as intended in a "dishdrainer" rack, only one wheel of the bicycle can be secured with any practical lock. In high crime areas, racks are littered with orphaned wheels hanging by their locks.

A "dishdrainer" rack is more or less acceptable to hold bicycles upright inside a guarded enclosure. But roll your bicycle in, back wheel first, and be careful of a reflector or light attached to the back of the bicycle's rear rack — it may be bent or broken as it hits the "dishdrainer's" top crossbar. Lock the rear wheel for a little more security. If you roll your bicycle in front wheel first, the wheel will turn if the bicycle gets bumped. Then the bicycle will fall and the wheel will get bent.

To secure your bicycle properly to a "dishdrainer" rack, lock it to the end, or sideways in the middle.

More modern bicycle racks are available now, which are simple, inexpensive, and secure your bicycle properly. Roll-in lockers for secure long-term storage are also available. If you are ever in a position to influence decisions about bicycle parking, remember this!

IF BIKES ARE PROHIBITED

You may live or work in a building where bicycles are not allowed inside and where secure parking is not available. The prohibition on taking bicycles indoors is often unreasonable though sometimes not — bicycles mix poorly in an environment of narrow stairways, fine woodwork, and plush carpets.

But it is reasonable for you to have some sort of secure parking for your bicycle. It is to your advantage — and it is usually to the advantage to your landlord or employer. Constructing and maintaining facilities for cars is very expensive; encouraging people to use bicycles is an effective way to cut costs.

If you are looking for a new place to live or work, one factor in your choice might be the availability of bicycle parking. But if you're stuck with no parking (or no *secure* parking as we've described it), put your imagination to work. Usually, there will be a workable solution. Since you spend time day after day in your home and place of work, you have time to investigate possible solutions.

Approach whoever is in charge of managing the building, in a friendly, cooperative manner. Often, bicycle prohibitions have been set down without thought, or are more sweeping than reasonable. But there always has been some real problem that brought them on. Listen to the concerns of the building manager, landlord, or employer with an open ear, and try to find a solution. It helps if you've done some legwork and already have a plan. For example, you suggest using a neglected first floor or basement storage room. It also helps if you make a businesslike offer to pay a reasonable rent for its use. You might split the rent with a couple of friends who are also bicyclists. The space could become your workshop as well as your storage area.

If you can't work out such an arrangement, look further. Perhaps your building or a neighboring one has an attended parking garage, and you could work out an arrangement to lock your bicycle there. A nearby resident or storekeeper might have a bit of extra space you could use. Be imaginative, and remember that time is on your side in your search.

If you own a car which you don't have to share with another driver, you could store your bicycle in the car as long as the car is parked within sight of the garage's attendant. Preferably, put the bicycle in the car's trunk, or cover it with a cloth, so it won't be seen.

A folding bicycle goes inside most buildings without problems — especially if it is in a carrying bag.

If you have to park your bicycle outside your living space, it helps to keep a small shopping cart with your bicycle to carry loads back to your living space. Or use a bicycle trailer, which also has other uses.

When you do maintenance work on your bicycle, you may have to take it to a friend's work area or else take its wheels off and carry it up to your living space wrapped in cloth.

The most difficult parking problems come when you are a visitor at a building that prohibits bicycles. Be sure to ask what the policy is as you plan your visit. Then take your trashmo bicycle — or if necessary a folding bicycle with a bag.

Someday, and it won't be long, bicycle parking will be everywhere. But for the time being, these are our best answers.

LONG-TERM STORAGE

If you're not going to be using your bicycle for a month or longer, it pays to take special precautions.

Protect your bicycle from rust. Store it in a dry place, and wipe it down (except for rubber parts and rim braking surfaces) with a rag lubricated with WD-40, LPS-3, or another rust preventative. You might also spray a bit of this into the frame's vent holes, and, with the saddle removed, down the seat tube. Don't use too much, or it will dissolve bottom bracket and headset grease.

Hang the bicycle up, or lay it on its side on a raised surface. Within a month or two, air will seep out of the tires. If the bicycle sits on a flat tire, it will be hard to get the tire to seat on the rim.

Do not turn the bicycle upside down on its saddle and handlebars. With dropped bars, brake cables will be damaged; also, parts near the floor are vulnerable to rust, rot, and rodent damage.

Store the bicycle in your own or someone else's private space. If possible, appoint someone to keep track of the bicycle for you. This person should know where to get in touch with you and when you are returning to claim the bicycle.

Leave a note on the bicycle explaining that it is yours and will be reclaimed.

Lock the bicycle. Keep one key, and give another to the person who is watching the bicycle, in case it must be moved. It's good, too, to have a third key stored away somewhere. Over a long period of time, keys get lost!

Check to see whether any insurance covers your bicycle where it is stored. If not, you might consider arranging for insurance.

If you can't find someone to watch the bicycle — put it in a locked area. Also, consider taking off some of the parts and storing them separately from the frame, to make the bicycle a less attractive target for theft.

When you claim the bicycle, bring tools, machine oil, chain lubricant, and an air pump. Inflate the tires and inspect the bicycle carefully before you ride it. Lubricate all parts which use oil. If you have been away for more than two years, have the bearings regreased; grease can dry out with time.

QUICK LOCKING TRICKS

You should always lock your bicycle if it will be out of your sight. In some situations it will be within your sight and you would be safe if you made the bicycle unridable. A thief would have to carry it, or would try to ride it and give up. Locking the bicycle takes time, so you might decide to use one of these tricks:

. . . If the bicycle has a quick-release front wheel, take the wheel off and bring it with you.
. . . If it has a quick-release rear wheel, loosen the quick-release skewer. The wheel will jam as the thief starts to pedal away.
. . . If you set one of the brakes, you'll likely stop a thief in his tracks.
. . . If your bicycle is a folding bicycle, fold it. Even better, remove the hinge key or nut, too.

If you use some of these techniques, you do take the risk of having to chase a thief. But it's easy to catch a thief who is carrying your bicycle. If you yell, the thief will usually drop the bicycle and run away.

These techniques may be used in combination with locking your bicycle in order to further discourage a thief. An incomplete bicycle is a poor target for theft.

THEFT PREVENTION

Remember, the thief has a lot to lose by being caught. Make this work for you. Definitely make your presence known, but leave the thief an escape route — don't get too close. If you are where other people can hear you, call out. The thief will almost certainly run.

Do not attempt to stop the thief unless you have complete confidence in your skills. A cornered thief is desperate. He may have an assistant standing lookout nearby, and you may have to deal with both of them.

If you see someone carrying your bicycle, give chase and call out, but again, don't get too close. The thief will usually drop the bicycle and run off.

If you surprise a thief riding your bicycle toward you, you might try pushing the bicycle over with a quick, hard kick or lunge. Don't make your intentions known in advance by yelling or making abrupt moves.

Violent theft is a vexing problem. You are vulnerable on your bicycle. It's easy for people to knock you down, and once you're down the fight is usually over. Though fortunately, violent theft is rare in most places.

If you are small or are a woman, your chances of being stopped are greater. Take this factor into consideration when planning your routes.

Learn about the bad spots from other bicyclists. Stay away from them; avoid bike-paths, bridge sidewalks, and other isolated areas at night. You are safest on well-traveled streets, moving along at a good speed. Ride the traffic lane of the bridge if you can.

Don't ride a flashy bicycle, and don't wear expensive, fashionable clothes or bicycle racing clothes which create the impression that your bicycle is valuable.

Thieves often dart out from behind bushes or parked cars, so stay away from the side of the street when traffic is light. Thieves sometimes approach you, riding two on one bicycle, then push you over and ride away, one on your bicycle. Steer clear. You can certainly outrace and outmaneuver them. Thieves sometimes hang out in gangs on street corners, waiting to trap bicyclists at traffic lights. Keep an eye out for them. Riding in bad areas, it's better to slow down for the lights in mid-block, then sprint through them, rather than to stop and wait at the corner.

If you see a group of people — usually young men — begin to move out into the street ahead of you to block your path, you have two choices:

If you're going uphill, or have time to get away, glance behind you, make a quick U-turn and sprint away.

If you don't have time or space to U-turn, put on speed and charge. First aim a couple feet to the side of one of your assailants to confuse him — then ride straight at the assailant. Yell loudly at the last moment, watch to see which way the assailant dives, and make a quick turn in the other direction.

You will have to deal with a red light as best as you can. If you must go through it, make a quick right turn into the cross street.

In any case, don't give in to your usual reaction and stop because thieves are in front of you. That's exactly what the thieves want you to do.

Generally, if you have been forced to a stop, or thieves come up to you while you're stopped, don't resist. Remember, the thief has already decided to use violence if necessary. You don't know to what lengths the thief will go. Better your bike than your life.

On the other hand, if you can set the brake with a reversed quick-release lever, or flip the chain off with your foot, you will force the thief to deal with your bicycle, not with you. You might then have the advantage. But be careful — don't press your luck if there's a weapon or more than one thief.

Ride with a friend if possible — it's safer.

You and other bicyclists in your community have a right to demand extra police protection, especially if thieves on bridges deny you access. Emergency telephones, and guards stationed at either end of bridge walkways, are a simple and effective way to stop theft. Police cyclists are effective on streets and bikepaths everywhere, against reckless riding as well as theft.

If your bicycle has been stolen, by all means report the theft to the police, both to aid recovery and to validate insurance claims. Collect on insurance if you can. Notify your friends, put a notice in your local bike club newsletter, and send notices to bike shops if you feel it might be worth the trouble. Note that losses due to theft are tax deductible.

Don't get your hopes up too high. The recovery rate for bicycles is very low. They're too easily transported, and it's too easy to repaint them and switch equipment around to make them unrecognizable.

Use the opportunity to get together a new bicycle better suited to your particular needs.

Think about the theft and how you might prevent a future one.

If you locate your stolen bike, first remember that the person who has your bike may not be the person who stole it. The person who has your bike may have bought it in good faith. Don't jump to any conclusions.

Even if it has been sold, the bike was once your property. Legally, you have a right to file claim to it, but you must get the police to help you. Should you find your bike parked, you can call the police to help you claim the bike. If you see someone riding your bike, you or a friend will have to follow this person discreetly until the bike is parked. Then call the police. If the bike is taken inside a building— unless it is a public building—the police will have to wait until it comes out again, or they will have to get a search warrant. When you call the police, explain clearly to them what has happened, so they won't drive right up to the door and arouse the suspicion of the person you have been following.

The police will take your bike, and will hold it for a while in order to check out your claim of ownership. However, if the person who had your bike bought it in good faith, you may legally have to pay this person for the bike. Stolen bikes are usually sold for much less than they are worth, so you will usually come out ahead by recovering the bike.

INSURANCE AGAINST THEFT AND DAMAGE

You can't buy separate blanket theft insurance for your bicycle. Because of the carelessness with which so many people lock their bicycles and the difficulty of validating claims (bicycles being unregistered), the cost of the insurance would be very high.

But you can buy blanket theft insurance under a homeowner's or renter's policy. This will usually cover your bicycle even when it is away from home. Check carefully with the insurance company. If necessary, get a bike provision written into your policy.

The subsidized Federal Crime Insurance program and some state insurance programs are designed to prevent the deterioration of good neighborhoods into high-crime areas. These programs generally will cover your bicycle and other possessions when they are inside your locked house or apartment. Call the federal government or state government information number in your area for information.

You can arrange for your car insurance policy to cover your bicycle and other possessions when they are locked inside your car. Still, it is best to pack them so a thief can't see them through the car's windows.

Some public transportation has insurance to cover your baggage. This is true of all airlines, but coverage varies on rail and bus lines. Coverage is usually for theft but not damage — your bicycle rates as a fragile item. Where insurance is not available, it is usually because baggage is carried in an open compartment or overhead rack. Then a thief has access to your baggage, but you're safe as long as you watch it when pulling into stations.

If you ship your bicycle as freight or by parcel post, you can and should have it insured. Bicycles are often stolen in shipment, so be aware of this.

Some U-bolt locks are sold with limited insurance against theft of your bicycle. Check when you go to buy a lock.

Remember that insurance may or may not cover the full value of your bicycle. Keep purchase records as evidence, but if you have improved your bicycle since you bought it, have it appraised at a bike shop. It is often complicated and time-consuming to settle an insurance claim, so the best insurance is to park and lock your bicycle carefully.

INSURE YOURSELF

Put aside three or four dollars a week out of the money that your bicycle is saving you. This is less than you would be paying in insurance premiums. Unlike the money you pay to the insurance company, it's still yours.

Keep a second bicycle so you'll have one to ride if the other gets stolen. The largest problem with losing a bicycle is the inconvenience of not having one to ride.

CHAPTER ELEVEN

CARRYING LOADS

Your bicycle carries you around, but it must also carry the things you need while riding and the things you need at your destination. You must provide for these needs.

ORGANIZING THE LOAD

There are several places to carry loads on your bike, and there's a certain order in which to use them. You organize the baggage in different bags according to purpose. Then you can attach and remove an entire bag at a time instead of rummaging and reorganizing for each trip.

A handlebar bag or small backpack carries supplies you need while riding, such as a raincape, a sweater, removable lights, snacks, maps, and a small tool kit. The handlebar bag is very convenient for this purpose because you can use it without getting off the bike.

If you're commuting and have to carry a change of clothes with you, a second bag is helpful. A saddlebag, behind the saddle, is a good choice.

The rear rack carries the bulkier, heavier loads, including a briefcase and items from the store. Additional bags called panniers may be attached to the sides of the rear rack next to the wheels for more load-carrying capacity. Front racks are sometimes useful when a child seat replaces the rear rack.

For the truly bulky, heavy loads like a week's groceries — the ones you "can't" carry on a bicycle — a bicycle trailer is the most flexible accessory. A trailer can also carry a child, and in some cases is preferable to a child seat.

EQUIPMENT TO GET STARTED

You may buy other load-carrying equipment later, but we recommend that you buy a rear rack right away. The rear rack is your carry-all, adaptable to many different sorts of loads. Buy and install a rack as soon as you take up using your bicycle for transportation. One exception: if you're installing a child seat on your bicycle, it takes the place of the rear rack. The seat may be used to carry baggage instead of a child, but you may need to install a front rack or basket or use a trailer when carrying the child and baggage.

The next purchase after a rack would be a handlebar bag, or small backpack — your "glove compartment."

Bicycle bags and racks are sold only at bicycle shops. Not all shops have a wide selection, so phone before you go out to buy.

CHOOSING AND INSTALLING A RACK

Several brands of aluminum rear racks are available in the $10 price range, including Pletscher, Kryptonite, and Schwinn. The top platform part of these racks that carries the load is solid enough, but the attachment to the bicycle leaves something to be desired — a single strut on each side and a clamp which may loosen and deposit the front of the rack on top of the bicycle's rear brake. A rack plate between the brake and rack attachments eliminates this problem, though the rack may still sway in use. The Schwinn rack is probably the best of the lot, attaching to the bicy-

This bicycle, used for point-to-point commuting, is equipped with a handlebar bag and saddlebag, though no rear rack.

cle's seatpost clamp bolt. Any of these racks will be able to carry a briefcase.

For a bit more money, you get a sturdier rack. The Karrimor, made of steel, is economical and solid. Blackburn, Eclipse, and others make more expensive racks — in the $25 range. These are of lightweight aluminum and have double or triple struts, making them very rigid.

Safe load limit for the least expensive racks is about 15 pounds; for the more expensive ones, about 25 pounds. However, to carry heavy loads, any of these racks can be reinforced as a do-it-yourself project and, surprisingly, the least expensive ones are the easiest to improve. When installing a rear rack, you must mount the bicycle's taillight and rear reflector out of its way.

CONTAINERS TO HOLD THINGS ON THE RACK

It's not convenient to carry the brown shopping bags on your bicycle's rack. They'll tear open and spill the contents all over the street. What you're looking for in containers is: convenience — not having to carry around things when you don't need them, economy — to save money, and durability — appropriate to the use. Some favorite choices include cardboard boxes — most merchants have an ample supply of them. The merchandise comes to the store in these boxes. A merchant will almost always give you a cardboard box instead of a bag if you ask for one — and if not, the merchant next door will. After you've been shopping by bike for a while, you'll have a collection of usable boxes, and you'll know which stores will give you boxes.

By using available boxes, you avoid carrying around an extra bicycle bag which you

have to remove from the bicycle when you park.

Some bicyclists bolt a plastic milk crate to the carrier. This is light, strong, and not valuable enough to be worth stealing from your parked bicycle. The milk crate is good for carrying small items which don't fill a cardboard box; the milk crate will also hold a standard shopping bag. On the other hand, the milk crate can be a problem if you need to carry more than it will hold, and it can get in the way when you don't need it. Fasten it to the rack with bolts and wing nuts so you can attach or remove it quickly.

ATTACHING A LOAD TO THE RACK

To tie your baggage down to the rack, carry several bungee cords with you.

A bungee cord conveniently threads through the rear rattrap of the Pletscher or Schwinn rack, so you can loop both ends over your load to the front of the rack.

For large items, it's best to use the bungee cords stretched out all the way for the highest possible tension. Secure the top of a large load to the saddle to help prevent sway.

When tying down the load, stretch the cords directly over the top of the load and down to the rack. Do not run them sideways under the load to the rack, or the load will slip around.

Be careful with bungee cords. They're very large rubber bands with metal hooks on the ends and dangerous if they come loose and snap at you. Nylon strap webbing (¾ of an inch wide) is available at surplus stores — a good alternative to bungee cords. It has some stretch but not enough to snap at you, or to dump a large load if half-tensioned.

Most loads have enough springiness to

absorb road shock well. But when carrying a heavy, hard object like a car battery or tool chest, put a foam rubber pad under it. If you don't, it will pound like a hammer on the bicycle's rack, frame, and wheels. Sooner or later something will bend or break. Avoid heavy point loads along the rack's rails. Spread loads with a box or board.

Be careful in securing any load at the front of the bicycle. Anything that gets caught in the spokes could stop the front wheel and send you over the handlebars.

CHOOSING AND USING THE HANDLEBAR BAG

Choose a handlebar bag of small to moderate size. A heavily loaded handlebar bag will make your bicycle awkward to steer, so it is better to carry bulky and heavy items like your lock elsewhere on the bicycle. You have to take the handlebar bag off the bicycle and carry it with you when you park the bicycle in a public place. So make sure your handlebar bag goes on and off the bicycle quickly. A shoulder strap is very useful when you're off the bicycle and many handlebar bags are equipped with one. If not, you could install one yourself. Straps are available at camping and surplus stores.

When you install a handlebar bag, you may have to move your bicycle's headlamp out of its way. Make sure you take care of this when you get the bag.

USING A SADDLEBAG

A saddlebag attaches with straps to loops at the back of the saddle. (Do not confuse it with a pannier, which attaches to the side of the rear rack.) To use a saddlebag, your saddle must have these loops — and most do. If you are short so your saddle is low over the rear wheel, you must either have a rear rack on your bicycle to support the bottom of the saddlebag or buy a special fitting to raise the saddlebag attachment point.

The saddlebag is ideal for carrying dress clothing or for use as an overnight bag. It interferes little with objects tied to the top of the rack, so you can use it to gain extra carrying capacity. For example, when shopping.

The saddlebag is very convenient to install and remove, but if you have a handlebar bag as well, you'll have both hands full carrying them when you park your bike. You may need three hands, when you consider your helmet, pump, and other removable accessories. The answer to this vexing problem may be a backpack.

HOW TO USE A BACKPACK

The most useful backpack for bicycling is one you don't use when riding — a large, frameless, inexpensive cloth one into which you stuff all of the items you remove from the bicycle when you park it. This backpack stuffs conveniently into your handlebar bag when you return to the bicycle.

A smaller backpack can serve well as a substitute for a handlebar bag on short trips, especially if you have to get on and off the bicycle frequently — for example, to carry your books if you're commuting between classes on a college campus. The small backpack is convenient to carry things you use only when you're off the bicycle. However, it's uncomfortable for longer rides, especially in hot weather. It must be low cut or narrow at the top so you can look back past it, and it must have a waist strap to keep it from riding up your back as you ride in crouched position.

Backpacks which meet these requirements are available at better bike shops.

A large, camping backpack with a frame is unsuitable for bicycling. It is very uncomfortable on your shoulders, and obstructs your view to the rear.

PANNIER BAGS FOR YOUR RACK

Pannier bags attach to the rack, and sit next to the wheel on either side. They carry the load well — low down, where it affects handling least. They're good for carrying large numbers of small items.

Of special interest to commuters is a "commuter bag" which is a pair of panniers in one piece, with a handle in the middle like a briefcase. This is very convenient for carrying personal papers and books. You can make instant panniers for shopping. Use two European-style fishnet shopping bags, the kind with wooden slats at the top. Tie the slats to the rack at the top and wrap bungee cords through the bottoms of the bags to secure them to the rack's struts. When you're not using your instant panniers, they take up almost no space. Most panniers, however, are made for long-distance bicycle tourists.

The best tourist panniers are easy-on, easy-off, of moderate size, and have lots of outside pockets to separate the small items (inexperienced tourists buy the larger panniers). You may find panniers useful for extra load capacity, or instead of a handlebar bag, though in fact few people use them for commuting or shopping — other containers are usually more convenient.

BICYCLE BASKETS

Some people prefer wire baskets over bike bags. The appeal of baskets is that you can throw anything into one without hunting for a container, and you don't have to remove baskets when you park the bicycle.

But baskets have drawbacks. They are heavy, clumsy loads which you have to carry with your bicycle everywhere. They make it difficult to get your bicycle into a car or up a narrow stairway.

Their most appropriate place is on a bicycle used mostly for shopping, and for this purpose, their convenience may outweigh their drawbacks.

The best side baskets are the Schwinn collapsible ones — these fold flat so they don't always stick out from the sides of the bicycle.

A small front handlebar basket is handy, but avoid buying a large one because it makes steering difficult.

Be careful not to put a valuable item like a handbag in sight in a basket, especially a rear basket. It may disappear while you're stopped at a traffic light. At the very least it could make you more vulnerable to theft.

These bungee cords are stretched sideways under the box and will allow it to slip and tilt. Attached at the front and rear of the cardboard box, the bungee cords would pull straight down and hold it securely.

RIDING WITH A LOAD

A load affects the way your bicycle behaves. The bicycle steers awkwardly, and may sway disturbingly. Proper attention to placement and securing of the load can keep these problems to a minimum.

It is most important to secure a load well. The most serious problems come from a load that flops and sways. A well-secured load has an effect you can compensate for, but a loose one will steer your bike.

A load has the least effect on handling if it is low down and close to the center of the bicycle. A heavy load high on the bicycle's rear rack can try to slide the front wheel sideways. Putting some of the load at the front, for example, in a handlebar bag, helps hold the front wheel down. But too much load at the front slows the steering.

When you start out riding with a load, test it. Before you move out into traffic, make a few turning and braking maneuvers to get the feel of your bicycle.

With a load, it helps to pedal quickly and lightly. Heavy, slow pedaling rocks the bicycle and will probably produce sway. Shift down to accelerate and climb; don't get out of the saddle.

If sway starts, stop it by steering with it. If you fight against it, you'll make it worse. "Catch" the sway just as you catch your lean to keep the bicycle upright. Think of the yardstick balanced on your finger. If it starts to lean to one side, you move your hand the same way to catch it.

As you ride, check the load from time to time to make sure things aren't working loose.

A load makes the bicycle heavier, so you can't jump it over bumps. If possible, carry little enough weight at the front that you can still yank the front wheel up over small obstacles. Then you're safer against being dumped by pavement cracks or railroad tracks. The greater weight on the tires will bottom them out sooner on the rims. You must slow down more for bumps, particularly for smaller bumps. Now, more than at any other time, make sure the tires are fully inflated. On a bicycle with skinny tires, imagine you're riding on eggshells. Tire, rim, and spoke problems are common when people don't temper their riding to a load.

A load makes you go slower primarily to protect your bicycle. On level ground, the weight has little effect on your speed since you're pushing mostly air resistance. Hills aren't so bad, either, if you think about it. An example: if you weigh 150 pounds and your bicycle weighs 30, a 60-pound load adds one-third to the total weight and slows you to three-fourths of your normal speed. With the appropriate low gear on your bicycle, you'll certainly get home in time with the groceries to prepare dinner.

CARRYING YOUR ACCESSORIES

Tools belong in a small pouch. The pouch can go in the handlebar bag. Some special pouches are made to clip under the saddle, good for light day touring, but for a commuter, just one more thing to strip off the bicycle when parking.

A pump belongs on every bicycle. Attach it to the frame with pump pegs. Don't carry the pump in a bag or on the rack because it'll stick out like a sore thumb.

Place your lock in a bag at the rear (it's too heavy to put at the front), lashed to the rear rack (the top of any rack or the side of a two-strut rack), or on its own special frame bracket.

A must item for hot-weather riding is a water bottle which attaches to the bicycle's frame in its water bottle cage. You can slip the water bottle out to drink as you ride.

Since all of these items (and some lights) are removable (without tools), you must take them with you when you park — in one of your bike bags or your frameless backpack.

USING A BICYCLE TRAILER

A bicycle trailer is excellent for carrying large loads. It can be used with any bike. Use it when you need it and unhitch it when you don't need it. Because you can use a trailer as a shopping cart, it is the best way to carry large loads when shopping.

A trailer hitches to the bike at the seatpost or rear carrier. Because the trailer's load is supported almost entirely by its wheels, it has surprisingly little effect on the way the bike rides. But there are a few things to remember. Lower gears will be needed, especially when climbing hills. To carry very large loads, you may want to change the gearing on your bike. You don't have to be careful of damaging your bike's wheels the way you do when carrying a load on the bike itself. But stopping distances will be greater, because the trailer's wheels have no brakes. You must be aware of the extra width behind you, especially when it swings to the side when you corner. And you can't thread your way between bumps or stopped cars with two wheels behind you which aren't in line with your bike's wheels.

At night, be sure to have front and rear lights or reflectors at both sides of the trailer, because of its extra width.

When attached to the bike's seatpost, the trailer will prevent you from using a child seat or putting loads on a rear rack. A good mechanic can attach the trailer hitch to the rear of the child seat or rack if necessary. The rack must be reinforced, and the drawbar may be shortened so the trailer doesn't follow too far behind you. At least one brand attaches to the rear axle, eliminating conflict with the rack.

Many brands of trailers are now coming on the market. Look for these features, depending on your needs:

. . . The ability to carry children or baggage. Some trailers carry children very well with a roll bar or high enclosure for safety.

. . . Usefulness as a shopping cart. It helps if the trailer is narrow enough to fit through a standard doorway. Some are and some are not. It also helps if the drawbar is short — or removable.

. . . A low center of gravity. A trailer needs a low center of gravity to be stable, because it is narrow.

. . . Large wheels. If you want a trailer that rolls easily, choose one with large wheels, though small ones are fine for shorter trips on good pavement.

. . . Ability to store. Some trailers tilt up on end to store compactly.

SPECIAL TRAILERS

For safe riding with a long load like lumber or a canoe, you'll need a three- or four-wheel trailer.

These are mostly do-it-yourself items — none are commercially available yet.

The three-wheeled trailer may be a single unit, just a one-wheel front, two-wheel rear tricycle with a drawbar to attach to your bicycle. Or it may be two units, the front wheel with its steering pivot and the drawbar, and the two-wheeled rear axle. Each unit clamps to one end of the long load, and the front unit attaches to the bicycle.

A four-wheeled trailer is similar. The front part of a four-wheeled trailer could be a commercial bicycle trailer, with a home-built pivoting platform on top. The rear part is a two-wheeled axle.

These trailers may seem strange, but they have their uses: to haul lumber around a construction site, or to pull a canoe down to the water.

SPECIAL LOAD-CARRYING BIKES

Tricycles and other load-carrying bicycles often are more effective than motorized trucks for short-distance hauling. They are slower, but their advantages are their low cost, quietness, ability to park in places where motorized vehicles are not permitted, and the absence of polluting exhaust fumes. For indoor warehouse work, vending, short-haul delivery work, and grounds maintenance work, they are often the most effective vehicles. These bicycles and tricycles are commercially available.

An ordinary small-wheeled bike such as a folding bike comfortably carries heavy loads because of the low center of gravity of its rack and the extra strength of its wheels. This bicycle carries heavy loads without any great sacrifice of normal riding qualities.

Many varieties of adapted bicycles perform delivery work and work the world around. A standard bicycle with a smaller front wheel carries a large load well.

One step further is the two front-wheeled tricycle widely used for deliveries and vending. In its most common form this is a bit

clumsy to steer. If one front wheel hits a bump, it tends to turn the entire front box. But on paved city streets, it is thoroughly practical.

A two rear-wheeled tricycle steers more easily. Use double freewheel drive to both rear wheels for best traction. Yet even with drive to only one of the two rear wheels, a two rear-wheeled tricycle is thoroughly practical on paved roads. A tricycle with two rear wheels can pull a two-wheeled semitrailer to haul long loads, making a simpler arrangement than a bicycle with a four-wheeled trailer.

BIKE AS A TOW TRUCK

By mounting a quick-release front hub firmly to your bike's rear rack, your bike can become a tow truck for another bike. In this towing jig, the quick-release hub is clamped inside an aluminum tube which is bolted to the rack. The rack is reinforced, because the towed bike places heavy side stresses on it. The towed bike's front wheel is removed and tied to the frame. The front fork is placed into the towing jig, and off you go. This is a do-it-yourself arrangement, not yet commercially available.

RULES OF THUMB: LOAD CARRYING

1. Carry the load on the bicycle, not on yourself. Don't carry anything in your hands. A small backpack is usable, but a large one is uncomfortable and dangerous.

2. Organize your load. For the commuter or shopper, the handlebar bag is the "glove compartment," the saddlebag is the wardrobe, and the rear rack is the carry-all.

3. Buy equipment as you need it. A rear rack belongs on any bicycle used for trans-

portation. It'll carry most items. Second on the list to buy is the handlebar bag, third the saddlebag.

4. Use available cardboard boxes on your rear rack when shopping. They save you time, money, and hassle.

5. Secure a load carefully, so it will have the minimum effect on steering and so it will stay put. Loose loads can dump themselves — and you. Things that get caught in the spokes can stop a wheel and send you flying over the handlebars.

6. Locate the load as low and as near the middle of the bicycle as you can. Balance it, with some of it up front for minimum effect on handling.

7. Make sure the load doesn't hide your bike's lights and reflectors. Buy light-colored bags for visibility.

8. Test the load by pushing on it, and test the bike's handling before you take it out into traffic. Check every once in a while as you ride that things aren't coming loose.

9. Adapt your riding to the load. Pedal lightly and quickly. Take it easier on bumps. Learn to compensate for slower steering.

10. Plastic trash can liners are handy to protect a load in case it rains.

11. Have a plan to deal with a load when you park your bicycle. Buy bags that attach and remove easily. A large frameless backpack is useful to carry the load when you're off the bicycle.

CARRYING PASSENGERS

The title probably makes you think of the Chinese rickshaw or Indian pedicab which are in effect tricycle taxis. These are for adult passengers who for one reason or another are not riding their own bicycle. There may be some use for these in our time and place — for example, to take an invalid for a quiet, pleasant stroll. But other forms of public transportation are more versatile than the tricycle taxi for most uses.

A TANDEM

A tandem provides a unique riding experience. It is a way that two people of different strengths and abilities can ride together comfortably. For teaching proper riding techniques it is an unbeatable tool. With two strong riders it is fun and fast — with twice the power and only 30 percent more air resistance, it travels 10 percent faster on level

Bike tows bike.

ground than a single bike.

A good tandem is expensive, and maintaining it is more troublesome than maintaining a standard bike, because it takes more wear and tear. Yet there are times when a tandem is the most effective transportation between two points:

1. When two people are traveling together to and from an event. This could be a good choice for two people who work at the same place and live near each other.

2. As a taxi for a visually impaired person. Also a tandem provides a fine opportunity for a visually impaired person to get aerobic exercise.

If you are riding a tandem alone to pick up someone, you must tie the rear pedals to the cranks so that the toe clips don't drag in corners.

There is much to learn about riding a tandem and taking care of one. If you are considering buying and using a tandem, avoid double trouble — find an experienced tandem rider to help you get started.

CARRYING CHILDREN

For many of us, carrying passengers means carrying children. There are several ways to carry children, depending on their age and the equipment you have available. When carrying very small children, especially, it is wise to take special safety precautions because they can't protect themselves in the event of a fall the way older children and adults can. Also, if you are pedaling and the child is not, remember that you must dress differently. The wind that cools you will feel unpleasantly cold to the child.

For safety, it is best to belt a baby into a roll cage like a race-car driver. Then the baby will be protected even if the bike falls over.

The good, safe way to carry a baby is in a child-carrier bicycle trailer or on a cargo tricycle. You may have to construct roll bars over and in front of the seat, if the cargo box doesn't extend high enough to provide protection. A padded bar across the front of the seat at high chest level lets the baby sleep while riding.

You may modify a rear child seat made for a bicycle similarly. The baby will be closer to you than when riding in a trailer, though not a tricycle. But a fall will likely be more disturbing to the baby, because it will be from a greater height. Don't ride with a baby in a backpack or carrier. If you take a fall, you could land on the baby. A front-pack carrier, on the other hand, is reasonably safe. Your arms and legs will protect the baby. You must use upright handlebars.

When riding with a baby on a tricycle or in a trailer, it is best to take low-traffic routes. There is some extra difficulty in traffic, because the trailer and tricycle are wider than a bicycle. Also, the baby is exposed to more concentrated exhaust fumes riding lower to the ground than you are.

You can continue to use a trailer or cargo tricycle from six months till riding age, but a child seat is the most common way to carry a child up to four years old.

A child seat should mount at the rear of the bike, like a rear rack. Front-mounted child seats are a bad idea because they disturb the bike's handling, and the child is in the way of the controls.

For safety, a child seat must have a high back and sides, and footrests. Get spoke guard plates which tie onto the bike's seat-stays; a child's foot can be very seriously injured if it goes into the spokes. The seat must have a seat belt, and if there is not a roll bar higher than the child's head, the child must wear a helmet for safety. A chest strap helps prevent the child's weight from shifting.

It is easiest to use a child seat with an open-frame bike, because the seat prevents you from swinging your leg over the back of the bike.

For a child more than four years old, a trailer or tricycle works better than a child seat on the back of a bike.

A CHILD ON A TANDEM

After five or six years old, a child can help pedal on a tandem. A child may find it very exciting to be in on the action, rather than just coming along as baggage.

A tandem is adapted for a child by installing a raised crankset which the child can reach. The crankset is attached to the rear seat tube, and the child sits in the normal rear position on the tandem. The rear handlebars will have to reach back far enough for the child.

To get the most use out of the tandem, you may wish to make it convertible so either a child or an adult can ride on the back. The raised crankset and child's seat can be attached and removed in minutes, if you use wing nut and quick-release fittings. By driving the rear wheel from the tandem's front crankset, you can tie the normal rear cranks horizontal to get them out of the way when using the raised crankset.

WHEN YOUR CHILD BEGINS TO RIDE

Most children love to ride bicycles. A bicycle is the only independent transportation children have that is faster than walking.

Up to the age of about 10, most children can't handle traffic. But they know the pedestrian rules, and can ride on sidewalks, bikepaths, and off-road trails. The most common accident is to ride straight out into the street without looking — warn against this. As children approach 10, they may be allowed to ride on very quiet streets. From about 10 to 14 they are ready to learn to use the streets in light to moderate traffic; from 14 on, to participate fully in traffic with proper instruction. The ages given here are rough guidelines. Base your decisions on your own child's abilities.

Proper instruction is crucial at all stages. Many parents, teachers, and police limit their instruction to telling children to keep out of traffic. This is good temporary advice, but like most advice to beginners, it should not be the final word. It is the same as telling children "don't go into the water" and teaching them nothing more about swimming. Children know that older people ride bicycles in the streets. Sooner or later, the children will take to the streets, with or without parents' permission. They must know that there is a right way to do it. If you are a parent of a bicycling child, or a neighbor of one, your example as a bicyclist is the most important factor in the child's learning to ride properly and safely. If you cultivate the idea that there is a correct, grownup way to ride, the child will likely want to learn how.

CHAPTER TWELVE

COMPLETE TRANSPORTATION

By using your bike intelligently, you can significantly expand its use. Transportation planners call this mixed-mode travel. You travel the longer distance by car, bus, boat or plane. At the beginning and end of the trip, and for connections, you use a bike.

This way, several people traveling in one car can each have independent transportation when the car reaches its destination. Or you can step off a train, plane, or bus in another city with your own way to get around. Your bicycle becomes the "glue" connecting different transportation systems. It has an almost magical way of smoothing out bad crosstown connections and eliminating the "stuck in the middle of nowhere" feeling you'd get while waiting to be picked up at a station or airport.

The best bicycle for mixed-mode travel is a folding bicycle. In a minute or two, it becomes a piece of luggage which goes on any bus, train or plane, or into any car trunk. A standard bike goes into many cars and onto many public carriers without disassembly.

BIKE AND WALK

For a very short trip, under one mile or so, walking is often faster and more convenient than bicycling, especially if you have to clothe yourself specially for bicycling, unlock and lock your bike, load and unload baggage, and walk part of the trip from where you've parked the bike. Walking's good for you, too. It uses your legs in ways bicycling doesn't.

If you're taking a longer trip to shop in a concentrated area, like a shopping mall, it makes sense for you to park your bike and walk between stores. But if you're shopping or running errands with stops spread even a little ways apart, you get around much faster by riding and parking at each stop. That's why it is in the interest of downtown merchants to provide convenient parking, and that's how bicycling can help preserve their stores and the downtown area. Bicycling can allow you to use stores near where you live to run your errands quicker than either walking or driving.

CAR AND BIKE

The car and the bicycle complement each other. The trips the bicycle is best for are the ones the car is worst for. That's because every car trip has a high startup cost in time, money, and wear on the car. Here's the measure of the startup cost:

. . . About 90 percent of the wear on your car's engine happens in the first 15 minutes of driving. This is because the choke pours liquid gasoline into the cold engine, washing oil from the cylinder walls. Also, the oil is cold and thick, leaving some parts of the engine unlubricated. It takes time to get everywhere it needs to be.

. . . Your car gets only about 10 percent of its normal gas mileage in a quarter-mile trip, 25 percent in a one-mile trip, and 60 percent in a five-mile trip, also because the engine is cold. It's burning extra gasoline just to warm the engine.

. . . On average, the time you spend looking for a parking place and walking from it to your destination doesn't change depending on how long the trip is.

So by riding your bicycle for the shorter trips it does best, you'll make your car last much longer, you'll save much more gas than you'd imagine, and you'll get where you're going faster.

If you have both a car and a bicycle and either breaks down, you have a "backup system." To transport heavy loads or passengers, you take the car (but don't write off the bike for this). You use the car for any trip you feel is too long or difficult to make by bicycle. As you become more experienced, you'll make more and longer trips by bicycle. It's all a matter of self-confidence.

SUCCESSFUL COMBINATIONS

CAR-BIKE #1

Suppose you live outside a city, and work in the city where parking is expensive. But it is too far for you to ride comfortably, or you have to take a bridge which doesn't allow bikes.

Then put your bike on the bike rack and drive most of the way to work. Park your car at a friend's house in a residential street or in a shopping center parking lot, for free. Then ride the rest of the way in to work.

You avoid the traffic jams and save your parking fee. At the end of the day you have the car in case you want to do some heavy shopping or pick up a friend.

If there is someone else who lives near you and works at the same place, you can do the "change horses" as a carpool, and save even more.

CAR-BIKE #2

If you have to take your car somewhere and leave it, say for repairs, or to lend to someone, take the bike along and ride it home. Do the same thing backward if you have to go pick up the car. By making a one-way trip on your bike, you save someone else a two-way trip in a second car. Even if it takes longer to get home on your bike, you come out way ahead on total time and money.

CAR-BIKE #3

Sometimes you'll want to go downtown shopping with a friend, in a car, but your friend has another errand to run afterward. Or you might decide to go out to dinner with someone from work; or you might be out late at night and tired, and someone offers you a ride home.

We've mentioned that you need to plan for round trips when you commute by bike. But if you have a folding bike, you can make one-way trips without worrying about how you'll get back. A bike with quick-release wheels will fit into most cars, but you may have to put it in the back seat rather than the trunk. That's a security problem if you park the car. Also the car's upholstery could be soiled.

A solution to the upholstery problem is to keep a car-bike rack at work to install on the car of whoever offers you a ride. Buy a bike rack which folds compactly enough to carry with you on the bike.

CAR-BIKE #4

Let's say that the food is terrible in the company cafeteria where you work. There's a little diner up the road a bit with good food. And you have a friend who works in another company nearby who might join you there for lunch.

But your car is parked way out in the parking lot every day. It takes you too long to get to it, get it started, drive it, and park it. Or perhaps you came to work on the bus and don't have a car. It's too far to walk to the diner. You don't have enough time to eat before you have to start back.

So keep a bicycle at work. Ride it to the diner, eat with your friend, and ride back. Save money, save time, get to see your friend, eat better food, and get some exercise on your lunch break.

THE "EMPTY TAXI" TRIP

Many people who advocate carpools correctly point out how inefficient it is to drive alone in a car. But there's an even worse situation than driving alone — the "empty taxi" trip in which one person is driving the car to pick up another. In an "empty taxi" trip, not only is the driver wasting time for this trip, the car is using gasoline and in effect has no passengers at all.

If your household has children, or handicapped or elderly people who can't drive, you may find yourself making large numbers of "empty taxi" trips. And in a one-car household, one person often will leave another off and then drive home because he or she needs the car later on.

If you make large numbers of "empty taxi" trips, it may make sense to own a second car, perhaps an older car which you can use for shorter trips. But a less expensive way to cut down on these trips is through public transportation and bicycling.

Since most "empty taxi" trips are short, you can replace them with bicycle trips. Children, too, once they are old enough to ride safely, can do most of their around-town traveling by bicycle. But for longer trips and for people who can't drive or bike, the best answer is public transportation. Without it, you have no choice but to make "empty taxi" trips. For this reason, public transportation is an essential service for a community to provide for itself.

BIKEPOOL #1

At the beginning and end of the trip in a carpool where people have to go in different directions, there's only one car! Using bicycles along with a carpool is an excellent way to eliminate "empty taxi" trips and make carpooling more convenient.

You go somewhere in the car and take bikes with you to use there. The "fan-out" bikepool is the most common bikepool, because it works beautifully for recreational trips, ranging from an afternoon jaunt to a summer vacation.

Everyone stashes bikes on the bike rack and piles into the car. You drive to a nice place. Then you take the bikes off the car. Everyone now can go exploring and sightseeing at his or her own speed. On a longer vacation you can often park the car and hardly use it until you drive back home. You use the bikes for visiting and errands. Children have independence, so parents don't have to drive them around.

The same plan also is very useful for shopping trips and errands. Suppose you live on a farm several miles from town. Then take two or three family members, or neighbors, and bikes with you when you go to town. Once there, you take your bikes off the car. Everyone runs errands. If you buy something too big to carry on the bike, you leave it at the store to pick up. At a prearranged time, you all come back to the car, or call in to a nearby phone booth. Then one person drives "sweep-up," picking up people, packages, and bikes until you're all back together. You not only save gas, but everyone gets more done because you don't spend so much time parking and walking.

BIKEPOOL #2

The most serious problem getting a carpool to go to work is organization. The person who drives on any one day has to get up early to pick up everyone else. And, on the road, the driver is out of touch with everyone else. If someone is late, everyone has to wait, or the later person loses the ride and the driver has made a useless side trip. If the car gets stuck or the driver gets lost, everyone is late. Carpooling to work is a great idea, but these problems discourage many people from using it.

By using bicycles to get to a carpool, you can solve all of these problems. Instead of the driver picking everyone up, everyone rides bicycles to the driver's home. Anyone who won't make it can phone in. The driver's car is already warming up when people arrive. The bicycles go into the garage or onto the car's bike rack. Everyone climbs into the car and drives off to work.

The driver saves gas, and everyone saves time. Instead of sitting in the driver's car while it makes the rounds, you enjoy an early morning bike ride.

For the ride home, you take the car to the driver's home and then ride your bike home. Or the driver may leave one or more people off at their homes. It is easy to organize this for the return trip because everyone is already in the car to plan the route together. One-way bikepooling takes the pressure off if the weather turns bad or if you have to bring home something you can't carry on the bicycle.

A large bike-to-carpool setup could have several cars ready to leave in the morning from the same spot, so the number of cars leaving would depend on how many people showed up. This way, nobody would be under any pressure to use the carpool every day, and nobody would have to make arrangements in advance for a ride. One car with a bike rack could be designated as a sweep-up car, and would pick up any rider who phoned in with bike trouble on the way to the pickup point.

BIKEPOOL #3

There are many ways to use a sweep-up car — commonly called a "sag wagon" by bicyclists. We've already mentioned its use in fan-out and funnel-in bikepools.

Here's another way to use a sweep-up car. You arrange with a group of people to ride bikes to work together, starting at one point. You're riding all the way, not switching to a car this time. But someone in a car starts out from the same point, following the same route and timed to arrive when you do. If any bicyclist has a flat tire or other trouble along the route, the car comes to the rescue. Bicyclists can take turns driving the car on different days, or there may be someone who works with you who drives or carpools the same route and will be happy to drive sweep-up.

Sweep-up service is most useful when a group of people is first trying out riding to work, and people are not confident of arriving on time. It is also helpful for a group of high-speed riders who like to ride their fast but finicky racing bikes to work.

Sweep-up or sag wagon service is a common feature of large bicycle rallies and road races. A car either follows the bicyclists or waits in reserve to pick up anyone who has trouble.

BIKEPOOL #4

Imagine someone who works with you and drives to work lives farther from work than you do, but a little off to the side. To pick you up for a carpool, this person would have to make a side trip.

So you ride your bike over to meet this person at some spot on the way to work. When you meet, you put your bike in the car or on a bike rack, and drive in to work.

This plan works even better if the spot where you meet is a diner or restaurant where the two of you can have breakfast together. Then whichever of you arrives first can order. As steady customers, you may even be able to arrange for a safe place to park your bike.

BIKEPOOL #5

With your bike, you have the choice of many different carpools. The driver of a carpool does not have to make special arrangements to pick you up; you only have to make sure there will be room for you in the car. Since most people still drive to work one or two to a car, you should have no problem. You could ride with a different person everyday if you wanted.

This way, you take a morning fun ride of any length you choose, finishing at the home of the person with whom you are carpooling to work. If you like to exercise and to explore different roads in your community, you will appreciate the variety. If one carpooling plan breaks down, you can instantly switch to another.

To set up a carpool-of-the-day arrangement for yourself, just talk it over with people who live within bicycling distance of you and drive to work. Get their approval and their phone numbers. Then, at work or by phone after work, set up your plan with the person you want to ride with the next day.

BIKE-CAR TRADEOFFS

If you live alone, you may need to keep a car just for yourself even though you use your bicycle for most trips. If you live in a household with other people who drive, you may get by with fewer cars by using bikes.

You will have to make some compromises to cut down the number of cars your household keeps. There will be times when two people want to use the car at once, and there will be times when one of you has to go out of the way to give another one a lift in a car. Most households are close enough to work out such conflicts. Some neighbors readily agree to carpooling arrangements. A large family or an extended group like a summer camp, school staff, or intentional community can keep cars for use by whoever needs them. The larger the group, the larger the number of people who share each car, because the need for cars averages out better from day to day. Also, it becomes practical to have specialized vehicles such as a bus, a heavy truck, and a small car for different uses. Motor pools have been used for many years in industry and government. If you can arrange one for your personal use, it will save you money and pay dividends in flexibility.

You get the most for your money out of a car, like any tool, if you use it often. There are fixed costs in owning a car, like its purchase price, insurance, depreciation, and deterioration (which occurs just from its sitting unused in the driveway).

Generally, it can be said that if you are a two-car family and use one car less than once a week, you'd be better off selling it. If you own one car and use it less than once a month, you'd be better off selling it. Then you depend on taxis, rental cars and trucks, delivery services, public transportation, and your bike instead. And you'll come out ahead.

Another way to cut costs is to keep an old car. The two largest costs in owning a new car are the purchase plan installments and collision insurance. The cost of gasoline will come in third behind these until it reaches about $4 per gallon. For occasional, around-town use, a car without collision insurance makes the best sense even if it gets poor gas mileage and may break down in a few months. If it breaks down or gets damaged in an accident, you get to make the simple decision — will it cost more to repair or to buy another?

THE RIGHT CAR FOR A CYCLIST

If you get into the habit of taking bicycles with you on trips, whether for recreation or for bikepooling to work, it's usually more convenient if the car is big enough so you can put the bicycles inside.

But even more importantly, if you're using bicycles for most of your short individual trips, you'll be using the car much less. The balance of needs for the car will change. You will use it mainly for longer trips, group trips, and trips to haul large, heavy loads.

So if you use bicycles for the short, individual trips, owning a truck, van, or large car with a utility trailer could be more economical for you.

CARRYING A BIKE ON OR IN A CAR

It's best for the bike if you can carry it in the car. If you have a van, truck, station wagon or hatchback, you'll have no problem. Inside the car, the bike is protected from the weather and more secure from theft. It's best if the bike is covered when you park, so a potential thief will not see it. A long cable lock from the bike to the undercarriage of one of the seats will discourage theft further.

A bike with wheels removed will fit into the trunk of a large sedan. It will also fit into the back seat of almost any car, even a Volkswagen beetle, though you're going to have to protect the upholstery.

Using large hooks with threaded attachments, you can hang up a bike on the inside back or side wall of a van or bus. Tie it in with bungee cords, so it can't rattle around.

These are the more secure and weatherproof ways to carry a bike. They're best for long trips, where you won't be using the bike until you get where you're going. But for shorter trips, it's more convenient to mount the bike on the outside of the car. It's easier on the upholstery, too. With a van or truck, you could just use hooks. With a car, you'll usually want a car-bike rack: a long cable lock is most practical for this use. If your car has an alarm system, you could also have a loop wired into it to set off the alarm if the bike is disturbed.

SELECTING A CAR-BIKE RACK

A car-bike rack makes carrying your bike easy with many cars. Some bike racks can carry as many as four bikes; even if you can fit a bike into your car, the bike rack is useful when more than one person needs to bring a bike along.

There are two main types of bike racks: those that mount on the roof, holding the bikes either upright or upside down, and those that mount on the rear deck or bumper. You can use an ordinary (nonbike) roof rack to carry one or two bikes, though attaching them takes extra time.

For commuting use, the rear bike rack is generally most convenient. The bikes and the rack go on and off the car quicker. Also, you can drive the car through a low garage door opening without damaging your bike. With a roof rack, you may someday do this by mistake, or have to get out of the car in a pouring rain just outside your garage door to take your bike down.

Earlier in this chapter, we recommended keeping a rack at work in case you have to drive away with someone after work. A rack for this purpose needs to fit a wide variety of cars and to attach and remove easily. Some are more versatile than others. But here are some things to look for.

Bikes on a rear rack may obstruct vision in your car's inside rearview mirror, and may be vulnerable to damage if you back into

something. Some hold the bikes so low they could drag on the ground as you go over bumps. Different racks work better on different cars. Make sure the rack fits the car.

For use on your car, try several racks until you find the one which works out best. Try to get the bikes above the bumper. Make sure bike tires and plastic parts will be away from the car's exhaust pipe because hot exhaust gases can melt them.

USING A BIKE RACK

Tie the bike down securely with bungee cords. If you care about your car's finish — or your bike's — watch for places where they might scratch each other; pad them or separate them. As we've recommended, keep the bikes above the bumper where they're safer; removing quick-release wheels often makes things easier. Keep bikes from obstructing the car's taillights.

As you drive, the extra weight of three or four bikes may affect the handling of a light car, so take this into account. The problem is not as severe if the bikes don't hang way off the back of the car. Remember the bikes when you back up. If the bikes overhang the sides of the car, take extra care driving through narrow passages.

Rain and dust are an extra problem for bikes being carried on a rack. High car speeds can drive them into the bearings and frame tubes. Sealed bearings are helpful, and so is a drain hole in your bike's bottom bracket, if you drive much with your bike in the rain.

If you go away from the car and leave your bike on the rack, you must lock it somehow. A long cable lock usually works best; you can thread it through the bike's wheels and frame and attach it to the rack, the car's bumper, or the trunk lid handle. If the rack can be removed without tools, or without unlocking the car's trunk, you'll have to lock the bike to the car or you could easily lose bike and rack together!

COST OF COMMUTING

Figures for commuting by car and by bike in Boston during 1978 came to $1,180 and $68, respectively. The figure for commuting by car included gas, tolls, parking fees, and extra wear and tear on the car. The figure for bicycling included the cost of the bike, spread out over its life; the cost of maintaining it; and the cost of taking public transportation on winter days when street conditions were difficult.

Savings for bike-car combination trips and bikepooling trips would be lower than for pure bike trips, but still considerable, assuming that you still own a car and use it for longer trips.

If family use of bikes means that the family gets by with one car instead of two, then add another $1,000 to the yearly savings.

PUBLIC TRANSPORTATION

Except for air travel, public transportation always has a lower cost than car travel. Public transportation saves you the trouble of driving and often gives you leisure time to work or read. Public transportation pollutes less and takes up less space — it's also safer. Rail travel, long-distance buses, and airplanes all can be faster and more convenient than driving, as long as you can get to the station easily.

Getting to the station is the problem with public transportation. That's where your bicycle enters the picture.

BIKE TO PUBLIC TRANSPORTATION

Let's assume that you have good public transportation service in your community, only you live too far from a station to walk there comfortably. Either you have to drive to the station, or you drive all the way to work and don't use the public transportation at all.

Then bike to the station instead. Avoid using your car for a short trip of the kind which wears it out the most quickly, and save gas. Leave the car at home so someone else can use it. Save a parking fee or save someone the time to drive with you and take the car back home. Even if your average trip time on the bike is a little longer than it is in the car, you can start out later without worrying about missing your train or bus because you're immune to traffic jams.

In many cases, it makes very good sense to bike to public transportation. The problem is, though, where to park it.

Your bike will be parked at the station all day, every day. It's got to be there and in working order when you get back every evening.

Several public transportation systems have installed bicycle lockers at their stations. These systems rent the lockers by the month. You sign up for a locker and you take a key. Then you roll your bike in every day and have peace of mind.

If your station already has lockers, and if they haven't all been taken, count yourself lucky. But chances are that you're going to have to use a little imagination to park your bicycle safely.

One solution to the problem is to keep a trashmo bike just for this trip — a $20 bike with a $30 lock. You use removable lights, or lights you wear, for your return trip after dark. Then you can lock the bike anywhere in the neighborhood.

Another solution is to make friends with someone who lives near or has a business close to the station. You then can arrange to park your bike at this person's place, either as a favor or in return for rent.

Some commuters keep two bikes, one for each end of their daily ride on public transportation.

BIKE AND CITY BUS, TROLLEY, SUBWAY, OR COMMUTER RAIL

Policies on carrying bikes vary from one place to another, and from one system to another even in the same city. You find out the policy by calling your local transit authority, or even better, by talking with members of the area's bicycle commuting advocacy group. But here are some guidelines.

BIKE AND INTERCITY BUSES

Almost all intercity bus services will take your bike, though most will require you to put it in a container. There may be an extra fee for the bike — call ahead to find out. Most bus companies do not provide the container, so bring your own. If the container is a bike bag, you can ride to the station, if it's a cardboard box, you can't.

Often, a bus will have an empty baggage compartment, and then the driver may let you put your bike in without using a container. You can't count on this, but if it doesn't matter to you whether you get on the first bus, you can try it. But remember that the bus will shake around quite a bit. If it's not in a container, your bike might slide around on the metal floor of the baggage compartment. Lay it on its left side to protect the drive train, and if possible wedge it in or tie it in with bungee cords so it won't move. Some buses have

baggage quilts which you can wrap around your bicycle to prevent damage. But expect a few scratches. You may have to adjust the fenders so they don't rub, and undo a few other minor damages.

Roll or carry your bike to the bus yourself. Load it yourself, or see it loaded. At stops on the way, keep an eye on the baggage loading and unloading. Baggage sometimes gets shifted from one bus to another, or gets lost temporarily or permanently. Don't let this happen to your bicycle.

TROLLEYS AND SUBWAYS

The situation on trolley and subway systems is mixed. Many trolley cars are very cramped; there's room only for a folding bike in a bag. On the other hand, many subway and commuter rail lines have ample room for standard bikes, and some have welcomed bikes on board. PATH trains between New York City and New Jersey take bikes during off-peak hours, as does San Francisco's BART system. The most advanced situation is in West Berlin, Germany, where nobody is allowed on the last car of any commuter train without a bike. For rush-hour use, a special car for bikers would seem the best solution when standard bikes are used; until bikers and transportation planners get together to work this out, a folding bicycle with a bag will solve the problem handily.

Even where bikes cannot be accommodated on all lines of a commuter rail system because of equipment limitations or revolving door turnstiles at stations, it makes good sense to work for exceptions where no alternate route exists. The PATH trains are an example. They are the only way a bicyclist can get between New Jersey and Lower Manhattan, because the Lincoln and Holland tunnels take only motor vehicles. New York and New Jersey bicyclists were successful in convincing authorities that the service was needed, and that it would provide extra customers during off-peak hours. It has turned out well for everyone. But as more people take to riding bikes to work, and as transportation funding allows, all-hour bicycle service on rail lines is the ideal goal for closing the "missing links" in the bicycle road network. You can help this along by working with your area's bicycle advocacy group.

BIKE AND RAIL

Amtrak will take a bike in a container on any train with a baggage car, between any stops with baggage service. Canadian and Mexican railways do not require a container. Due to a shortage of baggage cars and personnel, not all trains and not all stations have a baggage car service. Amtrak sells bike boxes, but they are not always available. Call to find out, or bring your own.

Security on Amtrak baggage cars is generally good, since baggage is loaded and unloaded only by the Amtrak baggage handler. If your bicycle is bagged, and in the overhead rack, return to your seat to watch it whenever the train is about to make a stop.

As of this writing, it is official Amtrak policy to take folding bikes as carry-on luggage. This is practical because the overhead luggage racks in railroad cars are usually much more spacious than those in buses. Also, trains are smooth — there is a much lower risk of luggage shaking loose. However, we strongly recommend that you put your folding bicycle into an unmarked bag before you carry it out to the train. Not all Amtrak personnel know that folding bikes are allowed. It doesn't work very well to get into an argument with the conductor of your train five minutes before it's scheduled to leave. And chain dirt on your fellow passengers' luggage can make

your situation even more precarious. But with the bike in a bag, there's no problem. Taken apart and hidden in a bag, a standard bicycle also fits the overhead racks.

OTHER TRANSPORTATION OPTIONS

There are several other modes of transport you can use with your bicycle in addition to the standard modes listed earlier.

SPECIAL BICYCLE SHUTTLE SERVICE

Shuttle service exists in some places to fill in "missing links" in the road network, particularly, through bridges and tunnels built during the dark ages when the car was king.

This service may take the form of bicycle vans, locking bike racks on the back of buses, or arranging for police or tollgate personnel to ferry bicyclists across bridges or through tunnels (mostly in rural areas and used by bicycle tourists). Where bicycle traffic is heavy, shuttle service can work efficiently as part of another service already provided, such as a bus service, or on its own. In rural areas where it serves primarily bicycle tourists, it may be combined with bridge police patrol work.

If traffic jams up in rush hour, it works better to ferry bicyclists on rail or boat lines. But where bridge and tunnel traffic moves smoothly, shuttle service can work very well.

Your local bicycle advocacy group or transportation authorities can tell you what shuttle service is available in your community. If it is available, use it. If there are problems with it, work to solve them. If there isn't any shuttle service, push for it or for another way to fill in the "missing links."

BIKE AND TAXI

Bicycling is supposed to save you money, so you may ask "why a taxi?"

Taking a taxi has its uses, though it isn't something you'd want to do every day. If you've managed to get rid of a car in your household by using bicycles, then using a taxi once in a while is going to cost you pennies on the dollar compared with what you're saving on the car.

A taxi is your bailout, your tow truck, and your delivery van. Take a taxi if your bike breaks down and you've got to get somewhere in a hurry; if, in the middle of a long trip, you come up on a tunnel or a bridge which doesn't take bikes; or if you're caught without your bicycle trailer and have to take home a new TV set or 60 pounds of groceries (or if you're riding off in another direction, just send the groceries home with the taxi to someone who's waiting to pick them up). The time you save by doing this is often worth the money you spend on the taxi.

When you hail a taxi or call the taxi company, explain that you have a bicycle and be sure to get a Checker cab or a station wagon. The Checker is most convenient unless you're carrying a long load that needs the station wagon — you can roll a bicycle right into the space behind the Checker's front seat.

BIKE AND BOAT

Almost all boat services will take bikes, though usually at an extra fee. Check ahead for the rules, fares, and reservations. Many coastal and river cities have commuter ferries, though many of these have been re-placed with bridges.

On a ferry you don't have to worry about your bike being stolen, because there's no place for anyone to ride it to. Just get back to your bike a few minutes before docking to check on it and prepare it to roll. It's most convenient to be either the first or the last down the gangplank.

One thing you do need to watch on a ferry: make sure your bike is out of the range of spray — or at least cover your bike. Salt water can get rust started very quickly.

HITCHHIKING WITH A BIKE

In a rural area where taxi service is poor, hitchhiking is your best bet to get to the next bike shop for repairs, or to cross a bridge which unexpectedly does not allow bikes.

Fewer vehicles can pick you up with your bike, yet your luck will usually be better. Drivers are not as afraid of you, because they can see why you are hitchhiking. Your luck will be even better if you display a large sign reading "ACROSS THE BRIDGE," "BIKE SHOP," or whatever your destination may be. You may want to carry a Magic Marker and a couple of sheets of cardboard with you in case you need them to make signs. Or hold up your front wheel — this is a well-known signal in Europe.

Because you can't tell how long you'll have to wait for a ride, hitchhiking makes sense only as a bailout. Hitchhiking also has its drawbacks. Some sensible precautions: don't hitchhike in cities; look for your ride if possible in a place where cars are stopped for other reasons besides your hitchhiking — at the phone booths at a bridge toll plaza, for instance. You pick your ride, instead of the other way around. Talk with the driver before getting into the car. Only accept a ride with someone who feels safe — families and police cars are best. Even where hitchhiking is prohibited, police will help you, because with your bike you are a person in distress, not a hitchhiker. Memorize the car's license number. Never let the car out of your sight while the bike is in it. Get out of the car at a public place where other people can see you.

BIKE AND AIRPLANE

Almost all airlines will take your bicycle. Some require a container and others do not. There may be a moderate extra baggage fee. Folding bicycles usually go as regular baggage, at no extra charge. Since they usually pack baggage into bins before it goes onto the plane, your bicycle is not much extra trouble for them. And there's not much of a theft problem. Airlines will insure your bicycle against theft, though not against damage. Have a "fragile" tag put on your bike's container at the baggage counter. Then the baggage handlers will likely put it on top of the other baggage.

Enough airlines rent or sell bike containers so you will never have to bring one with you, at least not to a major airport. If the airline you are taking does not have a container, get one at the ticket counter of another airline.

When transferring from one plane to another, try to pick up and hand over your bicycle yourself so it will be with you at your destination.

When possible, many travelers prefer to fly their bicycles without containers. They just tie the handlebars straight with a bungee cord between the front rim and the bottom bracket and turn the pedals around to face the inside. Their theory is that the bike will be treated more carefully if it looks like what it is. This is an unproven theory, but the bike certainly is

ready to ride sooner if it does come off the plane undamaged.

If your bike goes unpackaged you may have to pick it up at a separate place from the usual baggage carousel. Check with the skycaps at the carousel to find where to pick it up.

SHIPPING YOUR BICYCLE AS FREIGHT

When shipping your bike, it's best to break it down as small as you can. Then it's less vulnerable to damage and less likely to be stolen. Freight rates may be cheaper, too.

Use a heavy cardboard box, preferably double walled. Tie down all loose parts of the bicycle inside, or stuff the box with wood shreds, plastic peanuts, wadded newspaper, or a similar packing material. You can get this material for free at the receiving desk or in the trash of almost any industrial firm in your area.

Do not label the box conspicuously as a bicycle, but label it as fragile.

Insure with the shipper for the value of the bike. Have the bike appraised at a bike shop before you ship it, so you'll have firm evidence of its value. Allow plenty of time for the bicycle to arrive.

Ship by Greyhound package express, UPS, parcel post, or many trucking services. Use the Yellow Pages and call around to find which one will serve you best.

Shipping works best if you need to make a side trip on the way to the place you will be using your bicycle.

BIKES AS CARRY-ON LUGGAGE

A folding bicycle is best for daily short-hop travel using public transportation or a car. A regular bicycle takes too long to disassemble. But for longer trips between cities, the time you spend taking apart your bicycle and putting it back together is not as important. As we've noted, some public transportation, such as airlines, will take your bicycle without your having to do much to it. On a bus or train, or in a small car, you have more to do. The best thing for all situations is if you can make your bike into carry-on luggage. With a bike bag as camouflage, you can.

There are several different ways to take apart a bicycle for travel, depending on how small you have to make it.

1. Turn the pedals around to the inside and tie the front wheel straight with one of the toe straps. This is enough for many airlines.

2. Take the wheels off to get the bicycle into most cars.

3. Take off the front wheel, front fender, handlebars, pedals, and sometimes the seat to get the bike into most commercial bike boxes to travel by bus, train, or plane.

4. Take off the above plus the rear wheel, rear fender, and rack to get the bike into a commercial bike storage bag which is considered carry-on luggage on most rail and bus lines.

5. Leave the front wheel and front fender on the fork and take apart the headset. Remove the cranks for the most compact possible arrangement. This procedure is best if you're shipping your bike by freight.

BIKE DISASSEMBLY

1. Taking the wheels off is a quick way to make a bike a lot smaller. So quick-release wheels or wing nuts help. Hub gears take a little longer. Coaster brakes or other hub brakes are more difficult. They have a strap to the frame, besides the wheel nuts.

2. After the wheels, the next thing to take off is the fenders, if the bike has them. Fenders are also easily damaged without the wheels protecting them. Plastic fenders work best. To make it easy to remove fenders, run long fender bolts from the inside of the dropouts to the outside. With threaded dropout holes or epoxy glue, the bolts will stay in place by themselves. Use a nut and washer at the outer end of each bolt to hold the fender braces on. Where the fenders attach under the brake bolt nuts, you use a right-angled piece of sheet metal, such as a piece of reflector bracket, so you don't have to take off the brake bolt nuts. Use a rear fender which clips to the chainstay bridge, instead of bolting to it, so you don't have to use tools here.

3. To turn a front fork around backward for compactness, a centerpull brake cable hanger in the headset must clear the top tube, and you must be able to easily unhook the cable stirrup from the transverse cable.

4. To remove the saddle and seatpost, it's easiest if you use an Allen key seatpost clamp or a Sun Tour quick-release clamp. Mark the seatpost before you remove it so you can easily put it back to the same height.

5. To remove the handlebars, a stem with a wedge expander is best. The expander will usually drop down without hammering, or with a light tap. You can tie the handlebars to the top tube without disconnecting cables.

6. To remove the pedals or turn them around, make sure there's enough room to fit a common adjustable wrench in between the pedal body and the crank. Otherwise, you will have to carry a special pedal wrench. Some T.A. cranks do not have pedal holes all the way through — you can't turn the pedals around with them. Oil the pedal threads before replacing them.

7. Using a Shimano one-key release system, it is easier to remove cotterless cranks than to remove pedals. The one-key release fits most other brands of cranks besides Shimano, though not Stronglight or T.A. You can drill out Stronglight or T.A. steel dust-

caps to adapt to the Shimano system. Removing the cranks makes the bike substantially smaller; also, it protects the vulnerable chainwheels. But wipe off the axle ends and oil them before replacing the cranks to avoid excessive wear to the cranks' axle holes.

8. A rack attaches at the dropouts the same way as fenders do. If it attaches at the seatstays with eyelets or eyelet clamps, you can just pivot it down parallel to the seatstays. Racks such as the Pletscher must be attached at the seatstays with wing nuts for quickest removal.

9. A headset is quick to take apart and put back together if you use caged ball bearings. These are standard on Dura-ace and Campagnolo headsets, and you can buy them to fit many others. It also helps to mark the headset races so you can tighten them to the same spot without checking the adjustment.

10. If there's a light or generator on the front wheel or fork or fender, a plug and socket in the wires to the frame make it easier to separate them.

TOOLS AND SUPPLIES

To disassemble and reassemble your bike, be sure to have the following equipment in addition to your usual tools:

1. A thin wrench or a pin tool for the headset locknut.
2. A screwdriver for rack bolts.
3. A plastic bag to store headset bearing retainers; several small canvas bags from a surplus store for removed parts; and a bike bag or duffel bag large enough to hold the disassembled bike.
4. A rag to clean headset races after you've disassembled the headset.
5. Several bungee cords to tie disassembled parts to the bike frame.
6. Spare wheel nuts and fender bolt nuts in case you lose or strip any.
7. A 35 mm film can full of grease to relubricate headset bearings.
8. Hand cleaner and paper towels.
9. A small oil can to lubricate pedal threads, cotterless crank fittings, and nuts and bolts. Do not use grease here—it holds dirt, while oil washes it away.

Try the whole procedure out at home after you've prepared the bike, to work out snags and find out how long it takes.

Get to the station in plenty of time.

If there's not an obvious place to work on your bike, ask where there is one. It's at least moderately dirty work. You will find, however, the more proficient you become, the cleaner your hands will remain.

BIKE AND PUBLIC TRANSPORTATION

	BIKES ALLOWED	EXTRA CHARGE?	CONTAINER AVAIL-ABILITY	COMFORT	SECURITY	POSSIBILITY OF DAMAGE TO BIKE	CARRIER'S LIABILITY
URBAN bus, trolley, subway, rail	Folder, in bag. Other bikes off hours on some systems (usually rail).	Folder: no; other bike: usually.	None.	OK for distance covered.	Hold onto your bike—little problem.	You hold onto it—no problem.	At your own risk.
SUBURB to CITY bus, rail	Folder, in bag. Bike in container on bus with baggage compartment.	Folder: no; other bike: usually.	None.	OK for distance covered.	OK—watch at stops if bike is underneath bus.	Can get scratched, minor damage.	At your own risk, carry on; theft insurance in baggage hold.
INTERCITY bus	Bike in container.	Yes, if in box—no, if disguised in bag.	None.	OK up to 150 miles; sleeping is uncomfortable.	Watch stops; keep your bike on the same bus.	Can get scratched, minor damage.	Theft insurance.
INTERCITY rail	Bike in container on some trains; folder is carry on.	Yes, unless carry on.	At some stations.	To 250 miles or indefinite, with sleeping compartment.	OK in baggage car; be with carry-ons at stops.	Unless carry-on, can get scratched, minor damage. Some rough baggage handling.	Theft and damage insurance.
AIR	Yes. Container needed sometimes.	Sometimes, or counts against baggage allowance.	Almost all airports.	3,000 miles at a hop. Jet lag!	Good.	Can get scratched, minor damage. Occasional serious damage.	Theft, but not damage insurance.
TAXI	With open arms—Checker or station wagon.	No.	Not needed.	OK for distance covered.	No problem.	No problem.	Insured, but an unlikely problem.
BOAT	Just roll it up the gangplank.	Usually moderate.	Not needed.	Splendid.	No problem. Get back to bike before docking.	No problem, but keep away from salt spray.	At your own risk.

CHAPTER THIRTEEN

RIDING AT NIGHT

If you are going to be using your bicycle for reliable transportation, you'll be riding it at night sometimes.

With proper equipment and reasonable riding skill, you can ride at night with confidence and in safety. Riding in the city under streetlights, or on quiet country roads, is hardly more difficult than during the day. Many of the collaborators on this book commute home from work every night in rush hour during winter darkness. Here's how to do it.

EQUIP YOURSELF FOR NIGHT RIDING

Here's what you need. We'll go through everything quickly here, and review it in more detail in the following pages.

On dark roads, you need lights so you can see where you are going. But you always need lights so people can see *you,* even if you only ride under streetlights.

You need reflectors and reflective material on your bicycle to shine extra light back at drivers whose headlights are pointed at you.

You need reflective and light-colored clothing so people can figure out your size, distance, and speed.

You need riding skill and awareness to choose your path and to check out that other people see you when you need them to. A rearview mirror is extra helpful in some night riding situations.

Put it all together, and you light up like a Christmas tree — exactly what you want and need to do. Then, riding at night is not much different from riding during daylight hours.

The equipment isn't going to break your bank, either. On the average, to be safe at night you spend about $40. Some riders will spend as much as $100 for special, high-powered lights which are, in fact, very useful in some riding situations. But there's one plan we will put forward that won't cost you even a penny!

WHY YOU MUST HAVE LIGHTS

On dark roads, you need a headlight to see where you are going. But even under streetlights, you need lights so people can see you. The streetlights may be bright enough for you to see by, but when car headlights are glaring behind you, other people will not see you unless you have lights.

Your bicycle should be equipped with reflectors, but they're no substitute for lights. Reflectors shine light back only in the direction it comes from. They don't shine light back at pedestrians, at drivers of cars pulling out of side streets in front of you, or at drivers of cars going downhill while you're going up the next hill. These people need to see you, but they don't have headlights aimed at you.

Not only are you more likely to have an accident if you ride without lights, lights are required by law, and if you have an accident without lights, you are more likely to be legally at fault. You may be unable to collect on a damage claim. If you hit someone, you might be faced with a lawsuit.

Riding with lights is much more pleasant. When you don't have lights, it's nerve-wracking. You are repeatedly forced into slowing down, swerving, or stopping to get out of the way of people who can't see you. And in turn, these unpredictable maneuvers can cause an accident. So use lights.

LEGAL REQUIREMENTS FOR LIGHTS

A white headlight is standard, legally required equipment for all vehicles, because white is brightest to light the way. A red taillight is standard by custom and required by law to look different from the headlight.

A flashing amber light is standard as a caution signal, and you may use one in the front or in the rear in addition to your basic lights.

These are the basic, commonsense rules. Actual laws vary somewhat from state to state. Some variations:

All states except Massachusetts require a headlight. In Massachusetts, a white reflector is a legal but nonsensical substitute for a headlight.

Only four states require a taillight — Kentucky, New Jersey, New York, and Ohio. The rest allow a red rear reflector as a substitute. While a rear reflector may be adequate protection for casual riding, we still advise that you use a rear light. A red rear reflector along with a flashing amber taillight satisfies legal and commonsense requirements.

Four states prohibit attaching a flashing amber light to your bicycle, though you may legally attach one to yourself. These states are Maryland, Michigan, Rhode Island, and New Mexico. As you see, laws vary from state to state.

In practice, as with other legal confusions about bicycles, use common sense. That means use more and brighter lights than the law requires. There are very few motorists, police, or judges who will object to this, even if you violate a technicality of the law like a prohibition on flashing lights.

THE BEST LIGHTS

The best lights for you depend on the kind of riding you do. In the city, under streetlights, small battery lights make the best sense. You can easily slip them off the bicycle when you park, preventing theft. These lights aren't bright enough to see by, but that doesn't matter under city streetlights. Rechargeable nickel cadmium batteries now bring the cost of these lights down to pennies a day. These batteries and a charger are sold at better hardware stores.

Where there aren't any streetlights, you need a headlight bright enough to see by. The usual answer is generator lights. They have no substitute if you're traveling with the bicycle where it's inconvenient to use batteries.

Recently, however, high-powered rechargeable battery lights have become available. These are the brightest of all, best suited to commuting on dark roads in suburbs or rural areas — but you can't ride more than a couple of hours before recharging them.

Specialty lights — like the Belt Beacon flashing light, the Laser Light fluorescent tube, the leg light, and others — can improve

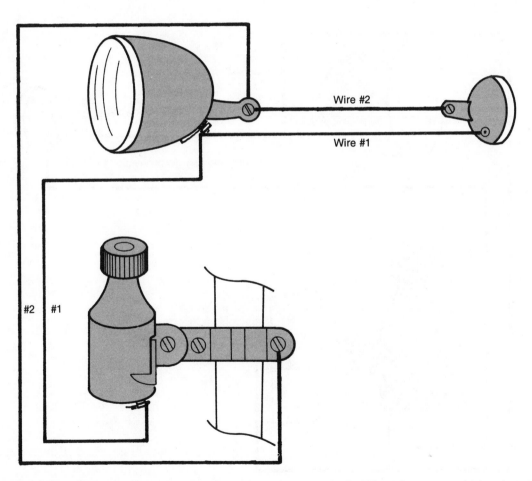

Double-wiring a generator light set. Wire #1 connects light terminals. Wire #2 connects the brackets that hold the generator and the lights.

your visibility. Except for the leg light, none of these shine white to the front and red to the rear, so they must be used along with other lights to meet legal requirements. The Laser Light uses a generator; the rest, batteries.

To summarize, remember to use: small battery lights for city riding, generator lights for long rides in the country out of reach of batteries, and high-powered rechargeable battery lights for suburban or rural commuting. Generator lights are the most adaptable

for a bicycle used in different situations. Supplement generator lights with Belt Beacons, since they go out when you're stopped.

Simplicity, low cost, and reliability are the main requirements you are looking for. The lights we recommend all provide good service, but bicycle lights get knocked around more than any other kind. Many people buy lights but soon give up on them because of their low reliability or the cost of batteries. We have practical solutions to these

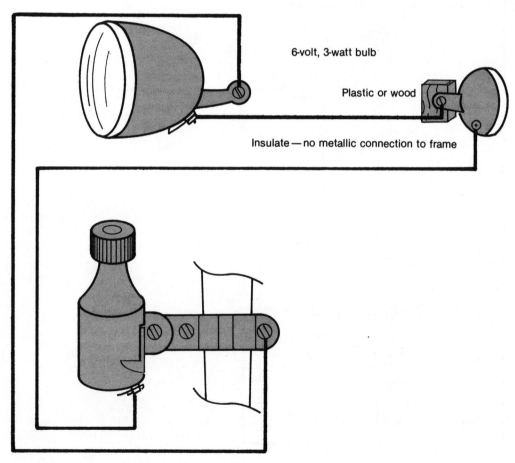

6-volt, 3-watt bulb

Plastic or wood

Insulate — no metallic connection to frame

A 12-volt, 6-watt generator may be used with two 6-volt, 3-watt bulbs connected in series. Insulate the light which is connected to the terminal of the generator.

problems. You'll have to go to a little trouble to modify some lights and keep them working, but the increased reliability justifies the trouble for all lights we mention here.

We'll start, though, with the lights that are the least trouble to use.

DEPENDABLE LIGHTS

The simplest lights to deal with are Belt Beacons and leg lights. Buy the Belt Beacon model that flashes 60 times per minute. Belt Beacons are almost problem free. Attach them to your bicycle, rather than your belt, for best aim. But remember, even if you use Belt Beacons front and rear, you need a white headlight to be legal. This could be a leg light. Buy French-made or Schwinn-approved leg lights. Imitations usually have serious problems. You need *two* leg lights to be seen full circle.

Leg light strap buckles are clumsy, and some tend to loosen. Solve the problem either of two ways: wear the lights on your arms where they slip on easily and don't get jarred as much, or sew Velcro onto the straps in place of the buckles. The Velcro treatment works beautifully, and the leg position for the lights is preferable — the motion attracts attention sooner.

CLAMP-ON BATTERY LIGHTS

There are three brands we recommend, though minor do-it-yourself improvements to all of them are needed to assure long and reliable service.

Berec English lights are the best of the lot. The taillight gives a near ideal fan-shaped beam pattern, which is very bright to the rear and sides. The headlight spreads the beam, too, but not so far.

The Berec headlight's handlebar mount-

ing bracket is its main weakness. The bracket is a potential hazard. It also is less than sturdy — usually breaking after a few months. And it puts the light where it interferes with handlebar bags. But it is a standard English bracket, and other brands are available to fit several positions on the bicycle. The headset variety is very common on English three-speed bicycles, available as a salvage item if your local bike shop doesn't have new ones. With a hacksaw, vise, hammer, and drill, this can be modified to fit elsewhere, in case you use a handlebar bag.

The Berec taillight is made to clamp to a seatstay. If you use wide tires or pannier bags, it will be obscured in this position. Attach it to a rack brace instead. A rack brace is too thin to hold it steady, so mount it upside down just under the top of the rack and tape it in place to prevent it from rotating to the side.

The Berec headlight is removed when parking by slipping it off its bracket; the tail-light, by removing the internals from the shell.

In this time exposure, the Ray-O-Vac taillight casts a steady beam; the leg light and Belt Beacon attract extra attention with their motion and flashing.

This is accomplished quickly, without tools.

Ray-O-Vac clamp-on lights are cheaper and more convenient to install than Berec lights, though less sturdy and with an inferior beam pattern. The concentrated taillight beam is uncomfortably bright for bicyclists overtaking you. The Ray-O-Vac's strong suit is the clamp mounting, which moves easily from one part of the bicycle to another, or to another bicycle, as needed.

The clamp, however, has problems. It slips — but if you tighten it so it doesn't slip, it may crack. The problem is easily remedied by stretching a ring cut from a discarded bicycle inner tube over the clamp's angle-adjusting ball. Any bike shop will have plenty of old inner tubes to give away. If you mount the clamp horizontally, stretch inner tube rubber over the jaws, too. Soapy water makes it easy to install the rubber.

Wonder and Rampar clamp lights are similar to Ray-O-Vac and have the same clamp problem and solution. These brands, however, use a bulb which is not widely available outside bike shops — and the Wonder light also uses a battery which is only available at bike shops. These are serious problems, since bike shops usually aren't open at night. Bulbs and batteries for the other lights are available at every drugstore and grocery store.

INSTALLING GENERATOR LIGHTS

Most generators have a roller that runs on the side of the tire. Make sure that the generator roller is exactly parallel to the tire, or it will drag sideways and cause rapid wear. Also, the tire should contact the center of the roller face, not the edge. The best tires for use with a generator have ribbed sidewalls to engage the roller. If your bike has lightweight tires with sides so thin you can see the fabric through them, you must raise and tilt the generator so it runs on the edge of the tire tread.

If you install a generator at the front wheel, be sure to place it *ahead* of the fork blade. If placed behind the fork blade, it can jam in the wheel if it slips loose, sending you flying.

Most generators rely on an electrical connection through the bike's frame. For greater reliability, double-wire the generator.

There have been considerable improvements recently in the taillights supplied with generator light sets. If your taillight is a small, bullet-shaped one, replace it with a modern taillight that has a curved mirror behind the bulb: with the same bulb, it may be more than ten times as bright.

AIMING YOUR LIGHTS

For your lights to work effectively, you must aim them. If you use a headlight just to be seen by, aim it straight ahead and level so it will shine directly at people who need to see you. Aim a taillight similarly — straight back and level.

Check the aim of these lights by rolling your bike toward and away from a wall. For level aim, the center of the beam should stay directly in line with the bike and at the same height as the light.

If you use your headlight to see on dark roads, check its aim while riding. Aim the light so its beam reaches the road directly in front of you and as far away as possible while still bright. Always keep in mind that however perfectly your lights have been aimed, the shock of your bike going over rough surfaces can throw the original set-up off. So check the "aim" of your lights frequently.

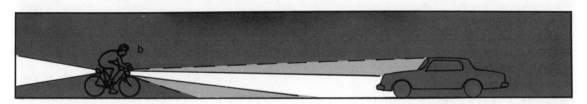

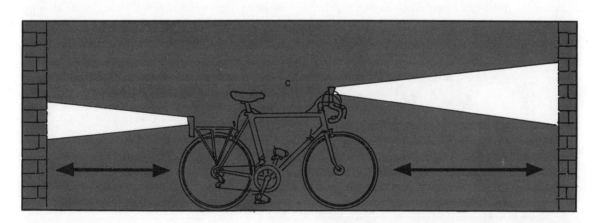

Aiming your lights. a) Flash your headlight to alert drivers and pedestrians by shaking the handlebars slightly. b) Mount and aim a headlight low; test aim as you ride. Aim it as high as possible. c) Mount a light to be seen by — headlight or taillight — high, and aim it level. Test aim by rolling the bike toward and away from a wall. The center of the beam should stay at the same height.

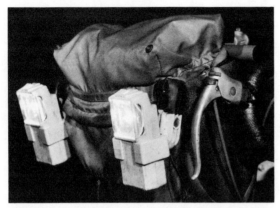

These two Ray-O-Vac lights are aimed slightly different for wider coverage. The grip of their clamps has been improved with inner tube sections. They clamp to the handlebar bag rack.

IF YOU DON'T HAVE LIGHTS

Here's a simple solution to a common problem — getting caught out without lights

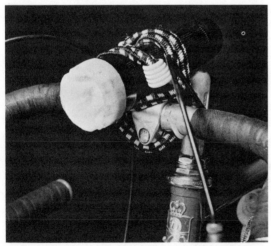

A flashlight strapped to the bicycle's handlebar stem with a bungee cord is an adequate headlight for city use.

as darkness is falling. This problem usually happens to people who don't ride much at night and don't own lights.

You don't need to own special bike lights. If you think you might be caught out after dark, just take along a flashlight, instead. A big, cylindrical one or a hand lantern is best — pocket-sized ones aren't bright enough. Take along an old white shirt, too. Or if you're caught at a friend's place after dark, borrow these items.

Lash the flashlight to your bicycle's handlebar stem or top tube with a bungee cord. Put on the white shirt, leaving it open at the front so it flaps in the wind.

Assuming that your bicycle has a rear reflector and pedal reflectors, you'll be reasonably safe with this equipment as long as you stay off high-speed roads.

If you want to be really serious about using a flashlight as your bike light, slip-in brackets are available at bike shops. If you do little night riding, the flashlight has a big advantage: if you make the flashlight serve two purposes, you aren't wasting money on batteries you aren't using.

USING REFLECTORS

For safe night riding, you must have lights. Reflectors only shine light back in the direction it comes from.

But reflectors are cheap and convenient to use. When they work, they can work very well, helping drivers to see you and increasing your safety.

Your bicycle probably already is equipped with reflectors — if it was sold since 1975, it had reflectors pointing in all directions. But some may be badly chosen, placed, or aimed. So we'll talk about how to make your reflectors work best.

This rear reflector made for bicycle use has three stripes which reflect light coming from different angles. The reflector must be aimed straight back and its stripes must be vertical for it to work as intended.

REAR AND FRONT REFLECTORS

A rear reflector may appear brighter than many bicycle taillights. It is cheap insurance in case your taillight bulb blows out while you're not looking. For these reasons, never ride at night without a rear reflector.

A rear reflector made for a bicycle has three parallel stripes which look slightly different. These make the reflector work for lights off to the sides as well as directly behind. Since two of the stripes are for the left and the right, some brightness is sacrificed directly behind where it is most needed. An automotive reflector, usually divided into six pie-slice segments, lacks wide-angle properties but is a bit brighter directly behind and is available in sizes up to a pie-plate 6 inches. Best advice: use the bicycle reflector first. It has a sturdy and waterproof plastic back. For highway riding use more than one bicycle reflector, or add a large automotive reflector—but seal its edges with epoxy or

An adhesive-backed "Hot Dot" patch of reflective film on the back of the cyclist's glove makes turn signals visible at night.

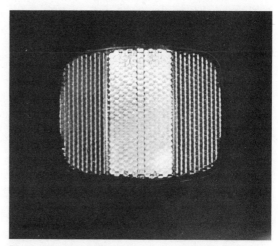

From directly behind, the bicycle reflector is active over only one-third of its area; not as bright as an automotive reflector.

bathtub caulk. If water gets in its back, it won't work.

If the rear reflector is under the saddle where a rear rack or saddlebag hides it, move it to the back of the rack or fender. If it's under 2½ inches across, replace it.

A standard rear reflector is red. Amber is brighter, and legal if you have another, red rear reflector or taillight.

Aim your rear reflector. Make sure it is pointed directly back. If it is tilted even slightly sideways, up, or down, it will not work at all. Also, the three parallel stripes of a bicycle reflector must point straight up and down, parallel to the tire. If they point sideways, drivers making turns out of side streets won't see the reflector as soon, though airplane pilots and glowworms will have an excellent view.

USE REFLECTIVE TAPE AND STICK-ONS

Scotchlight reflective tape is a valuable addition to your disc reflectors, which work best when cars are far away. The tape works best when cars are close, or for truck drivers in high cabs.

Good places for reflective tape are: the bicycle's frame, fork, and fenders, facing front, sides, and rear; the crank arms, as a supplement to pedal reflectors; and the inside surfaces of the rims, between the spokes. Yellow tape is bright, and legal for all directions.

Reflective tape works when wet and has excellent wide-angle properties. It is available at some bicycle shops and at industrial safety equipment outlets. These shops deliver C.O.D. by UPS, so you can shop by phone.

Reflexite plastic film reflective material, sold with a stick-on backing under the name "Hot dots," is brighter than reflective tape, but lacks wide-angle properties. "Hot dots" must face the light source squarely to work well, so you have less freedom in installing them than in installing tape. They're good at the backs of the fenders.

REFLECTIVE CLOTHING

Reflectors which attach to clothing are made of reflective cloth or tape, or plastic film. These reflectors are necessities. They must be usable with the different clothes you wear from day to day.

Trouser bands with Velcro attachments are the most comfortable ones sold. They add to the effect of pedal reflectors.

A reflective vest or sash helps round out your shape, and may be worn over any clothing. If you have a favorite windbreaker jacket for bicycling in cool weather, install reflective material on it to avoid having to add and remove an extra layer of clothing repeatedly as you warm up or cool down. Also install reflective material on your raincape. Understand that the most effective locations for the reflective material in a crouched bicycling position are not the same as when you are upright. For the rear direction, the reflective material must be at the lower back and in the upper arm/shoulder area; for the front, at the top of the shoulders. Many runners' safety vests sold to bicyclists lose most of their reflectivity in crouched position; this is especially true when they use Reflexite plastic film which lacks wide-angle properties. The familiar reflectorized triangle or "fanny bumper," odd as it may look, is in the right place. Reflective material on a belt or the waistline of bicycling shorts is a convenient alternative.

Reflective material on wristbands, the wrists of your jacket, or the backs of your gloves makes your hand signals visible at night. Adhesive "Hot dots" stick well to leather gloves, and are recommended. By turning your wrist, you alternate them backward and forward, so they blink just like car turn signals.

Your helmet is the highest perch for reflective material. Most helmets already have some, but installing more is a good idea. Pay special attention to your helmet's position when you're in a crouch. A band of reflective tape over the top front will increase your forward visibility to traffic coming from the opposite direction; one attached to the liner or rim inside the helmet at the back, your rear visibility to traffic coming from the rear. Yellow tape is brighter than red and is recommended.

We've presented many choices. In practice, trouser bands, something on the upper body — the vest, imperfect as it may be, is a workable available choice — the helmet, and gloves with "Hot dots" for signalling cover the need fairly well.

If you sew through Reflexite plastic film, seal around the stitches with Duco Cement or campers' seam sealer to keep water out.

Subject to the limitations mentioned above, Reflexite plastic film and Scotchlight tape work satisfactorily. Some varieties of Scotchlight reflective *cloth* lose reflective properties when wet.

RIDING ON
DARK ROADS

If you rarely ride on dark roads and are using a small battery headlight, move the light lower on the bicycle if possible and tilt it down to shine on the road.

You will have to ride slowly to keep inside the headlight beam. Don't overdrive your headlight. If you can't see clearly to ride in your normal position on the road, you'll tend to pull toward the center. That's dangerous

under nighttime overtaking conditions.

A small battery light with a nonstandard, brighter bulb will allow you to ride faster— about 15 mph. So will a three-watt generator set. With a six-watt generator, or high-powered battery lights, you'll rarely have to hold your speed down any more than during the daytime. One exception: with any generator, don't let yourself build up great speed down hill. You could burn out the bulbs. Keep an even, moderate pace.

Your eyes' dark adaptation makes an important difference for night riding on dark roads. If possible, turn off bright lights for the half-hour before you go out riding. Particularly, don't stare at a television screen, which is about 20 times brighter than normal room lighting.

TRIALS OF
NIGHT RIDING

Motorists who don't dim their lights do not recognize your bicycle as a "real" road vehicle. They react only to bright headlights.

If a motorist's headlights are blinding you, front-facing reflective material is effective. Have enough of it on the helmet, the bike, the pedals, and your clothing to identify you. A front disc reflector mimics a second headlight under these conditions. Flick the handlebars sideways to flash your headlight and signal the driver. The brighter it is, the more likely you are to impress a driver.

Have bright, well-aimed lights, and plenty of rear-facing reflective material. Moving or flashing lights are highly recommended. Be the brightest, most obvious thing in the motorists' view. Use a rearview mirror to check that each car will clear you as it approaches from behind. Check whether there is a second car behind the first one, and keep

COMMON COMMERCIAL REFLECTORS

	ENTRANCE ANGLE (WORKS UP TO WHAT ANGLE)	OBSERVA-TION ANGLE (HOW FAR VISIBLE FROM LIGHT SOURCE)	BRIGHT-NESS	PERFORM-ANCE WHEN WET	REMARKS
Automotive (SAE A) Reflector	Narrow (±20°).	Narrow.	High (varies with manufacturer).	Unimpaired though often poorly sealed.	Brightest for highway use at long distance.
Bicycle (CPSC) Reflector	Wide (±60°) if turned right way.	Narrow.	Moderately high — limited by 3-panel construction (varies with manufacturer).	Unimpaired.	Less bright than SAE directly back.
Bicycle Wheel Reflector	Wide (±60°) if turned right away.	Narrow.	Moderately high — limited by 3-panel construction (varies with manufacturer).	Unimpaired.	Mostly useful when stopped in intersection but may lose wide-angle properties depending on position of wheel.
Bicycle Pedal Reflector	Moderate (±45°).	Narrow.	Moderate — limited by size but aided by position.	Unimpaired.	May not work at stop if pedal not upright. Motion attracts attention. Low position catches low head-light beams.

track of it, too. Give extra attention to cars behind you when headlights from ahead of you blind the drivers — also watch out for drivers ahead making left turns, blinded by headlights behind you.

Occasionally, you may have to squint and look to the right side of the road to protect your eyes' dark adaptation, or even pull over to stop because you can't see where you're going. A narrow, dark, transparent visor on a helmet or on a cap under a helmet will let you keep track of the car while using the light from its headlights to see by.

Night riding is more difficult on un-

COMMON COMMERCIAL REFLECTORS—*Continued*

	ENTRANCE ANGLE (WORKS UP TO WHAT ANGLE)	OBSERVA-TION ANGLE (HOW FAR VISIBLE FROM LIGHT SOURCE)	BRIGHT-NESS	PERFORM-ANCE WHEN WET	REMARKS
Scotchlight Tape	Wide (±60°) in all directions.	Wide.	Low.	Unimpaired.	May be conveniently applied to most surfaces. Wide-observation angle makes visible closer to car.
Scotchlight Cloth (Limband)	Wide (±60°) in all directions.	Wide.	Low.	Does not work.	Reflective beads wear off surface.
Reflexite Plastic Film (Jog-a-lite)	Narrow to moderate. Wraps and folds, increasing angle.	Moderate.	Moderate.	Unimpaired unless water gets inside. Seal it if you sew it.	Gains wide-angle properties by wrapping around wearer but only when vertical. Quits when near horizontal.

lighted, narrow, high-speed roads with heavy traffic. Don't ride on roads like this unless you have to. Be aware that overtaking collisions are a serious risk under these conditions, though the statistics for overtaking collisions are swollen by bicyclists who protect themselves with no more than a single rear reflector and sometimes less.

Riding on lightly traveled rural roads at night can be a great pleasure. Imagine following your headlamp beam through a mysterious, softened landscape, outrunning the mosquitoes, and enjoying a free concert by millions of crickets. Think of navigating by the stars, and cooling yourself in the night air.

Most places in the city, too, there is very little traffic after midnight. Until the sunrise — and in the summer, until well after the sunrise — the streets are all yours. You ride free through their vast, empty expanses. The air is clean, free of exhaust fumes. You get to stare up at the buildings without worrying about traffic, and in the quiet you hear the city's little sounds — the buzz of the streetlights, the hum of machinery, the hoot of a switching engine in a distant railroad yard.

Many bicycling groups hold midnight rides. Save up some sleep and try one.

If you can work your schedule around to commute during the late night hours, night riding can become a very pleasant part of your routine.

NIGHT RIDING RULES OF THUMB

What follows are suggestions to help you ride safely at night:

. . . You can't make yourself too easy to see.
. . . Use lights front and rear, adequate for the conditions. Always use a white headlight.
. . . Flashing amber lights are OK in combination with a white headlight and a rear red reflector or taillight.
. . . Use reflectors — at least rear and pedal reflectors, and full-circle reflectors if you use generator lights.
. . . Use reflective tape for the high-cab truckers and for extra visibility by everyone.
. . . Use reflective material on your helmet, gloves or wrists (for signalling), back, and ankles.
. . . Wear light-colored clothing and use light-colored baggage.
. . . Understand how night equipment works and how it fails. Don't accept on faith that it works. Test it.
. . . Use your equipment actively. Flash your headlight at people. Wave your hand for a turn signal. Consider a leg light, or Belt Beacon, and understand the active role of pedal reflectors.
. . . Carry a backup lighting system and spare bulbs and batteries.
. . . Adapt your riding skills:
Check other people's behavior
Stay inside your headlight beam
Choose routes carefully
Be aware of the increased hazard of drunk drivers
Use a rearview mirror.

CHAPTER FOURTEEN

RIDING IN RAIN, SNOW, AND HEAT

If you are to use your bicycle as reliable transportation, you must be able to ride it in most kinds of weather which should not be much more of a serious inconvenience to you than it is to other travelers. And it need not be, if you learn to deal with it. Sometimes, the weather will inconvenience you a bit more than others, sometimes considerably less. (Ever try to carry a car over a snowdrift?)

RIDING IN THE RAIN

As long as you are comfortable, it can be easily pleasant to ride in the rain. It is easier to stay dry and warm riding a bike than in most other outdoor activities. The constant exercise of riding generates body heat, which warms you and evaporates moisture. The relatively steady riding posture allows your rain clothing to be open underneath, giving the moisture an escape route. And your feet are up off the ground, not pounding through puddles, so you don't need heavy boots.

EQUIPPING YOUR BIKE FOR WET WEATHER

Install fenders (also called mudguards) for wet-weather riding. These must be full fenders; "mini" fenders do little more than keep mud off your bike's brakes and headset bearings — an advantage you'll hardly appreciate if your face is full of mud. To keep mud and water off your feet, the front fender must have a mudflap which reaches almost to the ground. If the fender doesn't have a mudflap, cut one out of a corner of a plastic milk bottle and bolt it on.

Any bike can take fenders. Some racing frames do not have bolt holes for them, so you will have to attach the braces to the front forks and seatstays with rack seatstay clamps or chainguard clamps. The most convenient fenders for bikes with 26-inch and 27-inch wheels are plastic ones with adjustable braces. Clip off the ends of the braces after installing the fenders, so they don't stick out and scratch your legs. Make sure fenders are securely attached; a loose fender can roll around the wheel, causing a skid or a fall.

An internal hub gear is better in the rain than derailleur gears are, and it is much easier to clean off once you get home. If your bike has a leather saddle, a saddle cover is a good idea because rain is not good for leather. A plastic bag or elastic shower cap can serve as a saddle cover.

So that a rain cape will fit over them, don't loop your bike's brake cables too high above the handlebars. Upside down brake cable attachment to dropped bar levers works even better. And for night riding in the rain, make sure your lights and reflectors will be below the edge of the rain cape.

Wet weather will deteriorate a bike, so you may wish to keep a trashmo bike especially equipped for rainy weather, and another with sportier equipment for fair weather.

But you can do much to protect your bike. Fenders help the bike as well as you. It helps to plug the top of the seat tube and the bottom of the fork steerer tube. You can rustproof the inside of the frame. Touching up nicks and scratches in the paint will protect the outside. Cleaning the bike and rubbing it down with paste wax (except rims and rubber parts) will help preserve it from rust. Keeping moving parts well oiled and greased will prevent water from getting into them, and you may consider sealing the bearings or using sealed bearing components for an extra measure of protection. Seal bearings by wrapping pipe cleaners around the ends of the axles, between the part that turns and the part that doesn't.

Rim brakes don't work as well when wet as when dry. Chromed steel rims, the most common type on inexpensive bikes, give the worst problems. When you first apply the brakes, they will hardly work at all. After you have ridden 10, 20, or a 100 feet, they will dry out and catch.

Here are some solutions to that problem.

WET-WEATHER BRAKING CHOICES

1. Fibrax Brake Shoes
   Advantages: Easy to install, can be installed on any bike, cheapest way to get good wet-weather braking.
   Disadvantages: Still a bit hard to find, don't last as long as normal brake shoes; need to be cleaned occasionally.
   When to use them: When you have a bike with steel rims and need to get wet-weather braking the simplest way.
2. Coaster Brake
   Advantages: Commonly available, built into three-speed hub. Totally waterproof and very reliable.
   Disadvantages: Harder to control strength of braking — tends to skid rear tire. Works only on rear wheel. Overheats on long downhill runs. Complicated to repair — especially on the three-speed model. Only for one-speeds and three-speeds. Disturbs pedaling technique.
   When to use it: When buying a new one-speed or three-speed bike; by replacing the rear wheel of an older bike (wheels with coaster brakes are commonly available used). Use in conjunction with front and rear handbrakes.
3. Drum Brake, Disc Brake
   Advantages: Totally waterproof, available

for front and rear wheels for one-, three-, and ten-speeds.

Disadvantages: Some models are heavy. A front drum or disc brake puts a heavy strain on the front fork. Some models don't provide very strong braking, especially for the front. You usually must build up a new wheel to use one of these. May be expensive.

When to use: Use a rear drum or disc brake on a tandem or other very heavily loaded bike to prevent downhill rim overheating. On a new bike, when available. Works especially well with small wheels, as on a folding bike.

4. Aluminum Rims

Advantages: Besides improving braking, they are lighter, make your bike maneuver better, and they are much more often repairable than steel rims after being damaged. Widely available in most sizes.

Disadvantages: Braking is not absolutely positive at first in very wet weather. Buy a heavy-gauge aluminum rim; some light ones aren't durable.

When to use them: When buying a new ten-speed bike or rebuilding a wheel for an older bike. Aluminum rims are available in sizes to fit most bikes, but they are commonly sold on new bikes only if these are ten-speeds.

RAIN CLOTHING

The main item of clothing is the bicyclist's rain cape. This is a poncho specially tailored for a good fit in riding position. At the back, it has a belt tie or leg loops to keep it from flapping in the wind. At the front, it has thumb loops to hold it out in front of you over your arms like a little tent. A rain cape is inexpensive. You can buy a good one for $15.

The cape may be fitted with a hood to

The cyclist is wearing a rain cape, a poncho specially designed to protect you in bicycle riding position. The bicycle is a modified Raleigh three-speed, with aluminum rims for wet-weather braking and lightweight plastic fenders to keep down the road splash.

protect your head from the rain and to keep the rain from running down your neck. If you wear a helmet, remove the hood. A moderate rain will only wet your hair lightly through the helmet's ventilating holes. You'll be more comfortable with the helmet's ventilation if the weather is warm. In a cold or heavy rain, a helmet cover or elastic bathing cap will seal the helmet.

Depending on how hard it is raining, you may need more than just your bike's fenders to keep your feet and legs from getting wet. In a moderate rain, toe clip booties on your pedals are enough. Canvas shoes such as Bata Bikers can get a little wet without causing problems. Wool socks and other wool clothing shed water and stay warm even when wet. Plastic boots sold in five and ten cent stores will keep rain and mud off your feet. Even plastic food storage bags, tied over your feet by your leg bands, will do in a pinch, but be sure to cut holes in them underneath or you'll have steamy feet.

Passing cars may occasionally splash water on your legs. If the weather is warm so you're wearing shorts, you may tolerate this in return for better ventilation. In cooler weather, you'll want gaiters, rain chaps, or rain leggings to protect your legs and your trousers. But avoid rain pants because they cover more of you than necessary, and will become steamy inside.

What we've described is the bicyclist's classic rainwear. There is an alternative — the Gore-Tex rainsuit, made of a special material which keeps raindrops out but lets water vapor through. A Gore-Tex rainsuit can do a very good job of keeping you dry. A rainsuit gives you more freedom of motion, and has less air resistance than a rain cape. But it won't keep your bike's saddle dry, and it won't protect your hands and feet, so you'll need a saddle cover and waterproof gloves and boots. You still need fenders to keep mud out of your face and the bike's mechanism. The rainsuit is bulkier to carry than a rain cape and you have to get off the bike to put it on and take it off. And it is expensive — around $100. It will wear out quicker than a rain cape, too, because you sit on it.

There is some equipment to avoid: an ordinary hiker's poncho will flap in the wind and get in your way. A rainsuit which is not Gore-Tex will steam up inside so you'll get as wet as if you hadn't worn it at all. Rubber galoshes will blister your feet and won't fit toe clips. You may decide to use one of these items in an emergency but in the long run, they will frustrate you and make you dread riding in the rain. The equipment we recommend will let you enjoy riding in the rain.

RAIN RIDING EQUIPMENT CHECKLIST

Bring these items along if rain threatens:

. . . Your rain cape, rainhat, or helmet cover, and chaps.

. . . Your light boots or gaiters, and a pair of light gloves, if the temperature is below 60 degrees.

. . . Your saddle cover — or substitute an elastic shower cap or one of several plastic bags of various sizes, to protect your luggage from rain. Many backpacks and bike bags are not completely waterproof. Use plastic bags inside these. Also, wrap plastic bags over cardboard boxes or anything else you may be carrying.

. . . A dry pair of wool socks in case your feet get wet, and clean, dry clothing in case you have to look absolutely neat where you are going.

. . . An automotive antifog cloth, or a cloth with a few drops of dishwashing detergent on it, to keep your glasses and rearview mirror from fogging.

. . . Your bike cleaning supplies, and a small container of oil, if you're going to be away long enough to do any maintenance on your bike.

. . . A towel and hairbrush to restore your appearance.

SAFE RIDING IN THE RAIN

We've already mentioned that rim brakes don't work as well when wet. One or two attempts will convince you not to ride in traffic in the rain with steel rims and ordinary brake shoes. In riding which is not demanding of brakes, apply the brakes early to wipe the rims dry. But it's better to use brakes that work

Water beads up on an oil slick left by a car — slippery!

well in the rain.

In traffic, moderate your speed and keep an extra safety space around you. Everyone has the same traction problems you have, and most drivers will be taking it easy, too. Remember the road is most slippery in the first half hour of a rain, before the water has washed oil and sand off the pavement.

Ordinary rough asphalt and concrete are otherwise only a little slipperier when wet than when dry. You only need to take a little extra care with turning and braking. But watch out for patches which are shiny-smooth, oily, or doughy, such as smooth black paving tar, oil slicks from cars (water will bead up here), pavement paint stripes, wet leaves, and metal — manhole covers, and excavation cover plates. Don't turn or brake as you ride

over these. Steel-grated bridges, railroad tracks, and pavement reflector dots not only are slippery but will try to steer your bike for you. Avoid the reflector dots. Slow down or even walk across the grated bridges — they're very treacherous. Cross the railroad tracks slowly, at a right angle.

Don't ride through a puddle if you can't see to the bottom since it could be much deeper than you think! A puddle is a blind spot, just like a traffic blind spot.

These are a few extra things you may need to do to see well under wet conditions. Some rain hats and hoods cut off your vision, especially if you turn your head. Adjust or replace yours if it obscures your view. Rain droplets and fog may accumulate on your glasses and rearview mirror. Keep your anti-fog cloth handy. Soft contact lenses may be preferable to glasses in the rain, though a driving rain can sting your eyes. You may want glasses or goggles, even to wear over contact lenses.

Take extra care to be seen well on a gray, rainy day. We've suggested that the rain cape be bright yellow; Day-glo (fluorescent) material is even more effective. The extra proportion of blue light on a rainy day makes Day-glo shine very brightly. In case it becomes dark enough that drivers turn on their lights, keep your bike equipped with reflectors. And turn on your lights, too, as soon as motorists do. Remember, motorists have windshields — which may be fogged. Check carefully that drivers have seen you, especially if the weather is misty or foggy.

RIDING IN WINTER

One Boston cyclist says this about winter riding: "I found out that a bicycle is the best way to get around in winter. Walking is diffi-

A winter bicycle — a Raleigh Twenty folder, whose wide tires and open frame make it excellent for travel on slippery snow. The saddle is protected from moisture with a plastic bag.

cult, because the sidewalks are slippery even once they've been shoveled. But most of the time, the streets are clear. You can ride as fast as you want and never sweat. And you don't have to worry about scraping your windshield, shoveling out your car, or getting your engine to start. You never get stuck and you never

have to call a tow truck."

All of this is true, yet winter gives you some extra things to deal with.

PREPARING FOR WINTER RIDING

Many cyclists keep a special winter bike. Because road salt and sand wear a bike quickly, an older, less expensive, but sturdy bike is more appropriate for winter riding. An internal hub gear or single gear is much more weatherproof than derailleur gears; wide tires with deep treads go better in the snow than narrow ones. Toe clips and straps aren't suited to snow riding. Your winter bike spares the fancy bike for nicer days, including some nice, clear winter days.

The bike must have fenders to keep slush and sand out of your face! Adjust the back end of each fender so it is close to the tire, use tire savers, or make special scrapers. Then wet snow won't pack up inside the fenders. It could really slow you down.

Make sure your bike is well equipped with lights and reflectors for night riding; you'll have more of it in winter.

Controlling a bike on slippery surfaces is easiest with low handlebars since they allow you to shift your weight sideways over the front of the bike. Dropped handlebars are good, or turn flat handlebars over to put the grips lower.

You can make a studded snow tire by pounding large-headed galvanized roofing nails outward through the tread and clipping them short. Cut the tread out of another tire and put it inside to protect the tube from the heads of the nails. Use the studded tire only on very slippery days and on the front wheel. It will slow you down, but it will give you more steering control on packed snow and ice.

It is easiest to ride through the winter if

you ride into it. Keep on riding as the weather gets colder. Learn the joy of putting on full power without perspiring, and build up your collection of winter bicycling clothing as the need slowly increases.

Brush up on riding skills you'll especially need in winter: night riding, and riding on slippery surfaces — bikepaths often aren't plowed in winter.

WINTER CLOTHING AND WARMTH

Warmth that comes from inside is one of the great joys of winter bicycling. In a place like Boston, you can be truly comfortable in winter only with exercise that improves blood circulation and sets the body's fires burning brightly each day. It is a more common problem for bicyclists to feel too warm in winter riding than too cold. And winter has another compensation.

As long as the temperature stays below freezing, you never have to concern yourself about rain. So, in spite of the cold, you'll find it no harder to dress for winter than for autumn or spring. But you must dress right. If you're like most people, you throw a heavy overcoat or down parka over your normal indoor clothing. But this approach leaves your legs exposed. It's like insulating your house and leaving the front door open.

For bicycling, you dress like a cross-country skier. Your legs are especially important, because they are your motor. The lubricant in your knee joints thickens up when it's cold, just like the oil in your car's motor.

On your legs wear long underwear or tights under your regular trousers, or wear runner's warmup pants while riding, and change to your indoor clothes when you get to your destination.

On the upper body, wear several thick shirts and sweaters of increasing size, with the collars turned up. For convenience, they should open at the front — then you can take them off and put them on as you need without removing your glasses or helmet. Velcro is the best fastener for shirts though it will clog with lint on sweaters. Zippers with large handles are good, too — zipper handles have holes through which you can thread leather thongs or shoelaces. If possible, you want to operate the fasteners without taking off your mittens.

A skier's nylon windshell parka is ideal to wear on the outside. Yellow and bright orange, preferably Day-glo, are the best colors for this and the next one or two layers below it — in case you take them off. Or you could wear a runner's safety vest instead. Don't wear white, which is camouflage clothing against snow. Reflective tape on your clothing or sew-on strips cut from old leg bands are good ideas for night riding.

Use a handlebar bag or a box on your bike's rear rack to hold shirts and sweaters as you take them off. You will rarely need more clothing later in a ride than at the start, but take along a couple extra sweaters anyway, in case the weather gets colder before your ride home. As you warm up while riding, peel off layers of clothing to stay comfortable. At the top of long downhill runs, add a layer.

In very cold weather or for a short, slow ride, a down parka can keep you comfortable. But don't wear it unless you'll need it for the whole ride. Avoid wearing a long overcoat, which will interfere with your pedaling.

If you wear the clothes we've just suggested, you should be quite comfortable down to 0 degree F — or 10 degrees below, with the down parka and the sweaters.

Your hands, feet, and head need the most insulation, because they are farthest from your heart. Your ears and face get cold too, but your head has very strong blood circulation and radiates much heat.

On your feet, wear two pairs of heavy wool socks. If the outer pair is long, you can pull them over your trousers to keep the wind out. Down to about 10 degrees F in dry snow conditions, wear your tennis shoes or running shoes. For cold, wet conditions, if you must do much walking in snow, or if it is very cold, wear leather work boots. Waterproof the boots with mink oil or Sno-seal. Try to find boots with soles that aren't too wide or thick. Still, you may have to raise your bike's seat a bit and use wider pedals.

Keep your hands warm with heavy mittens. These should have a windproof nylon, leather, or plastic outer shell and an insulating liner. Ski mittens and snowmobile mittens are good. Avoid gloves with separate fingers — they insulate your fingers poorly. Three-fingered hunter's trigger mittens are best. They allow you to use your index finger to work the fasteners on your clothes or to stuff it in with your other fingers where it will stay warmer. Put reflective tape or cloth on the backs of your mittens (or the wrists of your windshell), for hand signalling at night. Waterproof the outsides of leather mittens, just the same as your boots. Your grip on the handlebars can compress the insulation in your mittens, so thick padding on the handlebars, such as Grab-On padding, can help keep your hands warm too.

On your head, wear a stocking cap, "trooper" style cap, or wool skiband, even under a helmet — and the helmet is highly recommended for winter ice and snow riding. Remove the helmet's sizing pads if necessary to make room. A raincover over the helmet will block the ventilating holes, if you find this necessary. Don't tape up the holes though, except with Scotchlight tape, because the glue on many tapes is bad for the plastic of the helmet.

Longer hair can make an improvement in winter comfort which you will notice!

Cold wind can make your eyes burn and water, especially as you start out. Glasses will probably give your eyes enough protection. Sunglasses are a good idea in any case when there's snow on the ground. Ski goggles are fine too.

When the weather is very cold, you'll need something to protect your face and also force moist exhaled air away from your glasses or goggles. A leather ski mask with a nose flap is good, though many cloth ski masks will fog your glasses. So will a scarf, if you wear it over your face. But any of the filter masks recommended later in this chapter will direct air downward, keep your face warm, and protect your lungs against the acrid smoke from cold auto engines.

If you wear a scarf to keep your neck warm, make sure it isn't long enough to get caught in the spokes.

When you exercise in cold air, your nose may run. It is normal and healthy for this to happen (it's how the inside of your nose protects itself from the cold). Carry a washcloth in your handlebar bag to blow your nose. A washcloth is much easier to handle than paper tissues when you're wearing gloves.

To enjoy a comfortable winter ride, eat right. You need more energy to keep warm. Eat a medium-sized breakfast. Stress cereal and avoid fatty foods before riding. They won't give you energy until too late, and they clog your circulation. Eat fresh fruit with your breakfast for vitamins and quick energy. On a long ride, take a snack with you.

Start out with clothing that has been kept in a warm place. You warm up quickly after starting to ride. If your clothes are warm as you start, you need one layer fewer. Very often you can get by without removing any layers as you warm up.

Remove layers of clothing before you begin to perspire. If you become hot, you'll get drenched with perspiration. Then, the first time you stop or go down a hill, you'll get cold, and you won't warm up again.

Ride briskly. As long as your head, hands, and feet are protected, heat from exercise banishes discomfort from cold. The faster you ride, the warmer you'll get.

Warm your hands by whirling them like windmills to force the blood into them.

At the end of your ride, wind down, or wait outside in the cold for a minute so you don't overheat when you go indoors.

Carry an extra pair of glasses, or run warm water over your glasses once you're indoors so moisture won't fog them.

YOUR WINTER SCHEDULE

The sun is out. The temperature is above freezing, but under you, reflected sunlight glares off an endless, wet expanse of slush, sand, meltwater, road salt, and rainbow-colored oil slicks. Your tires sizzle on the wet pavement.

How do you stay clean and dry on this fine, warm day?

Up to the waist, equip yourself for rain riding. Use waterproof boots, gaiters, chaps or leggings, and fenders on your bike.

Keep a change of clothing at your destination or in a saddlebag.

Be careful of how you store your bike. If you leave the bike outdoors, when it's clogged with slush, the tires can freeze to the fenders. But snow stuck in the tire treads will melt after you bring the bike indoors and leave tell-tale puddles with dirty tire marks in them. If you hang your bike vertically, meltwater can collect in the fenders and baptize you when you take the bike down again. Expect your bike to get dirty. Find a storage place where the snow can melt in peace, if the bike's clogged with snow. But take it to an unheated place once the snow has melted, so

warm rims won't get wet in snow as you start riding.

Most confirmed winter riders don't try to keep the outsides of their bikes clean until winter is over. It's just more trouble than it's worth. Excess cleaning of the outside of a bike can force dirt inside, into the bearings, where it does real damage. If you have one, ride a relatively weatherproof — that is, non-derailleur — bike, and seal the bearings. Oil an internally geared hub frequently to keep dirt washing toward the outside. Use machine oil. If the front hub, bottom bracket, or pedals have oil holes, oil them too. On the chain, use a light, nonsticking lubricant like LPS-3, but expect to replace the chain a bit sooner than you would in good weather. Still, it should last you through a season of winter riding.

RIDING IN SNOW AND ICE

If you have never ridden in winter, a streetscape of snow and ice may seem like one vast, scary expanse, a crazy place to ride.

In fact, you can get around on your bike very well in most common winter road conditions. You'll ride slower, but everyone else will be going slower too. You will have a greater advantage of shorter travel time and reliability over motorists than you do under clear conditions. Not only is it impossible to get stuck, but when motorists get stuck you won't get trapped in traffic jams behind them. In heavy snow conditions, two-way streets are commonly narrowed to one traffic lane as snow-plows pile drifts on either side. Two lines of cars commonly face off against each other in the middle of a block, and it is sometimes several minutes before everyone can make up their minds which line is going to back up.

Meanwhile, you pedal or push your bike

past, with a chuckle for the frustration you've spared yourself. Motorists have parking nightmares when half of the street parking places hold snowdrifts.

Biking under winter conditions is sometimes tough, but it isn't as tough as driving. Our experience is that biking is one of the best ways to keep sane and cheerful through a Boston winter.

There are several snow conditions which require different approaches to riding.

To ride effectively on a bad surface, you have to tune in to the surface and understand how your bike behaves.

The first time it snows, take your winter bike out and try it on a quiet street. Practice steering, braking, turning, and hill climbing on snow. Learn the little signals the bike gives you about the road surface: little skids, the crunch of snow and the sizzle of sand under the tires, and the many others. Then read these sections again; you'll get more out of them the second time.

SMOOTH ICE PATCHES

These patches appear in the road when a freeze follows a thaw. Check the weather forecast, feel the air, and look at puddles when you start out, so you'll know whether you must be on the lookout for ice. Wider tires have a bit better traction on smooth ice, but if the streets are mostly clear, you'll do better on average with your fair-weather, narrow-tired bike.

Temperatures can vary widely over the length of a ride, so keep checking for ice conditions as you go. Ice patches can appear even when there isn't any snow on the ground, usually from leaky water mains.

Read the ice as you approach it. As the temperature goes below freezing, ice will first appear as a white margin at the edges of puddles and runoff streams. Be careful of the

margins, though the center is usually still liquid at this stage. After a runoff stream has completely frozen, it will be very slippery but manageable if dry. If it has been sanded, it will be easy. Ice is worst when it is melting, with a film of meltwater on top either from rising temperatures or from salting without sand. And running water can wash off sand, too. Look for the high gloss of water, and the sparkle if it is flowing. Dry ice will be a bit rougher and less glossy.

When temperatures fall rapidly after a rain or where cars throw up spray from puddles, look for "black ice" — a film of ice so thin that it follows the shape of the gravel in the road surface. It may disguise itself as darker patches of asphalt, so be wary of it just after a freeze. Because it is so thin, it will evaporate in a day or two.

When you see an ice patch ahead, make sure it is smooth and level. Plan a straight path through, then slow to 15 mph or less and coast through. No pedaling, no braking, no turning. Keep going just as straight as you can so your tires are pushing straight down without sideways forces. Get down low on the handlebars with bent elbows for control. Keep your weight on the saddle so you can put a foot down quickly if you begin to fall.

If the road surface is banked, you may tend to slide sideways. Then plan a curved path instead of a straight one, so your tires are still aiming straight down at the pavement.

You may slip to the side unexpectedly due to banking or a sidewind. Keep your bike upright. With your hands low on the handlebars or with bent elbows on flat bars, you can swing your upper body sideways to keep your balance. Try this before you resort to putting a foot down.

If there is traffic behind you, make a slow signal and slow down well before you reach the ice. Make sure drivers behind you understand the problem and give you plenty of space. Then accelerate, so the cars will be well behind you. If the patch is long or a driver won't get off your tail, dismount and walk.

NEW SNOW

When the temperature of the road surface is below freezing, new snow will "dust" the surface and blow around. If the snow is still light enough that you can see through it, it will reduce your traction about twice as much as rain. If it is deeper, up to 2 inches or so, your tires will press it onto the road. You'll hear a crunching sound. You'll have to pedal harder, and traction will be less. But the "cupping" effect of the snow on either side of narrow bicycle tires will give you enough sideways traction for careful turning. Accelerating and braking will require more care than turning unless your tires have deep tread patterns.

When the road is wet, the effect depends on whether your tires push right through to the water or whether the snow cakes under them. You'll hear the crunching sound if it's caking and a splash if it isn't. If the snow is caking, it is quite slippery for accelerating and braking — a molten film will usually form between the snow and the tire. Still, the "cupping" effect will give enough sideways traction for careful turning.

You have to concern yourself with new snow mostly if you are at work when the snow begins. Still, you will have an easier time getting around in new snow than people who drove to work. Your employer will let you out long before riding conditions become very difficult.

A bike with narrow tires rolls easier in new snow, though one with wider tires has more traction. If you're riding to work and there's just a chance of snow, you're better off on the average taking the bike with narrow tires.

When the snow is deep your brakes may get wet. Cold, dry snow will wet the rims only for the first half mile after you've had the bike indoors in a warm place. Wet snow may keep the rims wet constantly. Snow which freezes on the rims may form either a very slick sheet of ice or rough crystals which make braking relatively easy. Check your brakes frequently, because their condition can change quickly.

Even when shallow, new snow can hide ice patches. When it is deeper or drifting, it can hide potholes and railroad tracks. Your best defense against these problems is to know your route. Take the same route every day so you know where the problems will be.

PACKED SNOW, ICE, AND SLUSH

These conditions are treacherous. Not only do they make the road slippery, they will force your tires sideways. If the packed snow, thick ice, and slush have been sanded, it's another story — and relatively easy riding. But we want to prepare you for the worst; no sand or a thaw which is washing it away.

Use your wide-tire bike, if you have one. Wear heavier clothing, because you'll be riding slowly (about 6 mph). Don't slow too much, because the effect of each little bump is reduced if you go over it faster. Keep your bike moving with gentle pedaling in a low gear. Your rear tire's slipping allows you to gauge the surface.

Get low on the handlebars so you can shift the weight of your upper body sideways. Expect your front wheel to slide sideways now and again. Ride in the middle of car tire ruts if possible, but steer so you don't have to climb up their sides. Steer the front wheel nearly straight as it slips sideways unless you have to force your way up over the edge of a rut. You may have to do this either to change your course or because you can't keep your balance without steering outside the rut. When you have to leave the rut, turn the front wheel sharply and jump it a little so it bites into the snow. As soon as it's over the edge, whip it back straight again to keep your balance. The rear wheel may slide along inside the rut for a while, but you can usually still control the bike. If you lose your balance, put down a foot.

Speed up a little before climbing a hill. Climb in a low gear, applying force all the way around the pedal stroke. Reduce your force whenever the rear wheel begins to skid. If you spin out, you'll just melt snow onto the tire and make it slipperier. If you can't get enough traction, you may have to walk up.

Take downhill stretches slowly. Use the rear brake lightly, and if necessary, drag your feet. A quick-release seatpost clamp is helpful so you can lower the saddle for a long downhill run.

Continuous packed snow is level enough so your tires and rims are safe from damage. Islands of packed snow on clear pavement and piles of frozen slush are as hard as curbs, and may be as high. Treat them as slippery curbs. Don't ride at them, and don't ride close and parallel to one unless you're ready to put a foot down.

VERY DEEP SNOW

This book attempts to be fair, and to recommend the best means of transportation for all conditions. For snow more than 3 or 4 inches deep, we recommend cross-country skis and snowmobiles. Our preference is for cross-country skis, because they are cheap and quiet. They put you in touch with the peacefulness of winter, property owners welcome them where they ban snowmobiles, and they keep you in shape for bicycling. But if you need to bring home a week's groceries, by all means use a snowmobile.

WINTER FALLS AND ACCIDENTS

You are likely to fall more often on slippery winter roads than you are in other seasons. That goes without saying. But winter falls are rarely serious ones. On a slippery surface, you can never go over the handlebars unless you actually run into something. Generally, you go slowly enough that, if you do run into something, nothing much happens. And the most common sort of fall, to the side, just lets you down on your shoulder and hip. Packed snow has approximately the same texture as the Styrofoam liner of a Bell Helmet, so you're unlikely to come up with anything much more serious than bruises.

Do wear a helmet though — you just might need it.

In the country, at least on back roads, you have to deal mostly with road conditions, and little with traffic. In the city, you may have to deal with traffic. In some ways, winter conditions work against you in traffic and in others they work for you.

In winter conditions, neither you nor motorists can brake or turn as quickly, and at times you may both have little control over your vehicles. You understand this, and so do most motorists — most drive slowly, keep a respectful distance behind you, and pass you only when there is plenty of room. It is sensible and courteous for you to pull over and let them go by, if they're short of room. At your winter speed, it won't add much time to your trip.

Once in a while, a motorist will tailgate you on a narrow, slippery street. If tailgated, put your feet down, slow down gradually, and stop. Then get out of the way. If you have a chance to explain to the driver exactly how you feel about the situation, do so. Be sure to point out that the law places the responsibility for an accident on the following driver. A safety vest with "STAY BACK" in large letters on the back may help.

Rough winter conditions can work for you because the the direction and speed of cars is more predictable — they can't turn, brake, or accelerate quickly. Use this notion to help build your safety space. Also, the worst conditions favor the best drivers. There will be less traffic. Timid and unskilled drivers will get stuck once or twice and then give up. Drivers who identify with the power of their engines will only get hopelessly stuck. The drivers who keep going in winter are the ones who are tuned in to traffic, the road surface, and the way their cars behave. Often, you can go on your bike when few if any motorists dare to go out. Winter conditions are more dangerous, yet you will find in most cases the really slippery places are only a small fraction of your total trip, small enough to deal with by walking or slowing. If a large part of your trip is slippery, car traffic is usually so tied up or so absent that you have little to worry about from it. You expect more falls, yet you compensate in your riding, because you know it's slippery. Statistically, few falls lead to collisions with cars, in winter or at any other time.

Winter bicycling is different, but not markedly more dangerous if you've had some practice and use caution.

HOT-WEATHER RIDING

Recreational bicycling is most popular in hot summer weather and for good reason. On a hot day a bike ride is more cooling than any other type of outdoor exercise except swimming. Most of a jogger's, roller skater's, or tennis player's energy goes to lifting body weight over and over. As a bicyclist, you lift your weight onto the bicycle once. Then, once you're riding, most of your energy goes to blowing air against your body. At a speed of 20 mph on level ground, about 90 percent of your pedaling effort pushes against air resistance, and about three-fourths of the air resistance is against your body — one-fourth is against the bicycle. Hills make you work harder going up but give you a free blast of air going down.

Long-distance bicycle tourists and racers take special precautions to prevent dehydration and other problems associated with prolonged exertion in hot weather. Over moderate bicycle commuting and shopping distances, you needn't be so careful. Still, there are things to know that will help make your hot weather trip a pleasant one.

HOT-WEATHER EQUIPMENT CHECKLIST

Clothing is important. A bicycle racer wears a tight-fitting wool jersey and shorts, which wick water to the outside. They may look hot, but they are in fact the coolest clothing for summer riding. Unless you're a hard-bitten commuter, you probably won't wear racing clothes, but your choice of clothing still can make a big difference.

Choose a shirt which covers your back down to the waist, even when you're in a crouched riding position. A swath of sunburn across the lower back can come as an unpleasant surprise after a summer ride. A cotton shirt will wick water out; a synthetic one will quickly become sopping wet.

The best shorts come halfway down to the knee and fit the legs fairly close so they protect them from chafing on the saddle. Again, wool is best but cotton is good. If you're making cutoffs out of an old pair of long trousers, don't cut them off too high!

Heavy wool athletic socks are the most comfortable. Thin socks get soaked and slippery. Wool socks wick away moisture and insulate your feet from the heat of the road surface.

Low-cut leather lace-up shoes with ventilating holes, like tennis shoes, work best for bicycling. The leather "breathes." Sandals would be cooler, but you can't use toe clips with them. Bare feet don't work on metal pedals, become very uncomfortable when you must stop on hot pavement, and are easily injured.

A few additional items of equipment are helpful:

An athletic sweatband helps cool your head and keeps sweat out of your eyes.

To keep the sun off your head, wear a helmet or bicycle cap. You may also want to wear a bandanna to protect the back of your neck from the sun.

Sunscreen lotion prevents sunburn on parts of the body which are not protected by clothing.

A small sponge, wrapped in a plastic bag in your handlebar bag or pocket, serves to wipe your face when necessary.

Sunglasses protect your eyes against bright light and insects. You'll want a cloth to wipe your glasses, too.

A bicyclist's water bottle in its cage on the frame allows you to drink without stopping.

Bring a towel, hairbrush, deodorant, and change of clothing in a saddlebag (not a backpack — it'll make you miserable in hot weather!) so you can spiff up after your ride.

It helps to make your bike more efficient. Check that the riding position is right for you.

A good saddle makes the most difference in hot weather. Get a leather or suede-topped one that "breathes." Try out dropped handlebars and toe clips. Once you're used to them, they'll let you ride just as fast with much less effort.

PREPARE FOR HOT-WEATHER RIDING

As summer builds up, ride frequently, and when you can, ride fast, so your body systems get better at handling the heat. They will get better exercise, just as your muscles strengthen. And the stronger you are, the more efficient you will be at producing energy, so you won't get as hot riding at any given speed.

Learn to *relax* as you ride, pedal fast, and put all your power into the pedals. Studies have shown that expert riders work only 40 percent as hard as beginners, so they only have 40 percent as much heat to dissipate.

Don't use excessive air conditioning in your home, workplace, or car. If you've prepared your body to handle the heat, you'll feel like turning the thermostat up anyway. You'll save on your electric bill, too.

The night before you ride and the day of your ride, eat your larger meals several hours before you will ride, at suppertime, and for a commuter, at lunchtime. When you ride, you want your blood to go to your skin and your muscles, not your digestive system.

Drink lots of water, and avoid excessive salt. Salt drives water out of your body. The night before, fill your water bottle one-third full and put it in the freezer, lying on its side. Before you leave, fill it the rest of the way. Then you'll have ice water to drink as you ride.

Eat a light breakfast, and take part of it,

an apple or orange, with you in your handle-bar bag. Or save breakfast till after your ride. Avoid fatty foods before riding or while you ride. Even vegetable oils are hard to digest, and make your red blood cells stick together, reducing circulation.

HOT-WEATHER RIDING TECHNIQUES

This is a bag of tricks for keeping cool and saving your energy.

Warm up, slowly increasing speed over the first mile so your breathing, circulation, and legs all build up in harmony.

Breathe deeply, and pedal fast enough so that you are always out of breath before your legs are tired. Breathing cools you, extra effort with your legs doesn't. Pedal steadily to keep your circulation — don't pedal and coast. If you don't feel comfortable pedaling steadily, your bike doesn't fit you right.

Sip ice water from your water bottle before you get thirsty. Your body won't tell you you're dehydrated until it's too late.

Avoid using the brakes unnecessarily. You need energy to get going again. On downhills, sit up and let the extra air resistance cool you as it slows you down. Keep turning the pedals to pump blood through your overheated leg muscles.

Choose your route carefully. Choose a route on the downwind side of a body of water, unless the wind is a strong headwind. Find a shaded route if possible. Avoid concrete expanses and steep hills if you can.

If your main need is to be really cool rather than to get somewhere fast, or if you have to climb a steep hill, gear down. Pedal slowly but don't strain, and breathe evenly and deeply. This is how Indian pedicab

drivers keep going in 110-degree heat, and they should know.

If you pedal fast right to your destination, you'll get off your bike and suddenly discover that you're hot! We weren't kidding about that wind blast. Unless you're headed for a swimming hole, wind down to a moderate speed for your last mile so you'll cool off.

CLEANING UP AFTER A HOT RIDE

If your workplace has a shower and lockers, you're lucky. You can take your morning shower at work. Often, a workplace will have a shower which is not in use. Or people may think of the shower as just for one special use; for example, you may teach in a school with showers at the gym. You can usually convince your employer to let you use a shower. People who like to go running during lunch hour will join you in making your request. Or you may chip in with other employees to have one installed.

But even if there isn't a shower, don't dread sweat! Fresh perspiration has little odor, and once you have wiped it off, it leaves none. Offensive odors are from bacterial action on stale perspiration, some held on the skin, but mostly in the clothes. A shower or wash basin at your destination will help you cool down quicker, but if you don't have one it is enough to remove your wet clothes, wipe yourself down with a towel, and give yourself five minutes to cool off. Then apply deodorant and put on fresh clothes. Unless the weather is very hot or you have been riding very hard, you will probably have to change only your shirt. If you have to wear special clothes at work, keeping a change of clothes there can be handy.

THE BIKE FOR BAD CONDITIONS

A bicycle can handle winter snows, soft sand, and rough hiking trails. It is the ultimate go-anywhere machine, because you can carry it anywhere you can't ride it. If most of your riding is on bad surfaces, consider owning a bicycle especially suited to them.

Use a bike with wide tires. For an adult, 26 × 2.125 inch tires are best, with knobby treads for soft surfaces. Aluminum rims are now available in all 2.125 inch sizes down to 16-inch. They make the wheels as light as possible and improve braking performance. You pay a moderate penalty for wide tires on good roads — maybe 15 percent of your speed.

A high bottom bracket lets the bike go over bumps without bottoming pedals.

Cantilever rim brakes or hub brakes work well because they don't have to reach around the wide tires.

Low gearing is needed to thread through difficult passages and climb steep trails.

A strong, reinforced frame takes the punishment of jumping, and of riding over rocks and tree roots.

Wide, flat handlebars allow more control.

Pedals without toe clips make the most sense when it is necessary to take feet off the pedals repeatedly, not because it is difficult to take them off, but because the toe clips drag and it is difficult to put the feet back in.

A quick-release seatpost allows lowering the seat for better control on long, steep downhill runs.

There are two types of bikes which are specifically made for rough riding:

1. The ballooner, mountain bike, or super cruiser has all of the features listed above and is usually equipped with multispeed derail-leur gearing. The ballooner is an adult bike. It can be very expensive, and is not yet in mass production. The ballooner is more or less a crossbreed between an old American fat-tire clunker bike, a dirt track motorcycle, and a high-quality touring bike.

2. The BMX (bicycle motocross) bike has 20-inch wheels, and is primarily a child's bike, though many teenagers and adults ride them. The BMX bike has high handlebars and a low seat — best for jumping over obstacles. These handlebars and seat prevent efficient long-distance riding since most pedaling is done in the standing position. The BMX bike usually has one-speed gearing for ruggedness, though special, rugged derailleurs are beginning to make an appearance. The BMX bike is widely available in mass production.

There are other types of bikes which do well on bad surfaces:

1. The classic American tank bike, clunker, or cruiser won't handle the pounding of jumps and rocky trails, but it cruises along well on dirt roads and beach sand. This sort of bike is enjoying a new wave of popularity as people rediscover its advantages.

2. The small-wheel folding bike or town bike with wide tires handles dirt roads and beaches well, but like the cruiser, it doesn't have the strength or the high bottom bracket for the rougher stuff.

3. The Raleigh Tourist, with 1½-inch tires, does reasonably well if ridden sedately.

4. Many European touring bikes and utility bikes, and in fact any bike with wide tires, have the advantage for soft or bumpy surfaces.

By selecting the right components, it is possible to upgrade many bikes for better riding on bad surfaces. A tank bike can be upgraded with a stronger front fork, better brakes, and multispeed gearing; a French touring bike with 650B tires would be converted to 26 × 2.125, and the frame could be reinforced to make an almost perfect copy of a super cruiser; wide rims and tires could go on any bike that will fit them.

SPECIAL CONDITIONS

Riding on rough surfaces poses a number of particular problems and challenges. With the wide tires, you can roll and jump over obstacles you'd have to walk over on a street bike. Your best bet to develop your judgment and learn the special techniques is to seek out an experienced off-road rider. Different surfaces present different hazards:

. . . Sand and mud are soft, like new snow. They slow you down and sometimes stop you. They may hide hazards. Unless you seal your bike's bearings, sand and mud can wear them quickly.

. . . Hard dirt is a good surface to ride on, but just slippery enough for spectacular rear-wheel skids in downhill turns. It's also hard on your bike's bearings.

. . . Gravel is slippery, like riding on ball bearings, and slows you down too.

. . . Pebbles and stones can roll your tires sideways, and you have to ride around the big ones or walk over them to save your rims.

. . . Grass and leaves are soft and slow, very slippery when wet, and can hide hazards.

. . . In the woods, sticks caught between your spokes are a hazard. Use lace-on wheel disks to prevent them from lodging across the bike's frame and ending your ride.

. . . On very rough terrain, fenders are a nuisance. Sticks get caught in them, and the back of the front fender can catch on rocks as you go down steplike edges. On sand, mud,

and wherever there is water, fenders keep you clean and keep dirt out of the bike's bearings. Many super cruiser bikes compromise with sealed bearings and a splash plate under the down tube. This at least keeps mud, sand, and pebbles out of the rider's face.

. . . Riding through water shortens the life of rims and spokes. Salt water is especially harmful; it can rust out a bike in a year or two. Stainless steel spokes or one-piece wheels and frequent sprayings with a light lubricant like WD-40 or LPS-3 will slow the damage. One way around the problem is to use an inexpensive, old tank bike as a beach bike. It has only one gear, but then most beaches are quite flat, anyway.

AIR POLLUTION

Depending on where you ride, it may make sense for you to protect yourself against unclean air. If you feel uncomfortable when riding or after riding, consider these measures:

. . . Choose your routes carefully. Often, you can find a route on back streets which is away from the worst pollution. If you can, choose a time for a trip when traffic is light or when wind or rain cleans the air. Learn to hold your breath as you pass through the exhaust from cars, and to come up for air in between.

. . . Be prepared to change your clothes after riding. Some materials, especially wool, goose down, and synthetics, pick up exhaust odors. Usually, it is enough to change your outer garments. The problem is worst in winter, when cold car engines throw out oil and soot.

. . . Some gaseous pollutants combine with sweat to form acids which sting your eyes. In hot weather, gaseous pollution is worst. Wear a sweatband to help keep the stinging sweat out of your eyes.

. . . If polluted air gives you headaches or a cough, consider wearing a filter mask. Even a handkerchief tied over your mouth helps. A simple paint spray mask, like a surgical mask, will be fairly effective in keeping out particulates, and the soot and oil mists from smoking cars. If you have a beard, the surgical mask won't seal well to your face. You'll need a more complicated mask with a rubber facepiece.

To keep out harmful gases as well as particulates, use a filter mask with activated charcoal cartridges as well as dust filters. The mask should protect against dust, mist, organic vapor, and acid gas. A standard industrial mask to this specification, such as the Norton model 7513 (7513-M for small face size), almost eliminates the odor and discomfort from polluted air. The Norton is probably the best brand of mask for bicyclists. Its facepiece is made of soft rubber, less of a hazard in a fall than others made partly of metal. The Norton's dual filters provide low breathing resistance except for prolonged sprints or climbs.

You can buy a paint spray mask at an automobile paint supply store or a well-stocked hardware store. The simpler masks can be found at industrial safety equipment outlets, in the Yellow Pages under "safety equipment." Shop by phone if necessary and have your mask sent C.O.D. by UPS.

Paint spray masks cost only about 25¢ each; a dust mask with a rubber facepiece, about $5; a respirator with activated charcoal cartridges, about $20. Buy extra filters and cartridges where you bought the mask. For the Norton mask, total expenses are about $30 per year if you use it every day.

Protect a Norton mask from water; if it gets wet from rainy day riding, take it apart, put the filter cartridges in a plastic bag, and dry out the remaining parts.

CARBON MONOXIDE

Motor vehicle engines are the most important source of poisonous carbon monoxide gas. Molecules of this gas attach themselves tightly to the oxygen-carrying hemoglobin in your red blood cells, leaving less hemoglobin to supply oxygen to your body. Prolonged riding in heavy traffic may dose you with enough carbon monoxide to make you feel dizzy and reduce your alertness. Still, studies have shown that bicyclists have lower levels of carbon monoxide than motorists, probably because we don't get caught in traffic jams, and we sit higher above the road. And in comparison with pack-a-day smokers, bicyclists have carbon monoxide levels ten times lower!

Not even activated charcoal filters can stop carbon monoxide. Fortunately, carbon monoxide does not irritate the lungs, and does not accumulate. You will breathe it back out again within a few hours. If you feel dizzy after riding in traffic, get out of the traffic and rest. Gauge your exposure so you'll know how much you can handle the next time. Remember that the transient effects of different poisons add to each other. If you wear a mask to keep out other poisons, carbon monoxide will bother you less.

WIND

Wind can speed you up or slow you down, and it can blow sideways at you so you have to lean into it to keep your balance.

A tail wind is an unexpected gift like a constant downhill ride. With a good 20 mph breeze behind you, you can fly along at 25 or 30 mph. A head wind is a tiresome annoyance. The same 20 mph breeze will slow you to about two-thirds of your usual speed, though the effect of wind on your travel time is less where traffic and red lights slow you too.

If you have an appointment to keep at the end of your trip, check the weather report or go outside and sample the wind. If there is going to be a head wind, allow yourself a little extra time beyond the normal travel time you know or have calculated.

In a head wind, you go faster if you use dropped handlebars and ride on the drops. Toe clips and a fast pedaling cadence keep you from tiring out. Also, it helps more than usual to wear compact, tight clothing and keep your baggage compact. If you can, choose a route sheltered from the wind by hills, buildings, fences, or vegetation. Wind shelter makes a real difference.

A wind gust from the side can push you sideways. The gust of wind leans you over, so you must steer away from the wind to keep your balance. Then you can turn the other way and lean into the wind. If you haven't had much practice riding, you can get blown off course. With practice, you will correct for wind so quickly you'll only move sideways a few inches.

Gusts of wind can occur in open country, but are most common where you move in and out of wind shelter — you can come out from behind buildings, for example, and get a gust of wind out of a side street. Air funnels through the openings in wind shelters at high speeds; with practice, you will learn to recognize such places and to watch for the little signs of wind like leaves blowing across the road.

As anyone who has ever driven a Volkswagen beetle knows, gusts of wind also come from large trucks and buses traveling at highway speed. Fortunately, once you have a little practice it is much easier to keep on course on a bike than in the beetle, but it would be a good idea to keep clear of large trucks and buses on the highway until you are confident about staying on course in gusty sidewinds.

The most serious problems with wind gusts from passing vehicles occur when the wind is coming from ahead of you or from your left. A wind from ahead adds to the speed of the vehicles, creating a stronger blast; a wind from the left is interrupted by the vehicles as they go by you, causing you to fall toward them momentarily. Give extra clearance under these wind conditions.

CHAPTER FIFTEEN

INSPECT, MAINTAIN, AND REPAIR YOUR BICYCLE

Your bicycle will treat you as well as you treat it. How well you maintain your bicycle is more important by far than how many gears it has, how light it is, or how much it cost when new. Gears that don't shift right, a bent wheel, or brakes that have gone out of adjustment can individually or collectively cripple your bicycle.

Bicycles deteriorate slowly. Problems creep up on you, so you hardly notice them. You get used to riding with brakes that are out of adjustment or a seat that slips. Your riding suffers because you're compensating for the bike's problems. Then, one day, the bike may really fail you or get you into an accident.

Obviously, you should not wait until your bike's performance begins to suffer. Learn to check your bike regularly and catch problems before they become serious. Then your bike will always be in top shape to ride, and you'll save a lot of money on repairs. Furthermore, a reliable bike will give you added confidence on the road.

WHO SHOULD REPAIR YOUR BIKE?

Who should work on your bike depends on what needs to be done, and on how much you know about maintenance. Here are some guidelines:

. . . A bike shop is the place to take your bike for most mechanical repairs and overhauls. Ask your bicycling friends which shops have the best mechanics and service.

. . . If the frame of your bike is out of alignment, bent, broken, or needs painting, you take it to a framebuilder who specializes in frame work. Framebuilders run independent businesses — most of them do not work through bike shops. Ask your bicycling friends where to go.

. . . To have wheels built, adjusted, or straightened, go to a professional wheelbuilder. Some wheelbuilders work out of bike shops, though many bike shops do not provide professional wheelbuilding services. A professionally built wheel will last several times longer, and the brakes will work better because the rims are straighter. A wheelbuilder can often save you money by repairing a bent wheel which a bike shop mechanic would have to replace. Bike racers and tandem riders can tell you where to find a good wheelbuilder.

. . . Certain common on-the-road repairs — such as patching tires — you should learn to do yourself. These repairs are simple; you can learn to do them in a few hours. You will save time and money, but you can do more.

LEARN TO FIX YOUR BIKE

Actually, you can learn to do most repairs on your bike yourself. A bicycle is a simple machine. Learning to repair it is relatively easy, and the tools you will need are basic and inexpensive. If you know how to fix your bike, you will save much time and money. Especially in the busy summer season, you may have to wait for a week to get your bike back from a shop, even for a repair which you could do in five minutes at home. And if you need to do a repair out on the road, you'll be glad you know how.

There are many good books about how to repair your bike. This book does not tell you more than you need to know for regular maintenance, because we'd only be repeating something you could read somewhere else.

We recommend that as you learn to repair your bike, you do it with someone who knows how. If you do an overhaul along with an experienced mechanic, you'll learn most of the basics.

A self-service bicycle repair shop offers you a workspace, tools, and a mechanic's help to fix your own bike. If you are inexperienced, you can learn there. Even if you are experienced at working on your bike, this shop will have all the tools you need, including those you use so rarely that it's not worth your time buying them.

Bicycle repair classes are available in many places through bike shops, bike clubs, schools, and adult education centers. A class is a good, systematic way to get started on learning to repair and maintain your bike.

INSPECTION

Every time you get on a bicycle you should first make sure that it is in safe, ridable condition. The four-part procedure described below covers the most important safety-related functions of the bike. If the bike is fit to ride, the whole procedure only takes about ten seconds.

1. The most important check is to squeeze both brake levers. They should move freely and smoothly, taking up the slack until the shoes touch the rim. Then you should feel firm resistance. The brake levers should not travel so far that they hit the handlebars. If both brakes are not working properly, you should not ride the bicycle until they have been repaired or adjusted. Brake shoes must contact the rim only, not the tire. If they contact the tire, they will wear through it very quickly.

2. Assuming that you are right-handed, use your left hand to lift the front of the bike about 6 inches off the ground. With your right hand, pinch the tire firmly to tell if it has a reasonable amount of air pressure. It should feel quite hard. If it feels OK, give the wheel a good spin. As the wheel turns, watch to see

whether it runs straight and true or wobbles from side to side. See if the wheel rubs on the brake shoes even for part of each revolution — you would have to pedal extra hard to overcome the resulting friction. The brakes should be adjusted and/or the wheel should be trued (straightened) so it can spin freely. If the tire rubs against the fork or a fender stay, this must be corrected or the tire may have a hole worn in it after just a few minutes of riding.

Rim wobble should be no more than about 1/8 inch. You shouldn't have to adjust the brakes so loose to compensate for rim wobble that they don't grip well. If you must, the bike is unsafe to ride. Rim wobble may be caused by slight bends in the rim, or by loose hub bearings. Loose bearings are more serious. Check for them by wiggling the rim sideways with your hand. If it shows more than the slightest amount of looseness, the bike is unsafe — the wheel may go into an uncontrollable oscillation as you ride down a hill.

Next, let go of the front of the bike and allow it to bounce on the front wheel. The purpose of this is to check for rattles. Rattles are an early warning signal of trouble to come. Bicycles in good working order do not generally rattle. If your bike does, you should find out why. It might be something merely irritating, like a loose fender ornament or reflector. Then again, it might be something serious, such as a loose wheel or headset, either of which could cause a serious accident.

3. Lift the rear end of the bike with your left hand, pinch the tire, spin the wheel, and drop the bike to check for rattles. When you spin the rear wheel, make sure that you spin it forward. If you spin it backward it will move the chain backward. You will get kicked in the shin by a pedal.

4. Examine the chain. It should be at least slightly wet with oil. If the chain is dry, it

TO LUBRICATE YOUR CHAIN

Lean your bicycle against something — preferably leaning to the right — then oil from the chain can't drip down onto the wheel. The pedals must be free to rotate. Use special chain lubricant.

Turn the pedals backward with the right hand, and hold the oil can in your left hand. With a regular oil can, drip oil on the chain just ahead of the lower pulley of the rear derailleur. With a spray can, squirt oil on the chain where it is wrapped over the small freewheel sprocket. Aim the spray directly forward so it lands on the upper length of chain.

Wipe the chain off afterward with a rag. The inner parts of the chain are what need oil, and extra oil on the outside will just attract dirt. If you get oil on the wheel, wipe it off right away — oil can rot the rubber of the tires and keep your brakes from working.

will create extra friction, and much of the work you do with the pedals will go into wearing out the chain instead of moving the bicycle over the road. If your bike has derailleur gears, a dry chain will make shifting difficult and noisy. Rust on your chain indicates neglect. You will probably have to replace the chain.

If you do not have derailleur gears, look at how the chain runs from the front sprocket to the rear and back again. It's probably too tight if it's straight as a midwestern road. This means binding and excessive friction and wear. You can feel the binding if you turn the pedals by hand. Chain sag indicates it is probably too loose, and it might fall off of one or both sprockets. Putting it back on is messy and inconvenient. If you have a coaster brake, you will lose your brake if the chain falls off.

Now you can feel safe to ride the bicycle. But as you ride, always listen for rattles and squeaks. The machinery of a bicycle is on the outside, so almost every mechanical problem will give you an early warning. A squeaking or rubbing sound means that you are wearing out part of your bicycle. A rattle or clunk means that something is loose and is again a serious danger signal. If your bicycle starts rattling, get off and check it right away.

BASIC TOOLS AND SUPPLIES

. . . Frame-mounted bicycle pump (make sure it fits your frame and the valves of your tubes)
. . . Tube patch kit
. . . Tire irons
. . . Tire pressure gauge (make sure it fits your valves — there are two common types)
. . . 6-inch adjustable wrench
. . . Medium-size flat-blade screwdriver (this will also fit most cross-slot screws used on bicycles; if not yours, buy a Phillips screwdriver too)
. . . Allen wrenches (to fit your bike's stem bolt, seat post bolt, and clamp bolt if they have Allen fittings — hexagonal socket in head of bolt)
. . . Oil. *Buy it at a bike shop.* Use bicycle oil, never "household" oil, which is vegetable oil and will gum up the insides of a three-speed hub.
. . . Chain lubricant. Buy this at a bike shop. This is a very light oil which evaporates and leaves behind a solid lubricating film. Used on the chain, it does not attract dirt as regular oil does.

Carry the tire-repair tools, wrenches, and screwdriver with you as your ride. They will get you through 95 percent of all on-the-road repairs. A small tool pouch is useful.

To do major repairs and adjustments, you will need more tools, but that's for another book.

TIGHTNESS TEST

The first part of the tightness test is to drop the bicycle and listen for rattles, as you do in your basic preride test. Dropping the bicycle will indicate most loose parts.

You should then go around the bicycle squeezing, twisting, and pushing all parts. Use a wrench to test that all nuts and bolts are snug. Parts that move, like brake levers and calipers, should have just the slightest wiggle on their bearings. Parts that are supposed to be tight, such as racks, lights, fenders, reflectors, brake attachment bolts, and brake shoes, should not wiggle at all. If they are loose, vibration will continue to loosen them and they will eventually fall off. Any part that falls off can be extremely dangerous, because it can catch in the spokes and lock the wheel. Be especially careful of the tightness of nuts and bolts which attach on the front brake, on the front fender, and on other parts near the front wheel.

WEEKLY MAINTENANCE

In addition to the daily check, every week or so there are three maintenance chores to be done. Oil your chain as described, and oil an internally geared hub. Check the tightness of nuts and bolts. Check your tire pressure with a pressure gauge and if necessary pump it up to the correct pressure.

Unless you live next door to a friendly gas station, the most convenient way to pump up your tires is with a floor-standing pump. You can buy a good one with a holding tank and a built-in pressure gauge for around $25. This type is much easier to use than the small hand pump you carry on your bike for on-the-road repairs. After you have inflated your tires to the correct pressure, pinch them as you do in the daily check-out. The correct pressure will generally be indicated on the sidewall of the tire. If in doubt, ask at a bike shop.

If you do have a friendly gas station next door, you can use their compressor, but don't trust their pressure gauge. Use your own pencil-type gauge instead. If you are using the type of gas station compressor that has a crank to set the desired pressure, it is safest to put the nozzle of the hose at a slight angle to the valve, so that some air leaks around as the tube is being filled, instead of having all the air go into the tube. This type of preselector

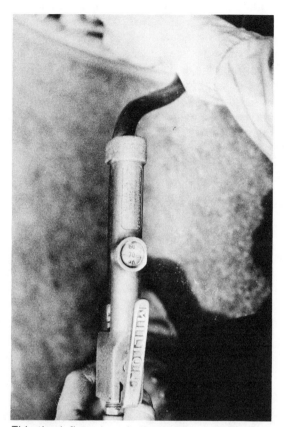

This tire inflator is safe if the lever is pumped in short bursts. The built-in gauge reads out the pressure in the tire when the lever is released.

This common gas station tire inflator may be used safely, with care.

gauge works by comparing the pressure in your tire with that set on the dial. If there is less air in the tire than the gauge is set for, it puts out a powerful blast of air, rings the bell, and measures again. The problem is that a bicycle tire has a much smaller volume than the automobile tires for which these devices were designed. With a bicycle tire a single blast from one of these can increase your pressure by as much as 20 pounds per square inch. If you set the dial for 75 psi, and your tire has 74 psi already, it could be up to 94 psi before you know it. This is assuming that the machine is correctly adjusted in the first place, which is a big assumption.

Some gas station hoses have a squeeze lever near the end, with a built-in gauge. This kind is safe if you use it carefully. Press the hose end down to the valve, squeeze the lever just for an instant — then release it and read the pressure in the gauge (it reads only when the lever is released). Do this again and again until the pressure in the tire is correct. Do not hold the lever down for more than an instant at a time, or you may blow out your tire.

The most dangerous gas station hoses are those with no gauge at all. Once you have placed the hose fitting against the valve of your tire, there is no control over the pressure. Sometimes the fitting catches on the valve, and then, in less than a second, the tire will overinflate and blow off the rim with a sound like a shotgun blast.

MONTHLY INSPECTION

Every month or so, you should give your bike a thorough inspection and perform routine lubrication, in addition to the daily and weekly check. Follow this schedule:

1. Check your brake and shift cables for fraying. These cables are made up of several strands of wire twisted together. If even one strand of the cable has broken, the cable should be replaced right away. The cables almost always break right near the end that attaches to the control lever. This part is easily visible on the shifter cables. To check the brake cables, squeeze the levers and look inside. It is a good idea to put a drop or two of bicycle oil in this section of cable at this time. When oiling derailleur shift cables, be careful

not to get any oil on the moving parts of the shifter levers, because these must have friction to keep the derailleurs from shifting of their own accord.

2. Check the brake shoes for wear. The shoes will have some sort of tread pattern cut into the braking surface to make them more effective in the rain. If they are worn past the tread area, they should be replaced. If your brake shoes are more than two or three years old, you might want to replace them anyway, because there have been major improvements in the materials used in the newer brake shoes. The modern types of composition give more effective braking than many of the older types, and they are quite cheap.

3. Make a careful examination of your tires. Look for bulges, cuts, and tread wear. Look for wear on the side of the tire if you use generator lights. If you have bulges in your tires, it means they are either incorrectly seated, in which case they will give a bumpy ride and may blow off of the rim without warning, or they have broken cords in the fabric that gives them their strength, in which case you are overdue for a blowout through the sidewall. If the tread is worn off of one or both of your tires, you will be slightly more likely to skid, and a lot more likely to get punctures.

4. Check your chain for stretch if you have derailleur gears. When a bicycle chain is new, each link is exactly 1 inch long. As the chain wears, it gets a little bit longer. This is not readily measurable on a single link, but can be checked easily on a one-foot length. Lay an accurate ruler or measuring tape along a one-foot length of the chain. Put one end at the exact center of one of the rivets (pins) of the chain; there should be another rivet perfectly centered at the 12-inch mark. If the chain is stretched less than 1/16 inch in the foot, it is alright. If the chain is stretched 1/8

inch or more, it has been left on too long, and the rear sprockets will be worn out of shape by the stretched chain. In this case, the chain and sprockets will have to be changed together, because a new, unstretched chain will not run smoothly on the old worn sprockets. The worn sprockets will wear out the new chain very quickly. If you keep replacing your chain when it gets stretched to the 1/16-inch level, your sprockets should last almost indefinitely.

5. To check wheel bearings, lift up each end of the bike in turn, and try to wiggle the wheel back and forth between the brake shoes. There should not be any significant play from side to side, except if you have internal gears. With three-, four-, or five-speed bikes, it is normal to have a little bit of play in the rear wheel. If there is excessive play, your bearings need to be adjusted (cone adjustment) or the wheels are not properly secured to the bicycle.

If you don't have excessive play in your wheels, you know that the bearings are not too loose. It is not so easy to tell if they are too tight. A good quick test for the front wheel is to lift the front of the bike off the ground to see if the wheel will turn of its own weight. Bicycle wheels are not balanced like car wheels, so one part of the wheel will be heavier than other parts. This will usually be near the valve, unless your wheels have reflectors attached to the spokes. Wherever the heaviest part of the wheel is, the wheel should turn by its own weight so that the heavy part is at the bottom. If the wheel does not turn when you lift up the front end of the bike, it might already have the heavy part down, so turn the wheel a quarter turn, stop it, and let go.

The wheel will normally swing back and forth like a pendulum several times before it finally slows to a stop, if your bearings are in good shape. If it stops in a jerky or abrupt manner, it is a sign that the bearings are too tight, too dirty, or in need of lubrication. Remove the wheel from the bicycle and check the bearings by hand if you are in doubt. Do this by holding the wheel steady and turning the axle. When turning the axle, use a very gentle grip with your fingertips. Turn the axle by revolving your wrist, not by rolling your fingers. If the axle feels at all gritty or hard to turn, the bearing needs to be adjusted or repacked.

You can test the pedal bearings for tightness by spinning or rocking the pedals. Also test the headset bearings once you have removed the front wheel, and the crank bearings once you have removed the chain.

Testing by lifting the bike up and letting the wheel turn does not work for the rear wheel unless you disconnect the chain, because when the rear wheel turns backward it takes the chain and crankset along with it, so you can't tell where the friction is. With derailleur gears, and a quick-release rear hub, it's easy to disconnect the chain — just take the wheel out, and when you put it back in, leave the chain hanging underneath.

To test the bearings with an internally geared hub or coaster brake, use another method. Spin the rear wheel forward. If the bearings are too tight, they will grab the sprocket and turn the chain and cranks forward — unless the crank bearings are too tight. It's normal for them to drift slowly — just so they don't grab and turn at full speed. If this test gives inconclusive results, try rocking the rear wheel sprocket from side to side. The sprocket's bearings are adjusted along with the wheel bearings, but they normally have play even after all noticeable play is gone at the rim. The sprocket should have a slight rock. If it does not move at all, the bearings are definitely too tight.

6. If your spokes are not tight enough, your wheels will not be as strong as they should be. Check spoke tension by squeezing two adjacent spokes together. They should be tight. Work your way around the wheel so that you feel the tension of every spoke, two at a time. If you find that some spokes are significantly looser than others, your wheel probably needs work. On derailleur-geared bikes it is normal for the spokes on the right side of the rear wheel to be tighter than those on the left.

Of all the jobs that a bicycle mechanic has to do, the most demanding and difficult to learn is spoke adjustment. For this reason you should not try to do any nonemergency wheel repairs yourself unless you have mastered all other basic aspects of bicycle repair. Even then, it is much easier to learn spoke adjustment by building up a new wheel with a new rim and new spokes than by trying to repair a damaged wheel.

A special warning: If you find that just one or two spokes are loose, do not tighten them. They are probably loose because your rim is bent, and if you tighten the loose ones you will only bend the rim more in the same direction.

YEARLY OVERHAUL

Once a year, your bicycle deserves a complete overhaul, in which all moving parts of the bicycle are taken apart, cleaned, inspected, replaced if necessary, lubricated, reassembled, and adjusted. A yearly overhaul will save you more than it will cost you, because parts that are beginning to wear out usually will wear out other parts along with them. Also, a complete overhaul is the only way to inspect, clean, and grease the bicycle's main bearings.

Unless you know how to overhaul your bicycle yourself, you will have to take it to a bicycle shop or an independent mechanic. Choose the shop or mechanic carefully, because thorough work is important in an overhaul. The easiest time to get an overhaul done is in the fall or winter.

The most common frame fault is a bent front fork. If you run into something head on, the fork is the most likely part to bend. If you look at the bike from the side, this type of damage is usually visible. Look at the line of the head tube — the upper part of the fork should be perfectly in line with it. The lower part of the fork bends forward. If your fork makes an "S" curve or is not in line with the head tube, it is bent, and should either be straightened or replaced. Do not assume that replacement is the better repair. If the fork has not been bent too severely, a good mechanic can straighten it. If the alternative is to install a brand "X" universal replacement fork, you would be better off having your old one straightened. On the other hand, if your bike is a major brand and you are able to get an exact replacement, then the new fork would be preferable.

Your fork can be bent to the side. Usually this would be in addition to a backward bend. If the fork is bent straight back, you would notice it as being a bit hard to steer. You also might have a problem with your toe clips hitting the front wheel. (Toe clips hitting the front wheel do not necessarily mean that your fork is bent. Many fine bicycles are built that way, especially racing bikes.) But if your fork is bent to the side, this will be much more noticeable and annoying: the bicycle will have a tendency to steer to one side. Test by riding without hands. You will not be able to ride without hands without leaning over to one side.

The most severe type of frame bend is caused by the same type of head-on collision that causes forks to bend back. This takes the form of bends in the top tube and down tube, right behind the head tube. In this type of bend the angle of the head tube is changed so that it becomes more nearly vertical. You will usually see a slight hump at the top of the top tube and down tube, and underneath the hump the tube may be wrinkled. If you see this type of damage on a used bike, don't buy it.

If you have a very valuable custom frame, it is possible to have a framebuilder replace the top tube, down tube, and head tube. This would make the frame as good as new, but

would likely cost as much as a new frame.

Another kind of bend is fairly common. This is where the rear stays of the frame are pushed over to one side, so they do not line up with the front triangle. This is not difficult to repair in many cases. All you need to check this is a piece of string and a ruler. Tie one end of the string to one of the rear dropouts (the part of the frame that the wheel attaches to), bring the string around the head tube and back to the other rear dropout. You now have string running up one side of the frame and back down the other. Make sure that the string

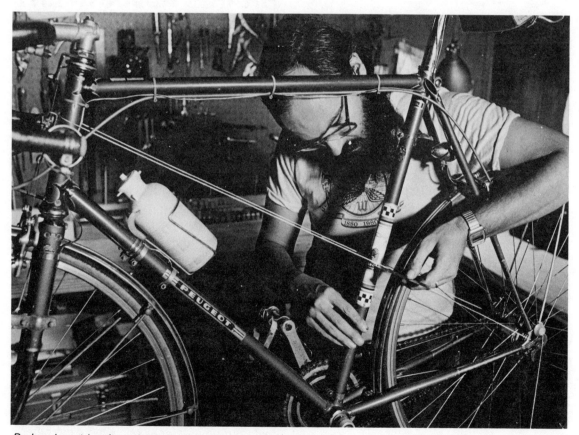

By looping string from the headset to the rear dropouts and measuring its spacing from the seat tube, the centering of the rear triangle of the bicycle's frame is tested.

is symmetrical at the dropouts. If it is coming around the outside of one dropout, it should go on the outside of the other dropout. Pull the string taut. Use a small ruler to measure how close the string passes to the seat tube at its closest point on each side of the bike. The distance should be the same on both sides. If it is not, your frame is bent.

If your frame or fork is bent because you ran into a tree, it may well make sense to have it straightened. On the other hand, if your frame or fork is bent in an accident that is someone else's fault, it is the responsibility of the person who is at fault (or that person's insurance company) to restore your bicycle to as good a condition as it was before they damaged it. In the last analysis, a bent and straightened frame or fork can never be quite as strong as new, even though it may be restored to the correct geometry. In such a case, you are owed a new frame or fork. In the case of the fork, this means an identical replacement. If an identical replacement is not available, a new frameset is in order.

BRAKE ADJUSTMENT

The most important part of your bicycle is the brake system. If your brakes do not work properly, they can kill you. A large number of cyclists accept inadequate performance from their brakes because they do not know how to maintain them. To compensate, they must ride slowly much of the time.

Your brakes are each made up of three parts: the levers on the handlebars, the caliper units that squeeze the wheel rims with rubber blocks, and the cables that connect the levers to the calipers.

The most misunderstood and most troublesome parts of the brakes are the cables. Each cable consists of two parts; the inner cable is a multistranded wire rope made of thin strands of steel. The cable has a metal fitting molded on to the end that connects to the lever. The outer cable, or housing, is a spirally wound piece of steel, similar to a spring. This is usually covered with a plastic wrapper to keep water from rusting the cable and to keep the cable from scratching the paint of your bicycle frame.

Each of these two parts is equally important, and neither will work without the other.

The brake lever on the handlebars is also

This frame has suffered serious damage from a head-on impact.

The cable housing on the left has been sloppily cut and will fray the cable. The one in the middle has been cleanly cut; the one on the right, ground to a smooth, flat surface — a professional job — though you can do it at home with a simple, flat file.

the side instead of being in line with the grabbing end. The handle ends are where the cable attaches. The inner cable fits easily through the small hole in the adjusting barrel on the caliper, but the outer housing cannot. The larger hole serves as a socket for the outer housing. When the brake is applied, the outer housing pushes down on this socket and moves the upper arm downward. The lower arm has a small bolt at its end, called the cable anchor bolt which has a small hole drilled crosswise through it that is just big enough for the inner cable to be threaded through. When the nut is tightened on this anchor bolt, the inner cable is pinched and locked in place securely. When the brake is applied, the inner cable pulls up on the lower arm and applies pressure to the other side of

made up of two parts: the movable part is the lever itself, and the stationary part that attaches to the handlebars is the hood. The inner cable attaches to the movable lever, so when you pull the lever it pulls the inner cable. The outer cable housing attaches to the stationary hood. Though the housing does not move when the brake is applied, it does just as much work as the inner cable, because the inner cable's pull cannot do any work without the corresponding push on the outer cable. The effect is similar to what would happen if you took a string of beads and pulled the string while holding one of the beads. The bead you are holding pushes the one next to it, which pushes the one next to it and so forth all the way along the string.

Brake calipers come in two basic types: sidepull and centerpull. What this means is that if the cable runs to the side of the caliper, it is a sidepull brake, and if the cable runs to the center of the caliper, it is a centerpull.

Sidepull calipers work just like a pair of pliers, except that the handle ends are off to

A carelessly installed wire basket kinks the brake cables, increasing cable friction so the brakes work poorly.

the rim. In the case of the rear brake on a "ladies" bicycle, the cable comes up from below, so the terms upper and lower should be reversed in that case.

Centerpull calipers work somewhat differently. The outer housing does not attach directly to the caliper, but to a fulcrum which is usually attached to the headset for the front brake, and to the seatpost bolt for the rear brake. Centerpull brakes use part of the frame (or fork) to do the pushing, because the outer housing attaches to the frame and so does the

This is a sidepull brake. Note the single pivot. The two brake arms are actuated — one by the pull of the cable and the other by the push of the housing.

This is a centerpull brake. Note that the cable pulls upward at the center, and that the brake has two pivots.

body of the caliper. The two arms of the centerpull caliper are joined together by a transverse cable. The inner cable from the lever hooks on to the transverse cable with a piece called the yoke, which has an anchor bolt in it to clamp the end of the inner cable. When the inner cable is pulled by the lever, it pulls up on the transverse cable, which in turn pulls up on the ends of the two brake arms.

The basic brake adjustment is the length of the cable. If the inner cable is too long or the outer housing too short, the brake will be too loose. When you squeeze the lever, the lever will travel unnecessarily far, usually until the lever hits the handlebars. Once the lever comes in touch with the handlebars, it does not matter how much harder you squeeze; the brakes will not get any tighter. It should not be possible to get the end of the brake lever to touch the handlebars. If it can do so, your brakes are not correctly adjusted.

If the inner cable is too short, or the outer

This adjusting barrel is located on a cable stop for a centerpull brake.

to use the wrench to loosen and tighten the anchor bolt, and one hand to pull the cable through the anchor bolt. Since most people have only two hands, there is a special tool made, called a third hand, to hold the brake shoes against the rim. You don't really need one of these, because a toe strap or a bungee cord wrapped around the caliper and tire will do the job just as well.

When you tighten the anchor bolt, it is very important that you tighten it the right amount. This is a rather small bolt and it has a hole drilled in it, so it is not very strong. It is very easy to overtighten it and break it. On the other hand, if you do not get it tight enough, your brakes may work normally in ordinary use until an emergency stop is necessary. In a panic stop you squeeze harder than usual on the brakes, and if the anchor bolt is not good and tight, the cable can pull loose. Just when you need your brakes the most they will fail altogether.

All experienced bicycle mechanics have learned how tight this bolt can be tightened without breaking it. The way they learned was by breaking a few when they were starting out.

housing too long, the brakes will stop you. However, when you let go of the levers, the brake will drag on the rim. The brake will be partly on all the time, and the bicycle will be very hard to pedal.

There are two ways to adjust the cable length: a coarse and a fine adjustment.

The coarse adjustment is made with the cable anchor bolt. To make this adjustment you need three hands: one hand to hold the brake shoes tightly against the rim (there is a spring that tries to push them away), one hand

The open-ended brake shoe holder on the left has been installed backwards. The brake block could slip out during a panic stop.

After you have broken a couple of these bolts your hands will know what the limit is. If you never break one, you are probably not tightening them enough. Lubricate the threads where the nut screws onto the anchor bolt.

A good test to see if the anchor bolts are tight enough is to squeeze each brake lever in turn with both hands. If you can't pull the cable loose with both hands, you certainly will not be able to with one hand.

The fine adjustment can be made without any tools at all, and is the one that should be used most of the time. This adjustment is made with a part called an "adjusting barrel." The adjusting barrel is a bolt with a small hole drilled through it the long way. The head of this bolt is usually "knurled" or textured, so you can turn it by hand. The head also has a

Front view of adjusting barrel.

A toe strap serves perfectly as a "third hand" tool while the brake cable length is adjusted.

larger hole going partway down, to serve as a socket for the outer housing. The inner cable goes all the way through the adjusting barrel, but the outer housing can only go partway in. The adjusting barrels are located in different places on different bicycles. They will always be at the end of a piece of outer housing. In the case of sidepull brakes, they are usually found on the upper brake arms. In the case of centerpull brakes, they are usually found on the fulcrum attached to the headset for the front brake, and to the seatpost bolt for the rear brake. Sometimes they are on the brake levers, where the outer housing attaches to the hood.

The adjusting barrel operates by changing the effective length of the outer housing. It can be slightly confusing, because turning it in the direction we normally think of as "loosening" makes the outer housing get longer, and makes the brake tighter. This is nothing to worry about — if you are not sure which way to turn the barrel to tighten your brake, try turning it one way and then squeeze the brake. Does it feel tighter? If so, you were turning it the right way. Does it feel looser? No problem — just turn it in the other direction.

It will make it easier to turn the adjusting barrel if you squeeze the brake shoes against the rim with one hand to relieve the spring tension on the cable while you adjust the barrel with your other hand.

If your brakes work poorly even though properly adjusted, this is generally due to excessive cable friction. Cables may be kinked or need lubrication. The remedy is to overhaul the cables, taking them apart to grease them and, if necessary, replace them.

REPAIRING FLAT TIRES

Beginning cyclists are afraid of flat tires because they don't have the tools or the know-how to repair them. After you have fixed a couple of them on the road you will come to look on them as only minor inconveniences, taking 5 to 15 minutes of your time.

To repair a flat, first decide whether you will need to remove the wheel from the bicycle. If you are just going to patch the tube, you may simplify the procedure by leaving the wheel on. If you are going to replace the tube or tire, as you must if they are badly damaged,

then you must remove the wheel.

If the flat is on the front wheel, all that is required is to flip the quick-release lever or loosen the axle nuts, depending on which type of hub you have. If the axle is held in by nuts, make sure not to remove them — just loosen them. That way you save time and you will not lose the nuts.

If the flat is on the rear wheel of a three-speed or other internally geared hub, first shift into high gear to release tension on the shift cable. Next, the cable must be disconnected from the hub. At the end of the cable nearest the hub, the wire cable connects to a cylindrical adjusting barrel. This adjusting barrel screws onto the small "indicator chain" or "bellcrank" depending on what type of hub you have. Unscrew the adjusting barrel from the indicator chain or bellcrank. Next, loosen (do not remove) the axle nuts holding the rear wheel in place. You will now be able to slide the wheel forward and down and out. Lift the chain off of the rear sprocket, and the wheel is separated.

Most people think that it is harder to take the rear wheel off of a ten-speed than a three-speed. This is not true if you know how.

The first step in taking the rear wheel off of a five-speed, ten-speed, or any derailleur-equipped bike is to shift the rear derailleur into the highest gear (smallest sprocket). This gets the chain as far as possible away from the wheel. It doesn't matter what gear the front derailleur is in.

Examine your rear derailleur. It has two large pivot bolts which probably have six-sided Allen heads. The lower one is the pivot for the cage (the cage is the part that the chain runs through). The cage rotates around the lower pivot to take up the slack in the chain as you change gears. The upper pivot is located just below the axle of the wheel. The whole body of the derailleur can swing back and forth on this upper pivot, and that is just what you want it to do. Take hold of the main body of the derailleur and pull it backward. Let go of it and it will swing back into its normal position by spring tension from the cage. Practice swinging it back as far as it will go. This is the action that will get the derailleur out of your way as you are removing and reinstalling the rear wheel. Once you are used to this idea, flip your quick-release or loosen your axle nuts. If your hub has axle nuts, notice which washers inside the nuts are outside and which are inside the dropouts. They should go back the same way when you put the wheel back on. Lift the rear end of the bicycle with your left hand, swing the derailleur back with your right hand, and push the wheel forward with your knee. Hold the derailleur back until you have disengaged the chain from the small rear sprocket. Now, lay the bicycle down on its left side so you don't bend the derailleur.

Now that you have removed the wheel from the bike, examine the tire carefully to see if you can discover what caused your puncture. It might be a nail or a tack, a small sliver of glass, or it might not be visible from the outside of the tire. It also might not be there anymore, but look carefully, since this is your best clue to the location of the hole. If you find the cause, make a note of where it is so you will be able to go directly to the correct spot on the inner tube when you get it out.

QUICK-RELEASE WHEELS

Quick-release wheels are terrific, but many people that have them don't know how to use them correctly. If you have quick-release wheels, there will be a single lever on one end of each axle. There will be a domed nut on the other end of the axle. This domed nut may have a very small handle to turn it by, or it may just be knurled (roughened to provide a grip to the fingers).

Some bicycles have one quick-release wheel and one solid axle (nutted) wheel.

The axle of a quick-release hub is hollow, and there is a long thin piece called a skewer that threads through it. The long handle is attached to one end of the skewer, and the domed nut screws onto the other end once the skewer has been threaded through the axle.

There are two small conical springs, one at each end of the axle. These go with the small end toward the middle. These springs are not important to nonracers — all they do is keep the skewer centered to save a couple of seconds when installing the wheel.

The common wrong way to use the quick-release is to use it as a wrench — turning it clockwise to tighten it and counterclockwise to loosen it. This is not only slow; it is impossible to get it tight enough this way.

The right way to operate a quick-release is to pull it straight out away from the hub and flip it over the other way. If it was tight, this will loosen it, and vice versa, assuming that it is adjusted correctly. Flipping the lever 180 degrees moves the part the lever is attached to in or out about three millimeters. This is all that is needed to clamp and release the wheel if the adjustment is correct.

The adjustment point is the domed nut on the other end of the skewer from the lever. This screws onto the skewer. The adjustment is how far it is screwed on.

If the domed nut is not screwed on far enough, you will be able to flip the lever easily, but it will not clamp the wheel in place securely.

On the other hand, if the domed nut is screwed too far onto the skewer, you may not be able to get the axle into the frame dropouts. Even if you can get the wheel in, you will not be able to flip the lever all the way over.

When the adjustment is correct, you will be able to make the lever flip all the way so it lies parallel to the bike, but it should require a fair amount of effort to do so. How much effort depends on the individual.

Quick-releases should be adjusted quite tight if you are a big, strong, heavy person. You'll put more strain on every part of the bike and the wheels may slip out of position.

Adjustments need not be so tight if you are little, weak, and light. You may not have the strength to operate the quick-release lever if it is adjusted too tight.

This adjustment is made with the wheel on the bike, and the lever in the loose position. You can either hold the lever and turn the domed nut or hold the domed nut and turn the lever, whichever you find more convenient.

The lever should point to the rear once it is tight so it won't get caught on a bush or something and be pulled open as you ride.

As a matter of convention, the skewer is usually put in so the lever is on the bicycle's left side, but you can do it the other way if you prefer.

The first tire iron is hooked over a spoke to hold it in place.

REMOVING THE TIRE AND TUBE

This is what you need tire irons for. If you don't have tire irons, spoon handles are the safest alternative. Don't use screwdrivers, which can easily make holes in the inner tube.

Start at a part of the tire that is not near the valve. The hardest part of removing the tire is the first part, and you should not complicate it by dealing with the valve at the same time.

If the edges of the tire are stuck to the rim, push them inward with your fingers until they are loose on the rim. Then use tire irons.

Start opposite a spoke that runs to the same side of the wheel as you are working from. Pull the hooked end of the tire iron toward you to pry up one edge of the tire at that one spot. Hook the notch on the tire iron to the nearest spoke so you will not have to hold it. Use a second tire iron two spokes away to pull out more of the same edge of the tire. If you are using three tire irons, the third goes two spokes to either side of the two that you have already hooked in place. When the third tire iron has been hooked to its spoke, there won't be any tension on the middle tire iron, and it will fall out. You can then leapfrog it over one of the other two and repeat the sequence.

After you have done this once or twice, the tire will no longer be tight on the rim. You can then remove the rest of this edge of the tire by sliding a single tire iron around the wheel between the tire and the rim.

With practice you will be able to do this job with just two tire irons. Many experienced mechanics don't need any tire irons at all, and do the whole job by hand.

Once you have pulled one edge of the tire off the rim, you can reach in anywhere that is not too close to the valve and pull out the inner tube. Pull the whole tube out except for the part the valve attaches to. Leave the valve in the rim until the tire has been removed.

The second edge of the tire comes off on the same side as the first. Once the other edge of the tire and the inner tube are out of the way, it should come off easily, without tools. If your tire is unusually tight fitting, you

Now a second tire iron has been inserted under the tire bead, increasing the length of it which is off the rim.

might need to use one tire iron to get it started.

Now that the tire has been removed it will be easy to pull the valve out of the rim and patch or replace the tube.

PATCHING THE TUBE

The first step in patching your tube is finding the hole. If you saw a nail or a piece of glass sticking out of your tire this should be easy. If it was a nail, it might have made more than one hole in the tube.

If the location of the hole is not obvious, it will be necessary to inflate the tube to find the leak. An inner tube is basically a rubber balloon. When a tube is inflated without the support of a tire holding it in, it can stretch out until it is a great deal larger than its corresponding tire. This stretching enlarges the hole and makes it easier to find. After pumping up the tube, disconnect the pump and hold the tube to your ear. Work your way around the circumference of the tube and you should be able to locate the hole by the sound of the air hissing out. If you are unable to hear the air leaking out, put on another tube. When you get home, you can immerse the old inflated tube in water in the bathtub and look for the bubbles. This should be used as a last resort, because you will then have to wait for the tube to dry before you can proceed.

Once you have found the hole, select a patch from your patch kit that is an appropriate size to cover the hole with a bit to spare. Most punctures are very small and can be patched with the smallest patches in your kit. If you are trying to repair a cut or a blowout, you will need to use a larger patch.

After selecting a patch, you must prepare the area of the tube that is to be patched. Use the patch as a guide, and buff the surface of the tube with sandpaper or the scraper that came with the patch kit. Buff an area larger than the patch. The inner tube was coated with talcum powder when it was made, and you must remove this. It will take a good bit of elbow grease to clean the tube sufficiently, especially if there is a molding line in the area to be patched. If there is a molding line under the patch it can provide an escape route for the air unless you completely sand it away. Once you have cleaned the area to be patched, keep your dirty hands and everything else away from it. The most frequent cause of patch failure is not cleaning the tube well enough.

Once the tube has been thoroughly cleaned, apply the cement. Note that this is not a glue. It is a type of rubber cement, and it does not work if it is wet. Put a small amount on the area to be patched and quickly spread it in a thin layer. Cover an area larger than the patch you will be using. Do not touch the cement once it starts to dry, because it should be smooth. If you used a thin layer it will dry quickly, if not, it will take a while. Do not apply the patch until the cement has thoroughly dried. The second most frequent cause of patch failure is trying to use the patch with wet cement — it will not work.

While you are waiting for the cement to dry, you can pass the time by checking your tire. You can tell much more about a bicycle tire by looking at the inside than the outside. Examine the inside of the tire carefully all the way around. Look for sharp things poking through, and for broken cords. If you find broken cords in the tire it is a sign that the tire should be replaced, because even though it may hold pressure at the moment, it is not to be trusted. If you have a serious cut or break in the fabric of the tire, you can make a temporary repair by putting a piece cut from the sidewall of an old tire in between the tire and the tube. There is no need to use cement for

this — air pressure will hold the blowout patch in place.

Note that the tire does not have to be air tight. If the air cannot leak out of the inner tube, there will be no leakage. The tire's job is to shape and protect the inner tube. The rubber patches for patching the inner tube are useless for patching the tire, because the tire is not made of rubber — it is made of cloth, which is then dipped in rubber to keep it from rotting and wearing.

By now the cement should be dry on your inner tube. The patch has a protective backing, usually of aluminum foil, plastic, or cheesecloth. Peel this backing off (being careful not to touch the exposed surface of the patch) and press the patch onto the tube. It should adhere right away. The other side of your patch may be covered with cellophane. If so, leave it on — it won't do any harm and it might protect the tube from sticking to the tire. The tube is now patched, and should be as good as new.

REPLACING THE TIRE AND TUBE

If you are putting in a used tube that has been patched, no special preparation is needed. If you are putting in a new tube, it will help to stretch it first. Put your foot through the tube and step on it and hold it down, while pulling the other side of the tube straight up in the air as high as you can reach. This will make it easier to fit the tube into the tire.

Some people like to put a very small amount of air into the tube at this point. Others prefer to work with the tube empty.

Start by putting the valve into the valve hole of the rim. If you have rubber rim tape to protect the tube from the spoke ends, it often is easier if you lift up the part of the rim tape that the valve goes through and put the valve through the rim tape first before putting it through the rim.

Next, put on one edge of the tire, so the tube is hanging out of the open side. Once the first edge is on all the way around, the next

An inner tube is a doughnut-shaped balloon. Inflated without the tire to hold it in, it expands.

Before installing a new inner tube, stretch it.

step is to tuck the inner tube into the tire. When you are putting the inner tube in, try to avoid twisting it or wrinkling it. It should not have any creases.

The inner tube should not pull the valve to one side or another. If your valve is sitting crooked, it is a sign that the inner tube is pulled tight on one side of the valve, and bunched up on the other. To prevent this, when you are installing the tube, start from the

When reassembling the tire to the rim, first place the inner tube's valve in the valve hole.

Get the tire started into the well of the rim.

Now, place one side of the tire inside the well of the rim.

Tuck the inner tube into the well of the rim along with the tire.

valve and tuck the tube into the tire, working your way about one-third of the way around the tire in one direction. Then go back to the valve and work in the other direction for the rest of the way around the wheel. This will provide an even balance of tension on the valve, and your tube will last longer. Note that even if you do this and install the tube correctly, the valve can still be pulled out of position if you walk or ride the bike without inflating the tire.

The hardest part of repairing a flat tire is now ahead of you — getting the second edge of the tire onto the rim. The hardest part of this is the last part, and the valve is a complicating factor. Therefore, you should make sure that the last part of putting the second edge of the tire on does not happen in the area of the valve. The surest way to do this is to start at the valve, and work away from it in both directions. You may be tempted to use tire irons for this task, but you should resist the temptation. In the vast majority of cases tire irons are not needed to put the tire back on. If you use them you have a very high risk of pinching the tube between a tire iron and the rim. This will put not one but two crescent-shaped cuts into the tube you have just finished patching!

You will have no trouble putting the first two-thirds of the tire on the rim, but after that it may get a bit difficult. Hold the wheel so the open part of the tire is on top facing you. Put the four fingers of each hand over the top of the tire and push the tire on either with your thumbs, or with the heels of your hands. Do not try to push in the middle of the gap, but work on the places where the edge of the tire crosses over the edge of the rim. Keep working first one side and then the other, back and forth, getting a little bit more on each time, and all of a sudden the last bit will pop over the edge and the tire will be mounted.

One last, very important step remains before you are ready to inflate the tire. You must

Once you have guided most of the tire onto the rim, pop the rest of the tire on with your thumbs.

make sure that the tire is properly seated into the rim. The most likely place for it to not be seated is right at the valve. Where the valve is attached to the inner tube, the tube has a reinforcing patch. Frequently the edges of the tire will be sitting on top of this reinforcing patch, and not be down in the bottom of the rim where they belong. If you try to inflate the tire in this condition, the edge of the tire will blow off of the rim at the valve, and the tube will burst. There are two types of holes in inner tubes which usually cannot be patched successfully — very large holes and holes close to the valve. This type of blowout produces a very large hole right next to the valve. Time for a new tube!

Once the tire and tube are in place, you can prevent the above problems very easily. Before you put any air in, push the valve almost all the way into the rim. This will push the reinforcing patch up into the tire where it belongs. Then push the tire down by its sidewalls to seat it properly. Then you can pull the valve back down and pump up the tire.

It is a good idea to put only 20 psi in at first, and then spin the tire to see if it is well seated all the way around. If it is not, you may have to do a bit of pushing and pulling to get it right. Once it is seated properly it can be fully inflated. If you have quick-release brakes, it is usually easier to inflate the tire before you put the wheel back on the bicycle. If you do not have quick-release brakes, you may find it difficult to get a fully inflated tire between the brake shoes, since the tire is wider than the rim. It may be necessary to remove one of your brake shoes temporarily or to put the wheel on before inflating the tire.

REINSTALLING THE WHEEL

To reinstall the wheel, you reverse the steps you took in removing it. But you must also be sure that it is properly adjusted.

A front wheel is the simplest. Slide the axle into the fork dropouts at the axle threads if they are dry, and securely tighten the axle nuts or quick release.

The wheel may not automatically center itself. Test by putting your fingers between the tire and fork, behind the brake at the top. Use the same finger of each hand. If one goes in farther, loosen the axle nut on that side and slide the axle down until the wheel centers. Note that the brake may be off center. If so, turn the brake until it is straight. Do not position the wheel to compensate for an off-center brake—then both the brake and the wheel will be crooked. A brake shoe may rub on the tire, and the bike will not steer straight.

After reinstalling the wheel, check the bearing adjustment as described earlier. Some bikes do not have locknuts on the front wheel bearings. The axle nuts serve as the locknuts. You may have to turn one of the bearing cones (between the fork blade and

spokes) to tighten or loosen the bearings if you have disturbed its adjustment while removing or reinstalling the wheel.

To replace the rear wheel on a one-speed or internally geared bicycle, first hold the rear end of the bicycle up. Wrap the chain around the rear wheel sprocket and then lower the bicycle down onto the wheel axle. Make sure all nuts and washers are in the same position inside and outside the dropout slots as they were before removing the wheel.

As you tighten the axle nuts, you must adjust the chain tension as described earlier—so it is not completely tight (it will bind and wear out the bearings), but not too loose (it will be likely to fall off). Adjust chain tension by loosening one axle nut, then shifting the wheel sideways at the front near the pedals. Then tighten the loose axle nut and loosen the other. Continue until the chain is correctly adjusted and the wheel is centered at the front where you have been shifting it sideways. Spin the pedals as you test the chain adjustment. Sprockets are never perfectly round, so tension will vary. The chain must be slightly loose even at the tightest place.

With a coaster brake, you must securely reconnect the curved arm which comes from the left side of the hub. This keeps the axle from turning when you apply the brake.

With a three-speed or other internally geared hub, you must reconnect the shifter cable. Screw the cable's adjusting barrel down onto the threaded part attached to the right side of the hub—but not all the way. Correct shifting depends on a correct adjustment. Most hubs have a mark for the middle gear, or you can correct the cable adjustment by testing the shifting. In first gear, the cable should be almost as tight as it can get. Beyond this, if the hub's gears are one too high or one too low for the shifter position, or if the hub slips in second or third gear, the cable needs adjusting. On the threaded piece where the adjusting barrel attaches, there will be a locknut to keep it from unscrewing. Tighten this locknut against the adjusting barrel so it will hold its adjustment.

A rear wheel on a derailleur-equipped bicycle is easier to reinstall, because the derailleur adjusts the chain tension. Lift the rear end of the bicycle up and put the wheel underneath, with the sprockets inside the chain. Then let go of the wheel and pull the derailleur back, just as you did when removing the wheel. Now you can lower the bicycle onto the wheel. Slide the axle into the axle slots. On most bicycles, slide it all the way back at the right side (some more expensive bicycles have adjusters for both sides). Before tightening the left axle nut or quick-release, make sure the tire is centered between the chainstays at the front, near the pedals.

CHAPTER SIXTEEN

SPECIALIZED BICYCLE ADAPTATIONS

People who are very tall, very short, handicapped, or need to carry heavy loads, need special bicycles. Even for normal commuting needs, adaptations are sometimes useful. For example, lightweight bicycles with internally geared hubs are not widely available, but are excellent for city commuting.

It may be necessary to build a bicycle completely from the ground up to meet a special need. Custom bicycle shops can do this, as well.

A CUSTOM-MADE BIKE

Bicycles are not only made in factories. Small shops can build them, starting with no more than piles of metal tubes, spokes, gears, and other parts.

Many small bicycle framebuilding shops have sprung up around the country, serving the needs of demanding bicyclists. Most of their production goes to racers and long-distance tourists, who want machines that fit perfectly and are designed with all features to order. There are builders who specialize in serving all special needs. A custom machine is expensive, but if it is the only one that will work for you, it is a bargain.

Besides building bikes, custom bicycle shops can do repairs and modifications which ordinary shops cannot — fixing a bent or broken frame, or adding a special fitting to the frame.

BIKES FOR TALL PEOPLE

Diamond frame bikes are mass-produced in seat tube lengths up to 27 inches, fitting people up to about 6 feet 4 inches. Actual seat tube length should depend on your leg length, so check before you shop for a bike.

But there are other considerations:

. . . The handlebars must be far enough away from you. If your arms are long, you'll need a stem with a long forward extension for efficient riding. Long-reach, deep-drop handlebars help, too. The top tube lengths of frames vary considerably. Choose one that's long.

. . . Long legs work better with long cranks. Toe clips also must be longer for large feet. Aluminum cranks are available up to 180 mm (about 7 inches) and steel cranks for American frames up to 7½ inches. Schwinn makes some sturdy, tall frames which can use these longer American cranks. But long cranks drag close to the ground, reducing cornering clearance — to deal with this problem you'll need to switch around some parts.

. . . Wheels, 27 inches, or the slightly smaller 700 C wheels, will fit most bikes made for 26-inch wheels, raising the bottom bracket ½ inch. Front fork clearance is usually tighter than rear-brake bridge clearance, but you may solve the problem neatly by using a fork made for a 27-inch wheel on a frame made for a 26-inch wheel — raising the handlebars 1 full inch.

. . . Top tube length becomes more of a problem with oversize wheels and long cranks — interference between the pedals and the toe clips is likely. In practice, this is not as bad as it might seem. The front wheel does not turn far enough to the side to hit the toe clips except in very slow riding.

If you are very tall, 6 feet 5 inches or over, or if you want the ultimate fit, a custom frame may be the answer. All of the frame fit problems evaporate if the bike is made especially for you. A very tall person has a special need for a long top tube: the high center of gravity requires the front wheel to be farther forward so braking force and downhill stability can be equal to a shorter person's. Mention these requirements to the framebuilder you choose, since the fashion is for short top tubes. These are best for racers who need maneuverability above anything else, but not for you. You need stopping power, too.

A custom frame will cost about $300, not what you'd pay for a bike to park at the local shopping center, though on the other hand, if you're tall enough, few thieves could fit over your bike to ride it off. We recommend an adapted bike for errands, and a custom bike if you want top-grade performance for touring and commuting.

Raleigh, Dawes, and Peugeot folding bicycles are sturdy enough for tall people. The Raleigh and Dawes have 20-inch wheels; a 22 × 1⅜-inch or 550A rear wheel will raise the bottom bracket to allow the use of long cranks. If this size does not fit the front fork, then use a fork made for it, such as the Peugeot fork. The Raleigh, with its nonstandard bottom bracket width, needs a Phil Wood crankbearing assembly to accept the longer, cotterless cranks.

The seatpost may not be long enough, but it is a simple matter for any welding shop to braze another seatpost to its top end as an extension.

Toe clip interference is never a problem on a small-wheeled folding bike, but if you need the handlebars farther away, it is a simple matter for a framebuilder to braze an extension into the single main frame tube.

BIKES FOR SHORT PEOPLE

You must be especially careful to buy a bicycle which fits, or to set one up so it fits.

Just like anyone else, you must be able to straddle the bicycle if it has a diamond frame.

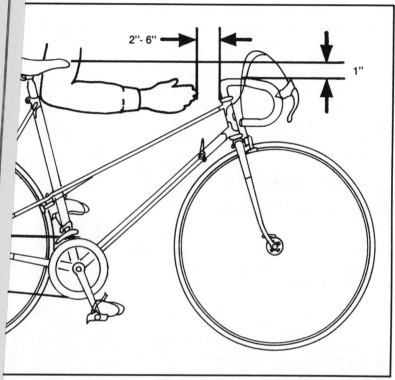

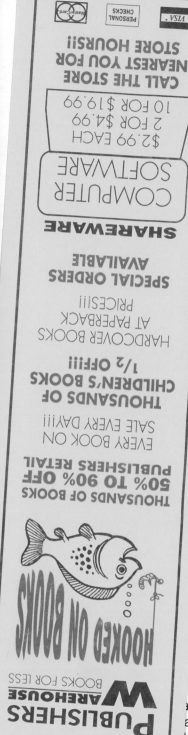

... lowered top tube of a mixte frame, but the handlebar distance and height
...est for distance is for there to be a 2- to 6-inch gap between your extended
...with your elbow against the seatpost. You may have to replace the handlebar
...orter or longer forward extension. It should be possible to lower the handle-
...low the top of the saddle.

...iirement.
... seat-to-handlebar
...t on any frame.
... with a ladies' or
... or too long, here

...d handlebars over
...andlebars are also
...ly on the drops, but
...lose enough to you.

... Buy a short stem. The steel stems sold
with three-speed bikes are shortest. Steel
dropped handlebars are available to fit these
stems. Some aluminum handlebars can be
made to fit by prying apart the opening in the
stem with a screwdriver. It's safe to do this
with a steel stem, though not safe with an
aluminum one.

... You can turn a stem around backward if
need be, to bring the handlebars even closer.

... Small hands need small brake levers.

"Junior" levers made by Weinmann and CLB, among others, are suitable. Order these through your bike shop.

These solutions will make your bike ridable, though it will be unnecessarily large and heavy, and harder to maneuver. Also, a handlebar bag or seat bag may drag on the tire or pound on the fender. A better solution is the following.

A BIKE WITH SMALLER WHEELS

Many bicycles with 26-inch and 24-inch wheels are sold, both internally geared and derailleur geared. When you buy one, check the following items:

. . . Brake levers must be small enough to fit your hands.
. . . Gears may be too low. Smaller wheels need a bigger chainwheel or smaller rear sprocket for the same gears. Gears can be changed easily.
. . . Avoid extreme chainlines in choosing your gear sequence. The chain stays of a 24-inch wheel bike are short.
. . . Crank length for short people is not a fully answered question. Wheel bikes that are 24 inches in diameter often come with 6-inch cranks, which are perhaps too short. Try longer ones on a friend's bike and see whether they feel better.

T.A. cranks that are size 160 mm (6.3 inches) will fit any 24-inch wheel bike if you use narrow racing pedals to improve cornering clearance.
. . . Get a rear rack that fits. A rack made for larger wheels will perch high above the rear wheel. Your bike may come with a custom-fitted rack. If not, replace the rack braces with shorter ones.

To upgrade a 24-inch wheel bike, start

A reversed handlebar stem brings the handlebars nearer for a rider with arms too short for this frame.

SHORT PEOPLE AND SAFETY

While most people on bicycles can see over the tops of cars, you may not be able to. It's to your advantage to learn to ride more assertively to put yourself where you can see and be seen. A safety flag makes more sense for you than for most people.

with the ten-speed you bought, or with a used Raleigh Space Rider three-speed frame. If you wish, you can build this up as a ten-speed. Good aluminum brakes, Nisi, Weinmann, or Ukai 24 × 1⅜-inch alloy rims, Fuji/Silver Star 80 psi 24 × 1¼-inch tires, and a T.A. 160 mm crankset with a Phil Wood bottom bracket for the Raleigh frame are recommended. You'll spend some money, but you'll have a bike that equals anyone else's.

A folding bike may be ideal for a short person for around town use, since it is adjustable to fit a small person. The handlebars on most folding bikes swivel forward and back as well as telescoping up and down.

HEAVY-DUTY BIKES

Some commercially mass-produced frames are designed for heavy use, such as the Raleigh Tourist and the Schwinn Superior.

A framebuilder can strengthen any diamond frame by adding twin lateral tubes, like the top tubes of a mixte frame. Or a custom frame can be built this way.

A heavy-duty fork is also desirable. A Raleigh Sports three-speed fork is unusually strong, suitable for a rider up to 250 pounds. Special tandem and mountain bike forks are even stronger. The fork must fit the frame and the wheel.

Framebuilders with tandem or mountain bike experience are the most familiar with heavy-duty construction.

HEAVY-DUTY WHEELS

The current fashion is for light, narrow wheels, but the small increase in performance these provide is lost when they bend or break under a heavy rider.

Here are several levels of strength for wheels, above the usual:

1. Up to 180 pounds rider/load weight, use any good quality rim that can take 1¼-inch (32 mm) or larger section tires; it should have 36 spokes, at 14 gauge (2 mm or .080).

2. From 180 to 210 pounds use a 1¼-inch high-pressure (90 psi) tire, or wider tire. The rear wheel should have 48 or 36 spokes with 13 (2.3 mm, .092) gauge spokes on the right side — 14 gauge spokes elsewhere.

3. From 210 to 280 pounds use 700C rims, with 700 × 35C tires, inflated to 75 psi. Wolber and Hutchinson tires are available in the United States in this size. Super Champion hook bead rims are recommended — 48 spokes rear, 40 or 48 front, 13 gauge spokes all around. Use Phil Wood or other heavy-duty hubs. Bicycle motocross hubs are also heavy-duty. These wheels will fit any bike made for 27-inch wheels. Alternately, use 650B or 26 × 1⅜ inches, both nominally 26 inches.

4. From 280 to 350 pounds, aluminum rims 26 × 1.75 inches and balloon tires, 26 × 1.75 inches, should be inflated to 55-60 psi, with 36 12 gauge (2.6 mm, .105) spokes per wheel. Rims and hubs may need to be drilled out for these spokes. For more strength, drill four holes to every three of the rim's original 36, making a 48-hole rim; space the holes evenly, using one of every three original holes.

5. Beyond 350 pounds, use moped wheels or small motorcycle wheels. Few people are this heavy, but these wheels may be useful for a cargo tricycle or trailer.

OTHER HEAVY-DUTY PARTS

For a very heavy rider or load, here are some other desirable improvements:

. . . Handlebars, stem, and seatpost should be steel. You'll bend aluminum.

. . . Brakes should be short-reach centerpulls

with brake booster antiflex straps. These are alright with tires up to a 35 mm (1⅜ inch) section, if clearance under the fork is kept tight. With deeper tires, you'll need cantilever brakes brazed to the frame. A rider or load over 250 pounds needs a rear hub brake as well to avoid overheating rims on long downhills. Operate the hub brake with separate control; a handlebar-end shifter is ideal. Do not use double cable brake levers, which prevent you from using the appropriate brake at the appropriate time. Phil Wood and Atom make 48-hole hub brake assemblies.

. . . Drive trains should not cause any particular problems. Good quality standard equipment works on tandems, so it will work for you. Use high-quality cotterless cranks, with one-piece right crank arm and spider, not the less expensive riveted kind. Avoid cottered cranks and tiny chainwheels. Use large sprockets at the rear instead for your low gears. Chains are rarely a problem. If yours is, change brands. Use a modern freewheel, all of whose cogs come off from the outside so it's easier to work on. The Sun Tour Pro-Compe tandem freewheel is highly recommended. Avoid excessive chain angles because they'll wear out the drivetrain faster than with a lighter rider. Avoid six- and seven-speed freewheels, except for the new narrow six-speed freewheels; extra-wide freewheels require extra dishing which weakens the rear wheel. For the greatest wheel strength, use a rear hub axle made for a wide six-speed freewheel, but with a narrower freewheel. Remove spacers from the right end of the axle and add them to the left to center the wheel. You may need to use a longer bottom bracket axle to center the chainwheels properly with this hub axle.

REINFORCED RACKS FOR HEAVY LOADS

The most important problem with a conventional rack is sidesway. Attaching the rack securely to the seatstays is not enough to prevent this. If you grab the back of the rack and push it sideways, you'll see why. One seatstay bends forward and the other bends back, allowing the rack to move.

The lower the rack, the better. Replace braces with shorter ones if necessary to get the rack down close to the wheel.

Extra braces from the middle rear of the rack to the bike's rear dropouts will triangulate the rack, cutting down on sidesway. Some of the more expensive commercial racks use such braces, though generally they are not designed for very heavy loads. You may have to add extra braces to another make of rack for such loads. The inexpensive Pletscher and similar racks have very sturdy main frames and are easily stiffened. Make braces of lengths of small diameter steel pipe, or seatstays from a junk bike, pounded flat and drilled for bolts at the ends. You might also run braces from the point where the rack attaches to each seatstay to a common point on the seat tube. Use chainguard clamps to attach these braces.

A plywood platform bolted to the top of the rack provides better support for large, heavy loads. Drill holes around the edges for bungee cords and straps. By attaching the platform with bolts and wing nuts, you can remove it when you don't need it.

BIKES FOR HANDICAPPED PERSONS

If you are handicapped, chances are that a special machine can let you ride pretty much like anyone else. Since the bike is a machine, it can be designed to use any muscle function. The exercise and mobility it gives you may change your life. The only handicaps which prevent using a bike are total loss of muscle function or severe disorders of attention, vision, or coordination.

If you have lost a leg or the use of a leg, you can ride a normal bicycle. A step-through frame is helpful for a weak leg or artificial leg, if you use one for riding. This is strapped into a toe clip before starting. A stiff knee requires a footrest-pedal which does not turn with the other one. A toe clip is needed for the normal leg, since it must pull the pedal up. Wide-range gears are fitted. You'll ride slowly up hills and not so slowly on level ground.

If you have the use of neither leg, a hand-powered tricycle works well. Average speed is about 12 mph. If you've lost an arm or the use of one, you can ride a normal bicycle with a short, flat handlebar. The single brake lever should operate the front brake. A three-speed hub with a coaster brake works well at the rear. You use the one-handed braking technique described earlier. Extra caution is needed in braking and on rough surfaces.

Even if you have the use of neither arm, you can ride an Avatar or similar recumbent bicycle. This design throws none of the weight forward, so you can easily control it with one hand or even with the shoulders, with a special linkage. Shifting can be done with knee levers if necessary. A person with the use of neither arm and only one leg could ride a recumbent tricycle.

Epilepsy, narcolepsy, and other conditions do not affect your riding if you are aware that an attack is about to come on. If you have attacks without warning, a recumbent tricycle with a reverse-operating brake will keep you upright and stop your travel in case of an attack. A tricycle is suited to a person with cerebral palsy or a similar coordination problem.

If you are deaf, you have no particular problems in riding beyond those you'd have if you were riding a moped. Then the sound of the motor would drown out the sounds of vehicles around you. You should have a rearview mirror and learn to use it well.

If you are visually handicapped you can ride on the back of a tandem. Also, people with reduced arm function can ride well on the back of a tandem, since there is no need to balance forces on the handlebars to steer.

For more information, write to Hand-Powered Cyclists of America, c/o Warner, 228 Winchester St., Brookline, MA 02146.

CONCLUSION

In no uncertain terms this book is a practical call to action. We feel very strongly that the individual, through his or her conscious decision to use a bicycle for commuting and for purposeful trips, can make a difference. And collectively, more commuters mean less oil consumption, less pollution, and less congestion in our cities.

But your presence on the road has great symbolic value as it represents a call to action to potential commuters. Through your dress, manner, and on-road behavior, you can be a high advertisement for bicycle commuting. You can truly participate in the recycling of America.

But there is more that you can do.

If you work with other bicyclists, you can actively improve conditions to make commuting safer and more convenient. Bicyclists have gotten together in many local, regional, and national groups to get the work started — preparing maps, exerting political pressure, publishing newspapers, and conducting educational campaigns. The Boston Area Bicycle Coalition is such a group, and this book grew out of its efforts.

Join a local group, or if there isn't one, start one. Join the League of American Wheelmen, too — it is the organization which promotes bicycling on the national level, and it is a valuable resource to all local groups. Inform yourself. Read *Bicycling* magazine and the other publications we've mentioned. If you own a building where you could install better bicycle parking facilities — or if you are otherwise in a position to encourage bicycling — do so. Above all, put the skills outlined in this book to use. Commute, in good health and in good spirits.

APPENDIX I
SOME STRAIGHT TALK
ABOUT BICYCLE PLANNING

For a thorough treatment of bicycle planning, we recommend the following books:

Forester, John. *Cycling Transportation Engineering.* Sunnyvale, CA: Custom Cycle Fitments, 1977. It costs $20 postpaid, $12 to members of bicycling organizations.

United States Department of Transportation, *Bicycle Transportation for Energy Conservation.* Washington, D.C.: United States Government Printing Office, April, 1980.

A few words are appropriate here, because bicycle planning is poorly understood by many people, including some bicyclists — there is potential for spending money on projects which later prove mistaken.

The principal problems are access, parking, education, and law enforcement.

Access means the ability to get to every street address by bicycle, by a convenient and reasonable route. Car-only streets, highways, bridges, and tunnels built when only cars were taken seriously, cut out bicyclists, pedestrians, and moped riders — a denial of the Constitutional right of free travel.

Parking means secure bike lockers, or a guarded area for all-day or all-night use, and modern bike racks which secure both wheels and the frame for short-term use. Parking does not mean the obsolete "dishdrainer" bike rack. This bends the wheels of modern bicycles, and prevents locking the bicycle securely.

Education means training millions of American bicyclists, who learned to ride as children, how to ride as adults — as responsible, law-abiding drivers of bicycles. This has the potential to cut the accident rate from 50 to 80 percent, making it the soundest investment in bicycle planning. Education also means training American motorists to respect and understand the role of bicyclists on the roads as equals.

Law enforcement means the passing of fair and consistent laws and their equal enforcement by police against bicyclists and motorists.

These are the major improvements needed. Road design improvements may also be helpful, but it is in the area of road design that the most serious mistakes continue to be made in bicycle planning.

Besides access, the main need is for general improvements which make the streets more friendly to bicyclists — wide curb lanes which a car and a bicycle can share side by side, traffic signals which respond to bicycles and cars alike, sewer grates which do not trap bicycle tires, and right and left turn lanes at intersections.

The main misconception and problem is in the construction of special bikepaths and bikelanes. Bikepaths are useful for recreational riding in parks, as low-pollution routes, and as short-cut routes. Bikelanes make sense to provide access across high-speed bridges. But where there is cross traffic, both have been statistically shown often more dangerous than riding in the street. And all too often, bikelanes and bikepaths have been an excuse for prohibiting bicycles on routes which are *safer, faster,* and *more direct* — an outright discouragement to bicycle transportation.

Yet in many places the majority of funding for bicycling has been spent on bikelanes and bikepaths. They are the first thing many people think of when the subject of bicycle planning is mentioned. Consider them carefully, as one part of a total bicycle transportation plan.

APPENDIX II
BICYCLE ACTIVIST
ORGANIZATIONS

Advocates of Bi-cology
c/o 9-3, Akasaka 1-Chomo
Minato-ku, Tokyo
Japan

Aktie Strohalm
Oudearacht 42,
Utrecht
Netherlands

Albuquerque Bicyclists of
   Alternative Transportation
106 Girard Blvd. SE
Albuquerque, NM 87106

Alternative Stad
Bryggargatan 8
Stockholm 111 21
Sweden

American Youth Hostels
National Campus
Delaplane, VA 22025

Amigos de la Tierra-Aepden
Campomanes 13, Madrid
Spain

Amis de la Terre
117 Avenue de Choisy
F75013 Paris
France

Amsterdam Autovrij
Sint Olofsport 4
Amsterdam
Netherlands

Ann Arbor Bicycle League
417 Detroit St.
Ann Arbor, MI 48104

Baltimore Area Bicyclists Association
333 E. 25th St.
Baltimore, MD 21218

Bicycle Action Committee, CBC
P.O. Box 12774
Seattle, WA 98111

Bicycle Commuter Service
1914 S.E. Ankeny
Portland, OR 97214

Bicycle Commuters of New York
5 Beekman St.
New York, NY 10038

Bicycle Federation of Pennsylvania
36 Sylvania Rd.
Hershey, PA 17033

Bicycle Institute of New South Wales
390 Pitt St.
Sydney, New South Wales 2000
Australia

Bicycle Institute of Victoria
G.P.O. Box 1961 R
Melbourne, 3001
Australia

Bicyclists of Iowa City
Box 841
Iowa City, IA 52240

Bikecentennial
P.O. Box 8308
Missoula, MT 59807

Bike ROAD
c/o Graff
2704 Stuart Dr.
Durham, NC 27707

Bikeways for Buffalo
308 Highland Ave.
Buffalo, NY 14222

Boston Area Bicycle Coalition
3 Joy St.
Boston, MA 02108

Bundesverband Buergerinitiativen Umwelt-
schutz e. v.
Hellbergstr. 6
D-7500 Karlsruhe 21
Germany

Burgeninitiative Westtangente s.v.
Cheruskerstra 10
D-1000
Berlin 62
West Germany

California Association of Bicycle
Organizations
P.O. Box 2684
Dublin, CA 94566

Cape & Islands Bicyclists
P.O. Box 1291
Vineyard Haven, MA 02568

Capital Bicycle Commuters Association
P.O. Box 1541
Sacramento, CA 95807

Central Arizona Bicycling Association
P.O. Box 3132
Tempe, AZ 85281

Coalition of Connecticut Bicyclists
510 N. Church St.
Naugatuck, CT 06770

Commuters by Cycle
c/o Carlson
2834 Calaverns Blvd.
Fairfield, CA 94533

Cyclebag
35 King St.
Bristol 1
England

Cyclists' Touring Club
Cotterell House
69 Meadrow
Godalming, Surrey GU7 3HS
England

Cykelgruppen for Uppsala
Box 2107
750 02 Uppsala 2
Sweden

Dansk Cyklist Forbund
Kjeld Langes gade 14
1367 Copenhagen
Denmark

Delaware Friends of Bikecology
108 Wayland Rd.
Wilmington, DE 19807

Dunedin Cyclists' Coalition
20 Gillespie St.
Dunedin
New Zealand

East Bay Bicycle Coalition
P.O. Box 1736
Oakland, CA 94604

Echte Nederlandse Fietsers Bond
Postbus 2150
NL-3440
Woerden
Netherlands

Energia Verde
Box 40612
Minillas Station
San Juan 00940
Puerto Rico

Energy Cycles
P.O. Box 51
Santa Barbara, CA 93102

Environment Liaison Center
P.O. Box 72461
Nairobi
Kenya

Environmental Protection Society
P.O. Box 382
Jin sultan
Pentaling Jaya, Selangor
Malaysia

Fedération Francaise des Usagers
  de la Bicyclette
7 Av. Forêt Noire
67000 Strasbourg
France

Florida Cyclist Association
c/o Hiller
P.O. Box 976
Miami, FL 33133

Foothills Group
c/o Wallace
765 Hertford Rd.
Winston-Salem, NC 27104

Freewheel Bike Co-op
3336 East 25th St.
Minneapolis, MN 55406

Friends of Central Park
Lenox Hill
P.O. Box 610
New York, NY 10021

Friends of the Earth
9 Poland St.
London W1V 3DG
England

Garden State Bicycle League
Box 7309
Trenton, NJ 08628

GRACQ
c/o J. deCoster
28 rue Ernest Gassart, 1180
Brussels
Belgium

Greater Kansas City Bicycle Coalition
c/o Haskell
4550 Warwick Blvd., Suite 1103
Kansas City, MO 64111

Greater Philadelphia Bicycle Coalition
P.O. Box 8194
Philadelphia, PA 19101

Gruene Radler bundesweit
Schelpsheide 39
D-4800 Bielefeld
West Germany

Hand-Powered Cyclists of America
c/o Warner
228 Winchester St.
Brookline, MA 02146

Indianapolis Bicycle Task Force
1426 W. 29th St.
Indianapolis, IN 46208

League of American Wheelmen
P.O. Box 988
Baltimore, MD 21203

League of Michigan Bicyclists
P.O. Box 13001
Lansing, MI 48901

Low Country Coalition for Alternative
   Transportation
1011-B St. Andrews Blvd.
Charleston, SC 29407

Maine Bicycle Coalition
P.O. Box 4544 DTS
Portland, ME 04112

Merseyside Friends of Cycling
20 Hilbre Rd.
West Kirby Wirral
Merseyside L48 3HH
England

Miami Valley Regional Bicycle Committee
1980 Winters Bank Tower
Dayton, OH 45423

Monde à Bicyclette
4224 Clark
Montréal, Québec H2W 1X3
Canada

Mountain Bicyclists
1200 Williams St.
Denver, CO 80218

Nova Scotia Cycling Association
P.O. Box 3010
South Halifax, Nova Scotia B3J 3G6
Canada

Ontario Bikeway Coalition
4776 Wyandotte St. E.
Windsor, Ontario N8Y 1H7
Canada

Ontario Cycling Association
559 Jarvis St.
Toronto, Ontario M4Y 2J1
Canada

Peace, Action, Development and
   Friendship Association
P.O. Box 50
Kingston 12
Jamaica

Pedal Power ACT
P.O. Box E305
Canberra, ACT 2600
Australia

Pedal Power Tasmania
Tasmanian Environment Center
102 Bathurst St.
Hobart, Tasmania 7000
Australia

Personal Mobility Committee
Suite 702, Transportation Bldg.
4th and Sycamore
Cincinnati, OH 45202

Pro World 99
A/C Grinberg
Casilla 60-Suc. 14
1405 Buenos Aires
Argentina

Roues Libres
475 rue Richelieu
Québec, Québec G1R 1K2
Canada

Roulavélo
C.P. 608
Alma, Québec G8B 5V4
Canada

San Francisco Bicycle Coalition
P.O. Box 22554
San Francisco, CA 94122

Santa Clara Valley Bicycle Association
P.O. Box 662
Los Gatos, CA 95030

Sociedad Conservacionista Arague
Apdo, 5115 El Limon
Maracay, EDO Aragua
Venezuela

South Marin Bicycle Commuter Coalition
c/o Lagios
135 Elinor Ave.
Mill Valley, CA 94941

Southern Bicycle League
P.O. Box 29474
Atlanta, GA 30359

Spokes
2A Ainslie Place
Edinburgh EH3 6AR
Scotland

Springfield Bicycle Club
1825 S. 5th
Springfield, IL 62703

Syklistenes Landsforening
c/o Leif Klyve
Storgt, 2
Oslo 1
Norway

Texas Cycling Committee
711 W. 32nd St., Apt. 133
Austin, TX 78705

Tidewater Bicycle Association
P.O. Box 12254
Norfolk, VA 23502

Todos En Bicycleta
Londres 161, L25
Col. Juarez, Mexico D.F.
Mexico

Toronto Cycling Committee
229 Brunswick Ave.
Toronto, Ontario M5S 2M6
Canada

Transportation Alternatives
133 West 72 St.
New York, NY 10023

Vancouver Bicycle Alliance
c/o Bernhardt
4554 Québec St.
Vancouver, B.C. V5V 3M2
Canada

Vélo Québec
1415 est Jarry
Montréal, Québec H2E 2Z7
Canada

Washington Area Bicyclist Association
1520 16th St. NW
Washington, DC 20036

Wright's Bicycle Co-op
3601 Woodland Park Ave. N
Seattle, WA 98103

INDEX

A

Accessories, for commuting, 11–18
Accidents. *See also* Collisions
    avoidance of, 134
    causes of, 134–35
    learning from, 139
    in winter, 248–49
Adjustments
    to brakes, 266–71
    to handlebars, 22–24
    to mirrors, 16
    to pedals, 25
    to saddle, 21–22
Adult trikes, 8
Airplanes, transporting bicycle on, 218
Air pollution
    filter mask for, 254
    and riding, 253–54
Audible signalling, 143–44

B

Backpacks, carrying load in, 198–99
Battery-powered lights, 227–28
Bell Biker helmet, 13
Bickerton portable bicycle, 6
Bicycle
    accessories for, 11–18
    carrying of, 70–72, 212–13
    customized, 281–86
    disassembly of, 219–20
    falls, 66–70, 248–49
    fitting of, 19–22

Automobile
    bicycle rack for, 213
    carbon monoxide from, 254
    carrying bicycle on, 212–13
    hitchhiking in, 217–18

Bicycle (*continued*)
    for handicapped, 286–87
    inspection of, 258–60, 262–64
    instructional, 40–44
    laws, 164–68
    lights, 224–30
        installation of, 228
        kinds of, 224–28
        legal requirements for, 224
    organizations, 293–98
    parking, 188–93
    parts, 3–4
    purchase of, 1–2
    reflectors, 230–32
    riding of, 44–47
    for rough riding, 252–53
    safety, 11–17, 230–32
    security of, 183, 185–88, 191–92
    shipping of, 218
    storage of, 189–91
    suitability of, 4
    tires, 64–65, 271–79
    tools for, 220
    transportation and, 207–18
Bicycler, mental attitude of, 160–63
Bicycle trailer, 201
Bicycling
    and carrying loads, 195–203
    clothes for, 11–12, 232–33, 239–45,
      249–50
    and passengers, 203
    in traffic, 75–139
Big Wheel, as alternative, 7
Bikelane, riding in, 128–29
Bikepaths, riding on, 125–28
Bikepools, 209–11
Boats, transporting bicycle on, 217
Brake(ing)
    adjustments, 266–71
    advanced, 56–57

    coaster, 30–31, 238
    levers, 24–25
    one-handed, 55–56
    rear-wheel, 52–53
    use of, 51–57
    in wet weather, 238–39
Brake levers, adjustments to, 24–25
Breathability, of clothes, 11
Buses, transporting bicycle on, 215

C

Cadence, 29–30
Car. *See* Automobile
Carbon monoxide, from car engines, 254
Carriers
    backpacks, 198–99
    handlebar bags, 198
    panniers, 199
    racks, 196–97
    saddlebags, 198
Catalogs, manufacturers', 2
Children
    bicycles for, 7–8
    learning to ride, 205
    as passengers, 204–5
    on tandems, 205
Clothes
    breathability of, 11
    cold weather, 11, 242–45
    colors of, 11–12
    comfort of, 11
    durability of, 12
    hot weather, 249–50
    rainwear, 239–40
    reflective, 232–33
Coaster brakes, 30–31, 238
Collisions. *See also* Accidents
    avoidance of, 136–37

with bicyclists, 137–38
with dogs, 138–39
learning from, 139
with pedestrians, 137
rear-end, 136–37
Communication, on road, 141–68
Commuting
accessories for, 11–18
adapting bicycle for, 8
distances, 170
and fatigue, 170–71
and nourishment, 170
times, 170
tips for, 169–70
Contact lenses, for riding, 15
Customized bicycles
for handicapped, 286–87
heavy-duty, 285–86
for short people, 282–84
small wheels, 284–85
for tall people, 281–82
Cyclometer, as measuring device, 176–77

D

Derailleur-geared bicycle, 5–6
Derailleur gearing, 33–38
Disassembly, of bicycle, 219–20
Dogs, collisions with, 138–39
Downhill riding, 59–62
Durability, of clothing, 12

E

Ears, use while bicycling, 141–43
Engraving, of bicycle, 184–85
Eye contact, and bicycling, 147–48

F

Falls
avoidance of, 66
learning how to, 67–70
types of, 69–70
in winter, 248–49
Fatigue, while commuting, 170–71
Fear, of riding, 75–77, 92
Fitting, of bicycle, 19–22
frame, 19–21
handlebars, 22–24
saddle position, 21–22
Five-speed bicycle, 32
Flags, bicycle, 17
Folding bicycle
advantages of, 6–7, 9–10
for mixed-mode travel, 207
Frame, proper fitting of, 19–21

G

Gear(s), 30–38
derailleur, 33–38
internal hub, 32–33
Glasses
for bicycling, 14–15, 244
cable temples and, 14

H

Handicapped, bicycles for, 286–87
Handlebar bag, 198
Handlebars
adjustments to, 22–24
distance, 23
height of, 22–23
tilt of, 23–24

Hand signalling, 155–58
Hazards, road-edge, 86–88
Heat, riding in, 249–51
Helmet, for safety, 13–14
Hot-weather riding
    clothes for, 249–50
    preparing for, 250–51
    techniques for, 251
Hub gears, internal
    advantages of, 32–33
    use of, 33

I

Inspection, of bicycle, 258–60, 262–64
Installation
    of bicycle racks, 196–97
    of lights, 228
    of tires, 275–79
Insurance
    on bicycle, 193–94
    on self, 194
Intersections, driving through, 103–5,
    109–11, 113, 131

J

Jackets, for bicycling, 243

L

Landmarks, navigation and, 175
Laws, bicycle, 164–68
    breaking of, 167–68
    obeying of, 167

and police, 164–68
Lights, 224–30
    aiming of, 228–29
    battery-powered, 227–28
    installation of, 228
    kinds of, 224–27
    legal requirements for, 224
Loading. *See also* Packing
    bicycle baskets, 199
    equipment for, 195–99
Locks, security, 185–88, 191–92

M

Maintenance
    flat tires, 271–72
    tests and, 260
    weekly, 260–62
    yearly, 264–66
Manufacturers' catalogs, 2
Maps, for touring, 173–75
Mask, for air pollution, 254
Mental attitude, importance of, 161–64
Mirrors
    adjustability of, 16
    as safety aid, 15–16
    use of, 151–52
Motorists, bicycling and, 135–36
Mounts, kinds of, 57
MSR helmet, 13
Mudguards, 237

N

Navigation
    by landmarks, 175
    with shadows, 176

by the sun, 175–76
Night riding
    equipment for, 223–24
    lights for, 224–30
    rules for, 236
Nourishment, while commuting, 170

O

One-speed bicycle, 30–32
Organizations, of bicycle activists, 293–98
Overconfidence, while bicycling, 161–62

P

Packing
    in backpacks, 198–99
    equipment for, 195–99
    in handlebar bags, 198
    pannier bags, 199
    on racks, 196–97
    in saddlebags, 198
Panniers, 199
Parking, of bicycle
    bicycle racks, 189–90
    indoors, 189
    long-term, 191
    short-term, 188–89
Passengers, 203–5
Patching tire tubes, 274–75
Pedals, adjustments to, 25
Pedestrians, collisions with, 137
Police
    dealing with, 164–65
    and laws, 164–68
Potholes, riding on, 62–64
Pro-Tec helmet, 13

R

Racks, rear carrier
    choosing of, 195–96
    installation of, 196–97
    loading of, 197–98
Railroad tracks, riding across, 65–66
Rain
    equipment checklist, 240
    riding in, 237–41
Rainwear, 239–40
Rear-wheel braking, 52–53
Reflective clothing, 232–33
Reflectors, 230–32
Repairs
    flat tires, 271–72, 275–79
    guidelines for, 257–58
    learning, 258
    patching tube, 274–75
Riding
    in bikelane, 128–29
    on bikepaths, 125–28
    downhill, 59–62
    fear of, 75–77, 92
    hazards, road-edge, 86–88
    in hot weather, 249–51
    in rain, 237–41
    safety and, 77–79
    on sidewalk, 123–25
    in snow, 241–49
    in traffic, 75–139
        intersections, 103–5, 109–11, 113,
          131
        lanes, 88–95, 97–101, 103, 117–21
        turning, 105–9, 132–34
    uphill, 58–59
Road surface, and tires, 64–65
Rough riding, bicycles for, 252–53
Route selection, 177
Rules of the road, and bicycling, 79

Rules of thumb
being seen, 149–51
on load carrying, 202–3
on night riding, 236

S

Saddle(s)
adjustments to, 21–22
dye coming off, 12
position for proper fit, 21–22
height, 21–22
horizontal placement, 22
tension, 22
Saddlebags, carrying load in, 198
Safety
clothing, 11–12
eyewear, 14–15
flags, 17
hand protectors, 12–13
helmets, 13–14
mirrors, rearview, 15–16
reflectors, 230–32
Safety zones, 154
Scootering, 72
Shipping, of bicycle, 218
Shoes, for bicycling, 16–17
Sidewalks, riding on, 123–25
Signalling
audible, 143–44
hand, 155–58
pointers on, 158–59
Snow, riding in, 241–49
Storage, of bicycle, 189–91
Subways, transporting bicycle on, 215–16
Sun
blinding drivers, 149–50
for navigation, 175–76

T

Tandem, children on, 203–5
Taxis, transporting bicycle on, 217
Ten-speed bicycle, 5–6, 9
Theft, of bicycle, 183–94
insurance against, 193–94
locks for, 185–88, 191–92
precautions for, 184–88
prevention of, 192–93
Three-speed bicycle, 5, 32
Tires
installation of, 275–79
removal of, 273–74
repairs to, 271–72
road surface and, 64–65
role of, 64
Toe clips, 16–17
ease of pedaling, 30
Tools, for bicycle, 220
Touring, maps, for, 173–75
Traffic, riding bicycle in, 81–129
Trains, transporting bicycle on, 216
Transporting, of bicycle
on airplanes, 218
on boats, 217
on buses, 215
cost of, 214
on subways, 215–16
on taxis, 217
on trains, 216
on trolleys, 215
Tricycles
for adults, 8
for children, 7
Trip
checklist for, 169–70
planning, 169–71
Trolleys, transporting bicycle on, 215–16

Turns, bicycle
    corners, 50–51
    practicing of, 47–51
    quick, 50

U

Uphill riding, 58–59

V

Visibility
    aids to, 224–33
    clothing colors and, 11–12, 232–33
Vision
    blind spots, 146–47

and eye contact, 147–48
widescreen, 144–45

W

Weather conditions, and riding, 241–51
Wet weather riding
    and brakes, 238–39
    clothes for, 239–40
    equipment checklist, 240
    preparing for, 237–38
    safety and, 240–41
Wind resistance
    effects of, 254–55
    problems with, 255
    riding position, and, 254–55
Winter riding
    clothes for, 242–45
    and falls, 248–49
    preparing for, 242
    in snow and ice, 245–48